Skilfully Passing the Solicitors Qualifying Examination (SQE)

Second Edition

Skilfully Passing the Solicitors Qualifying Examination (SQE)

Second Edition

Neeta Halai
Solicitor

Bloomsbury Professional
LONDON · DUBLIN · EDINBURGH · NEW YORK · NEW DELHI · SYDNEY

BLOOMSBURY PROFESSIONAL
Bloomsbury Publishing Plc
50 Bedford Square, London, WC1B 3DP, UK
1385 Broadway, New York, NY 10018, USA
29 Earlsfort Terrace, Dublin 2, Ireland

BLOOMSBURY and the Diana logo are trademarks of Bloomsbury Publishing Plc

© Neeta Halai 2023

All rights reserved. No part of this publication may be reproduced or transmitted in any form or by any means, electronic or mechanical, including photocopying, recording, or any information storage or retrieval system, without prior permission in writing from the publishers.

While every care has been taken to ensure the accuracy of this work, no responsibility for loss or damage occasioned to any person acting or refraining from action as a result of any statement in it can be accepted by the authors, editors or publishers.

All UK Government legislation and other public sector information used in the work is Crown Copyright ©. All House of Lords and House of Commons information used in the work is Parliamentary Copyright ©. This information is reused under the terms of the Open Government Licence v3.0 (http://www.nationalarchives.gov.uk/doc/open-government-licence/version/3) except where otherwise stated.

All Eur-lex material used in the work is © European Union, http://eur-lex.europa.eu/, 1998-2023.

British Library Cataloguing-in-Publication Data

A catalogue record for this book is available from the British Library.

ISBN:	PB:	978 1 52652 740 0
	Epdf:	978 1 52652 743 1
	Epub:	978 1 52652 741 7

Typeset by Evolution Design and Digital (Kent)
Printed and bound by CPI Group (UK) Ltd, Croydon, CR0 4YY

To find out more about our authors and books visit www.bloomsburyprofessional.com. Here you will find extracts, author information, details of forthcoming events and the option to sign up for our newsletters

Preface

The success of the 1st Edition of this book, worldwide, has resulted in this 2nd Edition. As the book has been recommended by universities, training providers, law firms, businesses and individuals, I knew that once the Qualified Lawyers Transfer Scheme (QLTS) was abolished, I would need to streamline the book and remove all the QLTS content.

Since the 1st Edition, the SRA have made minor changes to the core SQE functioning legal knowledge so it largely remains the same. The key change is to be able to clarify the understanding of the laws of England and Wales and where they differ.

The aim of this book is to help you pass the Solicitors Qualifying Examination (SQE) with confidence by understanding exactly what you need to do and how to do it. The three key steps are:

- **Plan**

    Know what you have to do and what is expected from you.

- **Prepare**

    Know how you will study for the SQE Part 1 and 2 by understanding what works best for you.

- **Pass**

    Execute your plan and preparation proactively to ensure you qualify as a solicitor.

The SQE came into force on 1 September 2021 and replaced all the existing routes to qualifying as a solicitor in England and Wales.

SQE Background

The SQE is new but it is actually based on an exam format called the Qualified Lawyers Transfer Scheme (QLTS) and very closely mirrors it. The similarities between the two are far greater than the differences. The QLTS was a set of assessments foreign-jurisdiction qualified lawyers had to pass to qualify as a solicitor in England and Wales. The standard of the SQE exam is the same as the QLTS: a newly qualified solicitor (Day One Solicitor).

This book is based on my experience and expertise in coaching and training lawyers for the QLTS and the SQE. Therefore, any reference to the QLTS is to reassure you that what I share equally applies to the SQE.

Through many years of working with lawyers on the QLTS, I found many common challenges and fears that equally apply to those clients I work with on the SQE. So the guidance and advice for the assessments remains the same and is relevant.

Preface

If you do not know much about performance coaching, you can read about what I do in Chapter 2, Preparing for the SQE. The lawyers come to me having studied the practice areas of the law they are assessed on and we work together on their legal and communication skills to deliver the law in a clear, concise, correct and comprehensive manner. That might sound quite easy, but many clients I work with say they underestimated the skills part of the assessments.

The goal is to share with you my many years of experience offering guidance, advice, practical tools and tips for what is considered a 'new' exam. For example, strategies are provided on how to deal with the practical issues you may face in the assessments, such as:

- feeling nervous and how to control this;
- not knowing the law and how to respond to a client or a judge asking a question;
- not knowing how to deal with emotional, vulnerable or challenging clients;
- feeling overwhelmed by how much studying you have to do.

This book will practically complement your academic studies.

A lot of the information specifically about the SQE comes from the Solicitors Regulation Authority (SRA). A generic reference to the SRA website (www.sra.org.uk) will be made throughout the book to avoid inaccurate references to links where the SRA website content may have changed. You should always check the SRA website for all up-to-date information on the SQE.

Studying for the SQE

I recommend you start with the following chapters to help you grasp what the SQE entails, before going into the chapters that detail the assessments:

- Chapter 1 The SQE Journey.
- Chapter 2 Preparing for the SQE.

Unless you are exempt, then read Chapter 3 on the SQE Part 1 Functioning Legal Knowledge Assessments. This is because you will need to pass this part before you can do the SQE Part 2.

Before reading any of the SQE Part 2 chapters on the assessments, I would recommend you read the following chapters because they provide core information referred to in the chapters that detail the assessments:

- Chapter 5 on Communication Skills.
- Chapter 6 on Managing Nerves, Fear and Failure.
- Chapter 7 on Writing in Professional English.

My suggestion is you read Chapter 6 on Managing Nerves, Fear and Failure with Chapters 5 and 7 because it will help you recognise feelings of nerves, anxiety or pressure before they occur, and provides tips and strategies on how to deal with them.

Preface

This recommendation means any duplication of core information that applies to many of the assessment chapters can be avoided. For example:

- For the oral assessments, read Chapters 5 and 6; then you can read Chapter 8 on Client Interviewing Skills or Chapter 10 on Advocacy.
- For the written assessments, read Chapter 7 on Writing in Professional English as a refresher and then you can read any of the chapters on the written assessments.

You can read Chapter 4 on Qualifying Work Experience (QWE) at any time. The section Types of Lawyers (para **4.02**) is beneficial for all qualified and aspiring solicitors. There is also a curriculum vitae (CV) template with guidance and tips on what to include in your CV in Appendix 4A.

You can read the following chapters on the SQE Part 2 in any order. These chapters focus on practical tips, what to expect when doing the assessments and how to prepare to pass them:

- Chapter 8 on Client Interviewing Skills.
- Chapter 9 on Writing the Attendance Note.
- Chapter 10 on Advocacy.
- Chapter 11 on Case and Matter Analysis.
- Chapter 12 on Legal Writing.
- Chapter 13 on Legal Drafting.
- Chapter 14 on Legal Research.

All the chapters have an appendix or appendices where more details on the assessment specifications and other information can be found.

My advice

There is no doubt that the SQE is a high-stakes professional exam that requires dedication, determination and discipline. These are qualities required by a solicitor, so even when it gets challenging and you feel like giving up see it as character building.

> *'Don't wish it was easier, wish you were better. Don't wish for less problems, wish for more skills. Don't wish for less challenge, wish for more wisdom.'*
> **Jim Rohn**

My goal is to help you qualify as a solicitor in the Senior Courts of England and Wales. My advice is do not compare yourself to other people's timelines for what they are doing or have achieved. Focus on what you want and why.

Sometimes preparing for the SQE can be quite an isolating experience. If you can relate to this, you can:

- speak to your employer, university or training provider; and

Preface

- share your experiences in the SQE Success group on LinkedIn.

Always take what works for you because your journey is unique to you. Be proactive and learn with passion and enthusiasm. One of my favourite quotes is:

> *'Live as if you were to die tomorrow. Learn as if you were to live forever.'*
> **Mahatma Gandhi**

To Your Success!

Neeta Halai
October 2023

This book has been written to help you pass the SQE. I welcome your thoughts and constructive feedback. Though I may not always be able to respond personally to every communication, please know that I always learn from it. Below are the ways you can connect with me:

LinkedIn Group: SQE Success

LinkedIn: Neeta Halai

Website: New Heights Training: (www.nh-training.co.uk)

Facebook: New Heights Training

Instagram: @neeta.halai

X (Twitter): @NeetaHalai

Acknowledgements

The book you are holding is the result of many people's encouragement, support and words of wisdom. Therefore, I cannot take full credit for it without mentioning some of those who were key players.

Bloomsbury Professional

First, I would like to thank Bloomsbury Professional for believing in this book. Thanks to Andy Hill, Head of Practitioner Publishing (Law and Hart), for your unwavering guidance and support. Thanks also to your marketing and editorial departments whose synergy has brought this book to life.

My Clients

This book would simply not exist without the lawyers, aspiring solicitors, students, law firms and businesses, I get to work with. Past and present clients, I am so thankful to each and every one of you. Without your support I would never have published this book.

Family and Friends

My dear friends and especially my 'inner circle' (you know who you are), thank you so much for all your encouragement and always being there for me.

Finally, I will forever be indebted to my wonderful parents, Samji and Radha Halai, for always being so supportive and encouraging in all my endeavours. Equally, I am thankful and so lucky to have four talented and inspiring sisters: Raj, Arti, Veena and Poonam. You are all my pillars of strength and guidance in different ways.

Thanks also to my brothers-in-law Zaf and Bhav and (gone but never forgotten) Baz – we all miss you.

Lastly, a big hug and thank you to Maya for helping me choose the colour for the cover of this book. You always have an answer for everything! I am continually learning from you.

Dedication

For my parents, Samji and Radha Halai

Your life stories and words of wisdom have made me who I am today.

Contents

Preface	vii
Acknowledgements	ix

Chapter 1 The SQE Journey — **1**
Introduction — 1
The Pre-SQE Journey — 2
The SQE Assessments — 7
Qualifying Work Experience (QWE) — 15
The Post-SQE Journey — 15
Chapter 1: Appendices — **19**

Chapter 2 Preparing for the SQE — **25**
Introduction — 25
SQE Registration — 27
How to Choose an SQE Course Provider — 27
Misleading Marketing and Advertising — 32
Studying Formats — 32
Students — 38
Aspiring Solicitors (Working) — 40
Qualified Lawyers — 40
Studying and Time Management — 41
A Study Plan — 44
Support Groups/'Study Buddies' — 47
Studying for the SQE — 48
Understanding the Competence Statement — 50
Preparing for the SQE Part 1: Functioning Legal Knowledge (FLK) Assessments — 52
Preparing for the SQE Part 2: Practical Legal Skills (PLS) — 53
Your Level of English — 58
Fitness to Sit/Reasonable Adjustments — 59
Pearson VUE Centres — 60
Chapter 2: Appendices — **62**

Chapter 3 SQE Part 1: Functioning Legal Knowledge (FLK) Assessments — **65**
Introduction — 65
FLK Assessments – Multiple Choice Tests (MCT) — 66
FLK Assessment Specification — 68
Professional Conduct and Ethics — 69
How to Study for the FLK Assessments — 69
Intellectual Thinking and Intuitive Thinking — 70
Practical Tips for Multiple Choice Questions (MCQs) — 72
Failing the FLK Assessments — 72
Chapter 3: Appendices — **74**

Contents

Chapter 4 Qualifying Work Experience (QWE) — 91
Introduction — 91
Types of Lawyers — 92
How does the QWE Affect You? — 95
Finding QWE — 96
Opportunities — 97
What Counts as QWE? — 98
Does the SRA Regulate the QWE? — 99
How is QWE Authenticated? — 99
When should you do the SQE Part 2? — 100
Good Quality Work Experience — 101
QWE Completed — 104
Chapter 4: Appendices — **106**

Chapter 5 Communication Skills — 117
Introduction — 117
What are Communication Skills? — 118
Challenges with Communication Skills — 120
Practising Your Skills — 120
The Connector — 121
The Communicator — 122
The Convincer — 122
Rapport — 123
Trust — 130
Appearance — 133
The Communicator — 134
Communication — 135
Intellectual Intelligence (IQ) and Emotional Intelligence (EQ) — 140
Time Management — 145
The Convincer — 149
Listening — 149
Questioning — 152
Impact: Persuasion and Influence — 155
Chapter 5: Appendices — **157**

Chapter 6 Managing Nerves, Fear and Failure — 165
Introduction — 165
The Different Zones of Experience — 166
What is Confidence? — 167
Controlling Nerves: Peak State — 168
Language Patterns — 168
Symptoms of Nerves or Fear — 171
The Brain — 172
Stored Patterns – Fight, Flight or Freeze — 172
Breathing — 174
Fear of Failure — 176
Fear of the Client or Judge — 178
Fear of the Unknown — 178
SQE Part 1 – Functional Legal Knowledge — 180
SQE Part 2 – Practical Legal Skills — 181
Fear of the Unknown for Client Interviewing — 181

Fear of the Unknown for Advocacy | 183
Failing the SQE Assessments | 185
Chapter 6: Appendices | **189**

Chapter 7 Writing in Professional English | **193**
Introduction | 193
Examples of Application of Law | 194
Identifying Your Writing Strengths and Weaknesses | 195
Your Level of English | 196
Letters | 196
Emails | 199
Paragraphs | 200
The Four Cs | 200
Commonly Misused Words | 203
Contractions | 204
Archaic Legal Language v Modern Plain English | 204
US and UK English | 205
Latin Phrases | 207
Spelling | 207
Punctuation | 208
Grammar | 213
Chapter 7: Appendices | **215**

Chapter 8 SQE Part 2: Client Interviewing Skills | **219**
Introduction | 219
Building Trust and Confidence | 222
The Assessment Criteria | 223
Unpredictable Clients | 224
Preparation Stage | 225
Property Practice | 227
Wills and Probate | 229
The Interview | 230
Chapter 8: Appendix | **243**

Chapter 9 SQE Part 2: Writing the Attendance Note | **245**
Introduction | 245
The Assessment Criteria | 246
The Purpose of an Attendance Note | 247
Post Interview – Failure to Address Key issues | 248
The Attendance Note Template | 248
Chapter 9: Appendix | **254**

Chapter 10 SQE Part 2: Advocacy | **257**
Introduction | 257
The Assessment Criteria | 259
Preparation Stage: 45 minutes | 260
Should You Skim Read or Scan? | 262
Advocacy Submission: 15 minutes | 264
The Beginning | 265

Contents

The Middle	266
The End	267
Handling Difficult Questions	268
Chapter 10: Appendix	**270**

Chapter 11 SQE Part 2: Case and Matter Analysis	**273**
Introduction	273
The Assessment Criteria	275
Report Templates	277
Contentious Matters	285
Negotiation Skills	285
SWOT Analysis	286
Chapter 11: Appendix	**289**

Chapter 12 SQE Part 2: Legal Writing	**291**
Introduction	291
The Assessment Criteria	292
Letters and Emails	293
Legal Writing: Sample Extracts	295
Emails	304
Chapter 12: Appendices	**306**

Chapter 13 SQE Part 2: Legal Drafting	**315**
Introduction	315
Legal Drafting – Business Law and Criminal Litigation	316
The Assessment Criteria	316
Types of Legal Documents	317
Business Law	318
Property Law	318
Criminal Litigation	318
Dispute Resolution	318
Wills and Probate	319
Language	319
Layout	322
Business Law – Drafting Clauses	322
Undertakings	327
Criminal Law – Defence Statement	329
Completing Forms	330
Chapter 13: Appendix	**332**

Chapter 14 SQE Part 2: Legal Research	**335**
Introduction	335
The Assessment Criteria	336
Legal Databases	338
Presenting Your Legal Research	338
Legal Research: Sample Extracts	339
Chapter 14: Appendices	**350**

Testimonials	**355**
Index	*361*

Chapter 1

The SQE Journey

'The journey of a thousand miles begins with a single step'
Lau Tzu

> In this chapter you will learn:
> - ✓ How to use the book if you are studying for the SQE.
> - ✓ What the SQE entails from start to finish.
> - ✓ What motivation is and how it can impact your journey.
> - ✓ Why choose England and Wales to qualify.
> - ✓ What common law means.
> - ✓ The different routes to qualification as a solicitor in England and Wales.
> - ✓ How you are assessed for the SQE Part 1 and 2 and what they include.
> - ✓ Whether you need to do Qualifying Work Experience (QWE).
> - ✓ What the admission process is to qualify as a solicitor once you have passed the SQE.
> - ✓ The difference between the role of the Law Society and Solicitors Regulation Authority (SRA).

Introduction

1.01 The aim of this chapter is to give you a 'snapshot' of what an SQE journey can look like from start to finish. If you have not read the Preface, I suggest you read it first because it tells you how to use this book.

This chapter is split into four parts as outlined below:

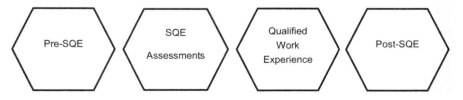

1.02 *The SQE Journey*

As the SQE Assessments and Qualifying Work Experience (QWE) have their own individual chapters only an overview of each is provided here.

All the chapters will provide detailed information and guidance with practical tips and tools. Some chapters also have exercises to support you through your SQE journey.

The SQE is a high-stakes professional exam. The aim of this book is to provide you with real practical tools and tips to help you successfully plan, prepare and pass it to qualify as a solicitor. It is not an academic textbook, there are many universities and training providers offering textbooks and materials from which you can learn the law.

The Pre-SQE Journey

• *Who is the SQE for?*

1.02   The SQE is for anyone who wants to qualify as a solicitor in England and Wales. This book is for students, qualified lawyers and aspiring solicitors and is also a recommended textbook by universities and training providers.

As I work with many different people, I will use the generic term 'lawyer' throughout the book to apply to all of you equally – especially as the end goal is the same for everyone – to qualify as a solicitor.

The book is aimed at helping you convert your academic knowledge of the law into practical and persuasive ways of communicating it, through your oral and written skills. For example, for the written assessments, you will see examples of writing with constructive feedback so you can get a real sense of what you should be aiming to achieve when practising mock papers. Even if your writing style is different, the constructive feedback may help you understand what to include and exclude in your answers.

Not every chapter of the SQE assessments will cover examples using all the practice areas of the law. Sometimes the point will be made by using just one or two practice areas. Those selected are not chosen for any particular reason. They are examples where I have provided more constructive feedback typically for similar issues. Therefore, if you find some of what is shared is not a problem area for you, you can just skip it. Have the confidence to use what works best for you.

What you will read are real examples of challenges experienced and shared by lawyers. The guidance, tools and tips offered are what I share in the coaching sessions with them. The type of coaching I do is called 'performance coaching' and you can read more about it in Chapter 2, Preparing for the SQE (paras **2.14** and **2.15**).

Your journey will be unique to you. It will be different depending on whether you are:
- a qualified lawyer from a foreign jurisdiction;
- an aspiring solicitor (working);

- a barrister in England and Wales; or
- a student.

You may not fit into any of the categories mentioned above (eg the CiLEX route or an apprenticeship route etc), or you may see yourself as belonging in a different category entirely. Your journey is yours and will be dependent on your personal and professional circumstances. As there are so many variables that can apply, you should use and adapt the guidance and information in this book to what works best for you.

The SRA has provided samples of what you can expect for both SQE Parts 1 and 2. These are available on the SRA website (www.sra.org.uk).

- ***Why Choose to Qualify as a Solicitor in England and Wales?***

1.03 In England and Wales, the law is often referred to as 'English law' and solicitors as 'English solicitors' but upon qualification your official title will be 'Solicitor of the Senior Courts of England and Wales'. This is because England and Wales share a unified legal system. So, even though Welsh law does exist separately to English law (mainly to govern issues within Wales), its judiciary applies English law. Scotland and Northern Ireland, respectively, have different legal jurisdictions and apply their own self-governing rules of the law and that is why you are not a 'solicitor of the United Kingdom'.

The laws of England and Wales are based on a common law system. Often, I have been asked *'What does common law mean?'* and *'Why is it called that?'* In Appendix 1A a brief explanation has been provided to help you understand.

England and Wales is one of the most respected legal jurisdictions in the world and it is a privilege to be a part of it. Most commercial businesses and lawyers use English as their preferred language and English law is seen as transparent, fair and flexible. The reputation of the judiciary and court system is also seen as independent and reliable. So, it should come as no surprise that those who wish to qualify as a solicitor and enter the legal profession of England and Wales are tested rigorously. This is to ensure high standards are consistently met, so the profession is not brought into disrepute.

Qualifying as a solicitor can help you expand your global legal footprint and open many professional opportunities for you. Some say, once you qualify as a solicitor in England and Wales, the world is your oyster.

The SQE is also available in the Welsh language. You can find out more about it on the SRA website.

- ***Why the SQE?***

1.04 The SQE is designed to end any bias or perceptions as to how someone qualifies as a solicitor in England and Wales. For example, many people think the traditional route through university and a training contract is better than an apprenticeship or any alternative route. The SQE hopes to end this perception by

1.05 *The SQE Journey*

offering everyone the same consistent approach in assessments, which is fairer and more transparent.

The SQE replaces all the existing routes to qualification such as the phased out Legal Practice Course (LPC). It provides one centralised and standard route for everyone. It removes the inconsistencies in exams that occurred with many different universities and training providers.

Therefore, unless you fall within the transitional period and continue with your chosen route, everyone who wants to qualify as a solicitor will have to do the SQE.

- ***Transitional Period***

1.05 If you fall within the transitional period you will have until 31 December 2032 to complete the LPC and qualify as a solicitor (as long as the chosen route remains available).

You may decide that you want to transfer to the SQE. If you are thinking of changing, check with the SRA if you are entitled to any exemptions (if you are a qualified lawyer) and whether they might be affected.

Once you have decided which route you will take you can focus on what it will entail. If you have decided on the SQE, the benchmark for all the assessments will be that of a newly qualified solicitor so the standard is higher than the LPC.

- ***SQE Exemptions***

1.06 Unless you are a qualified lawyer, there are no exemptions for the SQE.

If you are a qualified lawyer from a foreign jurisdiction or a qualified lawyer in England and Wales (eg a barrister with practice rights) you may be exempt from part or all of the SQE. This includes the requirement to have a minimum of two years Qualifying Work Experience (QWE). For example, to be exempt from the QWE, you will be required to show two years' professional experience to the standard expected of a newly qualified solicitor. Your knowledge, skills and competences in practice will need to be equivalent to the part of the SQE for which you seek exemption. That means your professional standard and experience will need to be 'not substantially different' to the SRA Competence Statement (more details can be found in Appendix 1B).

If you think you may qualify for an exemption, you will need to provide the SRA with evidence that your professional title and experience are equivalent to the SQE (or part of it).

The SRA have stated that there are two ways you can apply for an exemption.

- ***Agreed Exemptions***

1.07 You must have qualified through your jurisdiction's full legal qualification route and your professional legal qualification must meet the SRA requirements based on practice rights, competences and professional work experience. Law

Societies and Bar Councils can apply to the SRA for an agreed exemption for all the lawyers in their jurisdiction.

- **Individual Exemptions**

1.08 If your jurisdiction does not qualify for any agreed exemptions you can apply for an individual exemption from SQE Part 1 and/or SQE Part 2. Your application will be dealt with on a case-by-case basis.

If you are exempt from any or all of the SQE but the SRA has a serious concern about your level of English or Welsh, they can impose a language requirement when you apply for your first practising certificate.

You can only be exempt from the SQE parts as a 'whole' and not by practice areas of the law. This means that you could be exempt from the following:
- SQE Part 1: Functioning Legal Knowledge (FLK) – one or both days.
- SQE Part 2: Practical Legal Skills (PLS) – all of it because it is classed as one assessment (ie you are either exempt from all the oral and written assessments or none of them).
- QWE – the whole requirement.

If you are a student or aspiring solicitor who has completed the LPC but not secured a training contract you will not be exempt from the SQE. However, if you can show you have passed the LPC it could count as the equivalent means to satisfy the SQE Part 1, so you can directly register for the SQE Part 2.

You should look on the SRA website for the most up to date information on which countries have agreed exemptions and information on how to apply.

- **Different Routes to Qualification**

1.09 Where you start your SQE journey will impact how long it will take you to complete it and qualify as a solicitor. The image below provided by the SRA shows you an overview of what an SQE journey could look like depending on where you start:

* If approved, you may not need take all or part of SQE 1 and 2
** Applies to candidates who have not taken SQE 2

1.10 *The SQE Journey*

You will need to satisfy the following four stages (unless any exemptions apply):

(1) have a degree, apprenticeship or equivalent;
(2) pass the SQE two parts:
- Part 1: Functioning Legal Knowledge (FLK) Assessments;
- Part 2: Practical Legal Skills (PLS) Assessments;
(3) have two years of qualifying work experience;
(4) meet the requisite character and suitability requirements.

- ***Motivation***

1.10 It is a good idea to ask yourself why you want to become a solicitor. Interestingly, the two questions most law students are asked and find hard to answer are:

> 'Why law?'
>
> 'Why do you want to be a solicitor?'

Both of these are typical interview questions for training contracts or work experience, so it is a good starting point to think about your answers. If you are a student, then you may find the Venn Diagram in Chapter 4, Qualifying Work Experience, Appendix 4A (CV Commentary: Students) helpful. Throughout the SQE journey, asking yourself a 'Why?' question means you may end up refining your answers (that is good).

Most qualified lawyers are already clearer about why they want to become solicitors because they are not starting their legal career from the beginning. For some it is a professional requirement and for others there are personal reasons.

If you are clear about your reasons, then the motivation to achieve your goal is easier. That is not to be confused with the actual journey to get there – that may be fraught with highs and lows, but your motivation is what will keep you going.

> **'Sometimes it's the journey that teaches you a lot about the destination.'**
> **Drake**

Of course, the common goal is to successfully pass the SQE. What you need to do to achieve that success will be tested through your motivation.

Motivation is two-fold:
- extrinsic motivation – what people see; and
- intrinsic motivation – what people do not see.

Both are important driving factors for success; what drives you to succeed, however, will be your intrinsic motivation.

Sylvia Duckworth's the Iceberg Illusion gives a great illustration of success. It really captures what people might see as success, but not what the person might have gone through to achieve it. It is a good visual to apply to yourself and recognise that to achieve the success you want, you need to be prepared for what you might have to go through to achieve it.

Motivation is different for everyone. In the context of becoming a lawyer, extrinsic motivation might be perceptions of what you see about being a lawyer (such as status, appearance, money, lifestyle, results, workplace, stability etc). The intrinsic motivation experienced by lawyers is what you do not see (such as hard work, stress, work pressures, long hours, challenges, setbacks, emotional distress etc). It will be the motivation that fuels your ambition to qualify as a solicitor and how you progress in your chosen career.

Therefore, the Iceberg Illusion highlights nicely what an SQE success journey could look like from start to finish. You have no idea what your journey will be like until you start it. All you can do is be best prepared and well informed.

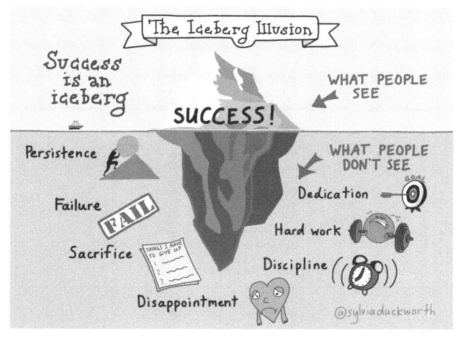

www.sylviaduckworth.com

The SQE Assessments

1.11 This section will look at what each part of the SQE entails and gives a brief overview of what you can expect to do. You can read about what to consider when deciding which university or training provider to invest in (unless you are sponsored) in Chapter 2, Preparing for the SQE (para **2.03**). You will also find practical suggestions on how to study for the SQE in there.

1.12 *The SQE Journey*

The SQE is made up of two parts: SQE Part 1 and SQE Part 2. Each part must be passed in the same sitting. For example, SQE Part 1 is two days and SQE Part 2 which tests your oral and written skills is split over several days. See the tables below for more details.

Unless you are exempt from any parts, the SQE Part 1 must be passed before you can register for SQE Part 2.

You will have six years from the date you sit your first SQE assessment in which to pass it. The six-year restriction only applies to the SQE assessments and not the QWE, which can be gained at any time. You can read more about how to cope with failure in Chapter 6, Managing Nerves, Fear and Failure (para **6.24**).

The Competence Statement (detailed in Appendix 1B) has heavily influenced the SQE and you need to understand how it can help you prepare for the assessments. The visual below will help you to understand how the SQE complements the Competence Statement requirements:

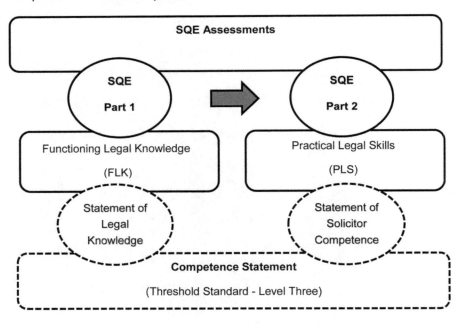

- **Professional Conduct and Ethics**

1.12 Remember, professional conduct and ethics will be tested throughout both parts of the SQE, so you must always bear this in mind and address it where necessary. Do not expect it to be specifically mentioned or highlighted. For example, it could be a conflict of interest or a confidentiality issue and you would be expected to proactively identify it.

In Chapter 3, Functioning Legal Knowledge (FLK) Assessments, Appendix 3A you can read more about what you need to study for this area. More details about each part of the SQE assessments can be found in their respective chapters throughout this book.

Something else that will not explicitly be highlighted but you may need to show are your negotiation skills.

- **Negotiation Skills**

1.13 You should be prepared to be tested on negotiation skills too. This is not assessed separately, but it could arise in SQE Part 2 and is a key skill for all solicitors. You may find that you need to demonstrate your negotiation skills in the following assessments:

- Client Interviewing Skills (and the Attendance Note).
- Case and Matter Analysis.
- Legal Writing.

Although negotiation skills are not specifically mentioned in the assessment criteria, it is reflected in providing client-focused advice. Therefore, you should look out for any language that asks you to advise a client on potential options, strategies, risks and benefits where you would demonstrate your negotiation skills in the oral or written assessments.

You can read more about negotiation skills generally in Chapter 11, Case and Matter Analysis (para **11.09**).

- **SQE Results**

1.14 The SQE is a pass or fail exam. You will be emailed your results and provided with a mark in the context of the assessments. You might have to share your results with your employer or a third party who requests a breakdown of them.

The pass mark for the SQE will vary between different sittings. This is to ensure consistency and fairness based on the ease or difficulty of the assessments.

Unless you are a qualified lawyer who is exempt from any or all parts of the SQE assessments, you will be required to pass the SQE Part 1 and 2.

The information and tables below provide a brief outline of what both parts of the SQE include.

- **SQE Part 1: Functioning Legal Knowledge (FLK) Assessments**

1.15 The SQE Part 1 will consist of two multiple choice tests (MCT) of 180 questions each, so a total of 360 multiple choice questions (MCQs). The focus of these assessments will be to test you on the fundamental legal rules and principles expected of a newly qualified solicitor. So, this part of the SQE can be seen as the 'academic' part where you need to learn the law and demonstrate your understanding. More details about this assessment can be found in Chapter 3, Functioning Legal Knowledge (FLK) Assessments.

The SQE Part 1 MCTs are 'closed book' which means that you cannot take any materials, notes or books into the assessment.

1.16 *The SQE Journey*

The table below shows what the two MCTs will cover on each day and they must be done in the same sitting (these will not be consecutive days):

SQE Part 1: Functioning Legal Knowledge (FLK) Assessments	
Day 1	**Day 2**
FLK Assessment One (FLK1)	**FLK Assessment Two (FLK2)**
180 MCQs	180 MCQs
Approximately 5 hours (plus a break)	**Approximately 5 hours (plus a break)**
• Session 1 – 90 MCQs (2 hours and 33 minutes) 60 Minutes Break • Session 2 – 90 MCQs (2 hours and 33 minutes)	• Session 1 – 90 MCQs (2 hours and 33 minutes) 60 Minutes Break • Session 2 – 90 MCQs (2 hours and 33 minutes)
FLK1 Subjects	**FLK2 Subjects**
Business Law and Practice*	Property Practice*
Dispute Resolution	Wills and Administration of Estates*
Contract Law	Land Law
Law of Torts	Trusts
Constitutional and Administrative Law and EU Law and Legal Services	Solicitors' Accounts
Legal System of England and Wales	Criminal Law and Practice
*principles of taxation will only be assessed in these subjects.	
Professional Conduct and Ethics	
You will be tested pervasively in all assessments.	
Location	
Pearson VUE centres in the UK and internationally.	
Dress Code	
Informal/Casual Wear	

- ### SQE Part 1 Results

1.16   The SQE Part 1 are pass-or-fail assessments against a set pass mark. If you fail FLK1 and/or FLK2 then you will have two further attempts to take the failed assessment within six years from the date you sat it. If you fail, more information can be found in Chapter 3, Functioning Legal Knowledge Assessments (para **3.08**) and Chapter 6, Managing Nerves, Fear and Failure (para **6.26**).

You can expect to receive your results around five or six weeks after sitting the assessment. If you pass and want the option to sit the next available SQE Part 2 assessments then you should have enough time to register for it.

• SQE Part 2: Practical Legal Skills (PLS) Assessments

1.17 The SQE Part 2 is classed as one single exam made up of 16 assessments which are split into two parts: oral and written assessments. It is made up of four oral assessments and twelve written assessments, where you are assessed equally on the law and skills.

These assessments are 'closed book' which means that you cannot take any materials, notes or books into the assessments.

For these assessments you use what you have learnt from the SQE Part 1, so not any 'new' areas of law, but you demonstrate your knowledge in a practical manner. You will be assessed in five practice areas of the law which will require you to have fundamental knowledge of the relevant substantive areas of law tested in SQE Part 1. The table below demonstrates how both parts overlap, but are not identical:

SQE Part 1 Functional Legal Knowledge	SQE Part 2 Practice Areas of Law
Criminal Law	Criminal Litigation
Contract and Tort	Dispute Resolution
Land Law	Property Practice
Trusts	Wills and Intestacy, Probate Administration and Practice*
Contract	Business Organisations, Rules and Procedures*

* throughout the book these subjects will be referred to as wills and probate and business law.

You will not be tested on the following areas of law (except for money laundering and financial services which may be examined in business law):

- legal system of England and Wales;
- constitutional and administrative law and EU law;
- legal services; and
- solicitors' accounts

For the SQE Part 2, you will need to demonstrate your ability to provide practical legal advice using effective communication skills. You will be assessed on your oral and written skills in a range of the practice areas of law mentioned in the table above. The key focus is on your ability to show your problem solving and advisory skills as opposed to just academic legal knowledge. The six areas you will be assessed on are as follows:

- Oral assessments:
  - Client interviewing (including writing an attendance note)
  - Advocacy
- Written assessments:
  - Case and matter analysis

1.18 *The SQE Journey*

- Legal writing
- Legal drafting
- Legal research.

Below is an example of how you may be assessed for the SQE Part 2 which is split into two parts for the oral and written assessments.

- **SQE Part 2: Oral Assessments**

1.18 The oral assessments suggested below can be done in any order.

\multicolumn{3}{c}{**SQE Part 2: Oral Assessments**}
\multicolumn{3}{c}{**4 Assessments**}
	Day 1	**Day 2**
Assessments	Criminal Litigation × 1 Property Practice* × 1	Dispute Resolution × 1 Wills and Probate* × 1
Advocacy	**Criminal Litigation**	**Dispute Resolution**
	Preparation: 45 minutes Advocacy: 15 minutes	Preparation: 45 minutes Advocacy: 15 minutes
Client Interviewing Skills and Attendance Note	**Property Practice***	**Wills and Probate***
	Preparation: 10 minutes Interview: 25 minutes Attendance Note: 25 minutes	Preparation: 10 minutes Interview: 25 minutes Attendance Note: 25 minutes
\multicolumn{3}{c}{*principles of taxation will only be assessed in these subjects.}
\multicolumn{3}{c}{**Professional Conduct and Ethics**}
\multicolumn{3}{c}{You will be tested pervasively in all the assessments.}
\multicolumn{3}{c}{**Location**}
\multicolumn{3}{c}{Pearson VUE centres in the UK only}
\multicolumn{3}{c}{**Dress Code**}
\multicolumn{3}{c}{Formal/Smart Office Wear}

❖ **Client Interviewing**

1.19 You will meet a client (the role will be played by an actor) and your instructions will tell you who the client is and some brief details about what they have come to discuss. You will be expected to take the client's instructions, address any concerns and, if required, provide some preliminary advice. The key objective is to build the client's trust and confidence for them to instruct you. You are assessed on the skills part only.

❖ **Attendance Note**

1.20 Straight after the client interview, you will need to produce a handwritten attendance note based on the interview. You will need to address what you gathered from the interview and identify any factual and legal issues as well as any next steps. You will be allowed to use your preparation and interview notes. The attendance note will be marked by an assessor (a qualified solicitor) and you are assessed on the law and skills for this part.

❖ **Advocacy**

1.21   You will be given a case study where you will be required to make a persuasive courtroom advocacy submission on a matter before a judge (a role played by a qualified solicitor). The submissions will be on dispute resolution and criminal litigation. You will act on the instructions and make an application which may include issues involving procedural or technical points of law.

- **SQE Part 2: Written Assessments**

1.22   The written assessments below can be done in any order and in either practice area of law (except for business law where you do all of them).

	SQE Part 2: Written Assessments		
	12 Assessments		
	Day 1	**Day 2**	**Day 3**
Assessments	Criminal Litigation × 2 Dispute Resolution × 2	Property Practice × 2 Wills and Probate × 2	Business Law × 4
Case and Matter Analysis	Criminal Litigation or Dispute Resolution	Property Practice* or Wills and Probate*	Business Law*
	Time: **60 minutes**	Time: **60 minutes**	Time: **60 minutes**
Legal Writing	Criminal Litigation or Dispute Resolution	Property Practice* or Wills and Probate*	Business Law*
	Time: **30 minutes**	Time: **30 minutes**	Time: **30 minutes**
Legal Drafting	Criminal Litigation or Dispute Resolution	Property Practice* or Wills and Probate*	Business Law*
	Time: **45 minutes**	Time: **45 minutes**	Time: **45 minutes**
Legal Research	Criminal Litigation or Dispute Resolution	Property Practice* or Wills and Probate*	Business Law*
	Time: **60 minutes**	Time: **60 minutes**	Time: **60 minutes**
	*principles of taxation will only be assessed in these subjects.		
	Professional Conduct and Ethics		
	You will be tested pervasively in all the assessments.		
	Location		
	Pearson VUE centres in the UK and internationally.		
	Dress Code		
	Informal/Casual Wear		

1.23 *The SQE Journey*

Below you will find brief details of each written assessment.

❖ Case and Matter Analysis

1.23 You will be given an electronic file of documents (not all of them may be relevant) where you will need to produce a written report for a partner based on your legal analysis of a matter. The matter could be something like reviewing a case file or transaction where you advise the client on the merits of what they want to do. You will be expected to identify the legal and factual issues as well as any legal risks. It should be client-focused advice where you may have to consider any options and strategies that may form part of a negotiation (where appropriate).

❖ Legal Writing

1.24 You will be required to write a letter or an email as the acting solicitor in the matter. It should be recipient-focused which sets out the law/legal advice and addresses any concerns raised. The recipient could be a client, expert, third party, the other side to a litigation or transaction matter or a partner within their organisation (this is a non-exhaustive list).

❖ Legal Drafting

1.25 You may be required to draft a legal document or a part of it. This may include drafting from a precedent, amending a document or drafting without either of them.

❖ Legal Research

1.26 You will be required to conduct legal research on instructions you receive on an email from a partner. Your written note should cover the issues and any advice the partner can give to the client. You should split your answer into two parts: advice to the client and legal reasoning (ie, key sources: precedents, legislation, authorities etc). You will be provided with primary and secondary sources and not all of them may be relevant.

• SQE Part 2: Results

❖ Marking Criteria

1.27 The SQE Part 2 is classed holistically as one single exam therefore, there is only one pass mark. Even though you get marked for each of the sixteen assessments (four oral skills and twelve written skills), you pass or fail based on your overall performance and not on individual marks for each of the assessments. You are marked equally on the law and skills for each assessment against Assessment Criteria using a grading scale. More details are explained in the relevant chapters.

You can expect to receive your results around fourteen weeks after sitting the assessment.

Qualifying Work Experience (QWE)

1.28   This can be done at any stage before the admission process.

- ***Qualified Lawyers***

1.29   If you are a qualified lawyer and have completed the SQE Part 1 and 2 (or are exempt), you can start the process of getting admitted onto the Roll of Solicitors (see the Post-SQE Journey (para **1.31**)).

- ***Aspiring Lawyers (Working) and Students***

1.30   If you are doing your QWE whilst you do the SQE Part 2, even if you pass the SQE Part 2, you will need to complete the QWE requirement of two years' legal work experience, before you can start the admissions process.

If you are looking for QWE, there is some guidance offered in more detail in Chapter 4, Qualifying Work Experience, Finding QWE (para **4.09**). The chapter will also provide you with help on how to create or improve your CV (Appendix 4A). This may be useful if you are a student looking for legal work experience or are a qualified lawyer looking to practise law in England and Wales.

Generally speaking, it makes sense to have some good-quality work experience before you attempt the SQE Part 2, otherwise you will probably find it very challenging. Chapter 4, Qualifying Work Experience (para **4.22**) looks at what amounts to good-quality work experience.

The Post-SQE Journey

1.31   You do not automatically qualify as a solicitor and get admitted to the Roll of Solicitors once you have completed the SQE assessments and QWE requirements. You have to apply through the SRA and complete the necessary paperwork to comply with the registration process.

This process can take a long time depending on your circumstances. For example, the pre-admission screening process can take up to four weeks, or if you have any character and suitability issues that need to be reviewed it can take up to six months.

If you are a qualified lawyer from a regulated profession, the SRA will require a Certificate of Good Standing from your home jurisdiction as part of the admission process. You should check how long this process can take so try to do as much preparation in advance as possible.

The Law Society does not deal with the admissions process. Many students and lawyers are sometimes unclear about the role of the Law Society and how it differs from the SRA. Therefore, in Appendix 1C there is a short explanation showing their respective roles.

1.32 *The SQE Journey*

- ## Admission to the Roll of Solicitors

1.32 The registration process means you will need to do the following:

(1) Validate your degree.

(2) Pass the SQE and share your results.

(3) Register your QWE.

(4) Pass the background screening (Disclosure and Barring Service (DBS)) and suitability checks.

(5) Complete the admissions application form and choose the date you become a solicitor.

Below is a brief explanation of what the DBS check and character and suitability check mean:

❖ Disclosure and Barring Service (DBS)

1.33 The DBS check is compulsory and you must pass it. If you are already a qualified lawyer in your home jurisdiction, you may need to provide further evidence of appropriate checks which can make the process even longer. Therefore, you should contact the SRA to confirm what their exact requirements are based on the jurisdiction in which you are a qualified lawyer. You should try to do as much of the paperwork as possible in advance, because the process can be time-consuming.

❖ Character and Suitability

1.34 If you are of good character, the process is straightforward and will be supported by the DBS check.

If you are not of good character (for whatever reason), you should speak to the SRA. Ask them to consider your character and suitability before you start the SQE. If your circumstances change during the SQE journey in a way which may affect your character and suitability upon admission, you should contact the SRA as soon as possible for an assessment. The last thing you want to do is to go through the SQE process and then realise that you do not meet the SRA requirements to qualify as a solicitor.

The SRA will take into account:

- Criminal conduct

    This is where the offence falls in the most serious category (likely refusal) or serious category (may refuse). Both categories and specific details can be found on the SRA website (www.sra.org.uk).

- Other conduct or behaviour

    This includes integrity issues, assessment offences (plagiarism or cheating), financial conduct, regulatory or disciplinary findings.

If the SRA is not satisfied with your character and suitability, you can only request a further assessment if there is a material change to your circumstances.

Once you pass the DBS check and character and suitability requirements you will successfully be admitted to the Roll of Solicitors and will become a qualified solicitor of the Senior Courts of England and Wales. Congratulations!

The day you are admitted you will be issued with an Admissions Certificate which you can download from your 'mySRA' membership account. An Admissions Certificate is different to a Practising Certificate.

- **A Practising Certificate**

1.35 Once you are a qualified solicitor, if you provide any work that amounts to reserved legal activity it is a criminal offence to practise law in England and Wales without a practising certificate. More information about what amounts to reserved or non-reserved legal activities can be found on the Legal Services Board website (www.legalservicesboard.org.uk).

Every year, all practising certificates need to be renewed by 31 October and last for 12 months.

Before you can apply for a practising certificate, you will need to abide by the SRA requirement and show evidence of continuing competence in accordance with the Competence Statement (see Appendix 1B).

- **Continuing Competence**

1.36 All practising solicitors must adopt the SRA approach to being assessed through continuing competence. This means you will be required to meet the competences and sign a declaration stating you are satisfied with your level of learning and development in relation to the law and skills required to practise as a solicitor.

The SRA does not dictate how many Continuing Professional Development (CPD) hours or days you must do to show continuing competence throughout the year. It is very much down to 'self-regulation' between you and the place where you work. You have to do what you believe is sufficient to meet the general requirements and legal knowledge for your practice area and level of experience (determined by the different Threshold Standards). More information on the Competence Statement can be found in Appendix 1B.

As the SRA has left it open to each solicitor or law firm to determine how they meet the Competence Statement, it has offered the following guidance:
- Step 1: reflect on your practice area;
- Step 2: keep up to date;
- Step 3: identify any learning gaps in your skills or knowledge; and
- Step 4: evaluate and keep a record.

The SRA is entitled to call upon you to produce evidence of what you have done to satisfy the Statement of Solicitor Competence and Statement of Legal Knowledge,

1.36 *The SQE Journey*

at any time. Therefore, you should record the details of everything you do that contributes to your personal and professional development.

> *'Success is a journey, not a destination. It requires constant effort, vigilance and re-evaluation'*
>
> **Mark Twain**

The SQE Journey – Top Ten Tips

(1) If you have any character and suitability issues, speak to the SRA sooner rather than later.

(2) Understand your motivations for why you want to be a solicitor; these will help you when times get tough.

(3) Check your SQE starting point and see if you qualify for any exemptions as a qualified lawyer or meet the equivalent means if you have passed the LPC.

(4) Think of the SQE Part 1 as the academic part that tests you on the substantive and procedural areas of the law through multiple choice tests.

(5) Think of the SQE Part 2 as the practical part that tests you on your knowledge of the law through your skills by doing oral and written assessments.

(6) Do not underestimate the skills part; it can be harder than learning the law and take more time. Marks for both the law and skills affect your pass/fail mark.

(7) Understand the Competence Statement and how it complements the SQE.

(8) Always bear in mind professional conduct and ethics for both parts of the SQE.

(9) The admissions process can be long, so do as much advance preparation as possible.

(10) Once qualified, you must have a valid practising certificate to practise law, otherwise you are committing a criminal offence.

Chapter 1

The SQE Journey: Appendices

Appendix 1A: Understanding the Common Law System of England and Wales

The following brief historical chronology of pre- and post-1066 (the Norman Conquest) describes how the common law system came about and got its name.

- Pre-1066
  - Customary law existed where local laws were created by members of the community based on their values and beliefs. These varied for different parts of the country.
  - There were no written records and laws were passed down orally.
  - This system created confusion and inconsistency throughout the land when community members tried to resolve criminal or civil matters.
- Post-1066
  - This was the start of the common law system of King William I (known as William the Conqueror), who introduced a more centralised system of government.
  - Later, this led to the development of the King's Court where King Henry II created a set of rules and procedures to be followed to ensure consistency.
  - King Henry II appointed skilled clerics to travel around the country to resolve disputes using his rules and procedures. This became known as using the 'common law'.

So, instead of a set of laws that are written down (codified law), the common law system is based on precedents (ie this means when a judge is deciding on a case, they will look at a decision of a previous similar case).

The English legal system is an evolving system that changes with the times and society's needs and requirements. New laws are made in Parliament (following a set process) and once they become law, it is the judge's job to interpret them and make decisions based on them. If it is new law and they have no previous precedent to rely on, they will be making a decision which will become a precedent for any future similar cases.

Therefore, it is essential as a lawyer that you keep up to date with the law as any changes can affect the advice you give a client. Any legal advice based on law

The SQE Journey: Appendices

that is outdated or incorrect could give rise to a negligence claim, and harm your reputation and credibility. It could also be a professional conduct issue.

Appendix 1B: The Competence Statement

An overview of the Competence Statement is provided below and it is made up of three parts:

1 Statement of Solicitor Competence

This broadly means the ability to perform the roles and tasks required by your job to a proper standard of service and competence – it is generic and applies to all practising solicitors.

The Statement of Solicitor Competence is made up of four sections, A to D. More details of what is specifically included within each section's headings can be found on the SRA website.

Sections A to D and top line headings should give you a good idea of what you are expected to know and be able to do as a newly qualified solicitor. These have also been included in Chapter 4, Qualifying Work Experience (Appendix 4B) to help you when completing your legal work experience 'diary' to evidence what you have done to develop some or all of your competences.

Statement of Solicitor Competence	
A – Ethics, professionalism and judgement	
A1	Act honestly and with integrity, in accordance with legal and regulatory requirements and the SRA Standards and Regulations.
A2	Maintain the level of competence and legal knowledge needed to practise effectively, taking into account changes in their role and/or practice context and developments in the law.
A3	Work within the limits of their competence and the supervision which they need.
A4	Draw on a sufficient detailed knowledge and understanding of their field(s) of work and role in order to practise effectively.
A5	Apply understanding, critical thinking and analysis to solve problems.
B – Technical legal practice	
B1	Obtain relevant facts.
B2	Undertake legal research.
B3	Develop and advise on relevant options, strategies and solutions.
B4	Draft documents which are legally effective and accurately reflect the client's instructions.
B5	Undertake effective spoken and written advocacy (in and out of court).
B6	Negotiate solutions to clients' issues.
B7	Plan, manage and progress legal cases and transactions.

Appendix 1A

	C – Working with other people
C1	Communicate clearly and effectively, orally and in writing.
C2	Establish and maintain effective and professional relations with clients.
C3	Establish and maintain effective and professional relations with other people.
	D – Managing themselves and their own work
D1	Initiate, plan, prioritise and manage work activities and projects to ensure that they are completed efficiently, on time and to an appropriate standard, both in relation to their own work and work that they lead or supervise.
D2	Keep, use and maintain accurate, complete and clear records.
D3	Apply good business practice.

2 The Threshold Standard

There are five levels of standards that need to be met and the levels will change as you develop and gain more experience working in legal practice.

- **Levels 1 and 2**

    Someone with limited experience (this might be someone with very little practical experience of working in a legal environment).

- **Level 3**

    Someone who is expected to meet the requirements of a newly qualified solicitor. This is the level the SQE assess you on.

- **Levels 4 and 5**

    Someone experienced (capable of dealing with more complex cases and transactions with a level of depth and mastery).

Below are the details of Threshold Standard level three from the SRA website which show you what you are expected to be able to do as a newly qualified solicitor:

Threshold Standard Level Three:

Functioning legal knowledge	Identifies the legal principles relevant to the area of practice and applies them appropriately and effectively to individual cases.
Standard of work	Acceptable standard achieved routinely for straightforward tasks. Complex tasks may lack refinement.
Autonomy	Achieves most tasks and able to progress legal matters using own judgment, recognising when support is needed.
Complexity	Able to deal with straightforward transactions, including occasional, unfamiliar tasks which present a range of problems and choices.
Perception of context	Understands the significance of individual actions in the context of the objectives of the transaction/strategy for the case.
Innovation and originality	Uses experience to check information provided and to form judgments about possible courses of action and ways forward.

The SQE Journey: Appendices

If you would like to read about all the levels, they can be found on the SRA website (www.sra.org.uk)

3 Statement of Legal Knowledge

The table below provides you with the headings of the subject areas of law that you are required to know at the point of qualification. For example, to avoid duplication of content, Chapter 3, Functioning Legal Knowledge Assessments, Appendix 3A provides some specific (but brief) details of what you are required to know for the SQE Part 1. If you want to read more about how the Competence Statement maps across the SQE (in more detail) you can find the information on the SRA website.

Statement of Legal Knowledge	
FLK 1	**FLK 2**
Business Law and Practice	Property Practice
Dispute Resolution	Wills and Administration of Estates
Contract Law	Land Law
Law of Torts	Trusts
Legal System of England and Wales	Solicitors Accounts
Constitutional and Administrative Law and EU and Legal Services	Criminal Law and Practice
Professional Conduct and Ethics	

Appendix 1C: The Roles of the Law Society and the SRA

Many students and lawyers do not know the difference between the role of the Law Society and the Solicitors Regulation Authority (SRA). What you need to know is that they have very distinct and independent roles. The SRA is funded and sits within the Law Society, but it is an independent regulatory body. Below are some examples to help you understand the key differences.

- ## *The Role of the Solicitors Regulation Authority (SRA)*

Website: www.sra.org.uk

The SRA is a regulatory body that protects the public and helps people in three ways:

(1) It ensures people have a fair choice in the market place for legal services.

(2) It ensures high standards from all solicitors by ensuring that they adhere to rules.

(3) It has a range of powers that allows it to discipline solicitors and law firms that breach the rules.

There are a range of disciplinary actions available to the SRA for professional misconduct. These range from a warning letter for a minor breach, to a solicitor

Appendix 1A

being struck off the Roll of Solicitors, or a law firm being shut down for a serious breach. Serious breaches are usually referred to the independent Solicitors Disciplinary Tribunal.

Ultimately, it is your personal responsibility to comply with the Code of Conduct. They are the rules that solicitors and law firms have to abide by to ensure compliance.

- ### *The Role of the Law Society*

Website: www.lawsociety.org.uk

The Law Society provides information and services to support solicitors. The main Law Society office is in Chancery Lane in Central London, but there are also regional law societies. There are many services provided by the Law Society and many law students, aspiring and qualified solicitors are not always aware of what it offers its members.

More information about members' benefits can be found on the Law Society website (www.lawsociety.org.uk). Below are a few examples:

- use of the reading room for informal meetings and catch-ups;
- use of the library to obtain expert help on a legal research issue;
- attendance at events and seminars (paid and free);
- discounts with various retail and business partners;
- a confidential and free ethics helpline;
- the opportunity to join different clubs (eg, the Law Society Arts Club).

Chapter 2

Preparing for the SQE

'Before anything else, preparation is the key to success.'
Alexander Graham Bell

In this chapter you will learn:

✓ What questions to ask different universities and training providers about their SQE preparatory courses.

✓ How to approach the SQE if you are a student, qualified lawyer or aspiring solicitor (working).

✓ Time management techniques and what to think about when making a study plan.

✓ How to identify your learning preferences and the different studying formats.

✓ How to ask for any reasonable adjustments (if required).

✓ Understanding the Competence Statement in relation to the SQE.

✓ The level of English required to pass the SQE.

Introduction

2.01 This chapter will start with what you need to do to register successfully online by creating an SQE account with the Solicitors Regulation Authority (SRA). It will help you think about what to consider when deciding which university or training provider you might want to use for the SQE. Whether you are a full-time/part-time student, an aspiring solicitor (working) or a qualified lawyer, your choices may impact your SQE experience.

If you have a sponsorship, your employer will probably have a preferred agreement with a university or training provider already in place. You should speak to them in the first instance.

If you are self-funding, then there are a lot of factors you may need to consider and cost will usually play a large part in your decision making of who to invest in.

It is important to know upfront that the SRA will not provide any regulatory assurances or oversight of any universities and training providers that offer SQE

2.01 Preparing for the SQE

preparatory courses. The SRA website does list and showcase case studies of training providers registered with them, however, this is not an endorsement of them. You still need to do your homework and research which one is best placed to meet your needs.

The SRA has stated it will not be setting out any specific requirements that the SQE preparatory courses have to follow. This means you have to be satisfied with the quality of the materials offered by any university and training provider. You want the quality to be at the level you are tested on which reflects the SRA Competence Statement and Assessment Specifications. See Chapter 1, The SQE Journey, Appendix 1B for the details of what is included in the Competence Statement and each of the respective chapters for the Assessment Specification details upon which you will be assessed.

The legal education market is competitive with the existing well-established law schools and many new businesses offering SQE preparatory courses. It can be quite daunting and confusing trying to figure out what the entire SQE includes. It can be even more confusing trying to compare who is best placed and experienced enough to offer you good-quality SQE materials and flexible study packages at competitive prices. The traditional approach to studying law has changed and this brings with it some new ways to be able to study law. You decide what works best for you.

This means that any SQE preparatory course you are interested in should be thoroughly checked by you to ensure you are happy with what is covered and at what depth. You may think the onus is on the university or training provider to tell you and no doubt they will, but you need to do your own homework and ask questions to make sure it is right for you. Below there is a list of questions you can ask to help you decide.

In a spirit of fairness, I will remain objective by not naming any universities or training providers. If you know who you will study with then you can skip the section on How to Choose an SQE Provider (para **2.03**) and go to Studying Formats (para **2.08**). If you do not know who to choose, my guidance around what to consider will be largely generic because you have your own personal and professional circumstances to consider. So, add your own questions to those set out below.

In preparing to study for the SQE, the focus on the law is tangible so easier to identify if you are on track or not. The focus on the skills part is intangible, so not as easy because it is varied and dependant on each person's skill set, personality and experience. You can read more on Communication Skills in Chapter 5.

I believe that one of the best ways to practise the oral skills I talk about in this book is by doing them in a real environment (ideally) face to face and receiving real-time constructive feedback from an expert.

> *'A lot of people have gone further than they thought they could because someone else thought they could.'*
> **Zig Ziglar**

What I do want to emphasise is that the nuances and what I share in this book will come across differently from what I do in person when working with lawyers.

To manage your expectations, the techniques and strategies that I use and share may not automatically work for you, just by you reading this book. This is because they are all tailored to each person I work with directly and how you interpret the writing in this book may be different to how I actually share it in person. Therefore, you should adapt what you read to suit you or find a coach who will help you tailor your skills specifically to your needs.

SQE Registration

2.02 One of the first things you should do is go to the SRA website to register and activate your SQE account. This will provide you with your SQE candidate number and once you log in you will need to upload photo ID to activate the account. The onus is on you to keep the ID up to date if it expires during the entire SQE process. Therefore, the SRA recommends a passport but there are other options too.

Once registered you will be able to complete all your assessment bookings and make any applications for reasonable adjustments or exemptions.

How to Choose an SQE Course Provider

2.03 If your employer is sponsoring you, this section will be less relevant to you. However, most people are usually self-funding, so the aim is to help you make an informed decision on which education or training provider to invest in.

Many universities and training providers have had to adapt their existing materials and create new ones. Those that offered the QLTS may be at a slight advantage because the SQE is heavily based on it, so they are not starting from the beginning but refining and developing their materials.

- *SQE Data*

2.04 As the SQE is still new it is important to point out that any data shared in its first year or so will be atypical and not reflective of future sittings. For example, many of those that have passed the SQE since it started may be foreign jurisdiction qualified lawyers or aspiring solicitors who had passed the LPC and are working (so not your typical full-time students).

Once the SQE is more established over the years, many university and training providers will be able to offer more data on the category of candidates and SQE pass/fail rates. Bear in mind that the data will be based on what the candidate decides to share or not. In the future, hopefully with a breakdown of more detailed data, it will make the decision process a little easier.

An internet search shows many of the established well-known universities or training providers. However, there are other smaller training providers who might be more cost effective and offer you a more personalised service. Look for independent statistical data if any of them suggest they are the best placed SQE provider in the

2.05 *Preparing for the SQE*

market (this means more than accepting their pass rate at face value and reading testimonials).

A lot of factors will depend on your personal and professional circumstances. Below are two tools I use with clients when a decision needs to be made and there is a lot of information and many options which can make the decision process difficult.

I hope my observations and suggestions help you work out which university or training provider you want to invest in.

- **Understanding Yourself**

2.05 Before you start looking at which SQE course provider to invest in, you need to know how you study best and what you prefer doing (eg classroom, online, blended, personal tutors, coaching etc). You also need to evaluate the following (a non-exhaustive list):

- The type of place where you work (if relevant).
- Your practice area and workload (if relevant).
- Your personal/family commitments.
- Whether you will require any flexibility in studying (if working full time).
- Whether work will support you and offer you study leave.
- How do you like to study?
- Do you want to do more classroom and online or online exclusively?
- How many hours of study can you do during the weekdays and weekends (you must be honest and realistic)?
- Are you looking for full time or part-time study options?
- What is your learning-style preference?
- Do you need any special adjustments or have any additional requirements to help you study?

Once you have figured out what you want to do, you can see what universities and training providers can offer you and whether their flexibility meets your requirements.

- **Understanding the SQE Course Provider**

2.06 There will be a lot of competition over what a university or training provider is prepared to offer you, especially if you are considering online materials only. Below are some observations from lawyers who studied online with different training providers or universities:

- The quantity of materials can be overwhelming.
- There are not many materials.
- The learning platform used is not user-friendly.
- The content is not well organised.

- There are mistakes and inconsistencies in the materials.
- The suggested answers for written assessment mocks were not a true reflection of how much you could realistically cover in the assessment time.
- The feedback for the oral assessments was not to the standard of the SQE Part 2 but more LPC level.

Therefore, speak to a training provider and find out what they are offering you and whether you can get a demonstration from them as to how their platform works, samples of their materials or a free trial to experience their services. Also, read the section on 'Misleading Marketing and Advertising' below before you decide.

Here are three key reflective questions to ask yourself after speaking to them:

(1) Who offers me the best service that suits my learning preferences?

(2) Who offers me the best price for what I am getting?

(3) Who offers any additional support such as, unlimited access to law tutors, skills coaching or improving my English language sessions (if required)?

If you are exempt from any parts of the SQE then your focus will be different to someone who has to complete both parts. You can read more in Chapter 1, The SQE Journey, SQE Exemptions (para **1.06**).

If you are self-funding, you can either choose to use the same university or training provider for both SQE Part 1 and 2 or you can use different ones for each part. You need to choose ones that best suit your learning needs and who offer you the best-quality materials. The training you will need to undertake for each part is different so do not take it for granted that one education or training provider will be equally good in quality and experience for both parts. For example:

- **University or Training Provider A**

    A very established training provider offering a good-quality experience for the SQE Part 2 (practical legal skills assessments) such as classroom environments, law tutor support and other study formats. However, for SQE Part 1 they do not necessarily have the best variety, depth and quantity of multiple choice questions for all the areas of law on which you are tested.

- **University or Training Provider B**

    A smaller and less-established training provider offering a good quantity and variety of multiple choice questions for the SQE Part 1 (Functioning Legal Knowledge) in a range of studying formats (eg online and digital). However, for SQE Part 2, they do not necessarily offer the best resources for the practical assessments, such as classroom, workshop or coaching experiences.

Find out what university and training providers are like; see how established they are and what they can offer you. Try to get a balance from them for *both* parts of the SQE and ask questions about each part, focusing on the part that needs more attention.

'Consciousness is shining a torch in a darkened room.'
William James

2.06 *Preparing for the SQE*

Do not be shy about asking probing questions – see it as doing your research before investing your money. You want to make sure you are getting what you are promised so you are not disappointed later.

Make a comparison list of universities or training providers you are interested in. Contact them prepared with relevant questions to see whether they are a good fit for you. Do not just accept generic statements at face value. The questions below are not about mistrusting any university or training provider – the majority are well respected and reputable. It is more about getting information in order to help you make a well-informed decision.

If the university or training provider wants you to invest in them, then they should be happy to answer all your questions. Also bear in mind, any big statements about how successful they are, should be backed up.

A university or training provider may say that their experience of the QLTS (now abolished) means they are well equipped for the SQE because of the similarities. That is a fair comment, but you can still ask them questions around their experience in offering both parts to ascertain whether they can provide the level of training you need for the SQE.

Below I have split the questions into three sections. Some are specific to training providers who did the QLTS. Then there are some questions specifically concerning the SQE and you can read more about what coaching is in Studying Formats at para **2.08**. The final section has some general questions on the SQE. The list of questions in each section is non-exhaustive, so add any other relevant questions appropriate for you:

- **Specific questions for training providers who offered the QLTS**
    1. What is your experience of the QLTS?
    2. How many years did you offer the QLTS (ie from when it started)?
    3. Who are your main category of candidates (ie students with no work experience, qualified lawyers or aspiring solicitors)?
    4. What are your SQE pass rates based on a detailed breakdown of different categories (eg types of candidates, age groups, how many candidates sat the exam etc)?
    5. What is the pass/failure rate?
    6. How many years did you offer the Multiple Choice Test (MCT) exam specifically for the QLTS (if they offer MCTs for other types of exams too, you want to be specific because the QLTS multiple choice questions are to the standard of the SQE)?
    7. For the SQE Part 1, how many multiple choice questions are provided for each of the areas of law assessed (not an overall figure)?
    8. For the SQE Part 2, what study format options are offered to help with the oral and written assessments?
- **Specific questions around SQE coaching programmes (if relevant)**
    1. What is your definition of coaching?
    2. What type of coaching do you offer?

3. What does the coaching process involve and how long is it?
4. Is the coaching face to face or online?
5. Do the coaches have any formal coaching qualifications?
6. What is their level of coaching experience and what is their specialism?
7. What is the coach's experience specifically for the SQE Part 2 (ie is it similar to that of the QLTS for client interviewing and advocacy)?
8. Do they have any specific coaching experience or qualifications using the psychology of human behaviour and emotional intelligence?

- **General questions around the SQE course**
    1. What is the blended learning ratio: the interactive (ie classroom, coaching, lectures) versus online (ie learning management platforms or digital apps) for each part of the course?
    2. Who are the majority of your candidates (ie qualified lawyers, aspiring solicitors or students)?
    3. What is the breakdown detail of data for the pass/fail rate?
    4. How many candidates are there in a classroom/lecture/small group tutorials/workshops?
    5. Are digital study formats (eg mobile/tablet apps) offered?
    6. What is the experience of the tutors/lecturers for SQE Part 1 and 2, respectively (eg teaching law, the Legal Practice Course (LPC) or the QLTS)?
    7. How often do you get one-to-one tutor time (if offered), with the focus on the law, as part of the SQE Part 1 and how long is each session?
    8. How often do you get one-to-one coaching (if offered), with the focus on how you use your skills within a legal context, as part of the SQE Part 2 and how long is each session?
    9. Do you offer any additional support (if required and specific to you)?
    10. Are the multiple choice questions and mock assessments an authentic simulation of the exam to offer an examination experience?
    11. How many MCT questions and mock practice papers are offered for all the subjects for each part of the SQE?
    12. Do you offer personalised constructive feedback for the written assessment mocks or is it suggested answers only?
    13. How many oral assessment mocks do you get to practise with a tutor (or coach) for the SQE Part 2 client interviewing and advocacy?
    14. If I were to fail, do you provide constructive feedback on how I can improve (ask them to specify what they do)?
    15. Are the law tutors practising/non-practising solicitors or academics (ie people who are not qualified solicitors)?

Academic lecturers are usually subject-matter experts from an academic perspective who can be engaging and inspiring which makes the process of learning the law more enjoyable. For the SQE Part 1, they may be able to really help you understand complex legal issues, technical points and help you grasp areas of the law that you find challenging.

Ideally, for the SQE Part 2, you want a practising or non-practising solicitor who has experience of working in practice. This is because they can enhance your learning experience and build your confidence by sharing practical tips of how you use the law in practice. This adds more value than just reading the materials. The SQE Part 2 assesses you equally on the law and skills based on realistic scenarios you may encounter in practice.

You can check with the university or training provider what the status is of their teaching staff. If they are a solicitor (even non-practising), their name should be on the Roll of Solicitors unless there is a valid explanation for it not being on there. You should check with the university or training provider if this is the case.

Misleading Marketing and Advertising

2.07 As mentioned above, most universities and training providers are reputable. They offer a great range of services and a variety of studying formats tailored to individual needs. If you are totally new to finding a university or training provider, then the choices can be overwhelming. Who do you choose? What do they offer? Who can recommend them? These might be some of the questions that go through your mind and you can read more about it the section called Understanding the SQE Course Provider (para **2.06**) to help you get some clarity and transparency.

What universities or training providers can do is use clever marketing to tell you how well established they are in providing the SQE courses based on their current or past courses and experience. For example:

University or Training Provider A

One might state they are the best SQE online training provider because they have years of experience of preparing lawyers for the QLTS exam (now abolished).

University or Training Provider B

Another might state they are the best SQE provider with an established history and reputation in the legal market.

Do not accept at face value sweeping statements you read or ones made by promoters of any SQE providers. The studying formats offered will be a huge part of your preferred learning style so ask questions to help you compare them.

Studying Formats

2.08 Many universities and training providers will offer a range of different studying formats to try to accommodate your learning preferences. These different studying formats can work well for the different parts of the SQE. Learning the black letter of the law can work well using several different approaches or a blended learning style. The skills can sometimes be referred to as 'soft skills' and it is important that you do not underestimate their importance. Many law firms do not like using the term 'soft skills' and choose 'core skills' or 'people skills' etc. In my opinion, it does not really matter what term they use because ultimately it all funnels down to the ability to communicate effectively. Chapter 5 on Communication Skills is a key chapter that I advise you to read before the chapters that deal with the oral assessments.

From my experience of working with many lawyers, they underestimate the skills part, often by focusing on the law. Knowing the law is a given, but the skills of how you deliver it confidently (orally and in writing) can take time to learn, especially when you do them to strict times for the assessments. The best way to learn skills is by practising them – not just reading about them. A whole range of studying formats are good for learning about skills in theory, but ultimately you will only get better if you do them.

> *'Knowledge isn't power unless it is applied.'*
> **Dale Carnegie**

Below are some of the different studying formats that may be offered.

- ### *Law Books*

2.09 The traditional approach of reading law books to learn the substantive areas of the law will probably be the most popular method. It is a good way to get the required depth and knowledge of the areas of the law. That may include using the traditional question and answer approach to test your understanding.

- ### *Digital Technology/Apps*

2.10 Some training providers will offer digital technology, such as apps that allow easy access to 'on the go' forms of study. For example, apps can be a great way to practise multiple choice questions for the SQE Part 1. This format complements reading the law books and allows you to test yourself in the format that you are assessed on. Ideally, you want multiple choice questions that offer you guidance on why your answer is correct or incorrect to help improve your understanding.

- ### *Classroom/Lectures*

2.11 The traditional face-to-face classroom or lecture option will suit many people and is a good way to get an interactive experience and also have the opportunity to work with other students. This format works nicely for both parts of the SQE.

- ### *Online*

2.12 This is a popular approach with the range of activities possible where you can work at your own pace and test yourself. The quality of the materials and variety will vary with different platforms or learning-management systems. A range

2.13 *Preparing for the SQE*

of different learning styles can be offered to suit your preference. For example, you can watch videos and do interactive exercises to test your understanding. You may also be able to do time-controlled mock tests when you are ready and track your progress. As a result of Covid-19, this studying format has prompted many law schools to adapt their traditional approaches and offer a much broader range of online studying options.

- ***Masterclasses***

2.13 These are a great way to test yourself with an expert once you have studied the law and practised lots of mock oral assessments. They are usually small groups and interactive so you can learn from watching each other and fine-tune what you do.

- ***Coaching***

2.14 This is quite a new offering by some universities and training providers. Coaching programmes vary and are tailored to each individual, so you want to know what coaching style is offered and what it entails. If you have no experience of working with a coach, then I will explain below what it can mean and share the type of coaching I do. It will offer you a better understanding so you can compare it to what you might be offered for the SQE. The coaching questions above will also help you get more clarity from what training providers are offering you and whether it works for you.

There are many different types of coaching (sports, lifestyle, business, executive etc) and many different definitions for it. Some people will be qualified through a certification programme and others will not have any formal qualifications. All coaches will have their own style and use different processes and tools which may not always work for everyone. Most importantly you need to connect with your coach and want to do it for yourself (you cannot be pushed or encouraged to do it by work, your parents or anyone else). You might think if it is helpful you would obviously want to do it, but, it can be hard work and usually involves you getting out of your comfort zone. You can read more about the different zones in Chapter 6 on Managing Nerves, Fear and Failure (para **6.02**).

Coaching is about encouraging learning and personal performance. Generally, a coach does not need to be a subject-matter expert. For example, many sports coaches to world champions are not champions themselves. However, for the context of the SQE, you do want a communication skills coach who understands the marking criteria used in the SQE. They do not need to be a lawyer but should know what you will be assessed on and how they propose to help you reach your goal from a skills perspective. It is not common to find a coach who is a lawyer and an expert in communication skills. A coach is not the same as a law tutor. A law tutor is an expert and knowledgeable in an area of the law and can help you learn and understand it. They are good at teaching you the law but may not necessarily have the same level of expertise and experience in effective communication skills.

Communication skills taught at law schools are delivered by law tutors where the skills usually form a part of the course materials. The focus is on basic communication skills but rarely covers content such as emotional intelligence, language patterns

Studying Formats **2.15**

or the psychology of human behaviour. These are essential skills for future lawyers and you can read why in Chapter 4, Qualifying Work Experience, Types of Lawyers (para **4.02**). Many law schools do not always fully appreciate the importance of soft skills with the focus heavily on learning the black letter of the law. Therefore, it is no surprise that the skills part is often undervalued by law students and lawyers. With the SQE, they have a chance to shift the balance to give communication skills equal importance to the law for the benefit of all future lawyers. The fact that SQE Part 2 tests the law and skills equally should be an indication as to what is expected from our future lawyers.

❖ Performance Coaching

2.15 The type of coaching I do is called 'performance coaching' and it is specific and contextualised to the SQE Part 2. My clients are qualified lawyers, aspiring solicitors and students, worldwide, so it is done in person or online.

The focus is very much on how to demonstrate your legal knowledge in a correct and comprehensive manner using your communication skills to maximise your marks. My approach is not the 'correct' way or the only way, because coaching models and processes vary for each individual. I have developed what I do over many years (from coaching qualified lawyers for the QLTS) and I have not had to adapt my approach or standard for the SQE Part 2.

I call it 'performance coaching' because the goal is to get you to 'perform' to the highest level which is 'superior performance' in the assessment criteria. You do this by communicating your legal knowledge (the law) in an effective and skilful manner (the skills). It is a style of coaching that allows you to perfect your technique with repetition and practice.

The coaching relationship is created to achieve a specific goal and is people-focused and task-focused, for a set period of time. It is adapted to your personality and language patterns, levels of experience and expertise. No two lawyers are ever the same. By that I mean you may have the same common issues as others, but your style and technique will always be unique to you. I work with you to enhance your authentic style, so it is not about getting you to try to copy my style.

My role as a coach is not to teach you the law but to test your knowledge of it through various scenarios to check how accurate you are and whether you are comprehensive in what you say. I assess how you advise a client and how you come across doing an advocacy submission in accordance with the Assessment Criteria using the grading scale. The grading scale assesses you on the law and skills and I work with you to get you to the highest Grade A (5 marks) which is 'superior performance'. You can read more about the Assessment Criteria and grading scale in each chapter that deals with the assessments.

During the coaching session, I observe how you explain legal issues or points and assess whether you articulate them in a structured, clear and understandable manner. Simultaneously, I observe and assess your body language (non-verbal), vocals (tone, intonation etc) and language (words) to see if you come across congruently. Chapter 5 on Communication Skills goes into more detail on this area. Usually, this is the part where the hard work starts because lawyers focus on the law

2.15 *Preparing for the SQE*

to the detriment of how they come across using their body language, vocals and language. For example, in client interviewing, I commonly find:

Skills

Your body language and facial expressions do not match the language used to greet a client and your advice often contains legal jargon without you realising it. Your keenness to explain the law in so much detail (when only preliminary advice is required) means you lose connection with the client by speaking at a fast pace (ie you are rushing because you are conscious of time).

Law

There is a tendency to advise the client by making assumptions before you get all the relevant information or address their concerns. By doing this (without asking questions) you miss out on key information or later realise your assumption may be incorrect which can cause confusion in the moment, wastes time and affect your confidence.

The performance coaching process I use incorporates the psychology of human behaviour, language patterns and emotional intelligence. These are three key areas we all use when communicating with people, and understanding how to use them all effectively can change your life personally and professionally. However, I appreciate your focus is on the SQE, so you do not need to know the theory, details or depth around how these areas work (unless you are interested in studying them later on). For you, it is enough that your skills coach or someone familiar with these areas can constructively pinpoint the following:

- what you do well;
- what areas you need to improve;
- their perception of how you come across;
- what you can do to adapt the areas that need improvement;
- how you can come up with a practice and repetition plan.

A coach will very quickly help you realise exactly what you do (your habits, behaviours and language patterns) and what you need to change (if anything). The feedback is instantaneous to help you realise (in that moment) what you do and how to break your current patterns of behaviour. This allows you to recognise what changes you need to make immediately. Then it is a matter of repetition and practise until it becomes natural and congruent with what you say. For example, you should be able to see and feel straightaway the difference from your original performance and your rehearsed new one. Chapter 5 on Communication Skills provides more details on how to improve your skills and Chapter 8 on Client Interviewing provides examples.

The performance coaching model is adapted for each of the assessments, so it is tailored to you, at your pace (regardless of your level of experience). The coaching process is bespoke because a standard approach does not work. A standard approach is generic and can be taught in a classroom-style lecture or large group workshop. There is nothing wrong with that at all, but for a tailored experience you will need help to figure out specifically:

- what areas you need to improve (Identify);

Studying Formats **2.15**

- how you will improve them (Strategy);

- when you will know you have improved (Evidence).

In my coaching session, you figure out the above with specific feedback to help you develop your capabilities. The process allows you to develop a sense of direction to help you understand what you need to do and *how* to do it – the process is driven by you. The responsibility is yours and you are accountable for your actions.

The coaching principles I use help your confidence in a practical way because you:

- learn for yourself;

- expand your skill competencies; and

- build on your advisory and problem-solving skills.

It is an extremely practical and focused experience. The goal is to give you a good understanding of how to explain the law and legal procedures in a way that is done skilfully through your communication style. It is not easy and it is the skills part that is usually the hardest part. The coaching process aims to help you improve not just to pass the SQE – but also for life in practice as a solicitor.

In the context of the SQE, the performance coaching gives you the tools to confidently deal with any situation that presents itself during the interactive oral assessments. The tools and techniques shared will build your confidence and help your performance on the assessment days. Chapter 5, Communication Skills is a key chapter to read with the details of how to take a practical approach to each assessment. The coaching process also covers how to deal with nerves and anxiety which are looked at in more detail in Chapter 6, Managing Nerves, Fear and Failure.

Any training providers that offer 'coaching' might not call it performance coaching. But, you have an idea of what it could entail for the SQE. They should be able to explain what coaching models and processes they use and you can always ask about their expertise and experience. What you should definitely expect is that it should be tailored to you.

The key is to connect with your coach. Ideally, your coach should be enthusiastic and passionate about being a coach, they should be invested in you and champion you to be the best version of yourself. It is not easy being a coach and working one to one can often be an intense process for both of you. It requires a lot of hard work and effort on both sides, but ultimately it should be a rewarding and valuable experience for both too.

So, if a university or training provider is offering you a coach as part of the SQE package, it can be a great tool. You have an idea of what you can expect from it and how it can help you pass the SQE.

Ultimately, who you decide to study with may depend on whether you are a student, aspiring solicitor (working) or a qualified lawyer working in your home jurisdiction. Below is some guidance for you to consider when making your choice.

2.16 *Preparing for the SQE*

Students

2.16 There are so many variables to being a 'student'. Some study full time whilst others are part time; some are domestic students (UK) and others international. Therefore, when I use the term 'student' it is not focusing on any particular type, so use what information works best for you and adapt it to suit your circumstances.

A traditional approach is to study a full-time degree course and you may decide to do a law or non-law degree.

- ***Law Degrees***

2.17 If you choose to do a law degree, it makes sense to speak to the universities to see what their law degree courses cover. For example, some universities are offering an adapted new vocational style law degree that may include an SQE preparatory course. Others may offer it as a 'top up' (sometimes offered as the equivalent of a Master's degree). More traditional universities have said that they will continue to offer their existing law degree as it is and you will need to do a separate SQE preparatory course. Some universities have partnered with training providers to work together and offer you incentives and discounts to do their SQE course. Remember, you should still make up your own mind and do your own research about who you decide to invest in.

If you want to be a City lawyer, you should know most City law firms will continue to recruit in the traditional way (at least for the foreseeable future). Therefore, it makes sense that you follow the path that appeals to them the most. In reality, City law firms have a recruitment process which includes a preferred status group of universities (eg Oxbridge or Russell Group). So, bear that in mind when deciding where you want to do your law degree because it could have some influence on the City firms you might be interested in.

If you are not interested in working for a City firm then you have much more flexibility in where you do your degree and whether it is more vocational than traditional. That does not mean you cannot change your mind. If you realise once you are a qualified solicitor (with experience) that you want to work in a City firm, it could be an option for you. By this stage, sometimes the focus shifts from your academics to your experience.

Some universities may also offer courses including a one-year legal work experience placement which could count as Qualifying Work Experience (QWE). This can be a really good way to experience what you want to do. A good question to ask yourself is *'what type of lawyer do I want to be?'* and Chapter 1, The SQE Journey offers you some guidance on what to consider in this area.

As a student without any legal experience, it can be difficult to know what path you eventually may want to go down. A good way to approach it is to think about what areas of law you are interested in and what types of businesses or law firms specialise in those areas. For example, if you are interested in organisations like Apple, Google, Amnesty International etc ask yourself what specifically (from a legal perspective) interests you. Also think about where your interests lie and what you enjoy reading about in the news, magazines and journals. In Chapter 4,

Qualifying Work Experience you can read more about tips on how to get some work experience (if required).

- **Non-Law Degrees**

2.18 If you do a non-law degree, you can choose any education or training provider to do the SQE preparatory course when you are ready. There are many choices and you can use some of the questions above in 'How to Choose an SQE Course Provider' at para **2.03** to help you decide.

- **Alternative Routes**

2.19 A solicitor apprenticeship is different to the traditional option of studying through the university route. It is a way to qualify where you 'earn while you learn'. Some law firms and businesses like Deloitte Legal (UK) and KPMG will offer solicitor apprenticeships. It means you work whilst studying to qualify as a solicitor. It is a popular concept for many businesses where they sponsor you whilst you work for them. The process of qualification is usually longer, but you will leave with less debt at the end of it. This means that you end up qualifying as a solicitor and being in a financially healthier position than if you were a full- or part-time student financing the SQE yourself.

The SRA does not have a definitive list of all the businesses that offer alternative routes to qualification. However, a good website called Prospects (www.prospects.ac.uk) does offer information and a non-exhaustive list of many law firms that offer solicitor apprenticeships.

As mentioned in the introduction, if you are self-funding, you do not have to do both parts of the SQE with the same education or training provider, so work out which ones suit your needs best.

Preparing for the SQE as a student means studying in different ways. The SQE Part 1 is more about learning the law in the traditional academic way. Most law students may find the adjustment easier than non-law students because they will be used to studying for law exams and will be familiar with some of the subjects and legal language. However, SQE Part 1 consists of two multiple choice tests and it may not be a format that you are used to doing. So, think about your preferred learning preference:

- Are you happy to self-study for all of the course?
- Do you prefer a more interactive classroom environment for the majority of your learning?
- Do you prefer an equal blend of both classroom and online learning?

For the SQE Part 1, you might want to self-study because it is more cost-effective but I would strongly recommend that you also practise in the multiple choice test study format.

The university or training provider you use for the SQE Part 2 is especially important because this includes the oral interactive assessments. Reading books on how to improve your interviewing and advocacy skills may be helpful, but it is a passive style of learning. For example, watching videos on how you should do client interviewing or advocacy is insightful to see how to do it, but you need to actually do it so you are learning through practice.

Aspiring Solicitors (Working)

2.20 If you are working and qualifying through an alternative route (such as a solicitor apprenticeship) and the law firm or a business is financially sponsoring you, they usually have a preferred training provider. If not, think about what will suit you best and offer you flexibility based on your personal and professional commitments.

Qualified Lawyers

2.21 Many lawyers I work with are commercial and corporate lawyers. Some are sponsored and others are self-funded. Commonly, their reason to qualify as a solicitor is because it gives them more credibility and puts them on an equal footing when working with English lawyers. Many are happy to continue working in their home jurisdiction and others say it is part of a work relocation package or they are already working in the UK, so it makes financial sense to do it. Overall, it also increases their leverage and opportunities by expanding their global legal footprint.

The SRA has stated that without any jurisdiction restrictions all qualified lawyers can do the SQE. However, if you are looking for any exemptions to the SQE then read Chapter 1, The SQE Journey, SQE Exemptions (para **1.06**) and also contact the SRA to see if you satisfy their requirements.

I have worked with many lawyers from civil law jurisdictions who say that studying the common law can be challenging because it is so different. Here are some issues to think about when you start studying:

- the general features of the common law;
- how common law lawyers think and reason;
- what sources of law may be used and relied upon.

It may help you to read Chapter 1, Starting the SQE Journey, Appendix 1A on Understanding the Common Law System of England and Wales if you want a brief summary of how the common law system came about and how it got its name.

- **Do you live outside the UK?**

    If you do, then you are limited in your options in terms of choosing a university or training provider that offers a host of options. Many will focus on training providers who offer the best online SQE preparatory courses. In this case, it would be useful to look at those that offered the QLTS and have developed their materials for the SQE.

- **Do you live in the UK?**

    If you do, then you have several options and a variety of study formats that may work for you. You need to work out what suits your learning style and work commitments (if relevant).

If you are working whilst studying then your options may be limited and you will have to be even more disciplined in your approach to the SQE. Motivation and time management will play a huge factor in your SQE journey.

Studying and Time Management

2.22 Time management has nothing to do with the law and everything to do with you. It applies to everyone doing the SQE and requires discipline, which can be challenging when there are many factors that can affect your studying.

Work out when you study best (think about whether you are a morning or a night person). There is no right or wrong answer; it is when you are at your best energy level, most alert and productive. That time should be the base starting point for you to be able to dedicate most of your time to studying with minimal distractions or disruptions (you will find examples of these in Appendix 2A).

The ways you study for the SQE Part 1 and 2 are different. The SQE Part 1 is a more academic approach and the SQE Part 2 more practical. The details of how to approach each of them practically will be shared in the respective chapters dealing with them.

A question I am often asked in relation to studying is *'Am I doing enough hours?'* There may be many universities or training providers who suggest that a certain number of hours should be studied each week to ensure you are on target.

My advice is that you know yourself best. Your personal and professional circumstances will play a huge part in how much time you can dedicate to studying during the weekdays and weekends. There are so many variables that can affect your study time, so try not to get too hung up or fixed on a given number of hours.

Everyone wants comfort and reassurance that they are studying enough hours and doing it right. However, I find it unfair to offer such a definitive answer. Everyone's personal and professional circumstances are different. Also, everyone has different learning preferences and ways they process information. For example, a topic that may take you one hour to read and understand, could take someone else double that time. All the variables mentioned above at para **2.05** Understanding Yourself could impact your studying times. You must have confidence in your own ability to know you have set enough time aside to study and be flexible about it. For any studying to be effective, you want to be in a peak state which means you are not tired. It is hard to study and you will not be productive if you are mentally and/or physically exhausted.

Here is a sample of what lawyers have shared with me about factors that have impacted their study time even when they have a study plan in place:

- what time they study;
- how tired they get;
- varied working day (unforeseeable issues);
- business trips;
- working long days;
- their personal commitments (young children, medical issues);

2.23 *Preparing for the SQE*

- getting distracted or bored;
- reading for the sake of reading (to feel better and meet their study plan targets).

The experiences differ for each person, day to day. Therefore, if you are worried about how you should approach the SQE and whether or not you are doing enough, I would suggest that you have a pragmatic and smart approach by creating a realistic study plan or a strategy that you know works best for you. The section on creating A Study Plan at para **2.25** will provide you with some tips to consider.

Unfortunately, only you can be the real judge of whether you are doing enough. You will need to manage your day-to-day routine and incorporate the SQE into it, as if it is a part of your daily life (at least until you complete it).

I would also advise you to be proactive in your studying approach so that if you realise you are struggling with a topic, you contact your education or training provider to find out about what additional support is available.

> *'Either you run the day or the day runs you.'*
> **Jim Rohn**

- ***Distractions and Disrupters***

2.23 We all have 24 hours in a day regardless of who we are and our personal or professional circumstances. So, the question is not about having enough time, because we all have the same. It is about how you are using your time.

A good way to work out how to fit in your studying is to breakdown your 24 hours. Identify when you are at your best energy level and schedule time around it to study (if possible). This does not have to be a long block of time.

If you find yourself saying *'I don't have enough time'*. Ask yourself: *'What are my distractions and disruptions?'* Disruptions are things that might happen more in a work environment, like interruptions where people ask for your help or call you – these are things that are beyond your control. Distractions are things like browsing online, using social media or checking your messages on your phone – these are things that are within your control. Both affect your time management. Below is an exercise that will help you work out what your distractions and disrupters are and how you can try to use your time more effectively. Sometimes you do not realise how much the distractions (within your control) actually affect your time management.

Exercise: Distractions and Disrupters

This exercise works best if you do it in a quiet place when you are on your own.

Instructions

Take one day – it can be any day. Think of every distraction and disruption throughout the whole day and work out how long they were and when they occurred. It might help you to write down a list of 24 hours starting with 6am. Below is a fictitious example from waking up to starting work:

Breakdown of 24 hours

6am: Wake up/Asleep etc

Breakdown times for shower/getting ready/breakfast/checking messages etc

7am: Shower/Commute to work etc

Breakdown times for commute/responding to work emails/reading/browsing social media/work from home etc

8am: Arrive at the office/Start work from home/Commute etc

Breakdown times for arriving in the office/coffee/catch up with colleagues etc

In Appendix 2A you can find some examples of what could be distractions and disrupters to help you with this exercise.

(1)   Start with the time you woke up and break your day down into hours.

(2)   Think about what you have done from the time you woke up to the time you went to bed. Break it down in detail – each hour and within the hours, minutes.

(3)   List everything, even if it seems irrelevant.

(4)   Look through your list and mark out what is routine (fixed) for you and what are your distractions and disrupters.

(5)   Think about what changes you can make to your routine (if any) and how you can manage any distractions to use your time more efficiently.

Reflection

Analyse how much of your time was disrupted and beyond your control and how much was a distraction that was within your control. Be honest.

You should get a good idea of what you do and when you do it. This will help you get an insight into how you use your time in a given day and help you create some structure to take some control of how you could use your time better.

No two days will be the same. Sometimes you do not have to make major changes, but you can make small shifts to your behaviour which can give you more time. For example, set a fixed time for how long and when you will indulge in your distractions – those are things you can control and when done spontaneously means you can lose track of how long you end up spending on them. Ideally, you want to study when you are in a peak state and not get distracted.

2.24 *Preparing for the SQE*

- **Pareto's Rule**

2.24 Pareto's rule is a good time-management tool which many businesses use, but for lawyers, professionally, it might not suit the type of work you do. However, when studying, the rule can help if you worry about whether you have done enough hours or think you need to study in long blocks of time to study 'properly'.

Vilfredo Pareto was an Italian economist in the twentieth century who observed that 80% of Italy's wealth was owned by 20% of the population. That rule provided many other examples and became known as 'Pareto's rule' or the 'Pareto principle' where 80% of the output is achieved with 20% of the input.

The rule works for the analogy of studying. For example, you can learn more (80% output) if you study in a peak state for shorter periods of time (20% input). This is contrary to thinking that studying longer hours means you learn more. It might make you feel psychologically better (eg thinking *'I spent a whole day studying so I feel better'*). The real question is: what did you actually learn in relation to how long you spent studying?

Therefore, use your time wisely. Get out of a fixed mindset about time and have flexibility rather than think you should wait until you have 'more time'. Of course, this comes down to your studying preferences, but I have often said to clients that a lot can be learnt or practised in 10 to 15 minutes using a range of different study material formats. For example:

✓ reading a short section or topic in a book;

✓ watching a short video;

✓ doing multiple choice questions; or

✓ practising vocal exercises.

It is just changing your mindset around time and recognising what you can do with it. Small changes can make a big impact. Therefore using your time efficiently and effectively will depend on your energy levels and whether you are studying in a peak state.

'20 percent of your activities will account for 80 percent of your results.'

Brian Tracy

A Study Plan

2.25 I coach many lawyers on time management. Therefore, what I share with you is insight to consider and to see whether a study plan helps or hinders you. A study plan can be a great time-management tool in helping you plan for the SQE. Most of the time it is beneficial when used as a guide to help you keep on top of your targets. However, you want it to be helpful rather than detrimental. Sometimes, what works really well for some people might not have the same effect for you. For example, you might end up feeling demotivated and spend more time worrying about the study plan, if you keep missing your set deadlines rather than focusing on studying. Therefore, you can create one but see how it works for you.

Do not blindly just go along with it if you start to realise that it is not having a beneficial impact on your studying.

Below are two examples of lawyers I coached on time management in work situations where you can see how what they did was detrimental to them, without realising it. The examples do not relate to study plans, but the principle is the same. I think you can apply it to the context of using a study plan and sometimes realise that factors or issues that are not time management or study plan related can impact your studying or work. For example:

Lawyer A

This lawyer used to create a to-do list every morning thinking it was helping him to meet his failed deadlines and organise his time better. Upon further exploration, he realised the to-do lists were not helpful at all and he actually 'hated' them. He resented the process of creating one every morning. It was not a productive or helpful way for him to start his day, but his behaviour was so habitual and subconscious, that he did not see its detrimental effect on him, because to-do lists are perceived as helpful. Working with him, he came up with a new way to work by creating a system to avoid missing deadlines and before he left the office (every evening), he would know what he would be doing the next day.

Lesson for you: A study plan might not be the best tool for you, so adapt it or find an alternative that works for you. Think about what normally helps you plan for when you work towards deadlines or targets. Also note the best time for you to make your plan.

Lawyer B

This lawyer created a to-do list that was so unrealistic (it would never be completed in a working day), that she never finished everything on it and this became her 'norm' and expectation. She left work every evening feeling low, guilty and unfulfilled. Her 'norm' had been created by her behavioural pattern (making unachievable to-do lists) so it was an expectation that the to-do list would never be completed. Upon further exploration, she realised having an unrealistic to-do list was not helpful. It was her way of ensuring that there was enough work for her to do and kept the pressure on in a way to justify her job and salary. So, the to-do list was a constant reminder that she was not doing enough (when she was) and this ultimately affected her self-esteem.

Lesson for you: Creating an unrealistic study plan which puts pressure on you to study harder will not necessarily motivate you. It could end up being more detrimental by affecting your self-esteem, which directly impacts your studying. It is important to have an overview of what you need to do overall. But, create achievable and manageable targets to keep you on track.

There is a well-known question which asks 'how do you eat an elephant?' Desmond Tutu very wisely answered 'there is only one way to eat an elephant: a bite at a time'. Therefore, do not overwhelm yourself by trying to do the impossible (ie trying to eat the whole elephant in one bite). This just means you end up feeling overwhelmed and not achieving very much at all.

Therefore, create and use a study plan but assess along the way how it makes you feel. A study plan is a good tool if used well, and its effect should be positive in keeping you on track with your deadlines and targets.

2.26 *Preparing for the SQE*

If you keep missing deadlines, it can spiral into negative thinking about failing the SQE because it can contribute to you feeling unprepared. It should be a warning to propel you to re-evaluate what you are doing proactively and help you realise the following:

(1) you are expecting to cover too much in the time frame set; or

(2) you are not doing enough (for whatever reason); or

(3) you are doing enough but there is too much to cover by the assessment dates, so you may need to consider an option to defer to a later date.

It is impossible always to know in advance how much time you need for each area of law until you start studying it. Some subjects may take longer than others, so you should have a flexible study plan to accommodate it.

'If you fail to plan, you are planning to fail.'
Benjamin Franklin

- **Fixed or Flexible Study Plan?**

2.26 If you do create a study plan, you can either create one that has fixed dates in place by which you will achieve targets set or you can have flexible dates depending on your circumstances at the time.

Many lawyers say to me they need to have set fixed dates to make them feel like they are working towards a deadline so they can be held accountable. Their reasoning does not come as a surprise and I understand their thinking. However, setting fixed dates can set you up for disappointment because it is often unforeseeable what your working weeks might look like in the build-up to your fixed date or how easy or difficult you find a subject. Therefore, having a flexible attitude towards the study plan is much more beneficial in the long run. Look at what you need to cover for both parts of the SQE and do the following:

- Work out an overview of the entire time frame you have to work within up to the assessment dates.
- Work out the order of the subjects you want to study.
- Create a more intricate plan of scheduled weeks rather than a fixed date.
- Keep track and adapt your weeks always having the overview in mind.

Having a flexible study plan can give you some advanced awareness of how your forthcoming week might look and you can adjust it accordingly. You are in control of what you will do and can make decisions around your week. It allows you to be more effective in what you do with your time and revise your schedule accordingly. For example:

- Busier week: adjust your schedule to compensate for it rather than miss your set date (if you set one).
- Quieter week: do more hours.

You might think by not having a fixed schedule there is a danger that you might not cover everything in the time frame and by the assessment dates. This will not happen if you have the overview in mind. Having flexibility is smart working by being proactive (by meeting or beating your target date) rather than reactive (missing your target date). The overview schedule and time frame never change, so you know by what stage you need to have covered all the subjects. The best analogy is that the goal is fixed (assessment dates) but the variables (studying, work etc) on how to achieve it can change and have to be monitored to ensure achievement.

You should sit down and go through the study plan with anyone (personal and professional) who may be affected by it and ask for their commitment to help you for the period of time you need to study to do the exams. It is a good idea to remind yourself and those affected that it is for a short-term goal or definitive period of time. So, when you find it challenging or someone else does, talk it through and find out how you can help each other and remind yourselves that the situation is not forever. If you are working and can take study leave or annual leave, make sure you book it well in advance to avoid any last minute or short notice refusals because of work commitments.

Some study days will be better than others. Remember, it is about the quality of information retained and not the number of hours studied. Achieving a set number of hours might make you feel better, but this does not necessarily mean you are engaged in effective learning.

Having a fixed schedule means you impose rules on yourself and will be reluctant to 'break' them. However, forcing yourself to study when you are tired or cannot concentrate properly to just 'tick the box' that you have done it, is not smart studying. It does not equate to effective levels of learning and understanding when you are not in a peak state. Ultimately, you are only deceiving yourself by thinking you have worked hard (which is probably true).

One way to ensure your study plan does not upset you if you miss a target date is by monitoring it (and it does not take much time at all). Keep checking it to see if you are on track and adapt it accordingly. The study plan you create is bespoke to you based on what you do and how many hours you can devote to studying.

Support Groups/'Study Buddies'

2.27 Sometimes it helps to have people you can talk to who are going through the SQE too and are at the same stage as you. It is important though not to compare yourself to anyone else, but share studying strategies and different ways of studying that could help others.

If you are studying full time you may be surrounded by other students and naturally gravitate to people you become friends with and end up supporting each other. Some subjects might come more naturally to you and others to your friends, so a combined effort to help each other can be useful. That is a good way to practise topics or procedures that you might have to explain in any of the assessments.

If you are a qualified or aspiring lawyer studying whilst working and primarily using an online training provider, it can be harder to meet others. If you work in an international firm, you may find there are other lawyers also doing it and

2.28 *Preparing for the SQE*

you can get together to discuss studying strategies. Alternatively, you could find others through online forums and members groups (eg LinkedIn, you can join SQE Success).

Some people prefer to study on their own and independently and others in a group environment. However, if you do want to work with others and they are compatible 'study buddies', there are many ways you can do it. Even if meeting up is not logistically possible, you can study through video conferencing facilities (such as Skype, Zoom or many of the other platforms available).

Studying for the SQE

2.28 Once you have decided who to study with, you need to know *how* to study for each part of the SQE. Here, the approach is not the same for both parts.

The key thing to remember about learning is it is state dependant – it is all about engagement. When you are enjoying or interested in what you are reading or doing, in a peak state, you are fully engaged in the learning process and it is effective. There are two pillars of learning:

- the pillar of intellect; and
- the pillar of experience.

For the SQE, you will be expected to meet both pillars. Intellect is primarily tested in the SQE Part 1 through Functioning Legal Knowledge (see Chapter 3) and your experience and application of using the law will be tested in SQE Part 2 through Practical Legal Skills (see Chapters 8 to 14).

The SRA has based the SQE model on the established Miller's pyramid which is used extensively for the assessment of professional competence. It assesses cognitive and behavioural competence. See Appendix 2B for an example of what Miller's pyramid looks like for the SQE.

How you study for the SQE will depend on whether you are studying or working. Of course, there are many variables in between, so you can read both parts and decide what is best for you.

- ### Studying Full Time

2.29 This category may typically include full-time students who after their degree (in law or otherwise) will go on to do the SQE.

It may be seen as a luxury to those who are working or do not fall into this category, especially if you do not have any family or personal commitments. The thinking is you should be able to commit to a study plan and be able to execute it without too many difficulties.

However, the danger is with time on your side, it is very easy to procrastinate. This means doing everything else (usually less important) than studying. Often it is easier to validate doing other things because you do not want to study for whatever reason: you might be overwhelmed with the amount you have to do, find the subject hard or boring etc. It becomes much easier to get side-tracked and fall into that false sense of security that you have time on your side until it catches up with you. It can also mean that you are less disciplined with a study plan and the time you give yourself to study. So, the question becomes: *'How effectively are you using your time?'* For example, if you are studying eight or more hours a day, how many of them are effective learning? To be most effective you want to study when in a peak state because low energy levels mean low concentration.

Reading for the sake of reading, to get through a book or topic is not smart learning. You are less likely to retain the information if you do not understand it so it can be a waste of your time. It makes sense to use your time wisely and set break times. It is suggested by many professionals and law schools that short bursts of studying are more effective than longer hours so they may offer you a more structured support and guidance.

The key for you is to make a plan around how many hours a day you can dedicate to studying and decide what you will do within those hours. Identify your learning preferences and be flexible to adapting them, if required. This is not about how many hours you *want* to set aside to study but realistically how many hours you *can* set aside – you must be honest with yourself. Then you can split the hours into smaller chunks of time to make the studying more effective. Include scheduled breaks and activities to break up your studying day.

- ***Studying and Working***

2.30 It is admirable if you are studying for the SQE alongside working full- or part-time, bringing up a family and/or have any other personal or professional commitments. You must be exceptionally disciplined and determined about how you will set time aside to study and have contingency plans in place for those unforeseeable days when your motivation will be tested. You can read more around motivation in Chapter 1, The SQE Journey, Motivation (para **1.10**).

Many lawyers with all the possible variables that affect their life whilst studying need reassurance around the issue of *'Am I doing enough hours?'* and the response is the same as I have shared in Studying and Time Management above at para **2.22**. The less pressure you put on yourself about 'set hours' per day or week, the more you will learn and be satisfied with the outcome. If you constantly judge yourself against the number of hours you study or the number of pages you have read in a law textbook, the focus can become a numbers game and you want to study smart.

Do not feel the pressure to block out several hours at a time if your lifestyle does not suit it. It is more about being as effective as possible with your time. So, small periods of time can be more manageable and doable than always thinking you will benefit more from longer periods of time or waiting until you have more time.

Have confidence and flexibility in recognising that some days you will hit your target hours and other days you will not. Do not panic or become complacent. There will always be more work you can do, but there is no point in pushing yourself when you are tired but feel compelled to carry on. For example, if you have had to work longer hours than usual one day or you have a young child who is ill so needs more time and attention, adapt your study plan for those days. If you had block hours set aside but realise you cannot do them, adapt and create smaller

2.31 *Preparing for the SQE*

bite-size study sessions and fit them in where you can. It might not be ideal or your preference, but it will help ease your mind and help you feel more in control. Start to think quality of learning, rather than panicking over quantity of time.

If you always work long hours (as many City lawyers do), then you must dedicate your non-working days to studying and think about sacrificing any social engagements. If you have no control over your workload, you do have control over your personal life and social activities.

You know when you study best. If you are a morning person, get up earlier and get a few hours of study in before work or any other commitments that require your attention. If you are someone who prefers to work at night, study when you know all your other commitments are met and the rest of the evening is yours to study.

You are not in a peak state to study if you are mentally and physically tired and your energy levels are low. It will inevitably mean you take longer to understand complex and technical areas of the law. Often, it is better to approach those areas when you are less tired and more alert; this is something to think about in the study plan stage. Even if an area of law is complex and hard, your ability to actively process the information will improve if you have more energy. So, save the hard topics for when you work at your best.

There may be lots of theories about how to study and when to study, but common sense would suggest that you listen to your body and work with it, rather than against it. So, if you are tired, respect your body and take a break, to carry on will affect your concentration levels. For example, have a power nap, do some exercise, meditate, have a shower – do whatever will help you relax mentally and feel energised physically. It is about having the attitude that it is not a waste of time but can help you study more effectively.

> **'Ability is what you are capable of doing. Motivation determines what you do. Attitude determines how well you do it.'**
>
> **Lou Holtz**

Understanding the Competence Statement

2.31 You can read about how the Competence Statement influences the SQE in more detail in Chapter 1, The SQE Journey, Appendix 1B.

The SQE Assessment Specifications are influenced by the Competence Statement which defines continuing competence for all solicitors. Therefore, it is important you understand that what you are assessed on reflects what you are expected to know and are able to do in practice.

- ### *What is the Competence Statement?*

2.32 The Competence Statement is a declaration where a solicitor certifies that they are competent to do their job, in line with their level of experience and legal knowledge. It is made up of three parts:

Understanding the Competence Statement **2.35**

❖ **The Statement of Solicitor Competence**

2.33 This is a general expectation of all practising solicitors and broadly means the ability to perform the roles and tasks required in your work to a proper standard of service and competence.

You must always bear in mind professional conduct and ethics for the SQE and can read more details about it in Chapter 3, Functioning Legal Knowledge (FLK) Assessments, Appendix 3A.

❖ **The Threshold Standard**

2.34 There are five levels of continuing competence. Level three is the standard required at the point of qualification as a newly qualified solicitor. This is the standard of legal knowledge and experience required for the SQE.

❖ **The Statement of Legal Knowledge**

2.35 This sets out the legal knowledge (law) that you are required to know as a newly qualified solicitor (Level three). This part influences how the SQE Part 1 assesses you on the law and how the SQE Part 2 builds on your knowledge in a practical way through your oral and written skills.

Below is a diagram of the parts that make up the Competence Statement. It is sometimes confusingly just referred to as the Statement of Solicitor Competence, but it is actually one part of the Competence Statement and underpinned by the Statement of Legal Knowledge.

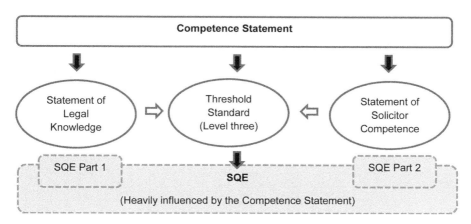

Therefore, you will need to demonstrate the general expectations of a solicitor in practice and the legal knowledge expected at Level three of the Threshold Standard: a newly qualified solicitor. The Threshold Standard has lower levels (one and two) and higher levels (four and five) depending on your experience, expertise and how you develop, in practice. That is why it is referred to as 'continuing competence' and you can read more about it in Chapter 1, The SQE Journey (paras **1.35** and **1.36**).

2.36 Preparing for the SQE

Preparing for the SQE Part 1: Functioning Legal Knowledge (FLK) Assessments

2.36 SQE Part 1 will assess you on the core legal principles and rules that you would be expected to know at the Level three Threshold Standard (a newly qualified solicitor).

- ## *The Assessment Specification*

2.37 You will be tested through two multiple choice tests; the end goal is to ensure your learning style complements this format. You can learn the law in the 'traditional' way by reading books to gain depth and knowledge, but rather than testing yourself in the 'traditional' way of writing answers to questions, you will need to get used to doing multiple choice questions where you will be given five possible answers and you have to select the single best answer.

You want to test your knowledge by practising as many multiple choice questions to the quality and standard expected in the SQE, in timed conditions. Chapter 3, Functioning Legal Knowledge (FLK) Assessments covers this part in more detail.

- ## *Multiple Choice Tests (MCT)*

2.38 You may hear many things about multiple choice tests. Namely that the questions can vary from being easy to difficult and a lot of it will be based on luck. That depends on your perspective. One easy question for you may be difficult for another and vice versa.

You may underestimate your level of knowledge (sometimes you know more than you think) and see it as 'luck' if the questions are ones you know the answers to whereas actually they might not be 'easy', but you just knew the answers. Whatever way you want to look at it, there are many different opinions and perspectives on them. The total number of questions that you are assessed on over the two days is 360. They cover a huge number of different areas of law, so you need to get into the frame of mind that you will not be able to rely on 'luck' to pass.

The subject areas of the law are vast and require a comprehensive and detailed understanding of the substantive and procedural areas of the law. If you think because they are multiple choice tests surface learning to cover the breadth of subject areas will be enough, you are setting yourself up for failure.

There is an argument that it does not really matter if you do not practise and test yourself with multiple choice questions, because if you know the law, it should be enough. Although that may be true, personally, I think that you will benefit from practising questions using the same format you are assessed on. It will help train your brain to get used to answering questions in that style and help you learn to deal with pressure and timing.

You should see SQE Part 1 as the foundation upon which to prepare yourself for SQE Part 2.

Preparing for the SQE Part 2: Practical Legal Skills (PLS)

2.39 The SQE Part 2 will assess you on the law and skills equally. It builds on your legal knowledge from SQE Part 1 in a more practical way. Although it may seem that the law and skills are separate, they are integrated. This means you need to be able to demonstrate that you know the law correctly and can communicate it in an appropriate style, in writing and orally. More about the skills part can be learnt in Chapter 5 on Communication Skills and Chapter 7 on Writing in Professional English.

Although the Assessment Specification and marking criteria show you how each of the parts are assessed, it is best to approach them holistically. They are intrinsically linked to assess how you perform and deliver your advice – whether that is for the oral or written assessments.

One reason for showing the law and skills separately might be to offer you guidance of what you are expected to do for each part. The requirements are more consistent for the law part for all of the assessments.

For the law you are assessed on it being correct and comprehensive, whilst always considering any professional conduct and ethics issues. However, for the skills part the requirements will depend on whether the relevant assessment is oral or written.

- ## *Assessment Specifications*

2.40 The Assessment Criteria will vary for each assessment for the skills part but remains largely the same for the law part (as mentioned above). The law and skills distinction shown in the Assessment Criteria is to help you understand what you need to demonstrate but leaves you to decide how you choose to do it. This is because communication skills are unique to each person's style. They are intangible so any ambiguity can be open to interpretation. For oral skills, read Chapter 5, Communication Skills and for a refresher on written skills, read Chapter 7, Writing in Professional English.

As the law is tangible, it is easier to assess (ie you get it right or wrong), unlike communication skills where there is no set 'correct' way which makes it more difficult to feel confident about your ability. The assessments for the skills part will be marked using a trained examiner's professional judgement as well as the description of the Competence Statement (Chapter 1, The SQE Journey, Appendix 1B).

The essence of SQE Part 2 is practical and tests you to show your knowledge and skills are to the standard of a newly qualified solicitor in legal practice.

> *'The essence of knowledge is, having it, to use it.'*
> **Confucius**

Below are some considerations for when to think about doing the SQE Part 2 depending on whether you are a student, qualified lawyer or an aspiring solicitor (working).

2.41 *Preparing for the SQE*

❖ **Students**

2.41   It makes sense that you attempt SQE Part 2 after you have some legal work experience, although this is not a requirement. See Chapter 4, Qualifying Work Experience (QWE) which provides more details of what you need to do.

Your QWE will help you for the SQE Part 2 because you are assessed on practical legal skills. The oral skills are tested through two assessments (client interviewing and advocacy) and the written skills are tested through four assessments (case and matter analysis, legal writing, legal drafting and legal research). More specific details about each of the six assessments can be found in their respective chapters.

You do not have to have experience in every practice area of the law on which you are assessed. Many of the skills you are assessed on (such as client interviewing and legal writing) should be transferrable skills to other practice areas of the law you are unfamiliar with even if you have not experienced working in them. For example, from a skills perspective generally you should be able to know how to conduct a client interview and write a letter or report.

You will be surprised how much you pick up and how much your thinking develops working in an environment where you are surrounded by lawyers. These are some of the 'intangible' skills and wisdom you learn which cannot be taught in books.

You may find it challenging to attempt the SQE Part 2 without any legal work experience. The SRA data shows those who have work experience performed better than those who did not.

❖ **Qualified Lawyers or Aspiring Solicitors (Working)**

2.42   From my experience of coaching and training lawyers for the SQE Part 2, many unexpectedly find preparing for the interactive part (the oral assessments) to be challenging. The common underlying difficulties include the uncertainty of knowing if what they were doing is correct and the fear of the unknown (how a client or judge might react or behave). For some qualified lawyers from foreign jurisdictions, the level of their fluency in English can also be an issue and this is looked at in more detail at para **2.44**.

Therefore, regardless of your background, years of industry experience, and subject-matter expertise you may experience levels of vulnerability that you are not used to feeling in your normal professional capacity. Your brain is hardwired to want to protect you, so it will work hard to take you back into your comfort zone.

If you are very experienced in client interviewing and/or advocacy, you may feel like you do not need much support in this area. The flip side of this situation is when you are experienced and have your own style which is influenced by your area of work. This means you may need to adapt your communication style which can be challenging, feel unnatural and outside of your comfort zone where you may need support.

The area of law you work in will dictate the types of clients you would normally expect to deal with in practice. For some of the assessments, you have to show you have versatile communication skills and an ability to adapt depending on who you are communicating with (eg, a client or a judge). Moreover, your communication style should be different depending on the practice area of the law you are being assessed on. It is here that many lawyers find it difficult to adapt their style so benefit from tailored coaching to help them very quickly understand what they need to do and how to do it. You can find out more about coaching in the section on Studying Formats (para **2.08**).

- ### *Practising Skills*

2.43 Whether you are a student, a qualified lawyer or aspiring solicitor, it makes sense to practise your communication skills with an expert first, in a safe and comfortable environment. You will be reassured and have appropriate guidance with constructive feedback on your performance. Then you can confidently practise with 'study buddies', friends and family, knowing that what you are doing is improving yourself with increased awareness. It allows you to have control over how much you practise until it becomes authentic and natural.

Grab every opportunity to practise if you know you need to improve a skill (eg read aloud if you are quietly spoken or practise your intonation exercises if you speak in a monotone voice). Read the section on Studying and Time Management (para **2.22**) because sometimes waiting for the 'right time' or 'enough time' means you miss out on valuable time to practise your skills. For example, even five minutes is enough for you to practise a vocal exercise. You will be surprised by the power of consistent repetition, so do not box yourself in by creating time-related boundaries which mean you may miss out altogether.

'We are boxed in by the boundary conditions of our thinking.'
Albert Einstein

Keep the momentum going of practising your skills in a contextual manner once you are comfortable with the skill in principle. This will make you feel more confident and come across as more authentic. It will take time but with more practise, it will become less awkward and more natural. Chapter 5, Communication Skills offers more detailed tips and guidance on this area.

Many lawyers have shared that they did not realise how hard the skills part is and wished they had practised it and paid more attention to it earlier. So, focus on learning the law, but equally focus on how you deliver it and get expert feedback in plenty of time before the assessments. This means that you are reinforcing behavioural patterns that might not come naturally to you when practising mocks in different practice areas of the law.

Some say they are used to cramming for exams when it comes to learning law. This may work for the SQE Part 1, but the SQE Part 2 assesses you equally on the law and skills so will not work as effectively from a skills perspective.

The sooner you know what oral and written communication skills you need to improve on, the more time you have to practise them. The more you practise them, the more confident you will feel about the whole assessment process.

2.43　Preparing for the SQE

> *'If you think you can do a thing or think you can't do a thing, you're right.'*
> **Henry Ford**

The interactive parts of the assessments primarily test your oral skills (except for writing the attendance note). You communicate what you have learnt (the law) and advise a client (an actor) or make a submission in the style of courtroom advocacy to the judge (a qualified solicitor). Therefore, you need to practise so you can perform confidently even when you feel overwhelmed, caught off guard or find yourself in a state of panic. Chapter 6 looks at Managing Nerves, Fear and Failure.

The written skills assessments require you to show what you have learnt (the law) and deliver it in a recipient-focused style which is clear, concise, correct and comprehensive.

Common concerns and questions shared by lawyers doing the assessments are:

- *What should I do if I can't answer the question?*
- *Will there be a clock in the assessment room?*
- *What happens if I go over time?*
- *How do I know what I'm doing is right?*
- *How do I deal with a difficult or challenging client?*
- *How should I deal with a question asked by the judge that I don't know the answer to?*

Many of these questions are dealt with in Chapter 8, Client Interviewing Skills and Chapter 10, Advocacy with practical tips and tools you can use.

The SQE Part 2 is there to test your performance on the day. This means you need to know the law and deliver it in a confident, clear and concise manner. You might think that the advice shared in this book focuses heavily on the skills part and that is correct. This is because knowing the law is a given otherwise you will fail and the skills are what you can really work on to ensure you deliver them to get the highest marks by demonstrating superior performance.

Many people will find the oral skills challenging and daunting, and the written skills are not easily conveyed in a clear and concise manner. The aim is to help you for the oral assessments to skilfully manage any unpredictable clients or unforeseen questions with confidence. The written assessments are computer-based so you can take some comfort that you do them on your own. Learning the law may be challenging and difficult too, but on the day of the assessments, you either know the law or you do not. How you manage your physiology and mindset is within your control and can have a huge impact on your performance on the day.

Chapter 6, Managing Nerves, Fear and Failure is incorporated in the coaching work to prepare you for how to handle nerves on the day and how they can affect your performance. However, if you have practised the skills, exercises and have the strategies in place, even if you do not know the law (you will score low), you should still be able to score high for the skills part. That does not mean you will pass the SQE Part 2 assessments on the skills alone. As explained in Chapter 1,

Preparing for the SQE Part 2: Practical Legal Skills (PLS) **2.43**

The SQE Journey (para **1.17**), the SQE Part 2 is assessed as one single assessment overall, that you pass or fail. So, the law and/or the skills could be the tipping point in you passing or failing.

There is no magic pill or set formula that works for everyone because everyone's ability and skill set is different. But all these skills can be learnt with practice and so become more natural. For example:

- you find making small talk with clients easier;
- you speak more confidently and persuasively doing an advocacy submission; or
- you recognise your writing style is in the active voice.

You can read more about this in Chapter 5, Communication Skills and Chapter 7, Writing in Professional English.

'You are tested on what you would do and how you would behave in practice.'
Solicitors Regulation Authority (SRA)

You need to get out of an 'academic' mindset and start thinking from a more advisory and problem-solving perspective. This is where your legal work experience can really help you.

Whether you are doing the SQE Part 1 or Part 2, at the final revision stage, you should be doing as many practice questions and self-assessment mock papers in the formats you will be assessed on. The more mocks you do, the better the idea you will get of what types of questions and scenarios you can expect to come across in the assessments.

A good way to test yourself whilst studying is to do a mind map. After you have read a topic or section of law, ask yourself: *'What have I learnt?'* The mind map exercise below will allow you to see how much you have remembered of what you have studied.

Exercise: Create a Mind Map

After each section, topic or whatever stage you feel is appropriate, set aside some time to do a mind map. It is a creative tool where you start with whatever comes to mind about what you have studied. Ideally, you move from the beginning to the end, in a structured order.

It is a good way to see a visual snapshot of what you have studied, and you can then go back to check if you have missed any key areas out.

Instructions:

(1) Close all your study materials or different study formats.

(2) Get a blank sheet of paper (A3 is better, as it is double the size of standard A4).

(3) Briefly write down what you remember and add in any key details or trigger words.

It can be helpful to use coloured marker pens for different key parts.

Reflection:

Did you remember everything you covered? What did you miss out? It is a good tool to use when trying to remember general steps for procedures or processes. For example, in property practice explaining the conveyancing process for buying or selling a house from pre-exchange to post-completion.

If you are interested in finding out more about mind maps, you can read about them on the Internet. This is recommended because they are a good tool used by many businesses and can help you see a snapshot of what you have studied.

Your Level of English

2.44 This is usually a concern for international lawyers and students for whom English is not their first language.

The SRA has not provided any guidance on the level of English required for the SQE. The problem is when the standard of English has not been set, non-native English-speaking lawyers or international students do not have anything to benchmark themselves against. This can make it difficult and can undermine your level of self-confidence if you feel your level of English may not be good enough.

My suggestions and opinions are just guidance and are not necessarily 'correct'. They are based on my experience of working with lawyers for whom English is not their first language and who have varying levels of proficiency in English. Sometimes their speaking skills can be an issue where they have a heavy accent and/or struggle with pronunciation and correct sentence structure.

Some lawyers have sufficient knowledge and understanding of English to pass the SQE Part 1 (Functioning Legal Knowledge) multiple choice tests because the key language proficiency tested is your reading skill. However, for the SQE Part 2 (Practical Legal Skills), they find it more challenging because all the skills are tested for language proficiency: speaking, listening, reading and writing. This is to demonstrate you can articulate the law correctly in English in the oral or written assessments to the standard expected of a newly qualified solicitor.

If you are uncertain about your level of English, a good benchmark to use is the International English Language Testing System (IELTS) which is used to measure the proficiency of people communicating in English. The Common European Framework for Reference (CEFR) has three user bands:

- basic;
- independent; and
- proficient.

The IELTS has nine levels which sit within the three user bands. My suggestion is that you should aim to be at a minimum level 7.5 which falls in the proficient user band. More details about the IELTS can be found on their website (www.ielts.org).

You will struggle to pass the SQE Part 2 if your level of English falls below what would be expected of a solicitor, and the suggested benchmark above should provide you with a good command of the language.

If you think your level of English might impact your studying for the oral assessments, my advice is first to find a native English speaker with whom you can practise conversational English, not the law. This will help you build up your self-confidence using the language. Then you can start working on how you explain legal concepts or procedures and offer advice by working with a law tutor or coach who can then prepare you for the assessments.

If you are still unsure about your level of English and want some expert advice, speak to your chosen university or training provider. They might be able to offer you reassurance over whether you will be able to use and understand their materials based on your level of English. They might even have ways to assess your levels of English to see if you are ready to take the SQE. For example, one of the challenges with the oral assessments is the area of pronunciation. If you are a non-native English speaker, Appendix 2C sets out ten sentences to provide you with an example of some of the challenges experienced using the English language where a word can be spelt the same, but is pronounced differently and has a different meaning.

Fitness to Sit/Reasonable Adjustments

2.45   Everyone will be assessed against the Competence Statement, which is detailed in Chapter 1, The SQE Journey, Appendix 1B and above at para 2.28.

In order to sit the assessments you will need to declare that you are deemed fit to sit them at the time you choose to sit them. If you have any mitigating or extenuating circumstances you believe could affect your performance during the assessments, you will need to raise them as soon as possible when you register online (see para **2.02,** SQE Registration). You will need to apply separately for each part of the SQE.

If you require any adjustments to be made, they will be reviewed on a case-by-case basis. You will be required to supply expert evidence as early as possible so any special requirements that need to be made are ready for you when you take the assessments.

- **What is Expert Evidence?**

2.46   This is required to ensure fairness to everyone. Expert evidence will typically be in the form of medical evidence, but can also include the opinion of an education specialist. The evidence has to be up to date and it will be reviewed by a solicitor.

For the SQE Part 1, because it is a computer-based assessment, reasonable adjustments could be allowing for extra time or offering a paper version of the exam.

2.47 *Preparing for the SQE*

For the SQE Part 2, because it is a mixture of computer based and face-to-face assessments, more tailored individual preparation is required. The assessment provider will ensure that a dedicated invigilation team is hand-picked, trained and briefed of the details of your reasonable adjustments for the assessments. Therefore, if you require any reasonable adjustments, you should raise them with the assessment provider at the time of registration or as soon as possible after it.

- ***Typical Examples of Reasonable Adjustments***

2.47 The SRA has a non-exhaustive list of reasonable adjustments that can be offered, such as:

- additional time;
- enlarged or coloured assessments;
- special seating or lighting;
- rest breaks;
- a personal assistant;
- an amanuensis (a person who writes on your behalf);
- a reader;
- a separate room and invigilation;
- specialist equipment;
- rescheduling of the assessment.

Everyone should have the same chance to qualify as a solicitor without compromising the standard and fairness of the assessments. Do not feel ashamed or embarrassed about any reasonable adjustments you may require, they are offered to be able to assist you and not prevent you from having a fair and equal chance to qualify as a solicitor.

'It always seems impossible until it's done.'
Nelson Mandela

Pearson VUE Centres

2.48 The SRA have indicated that Pearson VUE venues will be used for the SQE assessments in the UK and internationally. Most venues will be in city centres so you should be mindful of the fact that there is no control over traffic noise or building works.

Also, the centres are not exclusive for the SQE on the assessment days. Therefore, silence cannot be guaranteed. If you feel that noise could affect you on the assessment days, you can make a request for a reasonable adjustment (and if granted) you can use earplugs or noise cancelling headphones (not audio headphones).

As the centres will vary, you should bear in mind that the Internet speed might not be the same as you are used to working with and this can affect your timing in the assessments. The SRA website also mentions that for the written assessments there is a slight difference in the cut and paste functionality and you can see samples of how it works on the SRA website.

Preparing for the SQE – Top Ten Tips

(1) Find a university or training provider that caters for your learning preferences.

(2) Create a realistic study plan with flexibility and keep adjusting it.

(3) Focus on the quality of the learning rather than the number of hours studied.

(4) Make sure everyone affected (personally and professionally) can offer you support.

(5) Think about what study formats work best for you (classroom, online, coaching, blended).

(6) More time spent learning does not mean more is learnt: Pareto's rule.

(7) Take a break and listen to your body. You will study better in a peak state if you are mentally and physically rested.

(8) Create topic or subject mind maps to test yourself on what you have studied.

(9) If English is not your first language, aim for a minimum 7.5 IELTS score of English proficiency or equivalent.

(10) At the registration stage, tell the assessment provider if you need any reasonable adjustments.

Chapter 2

Preparing for the SQE: Appendices

Appendix 2A: Disruptions and Distractors

These can play a huge part in your day without you even realising how much time they take up. Here are some examples that can be from your personal or professional life (the list is non-exhaustive) and you can add in your own:

Disruptions	Distractions
Interruptions	Personal disorganisation
Waiting for answers/feedback	Perfectionism
Unnecessary meetings	Poor planning
Workload (too much)	Attempting too much
Poor communication	Indecision
Equipment failure	Social media
Shifting priorities	Fatigue
Conflicting priorities	Lack of self-discipline
Illness	Socialising/Chatting
Lack of authority	Procrastination
Revised deadlines	Cluttered workspace

Appendix 2B: Miller's Pyramid

The SRA use Miller's Pyramid (GE Miller, 1990) to assess clinical skills, competence and performance. It is extensively used for the assessment of professional competence in medical and dental training. Below is a model that can be found on the SRA website where I have explained how it would apply to the SQE.

Ideally, you want to make sure you have some qualified work experience (QWE) before you attempt the SQE Part 2 (although this is not a requirement by the SRA). The SRA data shows those with experience tend to perform better.

Appendix 2A

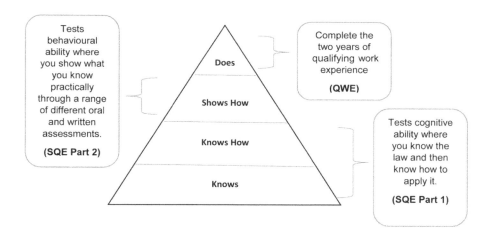

Appendix 2C: Pronunciation Exercise

Have a go at reading these sentences aloud. Focus on the words that are underlined.

(1) The plaster was <u>wound</u> around the <u>wound</u> very tightly.

(2) The man decided to <u>desert</u> his dessert in the <u>desert</u> due to the heat.

(3) There is no time like the <u>present</u> to <u>present</u> the <u>present</u> to the birthday child.

(4) They were too <u>close</u> to the window to <u>close</u> it.

(5) I did not <u>object</u> to the <u>object</u> that was shown to me.

(6) The <u>invalid</u> found her insurance policy was <u>invalid</u>.

(7) The <u>tear</u> in the dress brought a <u>tear</u> to her eyes.

(8) I had to <u>subject</u> the <u>subject</u> to a series of tests.

(9) A <u>row</u> broke out about who would <u>row</u> the boat to shore.

(10) I want to <u>live</u> my life privately and will never do a <u>live</u> documentary for TV.

Reflection.

There may be many words that you find difficult to pronounce. Always think of alternative words that are easier for you to say if possible. It is helpful to work with a native English speaker for this exercise if you need help with your pronunciation.

Chapter 3

SQE Part 1

Functioning Legal Knowledge (FLK) Assessments

> *'Knowledge is of no value unless you put it into practice.'*
> **Anton Chekhov**

In this chapter you will learn:

✓ How to study for the multiple choice tests (MCT).

✓ Tips on how to practically approach the multiple choice questions (MCQs).

✓ How to manage your time effectively for each assessment.

✓ What subject areas of law are tested on each day and which ones are required for the SQE Part 2.

✓ The difference between intellectual thinking and intuitive thinking.

Introduction

3.01 The SQE Part 1 Functioning Legal Knowledge (FLK) assessments will be the first step you need to pass before you can do the SQE Part 2. The FLK assessments consist of two multiple choice tests to assess your knowledge and understanding of the fundamental rules and legal principles expected of a newly qualified solicitor. They will not test specialist legal knowledge. You are tested by applying your knowledge to realistic client-based ethical problems and situations.

This is not a typical type of law exam where you write answers to questions using your knowledge of case law or legislation to support your advice. You will be tested through multiple choice questions and need to know, in depth, a number of different areas of law on which you could be assessed.

Unless you are a qualified lawyer and exempt or have passed the Legal Practice Course and can show equivalent means you will have to do the SQE Part 1.

3.02 *Functioning Legal Knowledge (FLK) Assessments*

More information can be found in Chapter 1, The SQE Journey, SQE Exemptions (para **1.06**)

The SQE Part 1 can be described as testing your intellectual ability. It is more an 'academic' assessment to test your knowledge of the substantive and procedural areas of the law. There is a lot to cover and if you think you can pass by selecting certain areas of the law to focus on and avoiding others, the chances of passing are slim.

You will cover more areas of law in the SQE than a law degree which covers mainly the substantive areas of the law.

However, you will not be required to recall specific case names, statutory or regulatory authorities, except where they are very commonly used (eg *Rylands v Fletcher* or the Civil Procedure Rules (CPR), eg Part 36 – offers to settle disputes etc). Therefore, although it may seem that you are not tested on the depth of the law, the assessments are in some respects more challenging because they cover such a vast range of subject areas of the law and topics on which you could be tested.

In Appendix 3A you will find details of the subjects you are required to study for the SQE Part 1. You will also see parts of the FLK that are relevant for the SQE Part 2, Practical Legal Skills assessments. So, there is an overlap in what you learn for both parts, but you are assessed using the law in different ways. Not every subject you learn for the SQE Part 1 will be tested in SQE Part 2.

Note that the assessment centre you choose may show the format of how the MCQs are presented slightly differently. You can log in your SRA SQE account and view a demo of what some sample questions look like in a Pearson Vue venue.

FLK Assessments – Multiple Choice Tests (MCT)

3.02 The MCT format of testing is not without controversy. It has brought into question the appropriateness and quality of authentically assessing how one can judge a person's knowledge and application of the law, when in practice it is rarely clear cut. Usually, there can be many variables affecting how you conclude what is the 'correct' or the 'best' way to deal with a situation or problem that presents itself.

The criticism (among many lawyers) regarding the format mainly comes down to the way it tests an individual. Typical comments in relation to MCTs are: *'You can guess the answer …', 'They aren't intellectually rigorous …'* and *'They bear no relation to what lawyers have to do in practice …'*

Kaplan is the sole assessor for the SQE. The experience and methodology used in the development of the SQE was based on the QLTS, a tried and tested format. The SRA supports the format of assessment because it allows for a rigorous and wider approach to testing the fundamental legal principles, in realistic situations, and over a larger number of topics. This means it reduces the chances of passing or failing by luck. It also offers more concrete consistency in marking without subjectivity.

FLK Assessments – Multiple Choice Tests (MCT) **3.03**

Many universities and training providers may offer you samples of what they have for the SQE Part 1 and you should look at them for the quality of the questions by comparing them to the samples provided by the SRA. You can read more about choosing who to study with in Chapter 2, Preparing for the SQE (para **2.03**). What you need to consider is what study formats are offered (eg online or digital apps). The digital apps are a great tool because they offer you the flexibility to test yourself whilst on the go and from anywhere in the world. You want to make sure you know and understand:

- the number of questions offered for each area of the law;
- the variety of topics covered for each area of the law; and
- how the quality of the questions meets the standard by which you are tested.
- the reason behind why an answer is right or wrong.

The SRA has provided 90 sample multiple choice questions (MCQs) on its website, which you can download and practice. They are split into 45 MCQs for each FLK respectively. All MCQs will have a scenario, lead in question and five options of which one answer is the single best answer.

They provide you with an idea of the types of questions you will be expected to answer, and the level and depth of knowledge required. Generally, the MCQs may vary in length (short or long) or style (eg set in transactions) based on the scenario.

It can be tempting to just have a go at the SRA samples before you start studying the law. It might be a confidence boost if you get some of the questions right, but it is a mistake to think you can pass the MCTs just through luck. It is inevitable that there will be questions that you will get right and wrong, but to think the 'luck' approach can work for you is a very high-risk strategy.

The sample questions will give you a good idea of the quality and standard you can expect from universities and training providers so make sure they are the equivalent and not too easy.

The MCTs cover a huge breadth of law, if not depth, in the way you are assessed. That does not mean it is easier because you are not expressing your opinion or reasoning. Multiple choice questions test your knowledge of detail and the thought process you have used to come to choose the single best answer without having to explain it. If your thought process is correct, you will choose the correct answer and where it is incorrect, you will choose the wrong one.

- **Distractors**

3.03 Sometimes the choice of answers will be based on common mistakes. In any scenario there may be a distractor or what is known as a 'red herring' which is not relevant. The reason for including it is not because the SRA want you to fail or to trick you. They use them to check you can identify common mistakes.

Some 'common mistake' type questions may attract a typical answer so when you see it as one of the five suggested answers you immediately think and feel confident it is correct. However, your answer may be based on what is often a

3.04 *Functioning Legal Knowledge (FLK) Assessments*

'common mistake' which shows your thought process. It is a way to be able to test your legal knowledge. You will be able to spot the common mistake if you know the law and therefore will choose the correct suggested answer.

FLK Assessment Specification

3.04 Below is the table reproduced again from Chapter 1, The SQE Journey, to help you understand what subject areas of the law you are assessed on for each day.

SQE Part 1: Functioning Legal Knowledge (FLK) Assessments	
Day 1	**Day 2**
FLK Assessment One (FLK1)	**FLK Assessment Two (FLK2)**
180 MCQs	180 MCQs
Approximately 5 hours (plus a break)	**Approximately 5 hours (plus a break)**
• Session 1 – 90 MCQs (2 hours and 33 minutes) 60 Minutes Break • Session 2 – 90 MCQs (2 hours and 33 minutes)	• Session 1 – 90 MCQs (2 hours and 33 minutes) 60 Minutes Break • Session 2 – 90 MCQs (2 hours and 33 minutes)
FLK 1 Subjects	**FLK 2 Subjects**
Business Law and Practice*	Property Practice*
Dispute Resolution	Wills and Administration of Estates*
Contract Law	Land Law
Law of Torts	Trusts
Constitutional and Administrative Law and EU Law and Legal Services	Solicitors' Accounts
Legal System of England and Wales	Criminal Law and Practice
*principles of taxation will only be assessed in these subjects.	
Professional Conduct and Ethics	
You will be tested pervasively in all assessments.	
Location	
Pearson VUE centres in the UK and internationally.	
Dress Code	
Informal/Casual Wear	

In Appendix 3A you can find an edited (high level) version of the Assessment Specification which highlights the areas of law you are expected to know for each of the subjects above. The key objective in relation to them is that you:

- apply the relevant core legal principles and rules to realistic client-based problems and situations; and

- consider any professional conduct and ethical problems.

For each of the FLK Assessments, the multiple choice questions may draw on any combination of the subject areas within each assessment.

Professional Conduct and Ethics

3.05 You will be assessed pervasively, so any of the subject areas could have a question that covers professional conduct and ethics. You might think the question initially relates to one practice area of the law but read it carefully. In Appendix 3A you can find some brief details of the SRA Principles and what you need to bear in mind when dealing with client-based scenarios and problems.

How to Study for the FLK Assessments

3.06 You will have a lot of reading to do. There is no easy way of getting around the subjects to understand them at the depth required, not just for the FLK assessments, but to help you use your knowledge of the law for the SQE Part 2.

You will be tested on 360 MCQs over two days. Each day will be split into two sessions of 90 MCQs each where you have two hours and 33 minutes per session, so approximately five hours per day. You will be given a 60-minute break between each MCT session where you can have food/snacks and leave the venue. However, you will need to re-register before the second session, so you should only take 45–50 minutes and ensure you have plenty of time to re-register. You can expect to be at the venue for a full day (around six hours, including the break).

The best way to study for the MCQs is to work out how much time you can spend on each question. For both days the format and timing will be the same. On average, you get around 1.7 minutes per question, which is not a lot of time when you consider that you have to:

- read the question or scenario;
- identify the area(s) of law;
- read the five possible answers; and
- choose the single best answer.

The question or scenario can also be developed into a 'rolling' fact pattern which means it may expand the scenario or transaction in a hypothetical manner to test your knowledge and understanding from different perspectives. It may also test you on different areas of law together. For example, a question on dispute resolution may also require knowledge of contract law. So, do not expect all the questions to fit neatly into just one area of law.

You should be strategic in your approach to each question. Do not spend too long on one question at the expense of other questions. This could lose you marks if you run out of time that can be the difference between passing and failing the FLK.

It is better to flag a question and go back to it so you have the chance to complete all the questions and maximise your marks.

3.07 *Functioning Legal Knowledge (FLK) Assessments*

When you have an idea of how long to spend on a question, it helps you gauge your time. You might complete a question quickly allowing you some extra time on another question when you need a little longer. It is a bit like trying to keep track of how much additional time you 'bank' to know how much longer you can spend on more tricky questions, but do not over-think it.

Most university or training providers will recommend a structured approach in relation to how to study and in what order to study the subjects. You can read Chapter 2, Preparing for the SQE to help you work out a study plan that can benefit you.

The 'traditional' study approach of reading law textbooks and testing yourself through exercises is usually the preferred option. Just because you are tested through multiple choice questions, does not mean you dismiss different ways of testing your understanding of the law. It is a good idea initially to test yourself using a wide range of different approaches such as the 'Question and Answer' style of exercises. The more you test yourself in different ways, the more confident you will feel about the depth of your understanding. It will help you for the SQE Part 2 where you use your oral and written communication skills to demonstrate your legal knowledge.

As the MCTs are computer-based, the focus will be on reading the questions properly and choosing a single best answer from five answers. You can only choose one answer for each question. The tests are 'closed-book' assessments so you will not be allowed to refer to any books or materials.

Some MCQs may be longer and others shorter based on the scenario so work with the information provided and do not make any assumptions or inferences. You may find some questions easy and others more difficult and that is your perception, based on your knowledge of the law. What you find straightforward or easy, another person might find hard and vice versa. The bottom line is if you know the law you will know the answer, and if you do not know the law you will not. The questions will test your legal knowledge and application of the law.

When you read the scenario all manner of questions or thoughts might go through your mind but you must focus only the information given. If you are in two minds about an answer, sometimes you should trust your gut feeling or intuition.

Intellectual Thinking and Intuitive Thinking

3.07 The purpose of the MCTs is to test your detailed understanding and application of the law. So, from the five suggested answers, there may be many variables to consider before you decide on your answer. However, this is what can cause confusion so do not make any assumptions or infer anything that is not in the scenario.

The challenge often arises when, under pressure, some of the answers to the question look similar. What do you do when your intellectual thinking is 'I know the answer', but you then doubt yourself because of another similar answer? One way to choose the best single answer is to not to over-think it and go with your initial gut-feeling or intuition, if you are not categorically sure.

You may be sceptical about this approach especially when you are trained to think methodically and logically. Most lawyers are risk-averse and fear failure only feeling comfortable and confident answering questions when they 'know' what the answer is or what they are doing (from past experience). However, if you do not know the answer, what can you do? When you are unsure, your intuition may help you.

Did you know that your gut-feeling is often referred to as 'the second brain' (the enteric nervous system) and both communicate with each other without you consciously being aware of it? Dr Valerie van Mulukom is a cognitive neuroscientist and explained that intuition or a gut feeling is not a random selection of feelings. It is often an emotional response informed by previous ideas or memories which are picked up subconsciously and unconsciously. Therefore, all the studying you do for the FLK assessments is not just cognitively absorbed by the brain.

You will do a lot of reading and studying on the different subject areas of law by the time you sit the assessments. The vast depth and breadth of the subject areas mean that you may not feel totally confident with all your levels of knowledge, but you may know more than you think.

There is neuroscientific evidence that suggests that intuition or gut-feelings are also the result of a lot of processing that happens in the brain. The reason why you might find it hard to understand how intuition works is because you cannot determine exactly when the subconscious nature of 'intuitive thinking' occurs.

Dr van Mulukom explains it as follows:

- Intuitive thinking is described as:
  - automatic;
  - fast; and
  - subconscious.
- Analytical thinking is described as:
  - slow;
  - logical;
  - conscious; and
  - deliberate.

In effect, the brain is always communicating with the gut. So, even though you may feel like 'analytical thinking' is the more dominant thinking style, both styles are complementary and work together – especially in difficult decision-making situations. You can read the full article from Dr van Mulukom in Appendix 3C.

Having said that, it does not mean you will pass the FLK assessments just on intuition or luck – that is highly unlikely. You are rigorously tested across a range of substantive and procedural areas of law, over two days of MCTs, amounting to a total of 360 MCQs.

Practising typical types of MCQs is a good way to assess what you do and do not know. Good mock practice questions will offer you an explanation for each answer as to why it is correct or incorrect, to help deepen your understanding of the law.

3.08 *Functioning Legal Knowledge (FLK) Assessments*

There are many opinions on whether practising MCQs does actually help you for the real exams. Some argue that if you know the law that should be good enough, but I believe training your brain to do MCQs by practising them, will benefit you. This will help you work in a set way and at a particular speed when answering questions. Speaking to many lawyers they find that the MCQ mocks are helpful in preparing them for the real assessments, so I recommend this way of testing yourself for the FLK assessments too.

If you are someone who panics or 'freezes' when you do not know an answer, Chapter 6, Managing Nerves, Fear and Failure will provide you with some strategies and techniques you can use or try out.

Practical Tips for Multiple Choice Questions (MCQs)

3.08 Remember to read the facts carefully because although you will have all the relevant information, there may be some distractors too (see para **3.03**). However, by carefully reading the facts and with your knowledge of the law you should be able to distinguish which is the single best answer.

There are too many variables to mention everything that you should look out for in the different types of questions asked. However, typically, you want to be aware of common factors that could affect your answers. For example:

- On a question of a person's liability – questions to consider amongst any distractors are:
    - Are you representing the person mentioned – are they your client?
    - Does your client owe a duty of care or is someone else responsible/liable?
    - Even if you represent the client, is there a professional conduct or ethical issue?

You may have some questions where you have to do calculations (eg working out inheritance tax). Read the facts carefully before you jump into identifying one of the five answers. All five answers are not arbitrary figures but based on common mistakes made. Therefore, your answer may be in the choice of five, but it will only be right if you have used the correct information. For example:

- On a question on inheritance tax – questions to consider amongst any distractors are:
    - Who is the beneficiary (eg child/children, spouse or nephew etc)?
    - What exemptions (if any) apply based on who the beneficiary is and any other relevant factors?

The key thing to remember is focus on the facts provided and do not make any assumptions or infer anything.

Failing the FLK Assessments

3.09 If you fail both parts of the FLK assessments you will have two further opportunities to re-sit them within a six-year period from the date you sat the exams. Your results will include a breakdown by practice area and show how many answers you got correct for each day of the assessment. Depending on your mark against the pass mark (if it is very low), it might be a good idea to take time to focus on the law before rebooking.

If you fail only one part (ie day one or day two), you will only be required to re-sit the day you failed within the same time frame.

If you use your maximum attempts within the six years, you will need to wait until the six-year period expires before you can re-apply. After six years, you can try again but any previous passes cannot be carried forward so, in effect, you have to start again.

If you find yourself in this situation, read Chapter 6, Managing Nerves, Fear and Failure for some guidance.

> *'In your thirst for knowledge, be sure not to drown in all the information.'*
> **Anthony J D'Angelo**

SQE Part 1 – FLK Assessments – Top Ten Tips

(1) Read and focus only on the facts before you choose an answer and do not assume anything.

(2) Watch out for the distractors (or red herrings) in any questions.

(3) Most questions will require an understanding of the application of the law.

(4) Keep an eye on the time spent on each question and be disciplined. It is better to finish all the questions than run out of time.

(5) Keep practising MCQs for all the subjects. Longer questions may require more time than shorter ones.

(6) Not all the questions will fit neatly into identifiable subject areas of law.

(7) Appendix 3A shows you what you need to know for both parts of the SQE.

(8) Do not over think; sometimes you have to go with your gut feeling or intuition.

(9) Professional conduct and ethics will be tested pervasively within any of the subjects.

(10) Have a strategy in mind as to what to do if you panic or 'freeze' during a question.

Chapter 3

Functioning Legal Knowledge (FLK) Assessments: Appendices

Appendix 3A: SQE Part 1: Assessment Specification

The SRA has provided a detailed Assessment Specification document. It includes much more detail than in this book. Therefore, if you want to know what specific parts of the Statement of Solicitor Competence apply to each area of law you should look at the SRA website.

The aim here is to give you a quick overview of the areas of law and Chapter 1, The SQE Journey, Appendix 1B provides you with an overview of the Statement of Solicitor Competence. These should give you a flavour of what you need: the requisite knowledge and competence required to provide a proper standard of service as a practising solicitor.

Your knowledge of the law is assessed in accordance with the Threshold Standard Level three which is that of a newly qualified solicitor.

Therefore, you may be asked a range of different types of questions where you have to show you can identify a legal principle or rule and understand the reason why it may apply to a client situation.

You would also be expected to know common case names, key statutory provisions and certain thresholds for tax calculations (ones that have been part of the UK tax system for a long time).

Professional conduct and ethics will not be specifically highlighted for any parts of the SQE but you would be expected to pick up on any issues identified.

Professional Conduct and Ethics

As mentioned in Chapter 3 (para **3.05**), you are assessed on this area pervasively throughout the SQE assessments. You will be required to consider any professional conduct and ethical issues (if applicable) and demonstrate you can act with honesty and integrity in accordance with the:

- SRA Principles;
- Code of Conduct (both for solicitors and firms);
- Statement of Solicitor Competence (a part of the Competence Statement).

Appendix 3A

In November 2019, the SRA simplified the standards and regulations that regulate the conduct of all solicitors. Below I have briefly summarised the seven SRA Principles just to give you an idea of what you should ask yourself when dealing with any client-based problems and situations. Are you:

1　upholding the rule of law?
2　upholding the public trust and confidence in the legal services provided?
3　acting with independence?
4　acting with honesty?
5　acting with integrity?
6　acting in a way that encourages equality, diversity and inclusion?
7　acting in the best interests of the client?

These SRA Principles underpin the separate SRA Code of Conduct for solicitors and law firms, respectively. The SRA website provides specific details for each of them to abide by the standards and regulations.

For example, under the SRA Code of Conduct for solicitors you would be expected to identify any conflicts of interest or confidentiality and disclosure issues that arise from client-based problems or situations, always bearing in mind the relevant SRA Principles.

- ## *SQE Part 1 – Functioning Legal Knowledge (FLK)*

You need to know the subject areas of law for SQE Part 1 as shown in the table below:

FLK Assessment 1 Subjects	FLK Assessment 2 Subjects
Business Law and Practice*	Property Practice*
Dispute Resolution	Wills and Administration of Estates*
Contract Law	Land Law
Law of Torts	Trusts
Constitutional and Administrative Law and EU Law and Legal Services**	Solicitors' Accounts
Legal System of England and Wales**	Criminal Law and Practice

* principles of taxation will only be assessed in these subjects.

** Note the SRA website shows these as separate subjects but they are included under The Legal System. Therefore, they are shown in the same way below in the table FLK Assessment 1.

Below you will see two tables split into FLK Assessment 1 (day one) and FLK Assessment 2 (day two) which show high level details of the topics you are assessed on for each day of the SQE Part 1. You should look on the SRA website for more specific details within the Legal Knowledge sections.

Functioning Legal Knowledge (FLK) Assessments: Appendices

• SQE Part 1 and 2 – Overlap

The two tables below are also useful to point out what you need (and do not need) to know for the SQE Part 2.

Where you see the label 'SQE 1 only' it means that you will not be tested on those subjects for the SQE Part 2. For example, you will not be tested on the following subject areas of law (except for money laundering and financial services which may be examined in business law):

- The Legal System.
- Solicitors' Accounts.

Where you see the label 'SQE 1 & 2' it means you are tested on your knowledge of the law in different ways for both parts of the SQE. For example, for SQE Part 1 you demonstrate your knowledge through the MCQs and for the SQE Part 2 you demonstrate your knowledge through oral and written skills assessments.

Where the subject does not have a label (eg contract, tort etc) you are tested on it for SQE Part 1 and it is a substantive subject you need to know for the practice areas of the law you are assessed in for SQE Part 2.

For the SQE Part 2, the label does not mean that you will do those subjects on any particular assessment day.

FLK Assessment 1

SQE 1 & 2

Business Law and Practice

Assessment Objective

The key things you need to do are:

(a) Apply the relevant core legal principles and rules to realistic client-based problems and situations; and

(b) Consider any ethical problems.

Assessment Areas

1. Starting a new business through the vehicle of a company, partnership, LLP or as a sole trader.
2. The management of a business and company decision making to ensure compliance with statutory and other legal requirements.
3. The interests, rights, obligations and powers of stakeholders in a business.
4. Financing a business.
5. Taxation of a business and its stakeholders.

Appendix 3A

6. The termination of a solvent business, corporate insolvency and personal bankruptcy.

Legal Knowledge

- **Business Organisations, Rules and Procedures**
    (1) Business and organisational characteristics (sole trader, partnership, different types of companies etc)
    (2) Legal personality and limited liability
    (3) Procedure and documentation required for incorporating a company/partnership
    (4) Finance (funding, security, distribution of profits, financial records)
    (5) Corporate governance and compliance
    (6) Partnership decision making and authority of partners
    (7) Insolvency (corporate and personal).
- **Taxation – Business**
    (1) Income tax
    (2) Capital gains tax
    (3) Corporation tax
    (4) Value added tax
    (5) Inheritance tax.

Dispute Resolution

SQE 1 & 2

Assessment Objective

The key things you need to do are:

(a) *Apply the relevant core legal principles and rules to realistic client-based problems and situations; and*

(b) *Consider any ethical problems.*

Assessment Areas

1. Analysis of merits of claim or defence.
2. Arbitration, mediation and litigation as an appropriate mechanism to resolve a dispute.
3. Pre-action considerations and steps.
4. Commencing, responding to or progressing a claim.

Functioning Legal Knowledge (FLK) Assessments: Appendices

5. Case management and any interim applications relevant to a claim.
6. The evidence needed and disclosure steps required in commencing, responding to, progressing or defending a claim.
7. Preparation of a case for a trial, the trial and any post-trial steps.
8. Procedures and processes relevant to costs involved in dispute resolution.

Legal Knowledge

- **Dispute Resolution – Principles, Processes and Procedures**
    (1) Different options for dispute resolution
    (2) Resolving a dispute through a civil claim
    (3) Where to start proceedings
    (4) Issuing and serving proceedings
    (5) Responding to a claim
    (6) Statements of case
    (7) Interim applications
    (8) Case management
    (9) Evidence
    (10) Disclosure and inspection
    (11) Trial
    (12) Costs
    (13) Appeals
    (14) Enforcement of money judgments.

Contract

Assessment Objective

The key things you need to do are:

(a) Apply the relevant core legal principles and rules to realistic client-based problems and situations; and
(b) Consider any ethical problems.

Assessment Areas

1. Existence/formation of a contract.
2. Contents of a contract.
3. Causation and remoteness.

Appendix 3A

4. Vitiating elements.
5. Discharge of contract and remedies.
6. Unjust enrichment.
7. Causation and remoteness.

Legal Knowledge

- **Core Principles of Contract Law**
    (1) Formation (offer, acceptance, consideration, intention, capacity)
    (2) Parties
    (3) Contract terms
    (4) Vitiating factors (misrepresentation, mistake, unfair contract terms, etc)
    (5) Termination
    (6) Remedies.

Tort

Assessment Objective

The key things you need to do are:

(a) Apply the relevant core legal principles and rules to realistic client-based problems and situations; and

(b) Consider any ethical problems.

Assessment Areas

1. Negligence.
2. Remedies and defences.
3. Occupiers' liability.
4. Product liability.
5. Nuisance and the rule in *Rylands v Fletcher*.

Legal Knowledge

- **Core Principles of Tort**
    (1) Negligence
    (2) Defences (consent, contributory negligence, illegality, necessity)
    (3) Principles of vicarious liability (occupiers' liability, product liability)
    (4) Nuisance.

The Legal System

SQE 1 only

Assessment Objective

The key things you need to do are:

(a) Apply the relevant core legal principles and rules to realistic client-based problems and situations; and

(b) Consider any ethical problems.

Assessment Areas

1. The Legal System of England and Wales and Sources of law.
2. Constitutional and Administrative law and EU law.
3. Legal services.

Legal Knowledge

- **The Legal System of England and Wales and Sources of Law**

    (1) The courts

    (2) Development of case law: the doctrine of precedent

    (3) Primary legislation: the structure of an Act of Parliament/ the Structure of an act of Senedd Cymru

    (4) Statutory interpretation.

    (5) The application of legislation made by Senedd Cymru and Westminster to England and Wales

- **Constitutional and Administrative Law and EU Law**

    (1) Core institutions of the state and how they interrelate

    (2) Legitimacy, separation of powers and the rule of law

    (3) Human Rights Act 1998 and the European Convention on Human Rights (ss 2, 3, 4, 6, 7, 8, 10 Human Rights Act 1998 and Schedule 1 the 'Convention Rights')

    (4) The place of EU law in the UK constitution.

- **Legal Services**

    (1) The regulatory role of the SRA

    (2) Funding options for legal services (private retainer, legal aid, insurance etc).

Appendix 3A

FLK Assessment 2

SQE 1 & 2

Property Practice

Assessment Objective

The key things you need to do are:

(a) Apply the relevant core legal principles and rules to realistic client-based problems and situations; and

(b) Consider any ethical problems.

Assessment Areas

1. The key elements of a freehold and/or leasehold residential or commercial property transaction.
2. Investigation of a registered or an unregistered freehold and/or leasehold title.
3. Pre-contract searches and enquiries undertaken when acquiring a freehold and/or leasehold property.
4. Steps in progressing a freehold and/or leasehold property transaction to exchange of contracts.
5. Pre-completion steps relevant to a freehold and/or leasehold property transaction.
6. Completion and post-completion steps relevant to a freehold and/or leasehold property transaction in each of England and Wales including remedies for delayed completion.
7. The grant and the assignment of a commercial lease and/or underlease.
8. The key lease covenants in a commercial lease and the law relating to their breach.
9. Security of tenure under the Landlord and Tenant Act 1954 Part II.
10. Taxation of property transactions through Stamp Duty Land Tax for land in England, Land Transaction Tax for land in Wales, Value Added Tax and Capital Gains Tax.

Legal Knowledge

- **Freehold Real Estate Law and Practice**

    (1) Investigation of a registered and unregistered freehold title

    (2) Pre-contract searches and enquiries

    (3) Law Society Conveyancing Protocol

    (4) Finance

    (5) Acting for a lender

Functioning Legal Knowledge (FLK) Assessments: Appendices

- (6) Preparation for and exchange of contracts
- (7) Pre-completion
- (8) Completion and post-completion
- (9) Remedies for delayed completion.

- **Leasehold Real Estate Law and Practice**
  - (1) Structure and content of a lease
  - (2) Procedural steps for the grant of a lease or underlease, deduction and investigation of title
  - (3) Procedural steps for the assignment of a lease
  - (4) Licence to assign and licence to underlet
  - (5) Leasehold covenants
  - (6) Remedies for breach of a leasehold covenant
  - (7) Termination of a lease
  - (8) Security of tenure under a business lease.

- **Planning law**
  - (1) Statutory definition of 'Development'
  - (2) Matters that do not constitute 'Development'
  - (3) Matters that do not require express planning permission
  - (4) Building regulation control
  - (5) Enforcement.

- **Taxation – Property**
  - (1) Stamp Duty Land Tax in England and Land Transaction Tax in Wales
  - (2) Value Added Tax
  - (3) Capital Gains Tax.

Wills and the Administration of Estates

SQE 1 & 2

Assessment Objective

The key things you need to do are:

(a) Apply the relevant core legal principles and rules to realistic client-based problems and situations; and

(b) Consider any ethical problems.

Assessment Areas

1. The validity of a will and interpretation of the contents of a will. The distribution of testate, intestate and partially intestate estates.
2. The law and practice in connection with an application for a grant of representation.
3. The law and practice of Inheritance Tax in the context of lifetime gifts and transfers on death.
4. The planning, management and progression of the administration of an estate including claims under the Inheritance (Provision for Family and Dependants) Act 1975.
5. The law and practice relating to personal representatives and trustees in the administration of estates and consequent trusts. The rights, powers and remedies of beneficiaries of wills and consequent trusts.

Legal Knowledge

- **Wills and Intestacy**
    (1) Validity of wills and codicils
    (2) Personal representatives
    (3) Alterations and amendments to wills
    (4) Revocation of wills
    (5) The interpretation of wills
    (6) The intestacy rules
    (7) Property passing outside the estate.

- **Probate and Administration Practice**
    (1) Grants of representation
    (2) Administration of estates
    (3) Claims against estates under the Inheritance (Provision for Family and Dependants) Act 1975.

- **Taxation – wills and the administration of estates**
    (1) Inheritance Tax
    (2) Income and Capital Gains Tax in respect of the period of the administration of an estate.

Land Law

Assessment Objective

The key things you need to do are:

Functioning Legal Knowledge (FLK) Assessments: Appendices

(a) *Apply the relevant core legal principles and rules to realistic client-based problems and situations; and*

(b) *Consider any ethical problems.*

Assessment Areas

1. Registered and unregistered land.
2. Freehold and leasehold estates, and legal and equitable interests in land.
3. Landlord and tenant.
4. Co-ownership.

Legal Knowledge

- **Land Law**
   (1) Nature of land (real and personal)
   (2) Title to land
- **Co-ownership and Trusts**
   (1) Differences between joint tenants and tenants in common in law and in equity
   (2) Proprietary rights (easements and covenants, mortgages etc)
   (3) Leases.

Trusts

Assessment Objective

The key things you need to do are:

(a) *Apply the relevant core legal principles and rules to realistic client-based problems and situations; and*

(b) *Consider any ethical problems.*

Assessment Areas

1. Express and implied trusts.
2. The fiduciary relationship.
3. Trustees' duties, powers and liability.
4. Equitable remedies.

Legal Knowledge

- **Trusts Law**

Appendix 3A

(1) Creation and requirements of express trusts
(2) Beneficial entitlement
(3) Resulting trusts
(4) Trusts of the family home
(5) Liability of strangers to the trust
(6) The fiduciary relationship and its obligations
(7) Trustees
(8) Trustees' liability.

Solicitors Accounts

SQE 1 only

Assessment Objective

The key things you need to do are:

(a) *Apply the relevant core legal principles and rules to realistic client-based problems and situations; and*

(b) *Consider any ethical problems.*

Assessment Areas

1. Transactions involving client money and money belonging to the authorised body.
2. Operation of ledgers and bank accounts; the payment of interest.
3. Breaches of the SRA Accounts Rules.
4. Accounting entries required; bills; obtaining and delivery of accountants' reports; obligations regarding record keeping.

Legal Knowledge

- **Solicitors Accounts**
    (1) Client money
    (2) Client account
    (3) Requirement to keep client money separate from money belonging to the authorised body
    (4) Interest
    (5) Breach of the SRA Accounts Rules
    (6) Requirement to keep and maintain accurate records in client ledgers

Functioning Legal Knowledge (FLK) Assessments: Appendices

(7) Operation of joint account; operation of a client's own account

(8) Third-party managed accounts

(9) Obtaining and delivery of accountants' reports; storage and retention of accounting records.

Criminal Law and Practice

SQE 1 & 2

Assessment Objective

The key things you need to do are:

(a) Apply the relevant core legal principles and rules to realistic client-based problems and situations; and

(b) Consider any ethical problems.

Assessment Areas

1. The core principles of criminal liability including *actus reus* and *mens rea*, specific and general defences, and participation.
2. The law, procedure and processes involved in advising a client at the police station.
3. The law, procedure and processes involved in pre-trial considerations.
4. The law, procedure and processes involved to meet the client's objectives.
5. The law, procedure and processes involved in magistrates' court and Crown Court trials, including sentencing and appeals.

Legal Knowledge

- **Criminal Liability**

    In relation to the specified criminal offences listed below:

    (1) Offences against the person (common assault: assault and battery, Offences Against the Person Act 1861 ss 47, 20 and 18)

    (2) Theft offences (Theft Act 1968 ss 1, 8, 9 and 10)

    (3) Criminal damage (simple, aggravated, arson)

    (4) Homicide

    (5) Fraud

    (6) Definition of the offence (*actus reus* and *mens rea*)

    (7) General defences (intoxication, self defence/defence of another)

(8) Partial defences (loss of control, diminished responsibility)

(9) Parties

(10) Inchoate offences (attempt to commit an offence).

- **Advising clients, including vulnerable clients, about the procedure and processes at the police station**

    (1) Rights of a suspect being detained by the police for questioning

    (2) Identification procedures

    (3) Advising a client, including vulnerable clients, whether to answer police questions

    (4) Procedure for interviewing a suspect under PACE 1984.

- **The procedures and processes involved in criminal litigation**

    (1) Bail applications

    (2) First hearings before the magistrates' court

    (3) Plea before Venue

    (4) Allocation of business between magistrates' court and Crown Court

    (5) Case management and pre-trial hearings

    (6) Principles and procedures to admit and exclude evidence

    (7) Trial procedure in magistrates' court and Crown Court

    (8) Sentencing

    (9) Appeals procedure

    (10) Youth court procedure.

    (11) Preliminary consideration for the use of the Welsh language in criminal proceedings

Appendix 3B: SQE Part 2: Assessment Specification

- *Functioning Legal Knowledge (FLK) for SQE Part 2*

The SRA website has more details of what you are required to know for the SQE Part 2. To avoid duplication the FLK Assessment 1 and FLK Assessment 2 tables have a label 'SQE 1 & 2' which shows you what you need to know for both parts of the SQE.

Where the subject does not have a label in the tables above, you can see below how it is a core subject that you need to know to help you develop your knowledge for SQE Part 2 practice areas of the law:

SQE Part 1	SQE Part 2
Functional Legal Knowledge (FLK)	**Practice Areas of Law**
Criminal Law	Criminal Litigation*
Contract and Tort	Dispute Resolution
Land Law	Property Practice
Trusts	Wills and Intestacy, Probate Administration and Practice
Contract	Business Organisations, Rules and Procedures

* Note the information on the SRA website shows this subject as Criminal Law and Practice and therefore it is called that in the table FLK Assessment 2.

The above just highlights at high level the areas of law to give you an idea of what is required. More specific details of what is covered in the 'Legal Knowledge' parts in the tables can be found in the Assessment Specification for SQE Part 1 and 2 on the SRA website (www.sra.org.uk).

Appendix 3C: Intellectual Thinking and Intuitive Thinking

Is it rational to trust your gut feelings? A neuroscientist explains

16 May 2018, article by Dr Valerie van Mulukom.

Imagine the director of a big company announcing an important decision and justifying it with it being based on a gut feeling. This would be met with disbelief – surely important decisions have to be thought over carefully, deliberately and rationally?

Indeed, relying on your intuition generally has a bad reputation, especially in the Western part of the world where analytic thinking has been steadily promoted over the past decades. Gradually, many have come to think that humans have progressed from relying on primitive, magical and religious thinking to analytic and scientific thinking. As a result, they view emotions and intuition as fallible, even whimsical, tools.

However, this attitude is based on a myth of cognitive progress. Emotions are actually not dumb responses that always need to be ignored or even corrected by rational faculties. They are appraisals of what you have just experienced or thought of – in this sense, they are also a form of information processing.

Intuition or gut feelings are also the result of a lot of processing that happens in the brain. Research suggests that the brain is a large predictive machine, constantly comparing incoming sensory information and current experiences against stored knowledge and memories of previous experiences, and predicting what will come next. This is described in what scientists call the 'predictive processing framework'.

This ensures that the brain is always as prepared to deal with the current situation as optimally as possible. When a mismatch occurs (something that wasn't predicted), your brain updates its cognitive models.

This matching between prior models (based on past experience) and current experience happens automatically and subconsciously. Intuitions occur when your brain has made a significant match or mismatch (between the cognitive model and current experience), but this has not yet reached your conscious awareness.

For example, you may be driving on a country road in the dark listening to some music, when suddenly you have an intuition to drive more to one side of the lane. As you continue driving, you notice that you have only just missed a massive pothole that could have significantly damaged your car. You are glad you relied on your gut feeling even if you don't know where it came from. In reality, the car in the far distance in front of you made a similar small swerve (since they are locals and know the road), and you picked up on this without consciously registering it.

When you have a lot of experience in a certain area, the brain has more information to match the current experience against. This makes your intuitions more reliable. This means that, as with creativity, your intuition can actually improve with experience.

Biased understanding

In the psychological literature, intuition is often explained as one of two general modes of thinking, along with analytic reasoning. Intuitive thinking is described as automatic, fast, and subconscious. Analytic thinking, on the other hand, is slow, logical, conscious and deliberate.

Many take the division between analytic and intuitive thinking to mean that the two types of processing (or 'thinking styles') are opposites, working in a see-saw manner. However, a recent meta-analysis – an investigation where the impact of a group of studies is measured – has shown that analytic and intuitive thinking are typically not correlated and could happen at the same time.

So while it is true that one style of thinking likely feels dominant over the other in any situation – in particular analytic thinking – the subconscious nature of intuitive thinking makes it hard to determine exactly when it occurs, since so much happens under the bonnet of our awareness.

Indeed, the two thinking styles are in fact complementary and can work in concert – we regularly employ them together. Even ground-breaking scientific research may start with intuitive knowledge that enables scientists to formulate innovative ideas and hypotheses, which later can be validated through rigorous testing and analysis.

Einstein valued intuition

What's more, while intuition is seen as sloppy and inaccurate, analytic thinking can be detrimental as well. Studies have shown that over-thinking can seriously hinder our decision-making process.

In other cases, analytic thinking may simply consist of post-hoc justifications or rationalisations of decisions based on intuitive thinking. This occurs for example when we have to explain our decisions in moral dilemmas. This effect has let some people refer to analytic thinking as the 'press secretary' or 'inner lawyer' of intuition. Oftentimes we don't know why we make decisions, but we still want to have reasons for our decisions.

Trusting instincts

So should we just rely on our intuition, given that it aids our decision making? It's complicated. Because intuition relies on evolutionarily older, automatic and fast processing, it also falls prey to misguidances, such as cognitive biases. These are systematic errors in thinking that can automatically occur. Despite this, familiarising yourself with common cognitive biases can help you spot them on future occasions.

Similarly, since fast processing is ancient, it can sometimes be a little out of date. Consider for example a plate of doughnuts. While you may be attracted to eat them all, it is unlikely that you need this large an amount of sugars and fats. However, in the hunter-gatherers' time, stocking up on energy would have been a wise instinct.

Thus, for every situation that involves a decision based on your assessment, consider whether your intuition has correctly assessed the situation. Is it an evolutionary old or new situation? Does it involve cognitive biases? Do you have experience or expertise in this type of situation? If it is evolutionary old, involves a cognitive bias, and you don't have expertise in it, then rely on analytic thinking. If not, feel free to trust your intuitive thinking.

It is time to stop the witch hunt on intuition, and see it for what it is: a fast, automatic, subconscious processing style that can provide us with very useful information that deliberate analysing can't. We need to accept that intuitive and analytic thinking should occur together, and be weighed up against each other in difficult decision-making situations.

Here is the link to read the article online:

https://theconversation.com/is-it-rational-to-trust-your-gut-feelings-a-neuroscientist-explains-95086

Chapter 4

Qualifying Work Experience (QWE)

'Nothing great was ever achieved without enthusiasm.'
Ralph Waldo Emmerson

In this chapter you will learn:
- ✓ What type of lawyers are required for the future.
- ✓ How the QWE affects students, aspiring solicitors (working) and qualified lawyers.
- ✓ What counts as QWE.
- ✓ How the QWE is authenticated.
- ✓ The standard of QWE you are expected to meet (Threshold Standard).
- ✓ What amounts to good-quality work experience.
- ✓ When to do the SQE Part 2: before, during or after the QWE.
- ✓ What and how to record your QWE using a template.
- ✓ Tips, guidance and suggestions of a CV template that works for the legal market.

Introduction

4.01 The Solicitors Regulation Authority's (SRA) introduction of the SQE aims to create a fairer system so smart and capable individuals can qualify as a solicitor in more flexible ways. The traditional way to qualify and be admitted as a solicitor in England and Wales has been by way of a training contract, but there are now various different ways to obtain Qualifying Work Experience (QWE) (see below). With the changing landscape of the way lawyers work, the onus falls on you to find the appropriate QWE to meet the SRA's requirements to be admitted as a solicitor.

If you are a qualified lawyer and exempt from the QWE or someone who has secured a sponsorship then some parts of this chapter (ie Finding QWE, para **4.09**) will not be relevant to you. So, skim read as many of the sections of the chapter as may be of interest to you. Aspiring solicitors will need at least two years of QWE unless exemptions apply (ie you are already a qualified lawyer from a foreign jurisdiction). The QWE does not have to be two consecutive years with the same law firm or

4.02 *Qualifying Work Experience (QWE)*

business organisation (like a traditional training contract). Your choice of where you work will undoubtedly help influence the direction of your career path as a lawyer. However, it will be your level of enthusiasm and interest which will help you discover what you enjoy doing and in which areas of law you enjoy working.

The purpose of the QWE requirement is to show that you have real legal work experience where competences to practise law as a solicitor have been proved and developed.

If you are a foreign jurisdiction lawyer looking to work in England and Wales as a solicitor or a student looking for QWE, you will need to have a good Curriculum Vitae (CV). In Appendix 4A there is a CV template with some tips and guidance on how to create a CV that is appropriate for the legal market in England and Wales. I have reviewed and provided constructive feedback to many lawyers and students so you can compare it to what you already have or, if you have not got a CV, it will help you create one from scratch. The template can be adapted to suit you.

The SRA has stated that you can use previous work experience to count as QWE before starting the SQE. This means that you have to be able to demonstrate that you meet some or all of the prescribed competences mentioned in the Statement of Solicitor Competence (you can read Chapter 1, The SQE Journey, Appendix 1B for more details). See What Counts as QWE (para **4.12**) below for more details about the requirements that need to be satisfied.

It is absolutely essential that you keep an accurate record of all your experiences. In Appendix 4B there is a template suggested by the SRA which has been adapted to include the competences in the Statement of Solicitor Competence to demonstrate that you have had the chance to develop some or all of them.

There is no set time period by which you have to complete your QWE (unlike the six-year limit for the SQE exams).

Types of Lawyers

4.02 The legal profession is changing and lawyers need to keep up with it. The traditional lawyer with a focus on just black letter law is not enough today and it has not been for a long time. Lawyers do not like change and when society changes and technology develops lawyers need to adapt to survive. Now, regardless of whether you work in a law firm or an in-house legal department, 21st century skills (outside of the knowledge of law) apply equally to all qualified lawyers and aspiring ones. For example, in-house lawyers might require less specialism with a more holistic focus on representing the whole business. Whereas, a lawyer in private practice might specialise in a particular practice area of law and represent a range of clients with billable hours and targets.

Ultimately, the areas of law worked in may differ, business models will differ and where you work may differ. However, one thing that is consistently true for everyone who wants to succeed and do well is the need for effective communication skills. I believe these communication skills extend to include being emotionally intelligent and understanding the psychology of human behaviour. These go beyond the traditional communication skills taught at most law schools. When you learn more about yourself and how you like to communicate and receive information it helps you identify how other people communicate when it is different to you. Having the ability to be flexible in your communication skills can make you not just a good lawyer, but a great leader. When you know how to use these skills confidently they can change your personal and professional life.

Law is a people business. Clients want to instruct and work with people they like; it makes it an enjoyable experience for everyone involved, even if it is a contentious matter. So, impressing clients with your knowledge of the law is usually the last thing they focus on. As mentioned before, it is a given that you should know the law. Therefore, from a client's perspective, it is an expectation and one you do not really have to prove to them. It is more important to get them to connect with you enough to like you, so they trust you and have confidence in your ability to do the work. What helps you do that is your communication skills (Chapter 5).

- **What Type of Lawyer Do I Want to Be?**

4.03 If you are a qualified lawyer and ambitious enough to want leadership roles in the future, then you want to be a role model demonstrating your expertise and skills. So, it is crucial that you ask yourself the question above. Even if you are happy in your role and have no desire to take on leadership roles and responsibilities (which is fine too), you should still ask yourself this question. A lot of insight can be drawn from personality profiling tools. There are many to choose from and Chapter 5, Communication Skills, Appendix 5D highlights some popular ones.

If you are an experienced lawyer, you will already be competent in the area of law you work in, but may want to focus on how to develop your skill set to become an exceptional and well-rounded lawyer.

If you are a student, start thinking about the question above. Rather than just focusing on the law, you should think about what skills are required to be a good lawyer. These skills play an important part in shaping your career as a lawyer. Any work experience or part-time jobs (not necessarily in law) have transferrable skills, so do not under-estimate their importance. These are looked at in more detail in Good-Quality Work Experience (para **4.22**).

Remember, the SQE Part 2 assesses you equally on the law and skills. This should tell you how much the SRA values not just a lawyer knowing black letter law, but one who can also deliver it skilfully too. According to the SRA initial data on pass rates, those who had work experience performed better than those without it.

- **The O-shaped Lawyer**

4.04 The O-shaped lawyer is a model introduced by Dan Kayne. The focus of this model is that it applies to the next generation of lawyers who will need to be well-rounded, utilising skills that complement their knowledge of the law.

The O-shaped model is more generic in its application and can be used by any qualified or aspiring lawyer regardless of the type of organisation they work in

4.04 *Qualifying Work Experience (QWE)*

(eg private practice, in-house, alternative business structures such as Deloitte Legal etc).

There is no doubt that aspiring lawyers will have the depth and breadth of legal knowledge, but the O-shaped model requires them to have a 'growth mindset' as opposed to a 'fixed mindset'. Law schools have a set way of training lawyers and that is required, but it needs to be adapted to move with the times. Lawyers are trained to be risk averse, as this protects them from the risk of failure. However, it also means that they miss out on potential business opportunities. The risk-averse style of thinking is useful and has its place, but lawyers also need to be trained at law school to have a 'growth mindset'. This involves them not being afraid to innovate and seek new and different ways to do things. The concept does not translate comfortably for many lawyers, because they have not been trained in this way and so feel uncomfortable with change. Therefore, the future O-shaped lawyer needs to be aware of the importance of the following words:

- ✓ Open – they should be open-minded and have a growth mindset.
- ✓ Opportunist – they should seek new opportunities and try new things.
- ✓ Original – they use creativity to problem-solve and be forward-thinking.
- ✓ Ownership – they should take ownership and be accountable for their work.

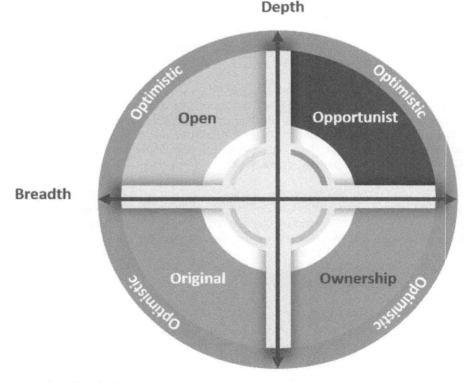

Reproduced with the permission of Dan Kayne (www.oshapedlawyer.com)

This model is shared to help you see and understand that whilst all lawyers need to know the law, only those with high levels of skills will stand out. The future lawyer needs to be ready to adapt, be agile, recognise and see opportunities as they present themselves.

Some law schools have started to recognise the importance of these skills and you should see what type of skills training they are offering and whether it incorporates what has been mentioned above to develop the O-shaped lawyer type of thinking.

Remember, your enthusiasm and work experience will shape and influence what type of a lawyer you become. Therefore, it is essential that you get good-quality QWE where you have good role models and mentors that can help you build your confidence to create your own style.

How Does the QWE Affect You?

4.05 This will depend on whether you are a qualified lawyer, an aspiring solicitor (working) or a student.

- ### *Qualified Lawyers*

4.06 You must be a qualified lawyer with practice rights otherwise you will need to do QWE. If you are a qualified lawyer in a foreign jurisdiction or a qualified barrister in England and Wales (with practice rights), you may be exempt from the QWE requirement. You should check with the SRA.

You will need to show the SRA that your qualifications and experience equates to the SQE requirements which are mapped against the Competence Statement (see Chapter 1, The SQE Journey, Appendix 1B).

If you satisfy the QWE requirement after passing both parts of the SQE (unless any exemptions apply), you can apply to get admitted onto the Roll of Solicitors (see Chapter 1, The SQE Journey, Post-SQE Journey, para **1.31**).

- ### *Aspiring Solicitors (Working)*

4.07 If you are an individual who has legal work experience from the place where you work or a number of different firms or businesses, you can check below in para **4.16** under How is QWE Authenticated? to see if it satisfies the requirements.

If you do not have any or enough QWE, you will need to have two years before the admission stage of qualification.

- ### *Students*

4.08 If you are a student who has little or no legal work experience, you will have to find QWE and there is a range of flexible ways you can do it which are listed below at para **4.12** under What Counts as QWE?

4.09 *Qualifying Work Experience (QWE)*

Finding QWE

4.09 There are many ways that you can try to obtain work experience – but you have to be open-minded and creative.

The Internet has made some things so easy; with the click of a button you are able to read lawyers' profiles and find out the history and facts about different types of firms or businesses. The downside is that law firms now expect you to know something different and current about them, rather than stating the obvious which is readily available from their website. Your CV should be tailored and that is what will make you stand out and give you the edge.

In the past you could only work in traditional law firms or legal departments, but now the legal market is expanding and changing. As such, it is open to much more competition and different ways of working. This means expectations are much higher, but you also have more opportunities to qualify as a solicitor, as opposed to the traditional approach which was through a 'Period of Recognised Training' such as a training contract.

There are many universities and training providers who will offer free advice and guidance through their careers service, so get some expert help if it is available. See Appendix 4A for guidance on how to create a CV for the legal market.

- ***Will Additional Qualifications Increase Your Chances of Getting QWE?***

4.10 When students find it hard getting work experience or a job in the legal sector, some think that by studying more and getting more qualifications (eg, a Master's degree) they will enhance their chances of getting work.

There is a lot of debate around whether a 'top up' option resulting in a 'Master's' is appreciated as a 'real' Master's. Many lawyers do not see it in this way and this may diminish its perceived value. You may feel doing a Master's in a specialised area of law will help you, but employers still want experience. Therefore, sadly, I do not think a Master's will significantly improve your chances of getting QWE.

The additional qualifications show the level of your intellect, but unfortunately that does not compensate for your lack of experience, which is what many employers are interested in. This is because if the work involves interacting with clients or other professionals then they want to make sure you have the skills or some experience to be able to do it professionally.

Do your research; be bold and creative. Popular law firms and businesses will always be competitive, but you have to be proactive and stand out. Be prepared to change your approach, rather than give up. Try not to take any rejection personally and remember a rejection now is not a rejection forever, it just means it is not your time now.

If what you are doing is not working, try something different. For example, it is great to have goals and be ambitious about where you want to work, but you have to deal with the present situation to get there. Therefore, without any experience, your chances are probably slim. You could start off by doing some voluntary legal work experience (locally) or through any pro bono law clinics at your law school (if available). You may be surprised by the skills (or tools) you develop and how they can help you with the SQE and your future. You also never know who you might meet. Remember, opportunities present themselves everywhere; you just need to be ready to see them.

> *'Do not wait: The time will never be "just right". Start where you stand and work whatever tools you may have at your command and better tools will be found as you go along.'*
>
> **Napoleon Hill**

Opportunities

4.11 Opportunities present themselves all the time and everywhere. They can also disappear just as quickly. They are there for everyone, but you have to spot them and grab them. For example, opportunities do not always present themselves in the most obvious manner or place. You could stumble upon an opportunity in any of the following ways (the list is non-exhaustive and you can add to it):

- work;
- networking;
- contacts in the legal profession;
- local members clubs/gym;
- neighbours;
- online forums;
- social media;
- courses/seminars;
- temporary work/part-time jobs;
- fellow students or work colleagues.

If you do not have any legal work experience and are keen to expand and develop your legal network, you have to be open-minded and professional. Naturally, it makes sense to meet lawyers in legal environments, but non-lawyers know lawyers or others in the legal profession too. So do not limit yourself because you never know who you might meet and what opportunities may present themselves. However, this is not a quick-fix solution to building contacts and connections; it takes time and you must have no hidden agenda – otherwise people will see straight through you. If you are interested in the person then the whole exchange and interaction becomes effortless.

Building authentic connections with people requires a real investment of your time and effort; it cannot be forced or rushed. The last thing you want is for someone to feel like you are 'using them' just to get what you want, rather than being genuinely interested in them. You have to build rapport and gain their trust and confidence (skills you are also required to show in the client interviewing assessment for SQE Part 2). Many people will be more than happy to offer you help and guidance if they can see you are being genuine.

4.12 *Qualifying Work Experience (QWE)*

You may find that having a mentor is a huge benefit because they can share their experience, wisdom and insight. A mentor is different to a coach; they can act as a sounding board for you when you want some advice. They do not need to be a lawyer but it is usually helpful if they are because they understand how the legal profession works and what you may be required to do in order to achieve your goal. A good mentor will help you build and improve your consequential thinking skills for any dilemmas or decisions rather than telling you what to do.

Therefore, meeting new people and developing your communication skills, inside and outside of a legal environment, will help you. This is looked at in more detail in Chapter 5, Communication Skills.

What Counts as QWE?

- ***Legal Work Experience***

4.12 Below are examples of what counts as QWE:
- formal training (like a training contract)
- working on a placement as part of your law degree
- working at a law clinic
- working at a voluntary or charitable organisation (eg the Citizens Advice Bureau)
- working as a paralegal, apprentice (or equivalent).

- ***Duration and Location***

4.13 Your QWE can be:
- two years (like a training contract)
- two years made up of four different organisations or law firms (no minimum requirement for each place)
- done in England and Wales
- done abroad
- paid or voluntary
- face-to-face or by using digital technology (eg virtual meetings).

- ***Organisations***

4.14 Typical types of examples of firms or organisations where you could gain experience could be:
- 'Magic Circle' law firms – large UK-headquartered global international city firms
- medium-to-large commercial/corporate law firms – national and international city firms

- niche or boutique law firms – specialist law firms which tend to be small
- high street law firms – tend to be local and small
- Government Legal Profession (GLP) – part of the civil service
- in-house legal departments of companies (eg Apple, Google, GSK, Tesco)
- Alternative Business Structures (ABS) – an organisation that is not a law firm (eg Deloitte Legal (UK), PwC, KPMG Legal)
- charitable or voluntary organisations (eg Citizens Advice Bureau, law clinics).

Does the SRA Regulate the QWE?

4.15 The SRA does not formally regulate any QWE during your employment or work experience. Also, the organisations that provide legal services do not need to be SRA regulated. As long as your work experience can show you have had a chance to develop at least two or more of the competences stated in the Statement of Solicitor Competence (Chapter 1, The SQE Journey, Appendix 1B) it can count as QWE.

The SRA recognises that businesses are different and a 'one size fits all' approach would not work effectively. Therefore, law firms and organisations know what is best for their target market. Employers are responsible for what amounts to 'full time' work when calculating your period of work experience and they are expected to take a common-sense view on what it means.

The level of flexibility offered to employers by the SRA (rather than formal regulation) could therefore be seen as benefiting you, rather than being a hindrance for the QWE purposes.

How is QWE Authenticated?

4.16 A solicitor will need to 'sign off' your QWE and will need to confirm the following:
- the period of work experience you have completed
- that the experience allowed you to develop your competences
- that there are no character and suitability issues.

The following solicitors can sign off your QWE:
- Compliance Officer of Legal Practice (COLP) (if the organisation has one)
- a solicitor in the organisation
- a nominated solicitor outside of the organisation but someone who has direct knowledge of your work.

The solicitor can be a non-practising solicitor which means they do not need to hold a practising certificate.

The solicitor who signs off your QWE is not signing off that you have met the SRA competences that will be tested in the SQE Part 2. They are confirming that you

4.17 *Qualifying Work Experience (QWE)*

have had the opportunity to do diverse and varied work which has allowed you to develop some or all of the competences as set out in the Statement of Solicitor Competence.

Every solicitor who signs off your work experience must bear in mind the SRA Principles and Code of Conduct that they are acting with honesty and integrity by not abusing their position.

If a solicitor unreasonably refuses to sign off your QWE, then you can report them to the SRA with supporting evidence.

When should you do the SQE Part 2?

4.17 There may be conflicting views as to when it is best to do the SQE Part 2, if you have a choice. The completion of QWE is a requirement for the admission stage only, but not a condition that has to be satisfied before you can take the SQE Part 2.

- **Before QWE**

  ❖ **Yes – I have legal work experience**

4.18 If you have some legal work experience which could count as QWE, it will help you when you attempt the SQE Part 2. You may not have legal experience in every single skill (eg client interviewing or advocacy) or all the areas of law you are assessed on, but your general experience should definitely boost your confidence. It will provide you with a real insight into what working in practice is like for lawyers. That confidence will help you with the assessments. You may not realise it, but you will observe how lawyers behave and speak to clients, pick up information and practical tips all of which might help you in some of the assessments.

  ❖ **No – I do not have any (or a lot of) legal work experience**

4.19 You might think it is a good idea to get the 'academics' out of the way first and then focus on getting legal work experience. This approach is similar to the traditional system of qualification, where you do most of your studying first (eg the Legal Practice Course), then do a 'Period of Recognised Training' such as a training contract before you could qualify as a solicitor.

The SQE Part 2 is not like the SQE Part 1. It is a sophisticated set of assessments that assess you on the law and skills expected of a newly qualified solicitor. Therefore, you would be expected to meet the competences set out in the Competence Statement (see Chapter 1, The SQE Journey, Appendix 1B) and each of the skills on which you are specifically assessed (in the Assessment Specification as shown in each relevant chapter).

SQE Part 2 consists of practical assessments, rather than 'academic' exams. Basically, they assess you to see if you are ready to enter the legal profession as a newly qualified solicitor (as opposed to a trainee solicitor). Therefore, the standard that you are assessed against is higher than the equivalent of the Legal Practice Course.

I have experience working with lawyers ranging from junior lawyers through to partners, all with varying degrees of legal work experience, subject matter expertise and levels of English. All of them find the assessments challenging. Therefore, it may be harder to pass the SQE Part 2 first time, unless you have some adequate good-quality legal work experience or you are doing a specialised preparatory course that can prepare you for it beforehand.

- *During QWE*

4.20 If you are working for a law firm or an organisation where they sponsor you to take the SQE, you will meet the QWE requirement with them. This type of set-up is typical of City law firms where you do all your QWE with them (like a traditional training contract). Your employers will work out with you the best time to do the SQE Part 2. Some employers will prefer that you do it before you start work and others may suggest you do it midway or at the end of your legal work experience.

- *After QWE*

4.21 If you are sponsored, what I say above applies and you discuss it with your employer. If you are doing several placements which are authenticated to count as QWE, you can decide when to do SQE Part 2.

Good-Quality Work Experience

4.22 The skills you pick up from non-legal work experience can be great transferable skills for law too. For example, a customer service role (where you may encounter dealing with demanding, difficult or vulnerable customers and a range of complaints), or an administrative role (where you may be filing, organising documents, multi-tasking and prioritising tasks and diaries). These skills can help you in legal practice. Do not underestimate them, and do use them in your CV.

> *'We are what we repeatedly do. Excellence then is not an act, but a habit.'*
>
> **Aristotle**

Having said the above, you do need to have good-quality legal QWE. You can look at the Competence Statement (in Chapter 1, The SQE Journey, Appendix 1B) which provides you with the standard you are expected to be at, upon qualification. Ask yourself, if you meet it and if not, what can you do to achieve it. You will only be deceiving yourself if you do not obtain good-quality work experience. Ultimately it could affect your confidence in the SQE Part 2 and in practice.

For example, poor-quality legal work experience might be if you are working in a small law firm where you are doing a purely administrative role for the majority of the time. It does not offer you a diverse and varied experience but you are still called a paralegal. There is nothing wrong with doing some administrative work, which is often expected. However, it would clearly be unsatisfactory if that was most of your work, all of the time.

4.23 *Qualifying Work Experience (QWE)*

If you want to be a confident, skilled and competent solicitor, then poor-quality work experience will not prepare you well for the SQE Part 2 and should not count as QWE. The chances are that even if you passed the SQE Part 2 and had legal work experience signed off as meeting the QWE requirements, your lack of self-confidence and self-doubt would probably affect your work. This is because the expectation of what work a qualified solicitor does is a given (at the level you go in at), so most employers will be less forgiving if your experience does not live up to your status (ie a newly qualified solicitor). It could also have much more serious implications for you because you could make costly mistakes (such as negligence) that could damage your reputation and you could also be called before the SRA for any breaches of professional conduct rules.

You are the only person who will know whether you are happy with the quality and variety of work and training you receive. If you have a good supervisor who sees your capabilities throughout the experience and provides you with an opportunity to discuss your personal and professional development, you can work out a plan together.

It is ultimately unfair on yourself, especially if you are self-funding, to sit the assessments without a full understanding of what you are expected to do for the SQE. You might think things will improve once you qualify, but often the contrary can happen where it can knock your confidence because you will be expected to do the work at the level you are taken on at, which is a fair expectation. The effect can mean you do not enjoy practising law and it can impact on your self-esteem because you question your own ability to do the work.

Good-quality training does not have to be in the most popular or largest City law firms or organisations. It can be in any of the accepted types of examples mentioned above at para **4.12**, What Counts as QWE. It will not always be easy and enjoyable, but it should provide a real insight for you as to what life as a lawyer is like in the area that you are working in. The variety and experience should allow you to develop your skills with proper supervision.

- **How Do I Know I Have Good Quality Experience?**

4.23 The value of work experience is very subjective. What you might think is great, someone else might think is average. The same can be said about people you work with; some people will like one lawyer's approach and style and another may not. You should feel confident about your experience in doing some of the skills you are assessed on, such as client interviewing and advocacy (doing presentations can be good experience if you do not do advocacy). Even if you do not have experience in all the practice areas of the law, you should be able to write letters and draft some legal documents for the practice areas you work in. These should be in a clear, concise and grammatically correct manner, to the level expected.

As there are no objective criteria for what constitutes 'good quality' legal work experience, then unless your employer is proactively involved, I suggest you take the onus of responsibility yourself. This means you and whoever is supervising you, will both need to be satisfied that you can meet the required standard. Practically, the best way to do this is by comparing the legal work you do against what you are expected to do as a newly qualified solicitor (see Chapter 1, The Competence

Good-Quality Work Experience **4.23**

Statement, Appendix 1B and the Qualifying Work Experience Template, Appendix 4B). However, it can be hard to determine confidently what you can do, so you may underestimate your ability. That is why it is important to have a good supervisor who is encouraging and supportive of your professional and personal development.

There are many tools that can help you assess how you are doing and there is always constructive feedback from the person supervising you which should be done in a supportive and encouraging manner.

A good tool is The Johari Window which helps you assess your communication skills and levels of self-awareness. It was a model developed by Joseph Luft and Harry Ingram in 1955 (the label 'Johari' derives from both their names). You can read more about this model by searching 'Johari Window' on the Internet.

Another good tool is the Conscious Competence Ladder which was developed by Noel Burch created in the 1970s. The focus was on the stages one goes through when learning a new skill: consciousness (awareness) and skill level (competence). You can also read more about this model on the Internet.

Below, I have specifically related the Conscious Competence Ladder to how you can assess your legal knowledge and skills within a working environment. It also complements the Johari Window by helping you to recognise your levels of self-awareness. The example provided is in the context of starting work in a new practice area of law (but you can use it in the context of your own work):

2. Conscious Incompetence	3. Conscious Competence
You know what you do not know. You realise you do not know the law in relation to what you have been asked to do, so will research it or ask for help.	**You practise what you know (knowledge and skills).** You know the law and can confidently and skilfully deal with clients, write letters, draft documents on matters etc.

1. Unconscious Incompetence	4. Unconscious Competence
You do not know what you do not know. Start work in a new area of law. You have to become conscious of your incompetence for you to shift into the quadrant above.	**You may have a new skill but do not realise it.** You do the skill so naturally it becomes easy and effortless. For example, having flexible communication skills for client interviews.

4.24 *Qualifying Work Experience (QWE)*

Good experience varies and there are so many factors that will impact it. For example, it can depend on the practice area of law you work in, the size of the law firm and the people. Generally, your experience should include doing things that you would be assessed on in the SQE Part 2 (it may not be all the areas) such as attending client meetings, doing or observing some advocacy, doing legal research, drafting legal documents or writing letters. Also, remember you may not have experience in all the practice areas of law that you are tested on. So, you will need to learn the law but some of your skills from your QWE should be transferable to other legal practice areas.

QWE Completed

4.24 Once you have completed the QWE and can provide evidence of it to the SRA, you have completed and satisfied the requirement (see Appendix 4B for a suggested QWE template). The solicitor who signs off your QWE will need to sign a declaration:

- setting out details of the work experience completed;
- stating that the work provided you with an opportunity to develop some or all of the competences; and
- confirming that there are no character and suitability issues that arose during the QWE.

If you have also completed the SQE Part 2, you are nearly there and can start the admissions process to be admitted to the Roll of Solicitors. You can read more about this in Chapter 1, The SQE Journey, Post-SQE section (para **1.31**).

> *'Don't worry about being successful but work toward being significant and the success will naturally follow.'*
>
> **Oprah Winfrey**

Qualifying Work Experience (QWE) – Top Ten Tips

(1) Get good-quality QWE (if applicable) otherwise you are deceiving yourself.

(2) Your enthusiasm for what you enjoy doing or reading about can be a good indication of what practice area of law you might find interesting.

(3) Do not take rejection personally. It simply was not meant to be or right for you at the time. That does not mean forever.

(4) Create or adapt your CV using the guidance and template (Appendix 4A).

(5) SRA SQE data shows it is best to have some QWE before you attempt the SQE Part 2.

(6) Getting additional qualifications may not increase your chances of getting legal work experience (if you do not have any).

(7) Non-legal work experience with relevant transferrable skills is helpful.

QWE Completed **4.24**

(8) Opportunities present themselves everywhere; you just have to see them.

(9) Use the QWE template (see Appendix 4B) to keep track and record details of your experience contemporaneously – you will need to show the SRA evidence of it.

(10) Compare your competence development with the requirements of the Statement of Solicitor Competence (see Chapter 1, The SQE Journey, Appendix 1B).

Chapter 4

Qualifying Work Experience: Appendices

Appendix 4A: Curriculum Vitae (CV)

Whether you are a student or a qualified lawyer, if you are looking to work in England and Wales, you will need to have a CV that reflects what employers look for in this legal market.

Although there are no set rules about CVs, I have reviewed many CVs for students and qualified lawyers. Some qualified lawyers from foreign jurisdictions or international students have CVs that reflect their culture, but what might be considered normal in their country might not work here. For example, CVs that read like an autobiography over multiple pages, with photos and certificates are not usually well received by legal recruiters in England and Wales.

The CV's content will be dependent on the person and their level of experience (if any). You can adapt the CV template below using the guidance based on whether you are a lawyer/aspiring solicitor or student. There is no right or wrong, but a CV is a reflection of you so do what will work best for you and be mindful of the tips shared.

For a CV to 'fit' what works for the legal profession in England and Wales, it is recommended that it is:

- two pages (maximum);
- uses the same font style throughout (Ariel or Calibri);
- black and white;
- structured and consistent with enough 'white space'.

I refer to a 'clean' CV as one that shows structure, consistency and white space. That means the body of the text should not have too many distractions (ie over-use of underlining, bold or italics for words throughout the main text of the section). It is also best to avoid using colours. See the CV template below and if you want to highlight the different sections, you could add a shaded light grey (or a non-obtrusive colour) border.

After the CV template below there are two sections on commentary for experienced lawyers and students which should be read in conjunction with the CV template.

Appendix 4A

Jane Doe

Email: janedoe@xxxxx.com **Mobile:** +44 (0)7900 012 456

Profile:

> This is where you have to capture the reader's interest so they want to read the rest of your CV. This profile part should not be more than a third of an A4 sheet of paper. Keep it punchy and concise with short paragraphs. Read Chapter 7, Writing in Professional English, The Four Cs (para **7.15**) and write in an active voice.
>
> **Lawyers:** Focus on your experience and expertise.
>
> **Students:** Focus on your academics, work experience and motivations to become a lawyer.

Employment:

Date	Job title	Company
[Start date–end date/present]	[Solicitor/Legal Counsel]	[Name, location]

Responsibilities:

- Evidence of deals or transactions with values (if applicable). Cases that involve complexities and technicalities.
- Sentences should be brief and bullet points short; use no more than a couple of sentences and avoid long paragraphs.

Date	Job title	Company
[Start date–end date/present]	[Add it in here]	[Name, location]

Responsibilities:

- Do not repeat the same responsibilities already shared in different jobs.
- Evidence of your negotiation skills, advocacy/ presentations etc.
- Demonstrate your vesatility in working independently and in a team.

Key Skills:

- **Languages:** [what languages you speak and at what level of fluency]
- **Leadership:** [evidence of leading a team, organising events, member's groups]

> - **Achievements:** [awards/recognition for deals or transactions]
> - **Public Speaking:** [Presenting at conferences, events, seminars, moots …]
>
> **Education:**
>
> | Year | Course | Organisation and Location |
> |---|---|---|
> | [2020] | Certificate [subject] | [Name of company, London (UK)] |
> | [1996–1997] | Postgraduate diploma/ MSc [subject] | [University of Name, New York (US)] |
> | [1991–1994] | Undergraduate degree [subject] | [University of Name, England (UK)] |
>
> **Personal Information:**
>
> Here you can mention your hobbies and activities in a bit of detail. For example, if you like reading (what genre/authors/magazines?), cooking (what cuisine?) art (what type/artists?).
>
> **Reference:**
>
> Referee details available upon request.

CV Commentary: Experienced Lawyers

The challenge for many lawyers is when they have a lot of experience they want to showcase everything and in detail. With the two-page recommendation, it is simply not possible to do that without making the CV come across as too content heavy. The CV space is precious. You need to leave enough 'white space' to allow your CV to breathe and not look crammed and too wordy.

The first thing the reader sees before reading your CV is its visual impact – either it pleases them or it does not. It is pleasing to the eye if the reader does not have to work hard or squint to read the text because they are helped by white space. To increase white space, you can extend the margins out a little to allow you more space to write, but make sure there is enough white space between each section and the text within each section (eg bullet points).

The emphasis of your CV should be on your legal work experience and less on your academic achievements. This is because the focus is on your expertise and skill set so it reduces the importance for your academic achievements to be the first section in your CV.

Below is guidance of what a CV for lawyers may include:

Appendix 4A

- **Name, Email and Mobile**

Note how you do not need to write 'Curriculum Vitae' or 'CV' at the top of the page like a heading. You can write your name and it can be in a slightly bigger type size to the rest of the CV.

Although some people still use the Times Roman typeface, Arial (text size 10.5 or 11) or Calibri (11 or 11.5) are more modern and probably preferable. You can use another font, but be consistent throughout the CV.

You do not need to include your address, date of birth, marital status, photo or nationality in this section or the 'Personal Information' section. The contact details you have provided will be enough for the reader to be able to contact you if they want to meet you or discuss anything relevant that could impact your employment status.

- **Profile**

You can write this part in the first person (eg 'I am ...') or the third person (eg 'Jane is ...'). Whichever style you use, keep it consistent throughout the CV. That means if you use the third person in the profile, do not switch to the first person in the 'Employment' section (see below) when talking about your experience.

The profile is the part where you have to grab the reader's interest to make them want to find out more about you. When a reader has lots of CVs to go through they may skim read for gist and scan for detail, so use figures (eg the value of deals or transactions or years of experience) to stand out.

In this part, less is more. Details can be added in the 'Employment' or 'Key Skills' section or can be explained if you are invited to meet them. Too much detail can lose the desired effect, so you want to spark the reader's curiosity with a key piece of information and leave the details for later on.

- **Employment**

Start with the most recent job first and if you have worked in a lot of places the oldest jobs may have to be omitted. Less recent jobs usually reflect levels of experience which you have now surpassed. Therefore, they do not add much value to your present employment prospects.

Also, make sure you do not repeat the same skills and experience in 'Responsibilities' even if they are different jobs. That is just duplication and does not add any value to what you have shown you can do. For example, if you have had a few jobs where you have been instrumental in leading transactions, rather than say this (which is very generic), be specific about what you did in each role that was different. That is evidence of your leadership skills and expertise without actually having to say it.

- **Key Skills**

This is an optional section and only really works if you do have a range of skills you want to highlight. You should not repeat details of what you include in any other sections here.

- **Education**

Although this section is important, it is usually more important when you are starting out in the legal profession, as opposed to being an experienced lawyer. By this stage, you will have surpassed the academic requirements by demonstrating your practical skills and levels of expertise.

Start with the most recent and include any personal and professional development certifications.

- **Personal Information**

This is the section where you can come to life and show the reader that you are human! It allows you to share a glimpse of your personality. It is an important section because it also allows for small talk if/when you are invited to interview or have a meeting.

Whatever you state in this section, make sure you can talk about it passionately. This will automatically mean you talk about it with more energy and naturally it will help you feel more relaxed and less nervous.

- **Reference**

There is no need to mention names and contact details of any referees at this stage.

CV Commentary: Students

If you are a student with no legal work experience, the focus of your CV will primarily be on your academics, followed by any non-legal work experience, key skills, hobbies and interests. Therefore, change the order of the CV template to suit you.

The challenge for most students is what to write in their CV. Many CVs may be one page, this is fine and expected if you cover everything needed. Do not try to write more unnecessarily to make it two pages, in the belief that it will add more depth. It will have the reverse effect and the reader will see that you are 'padding out' information rather than being concise and comprehensive.

Below is guidance of what a CV for students may include in the following order:

- **Name, Email and Mobile**

The same comments apply here as for experienced lawyers (above), so please read them.

- **Profile**

If you struggle with what to include in it, you could consider the following three 'whys':

Appendix 4A

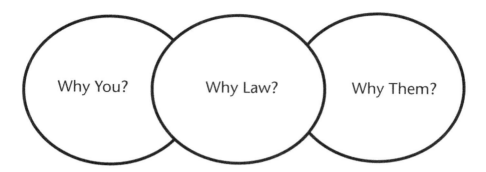

The 'why law?' part should help you write a good quality thought-through profile for the 'why you?' and 'why them?' parts.

- **Why law?**

  Many find this question hard to answer and it is often an interview question. It is good to think about why you want to study law and become a solicitor.

- **Why you?**

  This is the personal reason. You can state your work experience, motivation and key skills sharing what you are doing now. Do they complement skills required to become a lawyer? Why would you be a good fit for them?

- **Why them?**

  This is the professional reason. What value can you add to the business? Why should they take you on and invest in you?

  Your profile does not need to very long and it is optional but usually I would recommend having one.

- ***Education***

Start with the most recent and include any other certifications you may have got for personal and professional development.

- ***Achievements***

This section is optional and you should only include it if you have quite a few achievements you want to highlight but be selective. You could replace it with 'Extra-curricular Activities' if that works better for you, or include that too.

- ***Legal Work Experience***

I have suggested this as a separate section to highlight your legal work experience, so add it in before any general and non-legal employment. Again, this section is only relevant if you can show relevant experience. Include any paid or unpaid work (eg *pro bono*).

Qualifying Work Experience: Appendices

- **Employment**

Do not shy away from stating what your responsibilities are in your job, even if they are not law-related. Think about transferable skills because, worded cleverly, they can be interpreted to work just as well in a legal environment.

- **Personal Information**

The same comments apply here as for experienced lawyers (above), so please read them.

- **Reference**

The same comments apply here as for experienced lawyers (above), so please read them.

Appendix 4B: Qualifying Work Experience Template

You can find a downloadable template on the SRA website. Many firms will have their own digital versions. Below I have adapted the SRA template to include the Statement of Solicitor Competence to help you see what competences need to be met and how you need to demonstrate them.

The template is split into two sections:

- **Section 1 – Placement details**

In this section you record your placement(s). Remember, you can only have a maximum of four organisations and they should amount to a total of two years' full-time experience or equivalent.

The SRA will check with the solicitor(s) that they can confirm it has been signed off when you apply for admission as a solicitor.

	Placement 1	**Placement 2**	**Placement 3**	**Placement 4**
Organisation				
Start date				
End date				
How much of this time counts towards overall QWE requirement				
Name of individual signing off QWE				
Position				
SRA number				

Appendix 4B

- ## Section 2 – Qualifying work experience

The template refers to the Statement of Solicitor Competence Sections A to D which you can read about in Chapter 1, The Solicitors Journey, Appendix 1B.

The template includes sections of the Statement of Solicitor Competence which can be used for your current work experience and any past work experience. For any past work experiences, you will not need to complete Section D on 'Managing Themselves and Their Workload' because that section relates to current work experience.

Remember, you do not need to show all of the competences below for your QWE to be signed off. You have to show you have had a chance to develop some (or all) of them.

A – Ethics, professionalism and judgement					
	Competence	**Have I had experience? What was it/what did I do?**	**How can I evidence my experience?**	**What did I learn?**	**Do I need more experience?**
A1	Act honestly and with integrity, in accordance with legal and regulatory requirements and the SRA Standards and Regulations				
A2	Maintain the level of competence and legal knowledge needed to practise effectively, taking into account changes in their role and/or practice context and developments in the law				
A3	Work within the limits of their competence and the supervision that they need				

Qualifying Work Experience: Appendices

	A – Ethics, professionalism and judgement				
A4	Draw on a sufficient detailed knowledge and understanding of their field(s) of work and role in order to practise effectively				
A5	Apply understanding, critical thinking and analysis to solve problems				

	B – Technical legal practice				
	Competence	**Have I had experience? What was it/what did I do?**	**How can I evidence my experience?**	**What did I learn?**	**Do I need more experience?**
B1	Obtain relevant facts in a matter				
B2	Undertake legal research				
B3	Develop and advise on relevant options, strategies and solutions				
B4	Draft documents which are legally effective and accurately reflect the client's instructions				
B5	Undertake effective spoken and written advocacy in and of court				
B6	Negotiate solutions to clients' issues				
B7	Plan, manage and progress legal cases and transactions				

Appendix 4B

	C – Working with other people				
	Competence	**Have I had experience? What was it/what did I do?**	**How can I evidence my experience?**	**What did I learn?**	**Do I need more experience?**
C1	Communicate clearly and effectively, orally and in writing				
C2	Establish and maintain effective and professional relations with client				
C3	Establish and maintain effective and professional relations with other people				

	D – Managing themselves and their own work				
This section is only relevant for current work experience.					
	Competence	**Have I had experience? What was it/what did I do?**	**How can I evidence my experience?**	**What did I learn?**	**Do I need more experience?**
D1	Initiate, plan, prioritise and manage work activities and projects to ensure that they are completed efficiently, on time and to an appropriate standard, both in relation to their own work and work that they lead or supervise.				
D2	Keep, use and maintain accurate, complete and clear records.				
D3	Apply good business practice.				

Chapter 5

Communication Skills

'... practice your communication skills so that when important occasions arise you will have the ... style ... sharpness ... clarity and emotions to affect other people.'

Jim Rohn

In this chapter you will learn:

✓ How to use a range of tools and techniques to build on and improve your communication skills.

✓ How to recognise and understand the importance of intellectual intelligence and emotional intelligence.

✓ What key ingredients make up oral communication skills.

✓ About your own communication style and other people's preferences.

✓ How to effectively adapt and be flexible with your communication style.

✓ What measures to take to gauge your progress so you can see your levels of improvement.

Introduction

5.01 The purpose of this chapter is to provide you with some insight as to the importance of communication skills to help you continue to build on developing and honing your skills, effectively. They will serve you well and be useful long after you have completed the SQE and are into your journey as a solicitor.

The aim is to help you prepare for the SQE Part 2 (Practical Legal Skills) by sharing with you some guidance, tools and techniques I use when training or coaching lawyers. Remember, these practical and interactive skills will be relevant for the assessments where you are judged by a trained assessor (an actor), or a solicitor who will play the role of a judge.

Written communication skills will be looked at in more detail in Chapter 7, Writing in Professional English.

You may think whilst reading this chapter, *'how is this all really relevant for the SQE? I just want to know what to do'* but persevere and carry on reading. You

5.02 *Communication Skills*

need to have some understanding of what the skills are and their value before you can effectively use them in the assessments. This knowledge is underpinned by your own communication style and once you understand it, it becomes easier to learn how to improve it. Equally important is practising the exercises suggested to improve your communication skills in a way that is authentic to you. Once you recognise what is required and why, it becomes much easier for you to adapt your skill set confidently for whether you are doing a client interview or an advocacy submission.

This chapter is like the foundation to build on for the other chapters (such as client interviewing and advocacy). It helps you delve into the detail of how you can use your improved understanding of communication skills for the oral skills assessments. The goal is to get you to perform at a superior level – using your knowledge of the law correctly and comprehensively.

Also, bear in mind that you have picked up many of your communication skills and behaviours by watching and learning the behaviours of other people in your life. These can stem from your childhood experiences through to your current personal and professional life. Sometimes, it is subconsciously through watching and learning that you do things without being able to understand or articulate why you do them the way you do. These patterns of behaviours can serve you well and work to your advantage and at other times they are not helpful. They can be broken and replaced once you identify them. It can take time and you have to recognise it and have a strategy to change it.

I have worked with hundreds of lawyers, worldwide, from six of the seven continents. These lawyers come from different cultures, backgrounds and experiences. So, everything I share may or may not be relevant to you, but has been included for the sake of completeness or because it is something that has been raised quite often.

What are Communication Skills?

5.02 There are a lot of books and courses on this area and it can be a minefield. I aim to provide you with a basic understanding of how to specifically adapt your communication skills (if required) to ensure you score the highest marks possible for the skills part – that means delivering a 'superior performance', Grade A (5 marks).

Once you realise that you need to make some changes, those changes may feel uncomfortable at first, but eventually they will become more natural with practice and you will realise their benefit. So, it is important that you do not just passively read this chapter and think you *understand* what you need to do – but actually *do* the exercises and practise them several times and consistently. Knowledge is good, but taking action and practising is where you see the real results.

Remember that as well as knowing the law you will also be assessed on how you use your communication skills to offer legal advice to a client or make your advocacy submission persuasively and credibly to a judge. Therefore, approach studying the SQE Part 2 in a holistic manner, where you know the law and work on how you can deliver it effectively.

Once you feel confident that you have worked on your general communication skills through practising them, you can adapt them more effortlessly for the specific areas of law you are assessed on for the SQE Part 2. You can focus on your knowledge of the law (which it tends to be, naturally) and deliver it in a much more skilful and authentic manner that works for you.

Each chapter that deals with an SQE assessment will share its own Assessment Criteria and the standard marking criteria against which you are scored.

Remember, even the most skilful communicators have worked very hard to make it come across as effortless. Although everyone can improve their communication skills, it is not an overnight process that can be 'crammed' as you might have done for your law exams or the SQE Part 1. Communication skills take time, effort and practice to do well. They are always a work in progress and the more you reflect on how you deliver your skills the more aware you are of what you need to do. You have to have a real understanding of yourself and your communication style to help you recognise how other people's communication styles are different from yours and adapt yours effectively.

Learning how to be an effective communicator sometimes involves making a shift in your behaviour that may feel unnatural at first. If you recognise the positive value in making that shift, you will be more inclined to do it and it will be an authentic and natural change. Of course, the more you do it, the better you will become and as a result the more confident you will feel when you start seeing the results. As mentioned earlier, these skills will be beneficial for you not just for the SQE exams, but throughout your time in practice.

• *Why is Successful Communication Important?*

5.03   Everyone communicates the best way they know how. Much of how we communicate with one another is learnt through our primary socialisation (immediate family) and secondary socialisation (everything outside of the immediate family). To learn these skills effectively is not something you can do overnight and 'pass' an exam on. The types of skills I am talking about can be learnt through teaching, but have to be developed and practised consciously until they become a natural part of the way you communicate. That may mean learning new habits, but also unlearning some and doing them differently. Once you realise what you need to do and actually do it, it becomes effective communication.

It is easy when you work well with people; you do not think too hard about the way you communicate. However, the real test is learning how to adapt when you find someone you work with, or a client, 'difficult'. One way of looking at them is as if they are your teacher, testing you and giving you an opportunity to think about how you might want to change what you do to be more effective with them. Naturally, you might think *'Why should I change?'* and that is a valid question. However, if you want to get ahead you have to do everything you can that is within your control, and trying to make someone else change is not something you can do. It can be extremely rewarding and empowering when you have the tools that you can then adapt and use in any situation in which you find yourself. It is not about 'giving in' but about 'getting ahead'.

5.04 Communication Skills

Challenges with Communication Skills

5.04 Generally, a common theme among lawyers is that they focus heavily on the law, which is an essential and a given. You need to know it and understand it. However, knowing the law is one thing and being able to apply it in an articulate, persuasive, clear and concise manner is a different thing and often quite challenging. This tests your ability to understand the law – because when you understand something well, it is much easier to explain and you would naturally do it more confidently. Remember, you are equally tested on the law and skills, so very quickly lawyers realise that the skills part is not that easy and actually takes a lot of hard work. Unfortunately, the skills part is not something that can be learnt by cramming overnight or reading books: it is specific to you, your abilities and willingness to learn about yourself. It is also your ability to recognise the communication skills of others. This is what makes you an effective communicator and it takes time and practice.

Chapter 4, Qualifying Work Experience, has a section on Types of Lawyers (para **4.02**) which will be useful to read to understand how important communication skills are for lawyers.

- ***Experience: Too Much or Not Enough?***

5.05 I notice that for the client interviewing skills and advocacy skills there are some typical challenging areas that consistently come up for many lawyers. These affect lawyers ranging from junior level, with little experience, to senior lawyers and partners from 'Magic Circle' City law firms, who are very experienced and experts in their practice area of the law.

The problem is that junior lawyers lack practical experience and very experienced lawyers tend to be quite set in their ways as regards what they do and how they do it (which is to be expected). For client interviewing, I have to work with them to ensure their communication skills are aligned with the particular practice area and type of client they may encounter. The challenge is often to help them adapt their communication style in an authentic and natural way, so they deliver a superior performance on the day of the assessment.

For the oral assessments, you can read the list of common challenges experienced in Chapter 8 Client Interviewing Skills and Chapter 10 Advocacy.

> *'We learn by making mistakes, it's difficult,
> but that's not what defines you.'*
>
> **Patrick Mouratoglou**

Practising your Skills

5.06 There is a lot of advice about practising client interviewing and advocacy with family and friends or 'study buddies', which is a good idea. However, it is a better idea to work with a professional initially so you can identify very quickly what you do well and areas on which you need to work and improve. Once you have constructive feedback, it then makes sense to practise with others, because you will be very clear about what you need to do. Ideally, find someone who has expert communication skills so you know what areas you need to work on.

Most of the larger law schools will have tutors who can help you (usually they are lawyers but may not be experts in communication skills). They should be aware of what you need to do to meet the assessment criteria. If you are using a private training provider, it is definitely a good idea to check if they offer some level of interactive tutor support so you can practise with them. Also, make sure that the person you are allocated is a lawyer or someone who has the experience and the requisite skill set to help you assess your ability for the SQE. You can read more about choosing a university or training provider in Chapter 2, Preparing for the SQE (para **2.03**).

If you are practising with friends and family, it is a good idea to give them some guidance on the marking criteria, so they can offer you some constructive and appropriate feedback.

My advice is to focus on areas you need to improve and practise them every day, until they feel natural and an integral part of your behaviour. However, there is a danger you may come across as too prescriptive and scripted (like a robot, just going through the motions) if you try to learn it 'parrot fashion'.

Many lawyers I coach say that they did not appreciate how difficult it was to demonstrate the skills part until we actually started working together. As explained in Chapter 2, Preparing for the SQE, Performance Coaching (para **2.15**), this is an intensive process where you work to identify your strengths and weaknesses and are left with the ability to know what you need to practise to hone the skills required. The way the skills are learnt means that they will not just benefit you in taking the SQE but also when you are in practice.

If you are worried about the level of your English language skills, revisit Chapter 2, Preparing for the SQE (para **2.44**).

This chapter will be split into three key parts which all complement each other, and each part is equally important, so they are not ranked by level of importance. Here is a brief overview of what each part will cover:

The Connector

5.07 First impressions count and help create a confident performance whenever you meet anyone – it is all about the connection. This part will focus on:

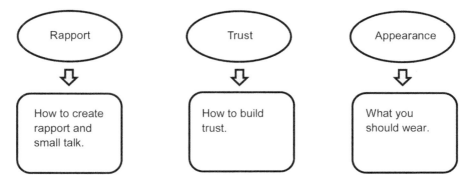

5.08 *Communication Skills*

The Communicator

5.08 Knowing what to say and how to say it are key to getting your message across confidently with clarity and conciseness. This creates an authentic and engaging connection in a structured, yet fluid manner. This part will focus on:

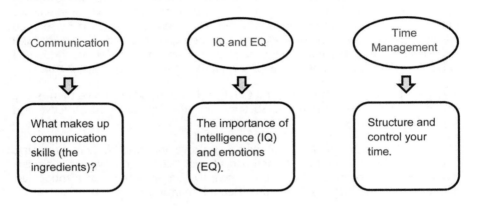

The Convincer

5.09 When you are alert and proactive, you are fully present in the situation. This instils confidence in your ability to communicate and connect authentically and persuasively. This part will focus on:

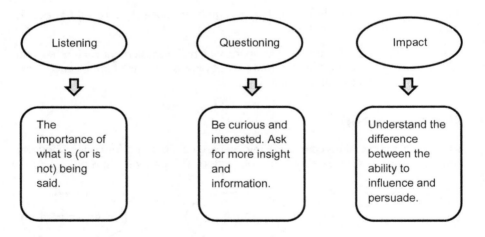

The Connector

> *'A smile is the shortest distance between two people.'*
> **Victor Borge**

5.10

> First impressions count and help create a confident performance whenever you meet anyone – it is all about the connection. This part will focus on:
> - **Rapport:** How to create rapport and small talk authentically.
> - **Trust:** How to build trust.
> - **Appearance:** What you should wear.

Rapport

> *'Rapport equals trust plus comfort.'*
> **Neil Strauss**

5.11 What is rapport and how easily can it be created? This two-part question is one I am often asked by many lawyers. Unfortunately, there are too many variables and so it is impossible to provide you with a comprehensive, definitive, 'right' answer. For some people, it is easy to create rapport and for others it is a difficult and sometimes an awkward experience. Often, the experiences you have meeting new people condition your beliefs around how easy or difficult it is to build rapport.

• What is Rapport?

5.12 The Oxford Dictionary defines 'rapport' as:

> *'A close and harmonious relationship in which the people or groups concerned understand each other's feelings or ideas and communicate well.'*

The Cambridge Dictionary defines 'rapport' as:

> *'A good understanding of someone and an ability to communicate well with them.'*

The definitions are similar in saying that to connect with a person you have to have the skills to be able to communicate well with them. However, from a practical perspective, to meet the definitions, you need to know and understand what you have to *do*, to 'communicate well'. This is often the challenge because in practice communication skills are not a strict set of defined skills which you can learn in theory and pass – in effect, they are not really measurable by a pass or fail.

Communication skills are individual and subjective. It really does come down to the individual person and who they are communicating with, on any given subject and at any given time.

5.13 *Communication Skills*

There is no set 'correct' way to build rapport, otherwise everyone would do it and it would be easy to identify and replicate. There are various ways and you have to work out what appeals to you most authentically and then make any necessary behavioural changes to improve your style.

Therefore, it is not possible to create an objective 'standardised' checklist of what communication skills are needed to create and build rapport effectively. Each of the skills may have differing degrees of importance, for what you want to achieve. For example, what works effectively for one person, might not have the same impact on another. So, there are many ways to create rapport effectively, you just need to have the skill set to adapt your communication style to create it in a comfortable way for you.

- **Building Rapport**

5.13 A huge part of building rapport does depend on the person you are communicating with and how receptive they are to you – which is out of your control. What is within your control is understanding you, your communication style and preferences. The more you work on yourself, the better you will understand and recognise the different forms of communication. This will help you when dealing with different types of people, because you will have learnt how to flex your communication style to achieve the desired outcome. We will look at this part in more detail under 'The Communicator' section (para **5.25**).

Most people I have worked with that find it easy to build rapport can never really articulate or extract what specifically makes their experience easy or enjoyable. Those that do not enjoy the process can often readily list and identify what they find challenging in trying to build rapport. Interestingly, the common challenges some lawyers share are:

- not knowing what to say or how to start small talk;
- not knowing what questions to ask; and
- finding small talk too superficial or fake.

Can you relate to this? What it says is that the people who do find it easy or enjoyable may not experience the same challenges suggested above – the most important one being that they are less likely to find small talk as superficial or fake. This makes it easier for them to ask questions authentically.

- **Building Rapport Authentically**

5.14 You need to have a strategy in place to help you overcome the challenges or beliefs you hold about building rapport (or any other reasons you negatively associate with small talk being superficial). You then need to practise until it becomes more natural. No one wants to do something consistently that they do not like doing, so this takes time and effort.

- **Overcoming Superficiality**

5.15 The reason why many people do not enjoy small talk is that they feel uncomfortable doing it. Whatever the reason, you should know that small talk can be done authentically and with practice becomes quite natural – but it does take consistent effort (initially) on your part to want to do it and change how you feel about doing it. Once you experience what it feels like to do it authentically, it will feel far from superficial or fake. You will realise the warmth of human connection can actually make clients (or anyone) who are 'hard work' easier to deal with. In turn, this can result in them being more amenable to what you have to say to them: good or bad.

Those of you who do not 'do small talk' or find it superficial will have your own reasons. These will often be based on your personal experiences of small talk (often called belief systems). Maybe you have had a few awkward encounters, felt embarrassed, self-conscious or shy in the past and so your beliefs around small talk will stem from these memories based on how you labelled the experience. So, whether in a social and/or professional environment, you will have subconsciously labelled your experiences as positive (enjoyable – it felt authentic) or negative (unenjoyable – it felt superficial).

- *Perception*

5.16 Your brain remembers these experiences so when it knows you are about to do something similar again (regardless of the environment or context), it will remind you of how you felt about the similar experience in the past. So, you will either feel fine about it (if it was an enjoyable experience) or nervous (if it was an unenjoyable experience).

You can read more about IQ and EQ in para **5.30** and how your brain works in Chapter 6, Managing Nerves, Fear and Failure (para **6.07**) and in Appendix 6A.

What you need to understand is that, regardless of the past experience, no two experiences will ever be exactly the same. Therefore, it will help you to think about the new situation as similar but different and remind yourself to be open-minded about it and have strategies and tools in place to help you.

- *Small Talk Topics*

5.17 Small talk is heavily connected to building rapport. British people are renowned for making small talk about the weather and it might seem superficial, but done with authenticity, it can be quite warm and endearing, especially when you inject some of your own personality into it. Generally, my advice would be to avoid controversial topics (politics, economic and social or cultural norms), until you get to know the person better. For the purposes of the assessment, you will not have time for prolonged small talk, so keep it simple.

Small talk is not formal, it is a type of ice-breaker done to relax people into having a connected conversation with you. If you are not relaxed when trying to make small talk (because you think it is superficial), it will inevitably come across in your behaviour which will affect the other person's response and sometimes create an awkward experience. So, you reinforce your negative experience by generalising it (eg small talk is always so superficial) and that becomes your belief, which in turn becomes a self-fulfilling prophecy.

5.18 *Communication Skills*

• *Small Talk Environment*

5.18 Many people over-think rapport in the belief that it is necessary to behave differently depending on whether you are in a professional or social environment. My advice is not to over-think it – just focus on the people. Think about trying to build rapport as meeting someone new at a party and having an informal chat with them. The interaction will be much more relaxed and warm, rather than formal and cold. You are connecting with a person, regardless of the actual environment in which you are meeting them. This applies to the assessment environment too – just because you need to be professional does not mean the small talk has to be formal. See it as an ice-breaker to help you start the interview with ease.

I have noticed that many lawyers I coach commonly associate being professional with being formal. This does not help them when trying to create rapport with a new client through small talk. It is because of their association of professionalism with formality that their body language and facial expressions appear stiff and forced. Their demeanour is not aligned with the informal language they use for the small talk to build rapport. The exchange comes across as unnatural and inauthentic.

Once they realise they can come across as professional and relax their body language, the whole verbal exchange feels better and instantly builds their confidence – and they immediately feel the difference themselves.

Small talk language is always professional but done in an informal way. It does not mean using slang or mimicking the client's language or behaviour to try to connect with them. That is more likely to offend them, rather than build rapport.

Remember, small talk is not made using formal language and you can read Chapter 8, Client Interviewing Skills, The Beginning (para **8.18**) which looks at how to use small talk questions at the start of the interview.

Building rapport will be an important part of the client interviewing skills assessment, when you meet the client (a role played by an actor). This means you have to get it right from the beginning – it sets the scene for how the interview will go. If it starts well, you will feel more confident about your ability and performance. If it starts awkwardly, then the chances are that this will affect your performance throughout the interview and make you feel less relaxed with the client.

So, it can be challenging to do all the following within a set time limit of 25 minutes:

- create rapport;
- make small talk;
- gather all the information;
- address any concerns;
- offer preliminary advice (where necessary);
- summarise the interview;
- identify next steps (if applicable).

Believe me, it can be done and it has been done well – when you are proactive. This means not panicking, but taking control of the interview by managing your client's expectations and your time.

Rapport **5.18**

The additional unforeseeable aspect is the type of client you may encounter and how they come across. The client will have very clear instructions on how to behave in playing the role and what information they can readily share with you or offer you if you ask them the right questions (this tests your listening and questioning skills which shapes the legal advice for your attendance note).

Remember, you cannot control how the other person will respond to you, but if you are more relaxed in your approach, they may mirror your behaviour too and relax. The conversation will flow better and the whole experience will be much more enjoyable.

A genuine smile might seem like an obvious thing to do when trying to build rapport, but I have lost count of the number of times when coaching lawyers I have seen them fail to smile from the moment they say 'Hello' and introduce themselves through to making small talk (if they do it). A smile is recognised worldwide as a sign of friendliness, warmth and sociability. It is one of the most impactful emotional triggers and one of the easiest things to do.

'A smile is the universal welcome.'
Max Eastman

The more comfortable you become making small talk, the more natural it will feel which means you will automatically want to smile. So, the exercise below is one that you can do at any time, without any preparation and in any social or professional environment – so you really have no excuse, but to give it a go (and keep doing it until you actually feel comfortable doing it).

The aim of the exercise below is to make you more confident when making small talk with someone you do not know by initiating it. This will be good practice for you for the client-interviewing assessment. For the assessment, you have to take the initiative with the client and build rapport very quickly and authentically – bearing in mind the time allocated for the interview.

Exercise: Make the first move!

This quick exercise is to help you get outside of your comfort zone if you never initiate small talk. For client interviewing it can enhance your performance of how you come across from the start of the interview and help build your confidence, which can score you high marks for the skills.

You do not have to be engaged in a long conversation with the person, but the aim is more about getting you used to smiling whilst asking an initial conversation starter question, comfortably, with aligned body language (very important) so you make small talk authentically. Once you get comfortable doing this, creating and building rapport gets much easier with every interaction and you start doing it automatically without too much effort.

Rule

The person you choose can be anyone; ideally someone new. You should try to get a mixture of different types of people from all walks of life. For

5.18 *Communication Skills*

example, it could be the person who serves you at a coffee shop, someone at reception in your gym or a social club, the cashier at a supermarket, someone in your work ... anyone you encounter on any day.

You need to do this frequently and the more you do it the easier it will become and the more natural it will feel.

Think about how you make small talk or have a conversation with someone you know very well – that is the feeling you need to experience – where your body language and facial expressions will be relaxed.

Instructions

(1) Smile at the person and say 'Hi' or 'Hello' (a soft genuine smile and eye contact is key).

(2) Follow that with: 'How are you today?' – or phrase it any way that comes natural to you. Make sure you are still smiling and looking at them (soft eye contact).

(3) Listen to their response and respond accordingly by linking into something they say (if possible).

(4) Then, leave them by telling them to 'Have a good day/evening'.

Debrief

Make a quick note (on your phone, diary or something you have access to immediately) so you can keep track of your progress – it is a good way to give yourself instant feedback and it should not take long at all.

(1) Think about how you felt before doing it

(eg I felt ... good/self-conscious/stupid/shy/silly/nervous)

(2) Notice the other person's response and facial expressions

(eg they smiled/looked surprised/confused)

(3) How did you feel after the exchange?

(eg I enjoyed it/hated it/felt nervous/felt excited/felt silly)

This quick but powerful exercise is a small step in getting you to make the first move to confidently strike up a quick informal conversation. In the client interviewing assessment, as the solicitor, you will have to take the initiative (not the client). Therefore, the aim of this exercise is to help you be natural and authentic, before you seamlessly move on to discuss the main issues.

The more pressure you put on yourself about being good at building rapport, the more unnatural and difficult it will feel to you. Remember, your interest in the other person or their issue, problem or whatever they are telling you about, has to be genuine. If it is, then it becomes an effortless exchange of information, with confidence. When you are not communicating congruently, it can create awkwardness and at worst mistrust which means the client does not have confidence in you and is unlikely to want to instruct you on their matter. We will look at this part in more detail under The Communicator section (para **5.25**).

> **Reflective Exercise**
>
> Examine what you do well naturally when you are with your friends or family in a social environment. How do you feel? What do you do? How do you speak to them? Think about how you could use some of those behaviours in a work-related context when meeting new people or clients.

The more you know yourself better, the easier it becomes – because building rapport is a bit like 'chemistry'; you cannot fake it. Sometimes it is there immediately and at other times it may take a little longer. However, people will know instinctively if you are genuinely interested in them.

- ***Commonality***

5.19 Naturally, it is human nature to be drawn to people who you see as similar to you or like you. Of course, it is easier to build rapport with these people much quicker than if they are different to you or you feel you do not have much in common with them. Having said that, when you place these types of 'rules' on what will make it easier or more difficult to build rapport with someone, this impacts on your experience without you even realising it. How? The minute you meet someone who you have something in common with, your brain knows what to do and it 'likes' them, so it becomes easier to talk to the person. The minute you realise you do not have much in common with someone, your brain will try to impose your 'self-belief' that the interaction will be more 'difficult' because you do not have much to talk about and so your brain will try to reinforce it, so it becomes harder to build rapport and talk to the person.

One way to overcome compartmentalisation is to shift your thinking to just wanting to find out more about the person – be curious. This approach will help you ask more inquisitive questions about someone you do not have much in common with rather than just 'shut down' and run out of things to say because you cannot connect on mutual interests.

- ***Cultural Appropriateness***

5.20 If you are an international student or a foreign jurisdiction lawyer, you need to also be aware of cultural differences. Body language itself varies hugely across different cultures. For example, what a Canadian person might perceive as arrogant, an American person might see as healthy confidence. Equally, what might be perceived as rude or inappropriate in the UK might be seen as warm and friendly in Africa. And, in some Asian cultures men and women do not shake hands, which might be perceived as rude in Western cultures. So, it is a good idea to have an open and honest conversation with a professional, tutor or native British

5.21 Communication Skills

national who can address any worries you have about the 'dos' and 'don'ts' of British etiquette.

Trust

> *'Trust is a product of vulnerability that grows over time and requires work, attention and full engagement.'*
>
> **Brené Brown**

5.21 Trust is essential in any relationship. In a professional setting, you simply cannot build great client relationships without trust, no matter how brilliant you might be at the law or the work you do. Usually the client is coming to you with a problem or asking you to give a transaction legal effect – their lack of knowledge or experience may make them feel vulnerable about the whole process and intimidated by lawyers. It is your job to build trust by offering them reassurance and transparency, as well as managing their expectations. The last thing that impresses clients is your knowledge of the law – that is a given and expected. What they want from you is confidence you can do what they need done. That confidence comes from them being able to trust you. Confidence does not mean not showing any vulnerability because you think it will affect trust levels – if anything, it can strengthen the bond of trust.

Your primary socialisation (eg family) may have taught you when growing up to be strong and not show weakness or vulnerability – all done with good intentions. These become your beliefs and can subconsciously impact your communication style and behaviour in your personal and professional life. These beliefs are then reinforced by secondary socialisation (eg law school) where you are trained to always be confident and brave – to avoid showing any vulnerability because it is often associated with weakness. So, it is natural that you may not see showing vulnerability as a strength.

Dr Brené Brown (a research professor, University of Houston) has done some great work on vulnerability. Her work reveals that showing vulnerability is the opposite of weakness; it takes courage. She says vulnerability is uncertainty, risk and emotional exposure. If you are interested in reading more about Dr Brené Brown's work, you can visit her website (brenebrown.com) and watch her TED Talk on Vulnerability. TED talks are short powerful talks online devoted to spreading ideas.

I do believe clients are more likely to connect with you if you can show vulnerability (which may be perceived as weakness) in dealing with their matter (when required). It is not being unprofessional or weak where there is an uncertainty and risk involved in the matter and what it means for you too. Sometimes, it may mean saying to the client that you do not know the answer and will need to check the law or that past successful results do not mean the same for their matter. That is not a weakness if it is said with confidence. It all comes down to how you communicate your response with credibility that determines how the information is received. You can read more about What is Confidence? in Chapter 6, para **6.03**.

This is a very important point for client interviewing, where you may have to provide preliminary legal advice. So many lawyers I work with get flustered when they do not know the answer to a question, which naturally affects their confidence. But rather than deal with it effectively, they often make the situation worse by feeling the need to talk (ie waffling) to disguise the fact they do not know the answer. Alternatively, they can advise in so much detail in an academic way (often making assumptions) so alienate the client. Either way, it does not help your confidence or credibility when you are only marked for skills (not law) for client interviewing.

- ***What is Trust?***

5.22 The Oxford Dictionary defines 'trust' as:

'Firm belief in the reliability, truth, or ability of someone or something.'

The key word to focus on in the definition is 'belief'. This is the perception the person or client has of you, which is determined by how you come across through your communication skills using your body language and verbal language. It is what they think about you and how you make them feel. They either have confidence in your ability or not. You may or may not say all the right things, but if the client walks away feeling unsure about you or dislikes you, then there is a high chance they will not instruct you. Remember, the law and skills are assessed equally, so aim for the highest possible marks in every assessment, especially for the skills part.

If you do not know the answer to something they ask you, how they feel about your response, will be dictated by how you react (your body language and facial expressions) and what you say (the tone and language used).

The client may be instructed on what they can and cannot tell you in the assessment. Sometimes you can be asked a question beyond the remit of your knowledge or what they have come to see you about and you have to deal with it. In reality, a client might do this and so the test is to see whether you handle it in a professional manner. Your response can leave your credibility intact or reduce it. You can still maintain your credibility even if you do not know the answer; it comes down to how you explain your reasoning to the client.

- ***Building Trust***

5.23 Trust can take a long time to build and seconds to break. Of course, if a person likes you they are more likely to trust you, because they can connect with you, hence, why building rapport is key.

Once you have connected with the client, even if you tell them something they do not want to hear or believe, they are more likely to accept it because they will trust you are doing it with their best intentions at heart.

Building trust does not mean you have to say everything that pleases the client to gain their trust. As a lawyer, you have to manage their expectations and skilfully and tactfully show empathy, especially if it is advice that they will not want to hear and it will be a difficult conversation.

If you are confident in how you come across, the client is more likely to believe you. How do you show confidence? Again, this is subjective to each individual and you can do a number of things like listening and have engaging body language which

5.23 *Communication Skills*

(without speaking) tells the client you are present, focused and alert to what they are saying.

When the client asks you about something you do not know the answer to, it really comes down to how you deal with it. If you feel compelled to offer 'something' as a suggestion and use language like 'maybe', 'I think' – that can sometimes create a level of uncertainty for the client. It can lead to misunderstandings with them forgetting the key words you said ('maybe' or 'I think') which results in inaccuracy. Therefore, the real skill is being able to tell them proactively and confidently how you propose to deal with their question and what you will do to maintain credibility and trust. For example, you could say something like:

> *'That is a very good question. Let me come back to you with an answer by close of business today. I don't want to say something to you when I'm not 100% sure about it.'*

The first and second sentence offers the client reassurance that they have asked a good question, not something silly or that you would have expected them to know. It is also time-framed so you must commit to it or do not say it. The tone can be neutral and quite factual for this part of the sentence. Done correctly, it is not patronising.

The third sentence shows some vulnerability because you do not know the answer (this is what can be perceived as a weakness). However, the confidence in the response of how you propose to get the answer – is a proactive stance. Because of the vulnerability, the tone should be more empathetic so a neutral or matter-of-fact tone will not be effective.

The client interview is a timed assessment so you have to have a strategy so you can take control of the interview right from the start. You will have no idea what type of client you will encounter, what their matter will be and whether it is something you can deal with competently in the interview or not. You will have some instructions but probably not enough detail because you only have ten minutes' preparation time.

Often, I have been told by lawyers that they have been advised to 'forget the small talk, there is no time for it.' I disagree; within a few minutes you can do the following without coming across as rushed:

- introduce yourself;
- engage in a little small talk;
- structure the interview.

To immediately jump into interview mode with a new client does not build rapport or trust and can come across a little rude and rushed. This can make you more nervous and does not help you which defeats the key objectives of building trust and confidence in the client interview assessment.

Remember, the client will still trust you if you cannot advise them comprehensively on the matter because you do not have all the relevant information. In fact, you are not expected to do that in the interview. You just need to provide preliminary advice, where appropriate. All the information you gather can be used in your attendance note which is where you write down any factual and legal issues identified. There is more information on how to write the attendance note in Chapter 9, Writing the Attendance Note and a refresher on written communication skills in Chapter 7, Writing in Professional English.

In practice, you would not offer any advice without full consideration of the whole position (otherwise your advice could be negligent) – that is what you need to get across to the client in the interview (if the situation requires it).

Appearance

'A good first impression can work wonders.'

J K Rowling

5.24 The reality is that it is human nature to make judgements about people when you first see them, so first impressions count. And, you want that first impression to be a good one. You want to come across as confident, and so dressing the part can psychologically make you feel better and more confident.

There is no set 'uniform' for lawyers but, typically, they wear smart suits. For the purposes of the SQE oral assessments, you should wear the smart attire that you would usually wear for a job interview at a law firm or a courtroom hearing.

So, for the client interview and advocacy, wear a smart suit in the colours that are traditionally associated with the legal profession, such as navy blue, black or dark grey.

For men, a conservative-coloured suit with a complementary coloured shirt and tie, with smart polished shoes.

For women, a conservative-coloured suit can be a trouser, dress or skirt suit which has a complementary coloured shirt or blouse and smart polished shoes.

If you are a practising lawyer, it might be similar to what you wear to the office or not (depending on where you work). If it is not, then you should consider the suggestions above.

If you are not used to wearing suits, try it out at home and make sure it feels comfortable for you because you will spend quite a long time in it; not just the time you actually do the assessments but from the time you register on the day.

I suggest that when you do some mock interviews or advocacy submissions, you practise by wearing what you will wear for the real assessments, so you can really visualise what you will look like on the day and how your clothes and shoes make you feel. Make sure what you wear is smart but comfortable. The last thing you need is to wear new shoes that may rub and hurt your feet.

I am often asked about make-up, hairstyles, jewellery, visible piercings and tattoos. My advice is your look should make you feel confident, not insecure or uncomfortable. However, it should also reflect how you want to come across to the client and judge and how they might perceive you. Traditionally, the legal

5.25 Communication Skills

profession in England and Wales is conservative and you want to stand out and be remembered for all the right reasons.

The Connector – Top Ten Tips

(1) Smile – it instantly connects you and helps you build rapport quickly and genuinely.

(2) Small talk is not formal, it is more of an ice-breaker to help you connect with the client.

(3) Rapport and trust are key to gaining any new client instructions.

(4) Trust is easier to build if the client likes you and believes in your ability to do the work.

(5) Confidence can include showing vulnerability (it is not a weakness) and can help build trust.

(6) You can still come across in a professional manner by being relaxed when making small talk with the client.

(7) Ensure you understand British cultural etiquette when meeting clients and in the courtroom.

(8) Appearance matters and first impressions count.

(9) Make sure you wear a smart suit in conservative colours and comfortable shoes for the client interview and advocacy.

(10) Practise doing the skills because they do take time and effort.

The Communicator

'If you can't explain it simply you don't understand it well enough'
Albert Einstein

5.25

Knowing what to say and how to say it are key to getting your message across confidently with clarity and conciseness. This creates an authentic and engaging connection in a structured, yet fluid manner. This part will focus on:

- **Communication:** What makes up communication skills (the ingredients)?
- **IQ and EQ:** The importance of intelligence (IQ) and emotions (EQ).
- **Time Management:** Structure and control your time.

Communication

> *'The single biggest problem in communication is the illusion that it has taken place.'*
>
> **George Bernard Shaw**

5.26 Communication skills are made up of three key elements that I call 'ingredients': visual, vocal and verbal communication skills. Generally, in any face-to-face communication, it is vital to understand the impact each of these three ingredients have, simultaneously, when you are communicating with someone.

Professor Albert Mehrabian did a study on the importance of non-verbal communication in the late 1960s. As a result of his research, which is contextualised to only communication that involves emotions and feelings (not communication generally), he devised the 'Communication Model'. Briefly, the model suggests:

- 55% of the meaning comes from your body language and facial expressions;
- 38% of the meaning comes from your voice;
- 7% of the meaning comes from your words.

Please see Appendix 5A for more information about Professor Albert Mehrabian's study.

The reason I have included the Communication Model in this section is because it is very relevant for client interviewing and advocacy. For these assessments you will probably be communicating with the client or the judge using emotions and feelings.

For example, if you are trying to influence and persuade a judge to your way of thinking then, with the evidence to support your submission, you will need to deliver it with emotions and feelings to make it come across as convincing. If you are talking to a client and need to convince them of what you are saying (if it is advice they do not want to hear) or show them empathy, then you will need to communicate with emotions and feelings, for them to believe you and your advice.

Emotions and feelings are not about appearing unprofessional or informal. Neither are they about communicating in an overtly emotional manner or over-reacting. Quite to the contrary, they form an essential part of the skills assessments in helping you score highly. More information about emotional intelligence can be found below in Intellectual Intelligence (IQ) and Emotional Intelligence (EQ) in para **5.30**.

Here are the three key elements in a bit more detail:

- ## *Visual Communication*

5.27 Visual communication is observing the person's body language (non-verbal communication) and inferring the meaning. It includes things like your facial expressions, gestures, posture and positioning.

- **Facial expressions**

    These are very important from the outset. It is what the client or judge would see first – before you even speak. So, it is important that you smile (which

5.27 Communication Skills

helps build rapport) and maintain soft eye contact (which helps build trust). Being professional and formal does not mean that you should come across expressionless or quite 'neutral'. If you try to hold back from expressing any emotional connection through your facial expressions, you may come across as unconvincing. This may make the client feel less inclined to trust you or the judge to believe you. That does not mean they think you are lying, but just that you are not convincing enough to influence and persuade them.

- **Gestures**

    These can include hand movements and nodding or shaking your head. Overuse of any of these gestures can become distracting, and underuse can make the client or judge question your credibility when you try to persuade them of your argument. You should not have to think about gestures; they should happen naturally.

    Remember, when you are speaking to your friends or family, you do not think about what gestures to use and when to use them. So, when doing a client interview or advocacy submission, trust that you will subconsciously do what is required naturally. Do not try consciously to avoid using gestures thinking that they will come across as unprofessional. On the other hand, if you tend to overuse your hand gestures so they become distracting, you will have to make a conscious effort to correct this and it will take time and practice to do this. The best way of being able to see your improvements is by video recording yourself doing a presentation.

- **Posture**

    An open, relaxed posture not only affects how confident you are but also how confident the other person perceives you. If your body posture is confident, your physiology will help your mindset become more confident too.

Exercise: Confidence Stance

Stand up as you would normally stand. Keep your legs aligned with your shoulders (ie shoulder-width apart), distribute your weight equally on both legs with your feet planted firmly on the ground.

Imagine a gold thread running up through your ankles, your legs and your back (ie spine), up through your neck and coming out through the top of your head.

Now, imagine that this gold thread is hooked to the ceiling. Your head should lift slightly – you have found your confident position.

Practise this exercise daily and you will find that it will gradually improve your posture.

Reflection

Sometimes all it takes is making small shifts to your body for you to look and feel more confident.

When your body language is aligned with what and how you are saying something, you become much more credible and confident.

There is a great TED talk by Amy Cuddy called Your Body Language May Shape Who You Are and you can find it on the TED website (www.ted.com).

- **Vocal Communication**

5.28 This is how you use your voice and it is made up of many elements and is a very powerful tool.

How you say something is open to interpretation based on the vocal elements used to project your message. Therefore, it is important to know what your natural vocal style is generally. For example, monotone, quietly spoken or fast paced. You may need to work to improve your vocals by using a range of different vocal elements which will seem unnatural at first. However, it is essential if you want to provide convincing and persuasive advice to a client or make a strong and credible advocacy submission before a judge.

Your voice is a powerful tool so you need to learn how to use it properly. Here is a quick summary of some of the key elements it is made up of:

- **Tone**

    This has to match the message; it is more about *how* you say the words (eg harsh, soft, angry, happy, authoritative).

- **Clarity**

    This is how you articulate your words. You need to open your mouth to form the letters correctly. If English is not your first language, you many need to work on your pronunciation of certain words.

- **Pitch**

    For the correct pitch, your voice can go high, low or natural – this will often depend on your energy levels. For example, on a serious topic you may speak in a lower pitch, but on a topic you get excited about you may become more high pitched and speak faster.

- **Volume**

    This is how loudly or quietly you speak which impacts on what you are saying. For example, the volume you speak at can make what you say sound authoritative (measured), nervous (quiet) or aggressive (loud or shouty).

- **Intonation**

    This is the rise and fall of your voice. For example, it is common for your voice to fade when you are coming to the end of what you are saying or your voice to rise when asking a question.

- **Emphasis**

    Where you stress a particular word you want to draw attention to, it can change the meaning of the context of what you are saying or the tone.

5.29 *Communication Skills*

The most important element that impacts your vocals is breathing, and you can read more about it in Chapter 6, Managing Nerves, Fear and Failure (para **6.12**). How you use your vocal elements can build your credibility in what you are saying so you are believed or can reduce it so the client or judge may not be convinced.

- ***Verbal Communication***

  ❖ **Language**

5.29 This is made up of the words you use to say what you want to get across. It is extremely important to make sure that you use the correct legal terminology in England and Wales and not your home jurisdiction's, which could cause confusion if interpreted differently. It is also a good idea to avoid using legal jargon with a client as this can make them feel alienated, which does not help build rapport and trust. This area is looked at in more detail in Chapter 7, Writing in Professional English.

Another tip to think about what language to use is to have in mind who you are communicating with and how they might like to hear your information or advice. If it is a judge, another solicitor or expert (ie a barrister), then legal jargon would be suitable; but this language would not be appropriate for a lay client. For the assessments, you should always have the recipient in mind.

For example, in client interviewing, without the danger of over-generalising and over-simplifying, you have to be prepared for a client who may be vulnerable and act accordingly. For client interviewing you are assessed in the following areas of law:

- **Wills and Probate**

  A client may want to instruct you to help them make a will or may be emotional over the loss of someone who has passed away and wants your help with the probate administration process or wants to contest a will.

- **Property Practice**

  A client may be a first-time buyer and nervous about the process of buying a home or a commercial client who may be more demanding with their business requirements on freehold or leasehold properties.

You can read about the potential types of 'Assessment Areas' in Chapter 3, Functioning Legal Knowledge (FLK) Assessments, Appendix 3A which gives you an idea of some common scenarios.

Once you have a good idea of the type of person you are dealing with you can think about how they come across and how you can simplify your language to connect with them. I often get told 'I don't want to come across as patronising.' Using simplified language does not mean coming across as patronising. *How* you come across when you say something (using your body language and voice) is what makes it come across or be perceived as patronising, it is not the actual words used.

Genius is in the simplicity of language. Using plain English shows you really understand something and can confidently explain it, which enhances your credibility.

Advocacy is a form of a presentation and before you dive into practising advocacy, it might be helpful to practise doing a general presentation to get comfortable with your authentic presenting style. This will help you when you do practise advocacy submissions. Advocacy is hard enough when you do not have experience of doing it, so it will help you to feel confident focusing on your presentation skills with a subject you are comfortable talking about.

> **Exercise: Do a mini presentation**
>
> The aim of this exercise is for you to very quickly realise how you come across when doing a presentation. You will get an insight into your body language, vocals and language used. Ideally, you want to find someone who has some experience or expertise in this area and can offer you constructive feedback (they do not need to be lawyer). You should then do the presentation again taking on board the feedback. It may not feel great and you may make mistakes, however it is a good idea to video record yourself so that you can review your progress.
>
> The idea is for you to do a presentation on a subject in which you are confident. This will provide you with a good idea of what you naturally do well because you know the subject matter.
>
> This is an exercise I do in the coaching sessions and workshops and although the body language and vocals are subjective to each person, the one area that comes up consistently for many lawyers is improving their structure. The point is picked up very quickly because it is a subject matter they know and it helps them see how the content could be better constructed. They then use their learnings and apply them to advocacy.
>
> **Instructions**
>
> Choose any topic for your presentation, it does not have to be law-related (eg a hobby).
>
> Preparation should not take too long for this exercise, around 10–15 minutes is enough.
>
> Stand up and do a three-minute presentation using no visual aids (Power Point, handouts etc).
>
> **Reflection**
>
> What worked well that you will use again and what area(s) need improvement and practice?
>
> - Design
>
> This is the preparation stage. What was the main aim of your presentation, did you get your message across? Did you have too much content or not enough? Was there a structure that could be followed easily?
>
> - Delivery
>
> This is the performance stage. How did you feel during the presentation and after it? Think about your body language, vocals and language used.

5.30 *Communication Skills*

Doing a confident advocacy submission means having a strong presence and vocals. If you feel you need to do some vocal exercises to help you provide a confident submission the exercise below might help you.

Vocal Exercise

If you need to work on your vocals because you realise (or it has been pointed out) that you speak in a monotone or are softly spoken, it can be hard to change the way you speak. Any change will feel unnatural and I suggest that for a short time, every day, you do what exercise works best for you.

Normally, I recommend reading a short children's story out aloud (as if you were reading it to a child). It might seem bizarre, but it is much harder to read a children's story in a monotone than an article or a document. The whole purpose of the exercise is to make you use your vocal range and elements in a way that you do not normally use them, so it will not feel natural. This exercise will take time and requires consistency.

I would also recommend that you record yourself each time to allow you to keep track of your progress.

Reading aloud will highlight any words that trip you up or you have difficulty pronouncing. Saying a word to yourself (internally) and out aloud are two different experiences.

You should also note down any words you pick up on whilst studying the law that you have difficulty pronouncing and create a 'word bank'. Practise them every day singularly and in the context of a sentence aloud.

Intellectual Intelligence (IQ) and Emotional Intelligence (EQ)

'Research shows ... emotional intelligence is twice as important an ingredient of outstanding performance as cognitive ability and technical skill combined.'

Daniel Goleman

5.30 Intellectual intelligence (IQ) and Emotional intelligence (EQ) are processed in different parts of the brain. In some cases, emotions can be processed subconsciously faster than intellectual thinking. This means you have often already decided how you 'feel' about something before you 'think' about it.

Many lawyers understand what is required of them from an intellectual and knowledge perspective. You have to study the law, understand it and skilfully apply it to any given scenario from various practice areas of law. However, understanding how their communication skills can make them more effective is much harder. I have observed many lawyers who lack emotional intelligence especially for client interviewing. When what they do is pointed out, the lawyers immediately understand what they need to do and realise they had underestimated the skills part which is more challenging than they initially thought.

Emotional intelligence is an area that is not only important for the SQE, but actually important for being an effective and smart lawyer. These are skills and competencies that are required for all lawyers and especially those who want to become exceptional role models and leaders, respected for the work they do.

Below is a brief explanation of what intellectual and emotional intelligence mean for most people:

Intellectual Intelligence (IQ)

5.31 Your IQ is associated with knowledge, intellect and the ability to comprehend complex information quickly and accurately.

There are many stereotypes associated with lawyers and one of them is that if you want to be a lawyer or are already a lawyer, you must be clever. Much of this perception stems from the weight placed on academic achievements required to become a lawyer and the related association with success.

In reality, high academic achievements do not themselves equate with being a good and successful lawyer. You need to have good communication skills and emotional intelligence, to complement your intellectual intelligence. A smart lawyer will have a good dose of both and understand the importance of both, in practice.

In the UK, traditionally, City law firms recruit high academic achievers, so they set academic criteria for the recruitment of students. Then, there are assessment days that will test various skills and competences as well as an interview. If they pass this competitive and gruelling process, they are offered the traditional training contract (two years' work experience) required to qualify as a solicitor or the equivalent for the SQE.

The SQE offers more ways for students to be able to qualify as a solicitor, outside the traditional approach. More information about the different routes to qualifying can be found in Chapter 4, Qualifying Work Experience, What Counts as QWE (para **4.12**).

For qualified and experienced lawyers, the focus is more on their years of experience in practice, as opposed to the grades they achieved back in law school. That is not to say the academic achievements do not matter, but as lawyers become more experienced and gain seniority, less importance is placed on their 'academics' and they are more likely to be considered for a role based on their knowledge, talent, expertise and skill set – especially if they are leadership roles.

Therefore, intellect and knowledge of the law are a given as a solicitor. It is the skills part that often becomes a minefield because there is no exact science behind it, but it forms an essential part of being a well-rounded, smart lawyer. This is why it forms part of the SQE examination. You should read Chapter 4, Qualifying Work Experience, Types of Lawyers (para **4.02**).

5.32 *Communication Skills*

The SQE rigorously assesses your knowledge of the law by using a range of different formats and styles. For the SQE Part 1 you have to learn the core substantive and procedural areas of the law. You have to demonstrate your understanding of the fundamental legal rules and principles through a broad range of subjects through multiple choice questions. This foundation of legal knowledge is what you need for the SQE Part 2.

The SQE Part 2 requires you to demonstrate your legal and communication skills by showing you understand and can explain the law and procedural knowledge, in a range of oral and written assessments. If you have legal work experience that should help you with this part because you are assessed on realistic client issues and problems or scenarios. For example, in client interviewing any legal advice should be offered in a problem-solving and advisory capacity, rather than in an academic way focusing heavily on the law. You can read more about Client Interviewing Skills in Chapter 8 and Writing the Attendance Note in Chapter 9.

More and more law firms are looking for lawyers who have the practical skills and commercial awareness of how to work with clients in an effective manner. They are looking for additional qualities and skills that fall outside the academic remit of the law.

In a competitive legal market, what good would a clever lawyer be without a client? How can a law firm or business survive and thrive if it does not have a healthy portfolio of clients, or clients leave because of their lawyers?

Even law firms recognise that lawyers need more than just intelligence to be successful. Many law firms' marketing focuses heavily on the client rather than the law. If you want to be a successful solicitor you will need to know how to build your own reputation, engage and develop client relationships and manage clients' expectations. The SQE Part 2 will assess you on your oral skills (client interviewing and advocacy) and writing skills (attendance note, case and matter analysis, legal writing, legal drafting and legal research). The focus is not just your accuracy in legal knowledge and advice, but whether you can confidently deliver it in an understandable, effective and professional manner to the recipient.

I am not playing down the requirement of intellectual intelligence, just increasing awareness that the skills part is tested equally as important as the law. The Solicitors Regulation Authority (SRA) clearly recognises that the skills are an essential part of being a good, well-rounded solicitor.

Emotional Intelligence (EQ)

5.32 The term EQ was first used in 1990 by two American psychologists called Peter Salovey and John Mayer. They defined 'emotional intelligence' as:

> *'the ability to manage one's own and others' feelings and emotions ... and to use this information to guide one's thoughts and actions.'*

Six Seconds is the largest non-profit international organisation that was founded in 1997 and is dedicated to the development of emotional intelligence. The aim of the organisation is to offer practical assistance to help people to perceive, understand and manage emotion and put that intelligence into action.

Intellectual Intelligence (IQ) and Emotional Intelligence (EQ) **5.33**

Six Seconds has built on the work of EQ offering this definition:

> *'Emotional intelligence is effectively blending thinking and feeling to make optimal decisions.'*

They believe that EQ is not your personality or about being 'too emotional', 'too nice' or 'touchy-feely'. It is also not the opposite of IQ; rather it works more holistically with it. You could think of emotional intelligence as being smart with feelings. But, because there are so many variables that make it up, it is harder to assess, unlike intellectual intelligence which is measurable.

Many of the lawyers I have worked with have heard or read about emotional intelligence but do not really understand *how* it is 'practically' used in everyday communication skills. I have chosen to include it in this book, because if you are aiming for superior performance marks, you will definitely benefit from understanding how to use it for some of the SQE Part 2 assessments.

- **Client Interviewing and EQ**

5.33 The common pattern I observe is that the lawyers I have coached and trained are very keen and focused on providing detailed and comprehensive advice – usually without actually having all the relevant information. This is because they do not ask enough, or good, questions so in offering advice they end up struggling and feel the pressure. It is important to ensure what you say is legally correct and that you know the law, otherwise you could be negligent. Stop and ask questions if you realise that in trying to advise the client you need more information rather than make assumptions. Remember, for the interactive part of the assessment you are only assessed on the skills, unless you are required to provide some preliminary advice. The attendance note will assess you on your knowledge of the law and writing skills. It will be a direct reflection of the information you have elicited from the client to advise them.

I have sometimes observed lawyers forget to introduce themselves and fail (or forget) to make any small talk with the client. This is the lawyer being very 'task-focused' and trying to get the information across to the client without using 'people-focused' skills. So, although the advice might be correct (or at times delivered too technically), this can make the client feel alienated. This is because no attempt (or very little) is made to build rapport or check that they have actually understood everything said. They do not acknowledge or recognise the client's body language or emotional language patterns used.

Ultimately, the key objective for the interview is you want the client to instruct you on their matter, and skilfully making some people-focused changes to your style can help you to achieve your goal.

I often point out to lawyers that you have to look at the client's demeanour and flex your communication style to work with theirs. This takes time and skill to learn because you need to learn what your own communication style preference is and then adapt it to other people's styles and language patterns. Once you can do it, it makes it easier to connect with them and you will do it naturally. See para **5.29** on Verbal Communication.

5.34 *Communication Skills*

If you hear a client talk about any concerns or worries (using emotional language), acknowledge it and address it, in the moment, reassuringly. For example, the client can raise any number of issues sometimes not related to why they have come to see you (non-exhaustive list):

- concerns about paying your fees;
- worry about their court hearing;
- anxiety over being sued or defending a claim; or
- anything that is important or worrying them.

You need to pick up on their body language, if you can sense they are upset or feel uncomfortable, and have the skills to deal with it, in that moment. You cannot ignore it (out of shock or embarrassment because you do not know what to do) and carry on asking questions or writing down notes. Often the untrained lawyer does not even realise the client's behaviour or language, may be masking worries or emotions through their language, until it is pointed out to them. If you have a client who is quite rude or dismissive, do not take it personally and get defensive. Always remain professional. This is an assessment to see whether you have the skills to deal with different types of clients.

You might think that the client interview is only 25 minutes long so you do not have time to spend on pleasantries and want to get to the heart of the issue or matter. But, none of what I am suggesting you do actually takes up a lot of time. If anything, that couple of minutes will add to your credibility and may make your time with the client easier. This is where you have to learn to skilfully and quickly deal with the client's unforeseen issues, as well as getting all the relevant information required, without coming across as flustered or rushed. It is a skill that takes time to learn, but with strategies in place is achievable with practice.

Being emotionally intelligent helps you build rapport and trust with the client and shows them that you genuinely care about them and their matter. This directly links to the client having trust and confidence in your ability to deal with their instructions – which is one of the key objectives of the skills part of the assessment. More details about typical situations and how to deal with them are set out in Chapter 8, Client Interviewing Skills.

You can read more about emotional intelligence on the Six Seconds website (www.6seconds.org). In Appendix 5B, I have shared an insightful article which explains why intellectual and emotional intelligence both need to work together.

- ### *Advocacy and EQ*

5.34 This is where you can maximise your marks on skills by creating a persuasive argument using language that powerfully makes your point and empathy through your body language and vocals where it is required. The emotional intelligence will be demonstrated by how you apply the facts to the law or legal principle relied upon.

Time Management

> *'Time management is a misnomer, the
> challenge is to manage ourselves.'*
>
> **Stephen Covey**

5.35 Chapter 2, Preparing for the SQE, Studying and Time Management (para **2.22**) focused on how to use your time for studying effectively. The focus here is to help you have a strategy in mind for managing your time for each assessment.

As mentioned previously, managing your time effectively has nothing to do with law and everything to do with you. You will need to be disciplined and have strategies in place so you do not waste time, get caught out or feel overwhelmed by the assessments. Use your time productively.

For the SQE Part 1, read Chapter 3, Functioning Legal Knowledge Assessments, for more information on how to work out a plan for studying the law and practising using the multiple choice format. As this is more structured than the SQE Part 2, it is easier to keep track of time and how long to spend on each question.

For the SQE Part 2, time management can be a little harder to work out because, although you are given set times for preparation and doing the assessments, you have no idea of the number of supporting documents (if any) you have to read and how that impacts your time. Therefore, for some assessments, time management is not just about the time allocated for each part of the assessment, but more about how you will use it to manage and prioritise what is relevant for you to use.

For the assessments, everything you need will be provided for you on the day because all the SQE assessments are 'closed book'.

For some assessments, you will have preparation time, so I will provide you with some practical guidance on how to manage your time during this stage. More details about what to do and how to prepare for each assessment will be dealt with in their respective chapters in this book.

- *Preparation Stage*

5.36 Preparation is key for being able to manage your time. It is essential that you have a strategy and template (where appropriate) that you use and practise with, so regardless of the scenario that presents itself, you do not get overwhelmed about how to deal with it.

In your preparation time, you may not have time to read, in detail, all the supporting documents in full if there are a lot of them. A part of the skills test is to see whether you can confidently sift through the documents and only use what is relevant. Therefore, it is good to remember that not everything provided may be relevant.

Typical types of supporting documents for the oral or written assessments could be (a non-exhaustive list):

➢ case law;

5.37 *Communication Skills*

- extracts of legislation;
- witness statements;
- a will;
- articles of association;
- a pre-sentence report;
- experts' reports;
- financial documents;
- Crown Prosecution Service file of documents;
- Forms (eg AP1, IHT205 or IHT400).

You need to get comfortable with the idea that there may be lots of documents, but you have a strategy as to how you will deal with them.

Reading is a key skill that will determine whether you use your time effectively or not. So, what is the quickest and best way to get through (potentially) a lot of information, in different documents? A good way to do it is to scan or skim read the documents. What is the difference? It depends on the type of document you are reading and what information you are looking for.

❖ **Scanning a Document**

5.37 If you are looking for something specific in a document, such as, a particular figure, section or key words you would scan the document to find it.

❖ **Skim Reading a Document**

5.38 If you needed to understand the gist of a document, you would skim read it rather than read it in detail. That means you would look for things to help you get through the document quickly, such as: headings, different fonts and styles, sub-headings, nouns, dates and places – factual information and then link it to form an opinion of what the document is broadly saying. This means that naturally you may miss out information that may be important, but you would have an overall idea of what it says.

Rudyard Kipling wrote a poem about asking powerful questions. It is called 'I Keep Six Honest Serving Men' and you can read the poem in Appendix 5C. The six questions are a good guide to help you think and decide what content you want to include and what can be left out.

This is just an example of the types of questions that can help you:

- *Who?* Who is this presentation/submission for? A judge – in which court?
- *What?* What is the most important point I want to get across? What are my key issues?
- *How?* How will I achieve the end goal? How will I separate the key issues?
- *Where?* Where will I put the content within each section and do I need sub-sections?

- *Why?* Why do I want to include this information? Why is the relevant or irrelevant?
- *When?* When will I finish? Close to 15 minutes.

This will help you focus on what you want to get across rather than get overwhelmed with the content and have no structure, so you do not know how to start. Remember, the preparation stage is really getting down to the crux of the content and working out what you want to say and where the information will sit.

You need to read the instructions carefully and make sure that the information you want to include relates to it and you create a structure that is easy to follow.

- ***Preparation Time for Oral Assessments***
  ❖ **Client Interviewing**

5.39 You will have a short amount of time for preparation (ten minutes) and then conduct the interview. You will have some instructions which will be your compass or direction as to what you need to address, advise or explore with the client. The purpose of the interview is for you to find out as much as possible about what the client wants to do. There might be some supporting documents, so you have to be smart about how you will use the time to think about what types of questions you want to ask the client. It is a good opportunity to brainstorm and think of specific issues you might want to explore. Do not make any assumptions but think of what questions to ask instead.

Having a template or a structure you will use for client interviewing and the attendance note are great time savers. It offers you some guidance so as to keep focused on what you want to include and what you exclude because it is not relevant. It will be helpful to practise using various templates and structures to work out what is most comfortable for you. You will need to memorise them because you will need to re-create them in your preparation time. You will not be allowed to take in any materials as all the assessments are 'closed book'.

Read the section on The Convincer below and in particular Listening and Questioning (paras **5.43** and **5.44** respectively) as well as Chapter 8, Client Interviewing Skills for more details.

❖ **Advocacy**

5.40 You will have 45 minutes' preparation time and a set of supporting documents, which you will need to go through to create a strong reasoned submission. You will need to read through the supporting documents quickly and have a strategy of how you will present the information in a coherent and structured manner.

Your instructions should be read carefully and in detail (and probably twice over, to make sure you understand exactly what you need to do). Unlike any supporting documents you cannot rush through reading the instructions. You may need to scan or skim read supporting documents (if there are a lot of them) to check their relevance. So, it is a good idea after reading the instructions that you think about what documents (if any) will support what you want to say. Prioritise them, weighing up whether you need to read them in detail, scan them or skim read them.

I doubt you will have time to write a 'script' of what you want to say and practise it, so my advice is to split the presentation into three parts: the beginning, middle and end. You need to work out what bit of information goes where and the bulk of it will usually be the middle section. When you decide what the key issues are, there may be a number of key points within them which you can include as sub-sections. See Chapter 10, Advocacy for the Advocacy Structure, para **10.04**.

- ***Preparation Time for Written Assessments***

5.41 This part is more tricky because you do not get told how much preparation time to spend for each assessment (Chapters 11–14). You must factor your preparation time within each assessment. This will vary depending on how many (if any) supporting documents there are to scan or skim read. For example, legal writing may require less preparation time (if fewer supporting documents) than legal research (expect lots of supporting documents and not all relevant). Having said that, you must have an idea of how to structure your answer and remember any templates that will help you.

Each written assessment will have a timer to let you know how long you have left in each assessment. Once your time is up you cannot continue or go back to the assessment.

The Communicator – Top Ten Tips

(1) Remember, visual, vocal and verbal are the three key 'ingredients' that make up communication skills.

(2) Body language speaks louder than words (in context). You may be saying all the right things, but if your body language is not congruent, it is less believable.

(3) First impressions count, so make a confident introduction with a smile.

(4) If you speak in a monotone or very quietly, practise using your range of vocals consistently and you will notice an improvement.

(5) A client who comes to see you wants someone who is confident – not just in how you look and come across, but also how you sound when you speak.

(6) Knowledge is key, but avoid using legal jargon with clients – as this can make them feel alienated (use plain English).

(7) Communicate using plain English for oral and written skills (where appropriate).

(8) Emotional intelligence is being smart with feelings. It connects you with the client and judge, builds your credibility and demonstrates your effective communication skills.

> (9) Be strategic with your time and know in advance how you will use your preparation time.
>
> (10) Get comfortable and practise how to scan and skim read documents.

The Convincer

'It doesn't matter how much we know, what matters is how clearly others can understand what we know.'

Simon Sinek

5.42

> When you are alert and proactive, you are fully present in the situation. This instils confidence in your ability to communicate and connect authentically and persuasively. This part will focus on:
>
> - **Listening:** The importance of what is (or is not) being said.
>
> - **Questioning:** Be curious and interested. Ask for more insight and information.
>
> - **Impact:** Understand the difference between the ability to influence and persuade.

Listening

'Most people do not listen with the intent to understand; they listen with the intent to reply.'

Stephen Covey

5.43 Listening is a very underrated skill. Many people do not really pay too much attention to it, and think it is pretty black and white: you are either listening or not. However, there are many different levels of listening which are looked at below in more detail.

Listening is an important skill, especially for something like client interviewing. You will probably already be feeling nervous and under pressure, because of the type of client you might get and the time limit. This means there is a high chance that instead of actually listening to the client, you will be listening to get the gist of what they say, whilst (probably) thinking about the relevant law or panicking if it is something you do not know about. In effect, doing what Steven Covey's quote above suggests, you *'listen with the intent to reply'* rather than *'the intent to understand'*.

When coaching lawyers, I notice many of them dismiss (ignore) information by making an assumption about its relevance without asking a question to clarify its

5.43 *Communication Skills*

importance. By doing this, you will often miss key information that can affect your preliminary advice and what you subsequently include in your attendance note (which is marked on the law and skills).

The pressure of thinking about what to say next or what question to ask often means that you are not fully engaged in listening. If this is visible from your body language, it can lead to a whole array of different interpretations from the client's perspective. They might feel any of the following:

- you do not understand them;
- you are not listening because you are distracted; or
- you are simply not interested in their matter.

Of course, this is not your intention at all, because you want to impress the client and come across as confident. So, you think about what to ask next to come across as engaged. But without having all the information or enough of it, it becomes harder to think of questions to ask. That is when it comes down to how the exchange of information is received and perceived.

Listening has many different levels ranging from the lowest level of ignoring (level one), through to the highest level of empathetic listening (level five). Here are the five different levels of listening that you may go through in any exchange of information, in any situation:

- **Ignoring**

    This is the most obvious where someone is speaking to you but you are not giving them any indication that you are listening to them. This is the lowest level of listening, because you can hear words being spoken but you are not paying any attention to them or responding.

- **Pretend Listening**

    At this level, you act like you are listening, but you are not. For example: whilst you are being spoken to about something, you are nodding and agreeing, but are actually focused on something else (most likely the law). Usually, most people can relate to this level in a personal/social situation (ie, distracted by work, mobile, TV etc). Remember, it is one of the quickest ways to start an argument with a loved one!

- **Selective Listening**

    There are two ways of listening selectively:

    - **You hear what you want to hear.**

        For example, when a number of things may be said but you only hear the positives that work for you.

    - **You get side-tracked onto a different thought process by a trigger word or phrase.**

        For example, a trigger word mentioned in conversation reminds you of something you need to do or it triggers a good or bad memory.

    Either way, selective listening affects the quality of the information you receive.

- **Active Listening**

    At this level, you are sending the person all the right signals (body language and facial expressions) that you are listening and you do not interrupt them too much. You also use a summarising technique called 'echoing' to ensure your understanding is correct. For example, you nod and make eye contact with them. You repeat something they said or 'echo' their point to ensure you have understood them correctly.

- **Empathetic Listening**

    This is the active level of listening, but higher. You are also listening for things that are *not* said through words. You observe the client's body language and facial expressions (the non-verbal communication) – it is a bit like listening with your eyes. This allows you to ask more probing questions where you feel it is appropriate. For example, in client interviewing you focus on what the client says and observe their body language. Where you think what they are saying and how they come across are not aligned this does not necessarily mean they are lying; it can just mean they may not be telling you everything. They might think the information is not relevant or it may be too sensitive so they want to avoid it. You then have to skilfully ask appropriate questions to get clarity and detail for an accurate understanding of the issue.

Exercise: Different Levels of Listening

Think of examples where you have used the first four levels of listening. They may have been with different people, at different times, locations or professional or social settings – they do not have to be recent examples.

Choose one listening level and think about a situation and how it played out for you.

Now, think about that same situation and how it could have been improved to make it a higher level of listening. You need to think about what you could have done differently to be a more effective listener.

For the client interview assessment, you should be aiming for the active or empathetic levels of listening. Use the echoing technique to allow the client to hear back what they have said and fill in any gaps of information they may have missed out.

Overall, good listening is not just about getting the information you need, but also ensuring that the client feels that they have been listened to and that you have fully understood their feelings and objectives.

> *'The spoken word belongs half to him who speaks, and half to him who listens.'*
>
> **French Proverb**

5.44 *Communication Skills*

Generally, by not interrupting you can get more information quickly. However, sometimes, if you are so focused on listening intently your facial expressions can come across as intense. The exercise below Listening Without Speaking lets you experience how it feels from the client's perspective. Listening is a fine balance to understand and ask questions for clarification.

Exercise: Listening Without Speaking

This is a quick one-minute exercise for you to know what it feels like when you are the person speaking and then the person listening, respectively.

You will need to find another person to do this exercise with you. One of you is person A and the other person is B. After you have done the exercise, you can swap roles (so person B asks the question to person A).

Person A's instructions

Ask the question: '***Tell me about your family?***' You are not allowed to ask any more questions or get into a discussion. You must keep neutral facial expressions whilst looking at person B for the entire minute. Stop person B when the minute is up.

Person B's instructions

You will be asked one question which you have to answer.

Reflection and Feedback

Question for person A: How did you feel not being able to engage with person B?

Question for person B: How did you feel when you were talking to person A?

Questioning

'Who questions much, shall learn much, and retain much.'
Francis Bacon

5.44 A good question can get the client to think of the situation or issue differently or find an answer they had not previously considered.

As a lawyer, when you are with the client, you should ask yourself: *'What is my strategy for asking this question?'*

- What am I assuming?
- What is built into the question?
- What is the client assuming?

Questioning **5.44**

Generally, questions beginning with 'why' are not usually powerful. They tend to offer a defensive response with justifications rather than good-quality information. Here is an example of asking the same question, but think about how the client might respond and how they might feel:

> *'Why did you do that?'*
>
> *'What made you do that?'*

Both questions can work, but there may be a difference in the quality of the response.

That does not mean you should never ask questions beginning with 'why'. If you know the answer will elicit a positive response, there is nothing wrong with it.

I have seen lawyers in client interviewing struggle to ask questions because they cannot think of them. Usually this is because:

- they are under pressure thinking about what to ask the client without getting enough information in the first place;
- they are distracted by whether they know the law in relation to the matter to advise on it;
- they have made assumptions about the situation and do not think a question is relevant.

Here is the problem – you are over-thinking. You cannot possibly come up with good open questions relevant to what the client is saying if you are preoccupied with thinking about what you will ask them. That puts unnecessary pressure on you and does not help you come up with good questions.

Without listening to the client attentively, it is too hard to come up with questions related to their matter. Clients will provide you with information (no matter how limited), but you have to listen to what they are telling you first and, from that information, it becomes easier to find your next relevant question. Therefore, closed questions are not helpful at the initial stage of gathering information.

Under pressure, it is easier to ask a lot of closed questions which naturally offer you very limited information. Therefore, they are not good starter questions. You also need to keep track of time, so you want to be able to control the interview and ask the appropriate types of questions depending on what stage of the interview you are in: the beginning, middle or end. It makes sense to ask open questions at the beginning of the interview because it allows you to get as much information as possible and then work your next questions based on the information provided by the client. Then in the middle section, you can 'drill down' on the information by asking more specific questions, to get clarity. Finally, towards the end of the interview, you can use closed questions which can confirm your understanding.

It takes skill, time and practice to ask a range of good-quality questions. There is no right or wrong approach and every situation is different. However, asking unrelated questions or repeating them, will reduce your credibility. It is fine for you to take a moment to reflect, think and look at your notes before you ask a question.

5.44 *Communication Skills*

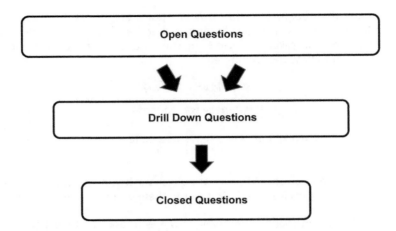

If you have a situation where the client cannot move away from their thinking because they are stuck or cannot see a way forward, then a hypothetical question is a good way to help shift their mindset. Hypothetical questions usually start with 'If ...' or 'Imagine ...' For example, if a client refuses to accept that they have a weak case and wants to carry on without considering all the implications, you could ask them:

'If you were to lose this case, how would it impact you financially?'

'Imagine you lost this case, what impact would it have on you financially?'

Here is your toolbox of questions that you can use to gather information:

Type of Question	Start with...	Reason to ask...
Open Neutral	When, What, How, Tell me	Allows an unrestrictive, unguided response.
Open Leading	When, What, How, Tell me	Allows a restrictive, guided response.
Drill Down	Clarify, Specifically, Exactly	Allows you to probe for detail and clarification.
Closed	Do, Is, Can, Did	Limits the scope of the answer to usually a 'yes' or 'no'.

Type of Question	Example	Commentary
Open Neutral	*What can you tell me about the family dynamics?*	No direction, unguided response.
Open Leading	*What would you like to do about this situation?*	Direction and guided response.
Drill Down	*Exactly what was your involvement?*	Specific details.
Closed	*Do you want to proceed with this?*	Narrows response to 'yes' or 'no'.

Asking good questions will also allow you to control the interview. The fear many lawyers have about the assessment is not knowing how to deal with the client if they talk too much or not enough. They do not want to seem rude by interrupting them. You need to learn how to manage the client in a skilful way without upsetting or offending them. This will take time but does get easier the more you practise it when you know what to do and how to say it. Then you will find yourself doing it effortlessly with confidence.

One strategy to use is a technique called 'framing'. You frame upfront (in the introduction stage, after the pleasantries and small talk) how you propose to conduct the interview. You tell the client that you will be making notes and if you interrupt them or ask them to repeat something, it is not that you are not listening, but because you need to ensure your notes are accurate. If you get their permission upfront, you do not need to keep apologising. This means the flow of the exchange is smoother and more connected.

If the client is not saying much at all, that is when open questions are good and one of my favourite ones is *'Tell me about ...'* as a starter question. It is an open neutral question which allows them to talk without any direction. Listen patiently and then when they start slowing down, or where you feel appropriate, you can ask an open leading question by linking into what they say. Use the table above for examples of the different types of questions when practising. You will see that you can use the same opening words for both types of open questions but choose which ones work best for your question.

More information for specific details of how to ask questions for the assessment can be found in Chapter 8, Client Interviewing Skills.

Impact: Persuasion and Influence

> *'Character may almost be called the most effective means of persuasion.'*
>
> **Aristotle**

5.45 The purpose of your client interview and advocacy is to influence and persuade the client or the judge through what you have to say. As you have seen from Professor Albert Mehrabian's Communication Model (para **5.26** and Appendix 5A), this type of communication requires you to focus not just on the actual words, but more importantly your body language and vocals too. Collectively, it brings your message to life.

In reality, it is most likely that your advice or advocacy submission will involve you communicating with emotions. For client interviewing, you may need to tailor your advice and make it more empathetic or persuasive to your client's situation. For an advocacy submission, you will need to make your submission with passion and conviction, so you come across as credible and confident. Speaking with passion does not mean speaking unprofessionally, informally or in an eccentric manner, but it means you are speaking with feelings about something you believe in and that you think is very important to persuade the judge to find in your favour.

5.45 Communication Skills

Often your personality is a good indicator of how hard you might have to work on the skills part. There are many personality profiling tools that you can do to help you get an insight into your personality preferences. When you know what your preferences are, there is a good chance you will be able to understand your preferred communication and language style better, as well as recognising other people's styles that are different to yours. Myers-Briggs Type Indicator (MBTI) is a famous one and as Isabel Briggs Myers said, 'It is up to each person to recognise his or her true preferences'.

You can find out more about MBTI on the Internet and in Appendix 5D.

> *'Communication is a skill you can learn. It's like riding a bicycle or typing. If you are willing to work at it, you can rapidly improve the quality of every part of your life.'*
>
> **Brian Tracy**

The Convincer – Top Ten Tips

(1) The listening exercises will help you recognise when you are listening at the various different levels.

(2) Try to listen to understand rather than worry about what question to ask next, which puts unnecessary pressure on you.

(3) Active listening means using good body language, and that lets the client know you are attentive and present.

(4) Practise asking good-quality questions which elicit good-quality answers.

(5) Make sure you have a range of question openers to help you decide what type of question to use.

(6) Get curious. Explore and ask a range of different questions if the information is not forthcoming.

(7) Have a strategy: start with asking open questions, then use probing questions, followed by closed questions.

(8) First impressions count, so to be convincing you need more than just good listening and questioning skills.

(9) Understanding your character can help you understand your behaviours and preferred communication style and those of others.

(10) To be a skilfully credible communicator, you need to be able to connect and convince, persuasively.

Chapter 5

Communication Skills: Appendices

Appendix 5A: The Communication Model

Professor Albert Mehrabian's book, *Silent Messages: Implicit Communication of Emotions and Attitudes* ((1981) Belmont, CA: Wadsworth) is currently being distributed by him, am@kaaj.com.

The Communication Model is often quoted but unfortunately misused. It should only be used in the context that the percentage numbers apply when a person is communicating about emotions. It does not apply to communication in general. He states that implicit expressions are not always more important than words and can be ineffective for communicating most referents denoted by words for example, where communication is factual (ie 'I'll see you tomorrow' or 'x + y = z').

Professor Mehrabian points out the limitations of the study, which is context dependent and is often over-generalised. In his book, Chapter 5 (Double-edged Messages) deals with communications where the verbal segment differs with or contradicts the nonverbal segment. The findings summarised in this chapter are often quoted, but unfortunately exaggerated.

Appendix 5B: Emotional Intelligence

I am a certified practitioner of emotional intelligence with Six Seconds and have seen how useful it is in developing and transforming people's communication skills. It improves your ability to understand yourself better and how you process emotions, enriching your emotional literacy. This in turn enables you to use your emotional intelligence to help you understand and communicate with others more effectively, authentically and confidently.

Six Seconds (www.6seconds.org) published an article below which highlights that Emotional Intelligence (EQ) is as important as Intellectual Intelligence (IQ). I hope that the extract from the article sparks a curiosity in you that makes you want to find out more about the importance of emotional intelligence. It will help you become a better lawyer and communicator.

IQ vs EQ: Why it matters what we measure

14 January 2020, article by Michael Miller

Both the progress and problems that define the Digital Era are the logical conclusion of 100 years dedicated to cognitive intelligence (IQ). What would emerge from 100 years dedicated to emotional intelligence (EQ)?

How many hours have you spent learning math and science in your life? Think about kindergarten all the way through high school or university. Hundreds, probably thousands? Even tens of thousands? And how many hours have you spent learning about emotions? How they work in our brains and bodies? How to recognize, label and transform them in yourself and others? For most people in the world, the answer is almost none.

Considering this, is it surprising where we find ourselves at this stage in history, as we enter the 4th Industrial Revolution?

We have smartphones, microbots performing heart surgery, and cars that can brake themselves to avoid accidents. But at the same time, we are lonelier, more frustrated, and more disconnected than ever before. It isn't that our education system has failed. It's been spectacularly successful, at least on the whole, at improving what it values, measures, and teaches. Let's look at the dramatic rise in cognitive intelligence over the past 100 years and the digital revolution it's fuelled, and then consider: What would happen if we adopted a different, more balanced approach for the next 100 years? What would it look like if we invested the same resources in emotional intelligence as we do in cognitive intelligence? Or even just 10% more than we do now?

IQ as the ultimate measure of success

IQ, the most common measure of cognitive intelligence, has become the basic standard in Western society of how smart someone is, and how successful they can be. In some ways, it has become a kind of cultural obsession. We've begun to test for IQ at earlier and earlier ages and produce literally thousands of products that promise to make your child the next Einstein. And because of the importance we give it, school curriculums have naturally gravitated toward prioritizing these skills, too. The result? IQ has steadily increased over the past century. Check out this graph:

Appendix 5B

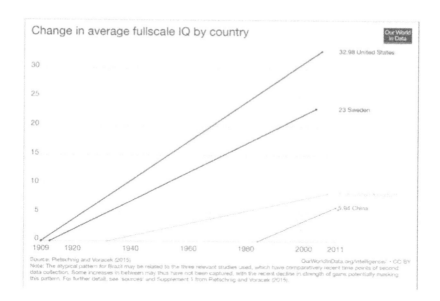

What does an IQ test measure? Verbal processing, logical reasoning abilities, mathematical problem solving, and working memory, among other things. But as even the test's founders acknowledged, it has many limitations. In a task-based test like this, you can only measure tasks that you can have people do right there in the testing room. That naturally excludes many types of intelligence, especially ones that are social or emotional in nature. Solving emotional problems is a type of intelligence we use literally all the time, but because it occurs in landscapes with constantly changing variables and a lack of clear, correct answers, it isn't as easy to measure as cognitive intelligence. So for the most part, we don't try.

But the reality, of course, is that life is messy. It occurs in these ever changing landscapes. Humans are social creatures, driven by emotion. High IQ scores are no guarantee of success. Many geniuses struggle to meet even their basic needs. It's not that cognitive intelligence isn't important. But it's far from the only, or even best, measure of success.

Research: EQ and success

Dan Goleman, then a columnist for *The New York Times*, became the first person to popularize the case against IQ as the ultimate measure of success, in his bestselling book: *Emotional Intelligence: Why It Matters More Than IQ*. He argues in his book, based on the research of Peter Salovey and John Mayer, that IQ accounts for only 20% of a person's success in life. And since he published that research, a growing body of evidence has confirmed his hypothesis. EQ is twice as predictive of performance as IQ. Check out this graph of EQ and life success, which is from a large, randomized and global sample of over 75,000 individuals.

Communication Skills: Appendices

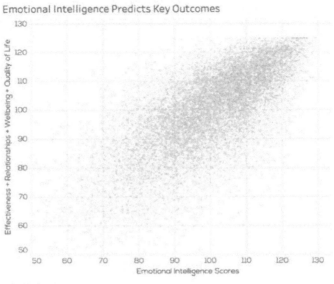

Total Eq vs. Overall.

What do you notice? I notice the white spaces in the top left and bottom right corners. These spaces indicate that there are almost no individuals who score low on EQ and high on Success – or vice versa. People with high emotional intelligence are likely to be doing well, to be effective at work, to have strong relationships, good health and a high quality of life. And people with low emotional intelligence? They are much more likely to be suffering, to be in poor health and unhappy with their social connections.

And what does EQ measure? The ability to identify your own and others' emotions, and recognize one's own patterns. The skill of seeing and weighing decisions, and connecting to yourself and others. This study used the *Six Seconds Emotional Intelligence Assessment*, a psychometrically valid test that has been used in over 150 countries. So does that mean we should abandon IQ tests in favor of EQ tests?

IQ or EQ? That's the wrong question

Let me be clear: I am not saying that cognitive intelligence isn't important. It is important, and has led to incredible advancements for human civilization. But you get what you measure, and right now we're only focusing on one half, or less, of the equation. And our most pressing problems right now aren't due to weapons that aren't powerful enough or computers that aren't smart enough. Our biggest problems are emotional, relational. Investing in one side doesn't mean abandoning the other. In fact, a growing body of research has found that social and emotional learning enables and improves cognitive learning. This isn't an either or situation. It's recognizing that these two types of intelligence need to work together.

Here is the link to read the full article online:

www.6seconds.org/2020/01/14/iq-vs-eq-why-it-matters-what-we-measure

Appendix 5C: Rudyard Kipling's The Elephant's Child

Rudyard Kipling's poem, 'The Elephant's Child' (www.kiplingsociety.co.uk/poems_serving.htm), describes the questions as six honest serving men:

I keep six honest serving men
(They taught me all I knew);
Their names are What and Why and When
And How and Where and Who.

I send them over land and sea,
  I send them east and west;
But after they have worked for me,
  I give them all a rest.

I let them rest from nine till five,
  For I am busy then,
As well as breakfast, lunch, and tea,
  For they are hungry men.

But different folk have different views;
  I know a person small—
She keeps ten million serving-men,
  Who get no rest at all!

She sends 'em abroad on her own affairs,
  From the second she opens her eyes—
One million Hows, two million Wheres,
  And seven million Whys!

The focus of the poem is all about curiosity and asking questions to gain understanding. Just like the poem refers to 'a person small' (ie a child) who ask lots of questions (often relentlessly), as a lawyer you should ask a variety of good questions to gain clarity rather than make assumptions.

Appendix 5D: Myers-Briggs Type Indicator (MBTI)

The information below has been provided with the permission of the Myers & Briggs Foundation (www.myersbriggs.org).

The purpose of the MBTI personality inventory is to make the theory of psychological types described by C. G. Jung understandable and useful in people's lives. The essence of the theory is that much seemingly random variation in the behaviour is actually quite orderly and consistent.

MBTI provides you with an insight without 'pigeon-holing' you into 'one type' because it recognises that we are all a blend of many types, but each person will have a preference. You complete a comprehensive questionnaire and it will work out your personality preferences for each of the four dichotomies specified.

The Myers & Briggs Foundation website under MBTI Basics (www.myersbriggs.org/my-mbti-personality-type/mbti-basics) provides a quick way to find out your preferences by answering the four questions below:

Extraversion (E) or Introversion (I)

This dimension measures how much an individual derives their energy from the external world over the internal world.

(1) Favourite world:

Do you prefer to focus on the outer world or on your own inner world?

Sensing (S) or Intuition (N)

This dimension measures how an individual processes information (relying on their five senses, practical and factual information or more on their intuition).

(2) Information:

Do you prefer to focus on the basic information you take in or do you prefer to interpret and add meaning?

Thinking (T) or Feeling (F)

This dimension measures how an individual makes decisions.

(3) Decisions:

When making decisions, do you prefer to first look at logic and consistency or first look at the people and special circumstances?

Judging (J) or Perceiving (P)

This dimension measures how an individual approaches the outside world.

(4) Structure:

In dealing with the outside world, do you prefer to get things decided or do you prefer to stay open to new information and options?

Results:

By answering the four questions on their website, you can find out your personality type, which will be represented by four letters (eg ESTJ, INTP, ENFP etc) from 16 combinations.

There are many licensed MBTI practitioners all over the world so you can search the Internet to find an organisation in your city or home jurisdiction if you are interested in finding out more about it.

Appendix 5D

Please note, there are many other personality profiling tools which measure different competencies and requirements. For example, DiSC, (www.discprofile.com) developed by William Marston is used in workplace settings to improve communication and teamwork. If you are interested in finding out more about this area of personal and professional development, it is worth doing your research. Some profiling tests can be done online (free) where you can get a profile but to be able to understand the results properly another option is to find a licensed practitioner.

Chapter 6

Managing Nerves, Fear and Failure

'Thinking will not overcome fear but action will.'
W. Clement Stone

> In this chapter you will learn:
> ✓ What are the different zones of experience.
> ✓ How to manage your fear and nerves effectively by creating a peak state.
> ✓ How to recognise your language patterns and how your self-talk can affect your state of mind.
> ✓ The difference between nerves and fear and how to deal with them.
> ✓ How your brain works when you feel nervous or fearful and how it affects your performance for the assessments
> ✓ Strategies to combat nerves immediately.
> ✓ How to understand the impact your thoughts and beliefs can have on your self-confidence.
> ✓ What to do if you fail and how to deal with it and move forward.

Introduction

6.01 This chapter will share lawyers' common concerns and how nerves and fear may generally affect you. It will then provide you with an understanding of how they can affect your performance during the SQE. Towards the end of the chapter, I will look at how to deal with failure and what you can learn from it.

The level of pressure and stress you are likely to experience preparing for and sitting the SQE assessments will be a real test of your strength, ability and motivation to achieve your goal of qualifying as a solicitor in England and Wales.

You will also experience a whole range of emotions including feeling nervous (and at worst, fear) whilst studying for and during the assessments. Nerves can affect you at any stage and can be a large contributor to whether you pass or fail the SQE. When you do not know how to navigate your emotions it can be even more confusing and stressful. Therefore, it is essential you understand how your brain works when you experience heightened emotions (read Appendix 6A).

6.02 *Managing Nerves, Fear and Failure*

If you are used to doing exams in controlled and timed environments, then you will be familiar with the emotions experienced. The SQE Part 1 is computer-based and the SQE Part 2 is a mixture of computer-based and interactive assessments. More information about each of the assessments can be found in their respective chapters and are touched on in Chapter 1, The SQE Journey and Chapter 2, Preparing for the SQE.

The aim of this chapter is to give you some insight into how to deal with nerves, fear and failure effectively for the assessments.

The Different Zones of Experience

6.02 There are many zones of experience that people can go through but I want to highlight three that I think you should always have in mind. These are:

(1) the pain zone;
(2) the comfort zone;
(3) the stretch zone.

The visual below shows the three zones and how you might feel about being in that zone and what you might do. Everyone wants to be in the comfort zone – the happy zone. This is where you are happy and content, but the problem is you are not growing. You might think that you are happy and content to live in this zone forever; it is safe and you know what you are doing. That is rarely ever the case. If you really think about it, after some time (or even a very long time) it can become boring and monotonous.

The arrows show you the direction in which you usually end up in a zone. Most people are in the comfort zone until they have to do something new. Then they are most likely to enter the pain zone (out of panic) which is not helpful. Slowly, they enter the stretch zone and before you know it, after a lot of experience and practice, it becomes part of their comfort zone.

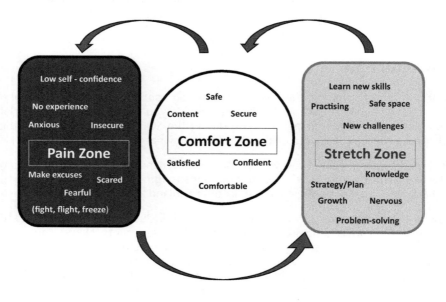

This is a good coaching tool that you can use when you have to do something outside your comfort zone by identifying which zone you are in and how to approach it. Without having a strategy or plan in mind about how to manage nerves and fear, they can affect your performance on the SQE and contribute to your failure.

The SQE will test your skills and knowledge of the law. Not all the skills will come to you naturally. This means you will have to move out of your comfort zone and work hard on them to pass the SQE. Whether you are a qualified and experienced lawyer or an aspiring solicitor (working), you may still feel out of your comfort zone doing something that does not fall within the remit of what you normally do in work. If you are a student you will be inexperienced in a range of skills and will have to practise these skills until they become comfortable (ie when you will feel confident about your ability to do them).

What is Confidence?

6.03 There is no strict definition that works because confidence is context dependent. However, just as courage cannot exist without fear or weakness, confidence cannot exist without doubt. Therefore, you can think of confidence as a skill that you practise when you doubt yourself or your ability. It helps you push past your fears and excuses.

The more you practise the stronger you will feel, and although your doubts may never disappear your confidence will continue to grow. You will start having more self-belief in your new skill or ability which will be evidenced by your actions (ie what you do). This will help you immensely for the assessments.

When you have to do something that is new and that you know very little about, ask yourself:

(1) What am I being asked to do (eg advocacy, draft a legal document, write a letter)?

(2) Which zone of experience am I in right now? (See the visual above.)

(3) What direction will I move in and what do I need to do to get there?

The chances are you will not be in your comfort zone, as this zone is the place where you know what you are doing and in which you feel safe.

If you find yourself in the pain zone straightaway (quite naturally) – this is not a helpful zone to be in for very long because it is being in the 'fear mindset'. It will not encourage you to learn and grow, but will instead give you permission to make excuses and validations for why you do not need to do it (which may be the case in real life, but not really a choice for the SQE). It is your brain's way of trying to protect you and keep you in your comfort zone doing what you are familiar with so you are safe. You might find yourself in the pain zone on the day of your assessments if you are unprepared. Read Appendix 6A to understand how our brain is hardwired to protect us.

You need to get into the stretch zone where you think with a 'growth mindset'. In this zone you can ask yourself questions such as, 'What is the benefit in doing this?' and 'How will learning this new skill make things easier for me?' For example, if

6.04 *Managing Nerves, Fear and Failure*

you do not like doing presentations (which means you will probably find advocacy challenging), watch an expert presenter, go on a presentation skills course or get a coach to work with you. Take small steps to build your confidence rather than immediately think 'I can't do this and it is hard'. Learning anything new will take time, practice and patience.

> *'The mind once stretched by a new idea, never returns to its original dimensions.'*
>
> **Ralph Waldo Emerson**

A small step in a supportive environment is much more manageable than trying to throw yourself in at an advanced level, where you would likely end up in the pain zone. It is hard enough that you need to know the law in a range of different practice areas and deliver it correctly and comprehensively. So make your life a little easier by getting some good experience for the skills part (without the law) and that will improve your self-confidence. For example, do a mini presentation on a topic of your choice to an expert and get some constructive feedback on it. You can then apply your skills to the law and you will have a very different experience. The exercise mentioned can be found in Chapter 5, Communication Skills, Verbal Communication (para **5.29**).

Getting into the stretch zone allows flexibility and growth to build your confidence at whatever skill you are learning. You will feel nerves in the stretch zone too, but in a safe and supportive environment they are manageable. You may make mistakes you will learn from and one day, that new skill will take you into your comfort zone enabling you to continually improve it by advancing your skill set. Even when you master a skill, you learn ways to improve it so the cycle of learning and growing affects your personal and professional development.

Controlling Nerves: Peak State

6.04 In attempting any exams, it is absolutely natural to feel nervous. However, you need to know how to manage your nerves. That means you have to have strategies that will help you deliver a superior performance on the day. How do you do that?

Superior performance scores come from being in a peak state and that starts with your body. So, when you are in a peak physical state your physiology and brain are operating at a high energy level. What you say to yourself (negative or positive self-talk) impacts how you feel directly and that shows up in your body language, which can affect your performance.

> *'The immune system is constantly eavesdropping to self talk.'*
>
> **Deepak Chopra**

Language Patterns

6.05 Nerves are a by-product of what we say to ourselves, which our brain processes and our body experiences. The brain cannot directly process negatives.

For example, if I said 'do not think of a pink elephant' it is hard not to think about one or visualise it. So, when you say something along the lines of 'I do not want to feel nervous' – the brain is processing it without paying attention to the negative word 'not' (ie 'I do want to feel nervous') and so the focus becomes feeling 'nervous'. The more you keep saying the sentence, the more you are, indirectly, reinforcing the feeling of nervousness because your brain is then routing itself to help you experience that state, through your physiology. You then experience nerves through your body (by how you use your body language, voice and words). You can read more about how your brain works in Appendix 6A and how it affects you in Chapter 5, Communication Skills, Intellectual Intelligence (IQ) and Emotional Intelligence (EQ) (para **5.30**).

When speaking to many lawyers about how they feel about the interactive oral assessments they usually say something like the first sentence below. When I ask them to re-phrase it into a positive sentence, I often hear something along the lines of the second sentence below.

First sentence　　　　　　　　　　　　　　**Second sentence**

Although the second sentence is good, the problem with it is that it is too general and needs to be contextualised. So, I ask them to drill down and be more specific. You need to ask yourself:

(1)　What do I specifically want to feel confident doing?

(2)　How will I know when I have achieved it?

Simply putting the word 'confident' in the sentence is not very helpful because it is too abstract and everyone's definition of what it means will be different. You have to ask yourself more specific questions to get clarity over what tangible 'evidence' you will look for in your body language, voice and words. Also identify how you want to feel and label the emotions so that when you feel them, you recognise it. Once you have identified what you need to *do*, in context, it is much easier for you to achieve it and feel confident about it.

For example, a better statement might be:

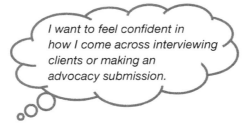

6.05 *Managing Nerves, Fear and Failure*

The above response deals with the first question above. You have to follow it up with the second question, so a good complete response would be:

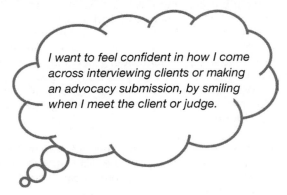

Then you start thinking about confidence in the context of interviewing clients or making an advocacy submission:

- what you need to do;
- what behaviours are required to come across as confident;
- who are the role models whose style you like and what is it that you specifically like about them:
    - what they do (their body language)?
    - how they communicate (use their vocals)?
    - what they say (the language used)?

Remember, when your 'self-talk' is phrased negatively or even when you are speaking to someone about the exam, you need to train your brain to recognise what language pattern you are using: is it 'away' language (what you do not want) or 'towards' language (what you do want). For example:

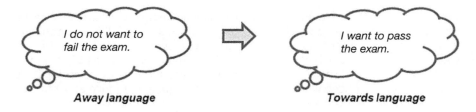

You will be surprised how small shifts in language patterns and thoughts can have a big impact on how you feel and how you come across (your state).

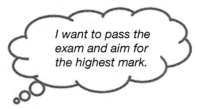

Towards language – more specific

Symptoms of Nerves or Fear

6.06 As long as you are learning, or trying new things or experiences, nerves will never go away and you will be outside of your comfort zone. This is part of the 'growth mindset' where you are continually stretching yourself to learn and improve yourself professionally and personally.

I often say, when you are about to do something that is important for the first time, if you do not feel nervous that is when you should be worried. Think of nerves as a good way of telling your body you are about to do something very important and it is time to focus. It is a bit like an alarm clock to wake you up and make you alert. The immediate association of feeling nervous usually has a negative connotation to it. However, if you turn it around to recognise that it can actually help you as a warning, it becomes an ally and has a positive connotation. This altered view directly impacts your physiology.

> *'The great thing ... in all education, is to make our nervous system our ally instead of our enemy.'*
>
> **William James**

Typical symptoms of feeling fearful or nervous are emitted throughout your body, such as:

- trembling;
- sweating;
- clammy palms;
- increased heartbeat;
- butterflies in your stomach; and
- shallow breathing.

Notice, how some of those same negative symptoms are what you can also feel when you are excited too (positive symptoms). Therefore, how you think about something has a major effect on how your brain and body responds to it. In effect, a smile can be the difference between feeling fear or feeling excited. Remember, positive thoughts and feelings are just as contagious as negative ones.

You may think managing nerves is easier said than done. However, it is possible to have strategies in place to help you when you can feel yourself getting nervous. The first step is recognising when it happens and what part of your body is reacting. Using the exercises suggested below, the Six Second Pause (para **6.11**) or breathing exercise (para **6.12**) can help.

A good idea is to get an expert to observe you doing a client interview and advocacy submission and provide you with constructive feedback. I would also suggest you video yourself, so you can watch what you do. Notice what your body language reveals and how your voice comes across:

- Do you smile?
- Does your posture contract and do your shoulders droop?

6.07 *Managing Nerves, Fear and Failure*

- Does your voice sound shaky or your throat dry up?
- Do your palms get sweaty or clammy?
- Do you find yourself clenching your hands together?
- Do your neck and face go blotchy?

My suggestion of recording yourself might sound painful because it can make you feel self-conscious, but you will get a real insight into what symptoms you are affected by so, when you get stressed, you can learn how to manage them to help you get into a peak state. It is also a good idea to record yourself wearing what you will wear for the oral assessments to see how you look and come across. More importantly, you can see how comfortable you feel with what you have chosen to wear.

The Brain

6.07 Lawyers like to understand tangible things and like to work with facts and evidence. So much emphasis and focus is placed on being clever (ie brainy) because learning the law is not easy. So naturally the focus is on intellectual intelligence – but this is just one part of your brain. You can read more about this in Chapter 5, Communication Skills, Intellectual Intelligence (IQ) and Emotional Intelligence (EQ) (para **5.30**).

Although you have one brain, it has multiple parts that are all deeply interconnected and work simultaneously. There are three parts of the brain that influence our thinking and the way we behave:

- the Brain Stem – responsible for your basic function (ie digestion and heart rate);
- the Limbic System – responsible for your memory, attention and emotions; and
- the Cerebral Cortex – responsible for speech, decision-making and problem solving.

Before you read Stored Patterns below it will be helpful to read Appendix 6A where Dr Sue McNamara of Six Seconds provides a brief and simplified explanation of what happens in the brain when our emotions 'hijack' our logical thinking. This can happen to you during the assessments.

Stored Patterns – Fight, Flight or Freeze

6.08 Some people experience fear which is stronger than feeling nervous and the symptoms are very similar, but heightened. Often you feel fearful where your brain perceives a threat in an environment and your reaction can be any one of three things: fight, flight or freeze. They may be reactions that are based on previous experiences.

- ***Fight***

6.09 Fight is when you take on the threat to protect or defend yourself and you become defensive. For example, in client interviewing or advocacy, if you feel challenged by the client or judge, your limbic system will perceive it as a threat and

Stored Patterns – Fight, Flight or Freeze **6.11**

let your amygdala know which will react based on a stored pattern. So, you may react in a defensive manner (ie use more curt, direct or unprofessional language) if you have felt challenged in a similar way in the past.

- *Flight*

6.10 Flight is when you run away from the threat or try to escape. For example, you might have a panic attack or feel so emotionally overwhelmed you decide to leave the assessment or do not turn up on the day.

- *Freeze*

6.11 Freeze is when you become immobile, you may have heard the saying 'scared stiff' where your body will immediately react by stiffening up and your muscles tense. For example, you are in the middle of your advocacy submission and the judge asks you a question and you do not know the answer. You may freeze and panic. Your brain has perceived the situation as a threat, meaning it needs immediate attention, so the amygdala reacts (it may or may not be a stored pattern) but you freeze (your body and muscles tense up). The result of this situation can derail how you perform for the rest of your submission because you cannot focus on getting back on track.

You might be thinking, why is there so much emphasis on how the brain works? The aim is to get you to understand what happens if you experience a 'fight, flight or freeze' moment on the day of the assessments. No one prepares or plans for it to happen. So, if it happens to you, you might not understand how it happened (emotionally) so you may naturally try to 'label' the experience (logically). Understanding helps you gain perspective of what happened and helps you navigate your emotions.

What is the strategy to manage feeling fearful or nervous? Engage a Six Second Pause, where the cerebral (pre-frontal) cortex is engaged in a six-second window, by recalling a challenging task. Anything that engages logic. This has to be practised prior to the assessment that is making you nervous but at the same time it cannot be so easy that it can be recalled without thought.

Six Second Pause Exercise

When you start to feel nervous, think of a challenging task (if it is not challenging it will not work).

For example:

- Counting backwards from 10 in a foreign language
- Doing a tough maths challenge
- Name 10 countries beginning with 'S' (or another letter if that is too easy)

Add your own tasks – but make sure they are challenging for you.

Reflection

How nervous do you feel immediately after doing the task?

6.12 *Managing Nerves, Fear and Failure*

Another good strategy to manage nerves or fear is thinking about your breathing. It is something you do naturally every day, so you may not give it much attention. Learning a good breathing technique will help you calm down and relax your physiology.

Breathing

6.12 Breathing deeply is one of the most important things you can do to gain control of your physiology. It is highly effective if you train yourself to know when to do it and how to do it properly. Breathing patterns vary with each emotion (joy, stress, sadness, fear etc). For example, if you are stressed or nervous, your breathing is likely to become shallow and you will feel as though you are breathing higher in your chest.

Conscious deep breathing, at the exact point you recognise the shift in your body language or voice can make all the difference to how you perform on the day of your assessments. If you practise consistently, your body will naturally change its state and become calmer and more relaxed.

As you go about your day-to-day life, you do not consciously stop and think about whether or not you are breathing, you just do it. Most of us have forgotten how to breathe properly or appreciate how crucial it is to the way we use our voice and speak. How you breathe changes depending on how you are feeling.

You will only think about your breathing if it becomes irregular or does not feel normal. So, focusing on your breathing is a good technique to distract the brain when you feel nervous. Basically, your mind cannot think about feeling nervous or fearful when you consciously take deep breaths or when you express gratitude (this is also a technique used to shift the feeling of fear). Expressing gratitude is thinking about what you are grateful and thankful for and, whilst focusing on that, you cannot focus on fear at the same time.

> *'Being aware of your breath forces you into the present moment ... Conscious breathing stops your mind.'*
> **Eckhart Tolle**

Therefore, this is a great tool to use because you can do it anywhere and at any time. It allows you to compose and centre yourself. I suggest that you start taking a few deep breaths before you practise your oral assessments and notice how you feel. You want to link that feeling of calm and control by deep breathing (as opposed to 'regular' breathing), when you start to feel nervous. When it happens, you have to immediately connect the two to shift your physiology and state (energy). Getting used to conscious breathing at the right time, takes patience and practice. Initially, you may feel awkward, embarrassed, giggle, and find it a bit strange. You might question how many times you have to do it, for it to actually work and when you do not see the results immediately you might want to give up. However, if you persevere and do it consistently, you will experience the calm effect (through the change in your physiology) and this is what you need to help you on the days of your assessments when you start to panic or feel nervous.

Think about your habits, which are things you do without having to think about them: some might be good ones and others not so good. A habit is something you do not question and end up doing automatically. Usually, a habit will only come to your conscious attention when you want to change it.

You want to create a new habit (conscious deep breathing), so you do it automatically when you get nervous.

'Breath is the link between mind and body.'
Dan Brule

Below is a good breathing exercise that can be done anywhere and at any time. It is so simple, yet, it does take some practice. Once you know how the breathing pattern works and how your body should be responding to it, when you inhale or exhale it changes your physical and mental state.

If you are not used to doing any breathing exercises, you may find it strange at first and need to put more effort into it by doing it for a longer period of time, just to get used to it. I suggest trying to do it daily and consistently, until it feels natural. Once you start doing it more frequently, you will start to feel the positive effects of it more quickly, which will help you for the assessments.

You may be thinking that you do not have the luxury of time on your side to do the deep breathing exercise. It can be done in seconds and once you know what to do, it becomes much quicker, easier and more effective – regardless of where you are. The results are instantaneous too because you are familiar with the technique.

Breathing Exercise

This exercise can be done standing up or sitting down. Initially, I would suggest you do it sitting down. When comfortable with the technique, you can try it standing up.

Sit on a chair, sit up straight with your back against the chair and feet flat on the ground. Your shoulders should be straight and your hands should be relaxed in front of you (the palms of your hands facing down and resting on your thighs).

You should breathe in deeply through your nose (inhale) and breathe out slowly through your mouth (exhale):

- Inhale for four counts (Inhale, 2, 3, 4)
- Hold your breath (Hold, 2, 3, 4)
- Exhale for four counts (Exhale 2, 3, 4)
- Hold your breath (Hold, 2, 3, 4)
- Repeat the deep breathing cycle.

You may need to do this many times until your mind and body sync. Initially you may need to do it more frequently to familiarise yourself with the technique until you get used to it.

6.13 *Managing Nerves, Fear and Failure*

From my experience of working with lawyers, it is usually the oral assessments they feel most nervous about and this breathing exercise helps them. I suggest you do the exercise before the client interview and advocacy to help calm and centre yourself.

Below are the three most common fears shared by some lawyers:

- fear of failure
- fear of the client or judge
- fear of the unknown.

Fear of Failure

6.13 Fear of failure is always contextualised. It is something that most people experience when they are about to do something that feels uncomfortable or scary because it is new for them.

Alternatively, fear of failure can come from your past experiences. For example, where you may have failed exams so you feel there is a chance that it could happen again. Although that is a possibility for everyone, that does not mean there is a higher chance of it happening to you.

If you are fearful because of your past experiences, you can have a plan and strategy to identify what went wrong and what you will do differently, so it can help you prepare better. However, you must realise that there are no two identical experiences. So, although it might make you feel better to have a strategy and plan (that is definitely a good thing), there is still an equal chance of you passing and failing – which is not related to your past experience.

- ***Fear of Failure – Direct Experience***

6.14 This is where you have done something in the past and it did not go well for you. Whatever you felt at the time, you believe and feel that failure may happen again. You believe that you will experience those same (often intense) emotions. In reality, there is nothing to truly suggest that a repeat of the past will happen in the future.

- ***Fear of Failure – Indirect Experience***

6.15 This is fear of failure by indirect association and happens where you have watched someone else do something or someone tells you about their awful experience. What you see or are told affects you emotionally (indirectly). You did not experience it personally; but you felt so relieved that it did not happen to you. However, when you think about having to do something similar, you immediately remember it and it feels very real.

A common fear shared by many lawyers is a lack of sufficient knowledge of the law. It is easy to say you need to work harder so you know it. In fact, that type of response is not very helpful because most lawyers do work hard. If you do fail on

Fear of Failure **6.15**

your knowledge of the law, you may realise that you did not dedicate enough time to study because of your personal and professional commitments or your level of experience was inadequate. You can read more around this in Chapter 2, Preparing for the SQE, Studying for the SQE (para **2.28**) and about each assessment in their respective chapters.

Feeling fear is different to feeling nervous. Although the symptoms might be the same, they can vary and make you feel outside of your comfort zone. For example, meeting clients might be something you do or have experience of doing, but you feel more nervous or change what you normally do because you are being assessed.

Sometimes people do not know the difference between nerves and fear and use the terms interchangeably. Although there are similar symptoms, being nervous is much more manageable. Therefore, it is important to label your emotions correctly, because all emotions are data and this data will allow you to understand your feelings better and help you work out the correct response required.

The fear of failure comes down to your attitude and how you want to think about a situation. For example, from a skills perspective, if you have done a client interview or presentation that went badly, those experiences happened and are in the past. You can definitely learn from them, but they cannot be identically replicated. That means, even if you did a client interview or presentation again and it did not go well, it would not be identical to the previous experience. However, your belief about not being very good can become stronger and be reinforced. Your beliefs are very powerful and the stronger they get the more convinced you become that they are true. So, you have to keep your beliefs in check by reassuring yourself that just because the previous experiences were not good, it does not mean all your future experiences will necessarily be the same. The more you reinforce 'fixed' beliefs the stronger they become and that can then become your reality. Therefore, it does not make sense to worry about failing something that you have not yet done. Do not let your past experiences dictate your present or your future.

> ***'Fear is past based and anxiety is future based. Neither exist in the present.'***
> **Neeta Halai**

I am not suggesting you ignore past failures. On the contrary, I am suggesting that you put them into perspective by recognising:

- what you did;
- why it went wrong; and
- what you can do to ensure you do it better next time.

You should learn from your failures (the past) and use what you learn from them (in the present moment) to move forward (the future).

It is an unachievable expectation to set yourself up to know '*all*' of the law. Of course, you need to study it diligently and in depth for the SQE Part 1 and 2. However, you have to contextualise it accordingly and use what study formats and styles work best for you. Putting so much pressure on yourself to learn 'all' the law can be counter-productive. In trying to satisfy this unachievable goal you might quickly get through

6.16 *Managing Nerves, Fear and Failure*

the materials on a subject to feel better about covering it all, but not understand it fully. Covering everything might make you feel better but it weakens your overall position for the assessments, increasing your chances of failure.

Remember, worrying about failing or past failures will lower your energy and ability to concentrate. So, instead of worrying or feeling guilty about what you should or could have done, focus on what you need to do now for the future.

Fear of the Client or Judge

6.16 This fear is more relevant for the oral assessments for the SQE Part 2 which assesses you equally on the law and skills. Namely, the client interviewing and advocacy assessments.

Fear of the client or judge is often two-fold. It is fear and worry about what they think of you and what they might ask you. The more you focus on what they think about you, the more self-conscious you become in the situation. They may pick up on your body language which will show you are nervous (even if you do not think you are showing it). It is normal to feel nervous initially, but the nerves should disappear quite quickly after you start to allow yourself to deliver a confident client interview or advocacy submission. Fear of the unknown is what they might ask you around questions that you do not know the answer to and how you will come across or be perceived. This is looked at in more detail below in para **6.19**.

- ### *Client Interviewing – The Client*

6.17 You might feel anxious because you do not know what type of client you will be meeting. You have to work with the information you have in your preparation stage and that might offer some clues. Regardless, with practice and experience you should feel confident in how you will deal with any type of client. Chapter 8, Client Interviewing Skills looks at the assessment in more detail and below in para **6.22** you can read more about the fear experienced around client interviewing.

- ### *Advocacy – The Judge*

6.18 You might feel anxious because you do not know what the judge will be like. That should not really matter, but it is human nature to feel nervous. Allow yourself to feel the nerves (they are a good ally) and feel confident that you have a structure in place to know what you have to do in the time allocated. Also, remind yourself of any prepared phrases for when you do not know the answer in case the judge asks you any questions. Chapter 10, Advocacy looks at the assessment in more detail and below in para **6.23** you can read more around the fear experienced around advocacy.

Fear of the Unknown

6.19 Another common concern among lawyers is a fear of the unknown. This can be fear of not knowing the law or how to deal with an unexpected situation.

Fear of the Unknown **6.19**

Fear of the unknown is very natural and you may see it as a 'threat' because you do not know what to expect from the assessments and the client or judge.

For the SQE Part 1 and the SQE Part 2 written assessments – it can be less daunting and intimidating because it is something you experience on your own. However, for the oral assessments the fear of the unknown involves another person so this adds more pressure which makes you feel even more nervous (eg 'I do not know what they will be like or what they will think of me').

The client or the judge can make you feel nervous because they may ask questions you did not expect. A client's behaviour may be more unpredictable than a judge's (eg vulnerable, upset or anxious etc). This can have the following effects:

- you lose your train of thought;
- you forget what you are saying;
- you miss something they say;
- you panic and start waffling in trying to answer their question when you do not know the answer.

These situations occur out of the blue and the shock of feeling out of control or being caught off guard can affect your confidence (as explained above in para **6.08** Stored Patterns – Fight Flight or Freeze).

In these situations, my advice is that you need to have a strategy to know what to do if it happens and to get comfortable with the idea that it could happen in real life too and not just in the assessments. Having good strategies to deal with unexpected situations confidently can take the pressure off you. It takes real skill and practice not just to know what to do (in theory), but actually do it (in practice). For example:

- recognise when you become stressed and use the Six Second Pause and deep breathing exercises (as appropriate);
- adapt your language so that the client or judge can relate to it;
- come up with a credible response if you do not know the answer to a question. For example:
  - for client interviewing – tell the client you will find out and get back to them after the meeting;
  - for advocacy – tell the judge you do not have the authority/rules in front of you so cannot give them an answer now.

Chapter 8, Client Interviewing Skills and Chapter 10, Advocacy, have examples of what you can say in the assessments when caught off guard.

The last thing you want to do is reinforce a failure for something you are about to do. It would be like running a horror movie in your mind where all the questions are ones you cannot answer, or the client interview or advocacy goes horribly wrong. Your body language will change to reflect your thoughts and recreate those feelings and emotions that support your thinking – you do not want to be the star of this movie!

So, imagine running the same horror movie in your mind but you visualise yourself this time:

6.20 *Managing Nerves, Fear and Failure*

- wearing a smart suit and how you look (your appearance);
- reading the questions and getting through the instructions in a calm and focused manner;
- doing your advocacy submission confidently and persuasively;
- looking confident in your comportment, gestures and facial expressions (your body language);
- sounding confident when you speak (your voice);
- greeting the client with a smile and engaging authentically whilst taking their instructions; and
- writing your structured attendance note in legible handwriting.

The above is the type of movie in which you would like to play the starring role! The power of your imagination can become your reality. Now, with this type of thinking, your body language, voice, feelings and emotions are congruent with your physiology. You are in a peak state and that helps you perform at your best.

Remember, the past and the future do not exist. So, feeling anxiety, stress or fear about what you have done (in the past) or something that might happen (in the future) is a waste of your energy. Only the present moment (now) exists, so imagine how you want it to be and your thoughts and feelings can actually reinforce it and make it your reality.

It comes back to controlling your nerves by being in a peak state. When you are in a peak state you can become the architect of your future.

'Fears are nothing more than a state of mind.'
Napoleon Hill

Below I will focus on how to manage your fear or nerves specifically for each part of the SQE.

SQE Part 1 – Functional Legal Knowledge

• *Multiple Choice Test*

6.20 This part of the exam will just test you on the law. It requires you to have control of your emotions by remaining calm and not panicking when you read a question that you do not know the answer to immediately or which causes confusion. Even in a panicked or stressed state, you need to keep an eye on the time allocated to each question and be disciplined enough to know when you have to move to the next question. You can always flag the question to come back to it. You do not want to jeopardise your chances by running out of time and not finishing the test.

When you panic, your body reacts and you need to have a strategy in place to do something different, very quickly. When your body is stressed, you are not performing in a peak state. Remember the breathing exercise to calm you down and help your physiology return to its normal state. It might even help if you close your eyes (not look at the computer screen) whilst taking a deep breath, and when you open your eyes, you re-read the question and choose an answer without over-thinking it. Those precious few seconds looking away from the computer screen and taking a deep breath, will make a difference to your state. It will make you feel calmer even if you do not know the answer.

I know time is of the essence in the assessments so you do not have the luxury of it on your side to spend a lot of time doing a breathing exercise. However, a few seconds is all it takes and it can help your physiology calm down so you feel more in control and can focus on the next question.

Chapter 2, Preparing for the SQE (para **2.36**) and Chapter 3, Functional Legal Knowledge (FLK) Assessments give you practical tips and more details on how to study for the multiple choice assessments and how to approach them.

SQE Part 2 – Practical Legal Skills

6.21 The SQE Part 2 exam consists of 16 assessments that test your legal knowledge through your oral and written skills.

As I mentioned above, it is usually the oral parts of the assessment that most people feel daunted by, so I will focus on only these areas below. My advice and strategy for the written part of these assessments (case and matter analysis, legal writing, legal drafting and legal research) is essentially the same as for the SQE Part 1 above because they are also computer-based assessments. You can also read more about each of the written assessments in their respective chapters for more details.

If you have no legal work experience or very little experience for the oral assessments, you are most likely to find them challenging. I coach many experienced lawyers who all share how nervous they feel about the oral assessments. Therefore, you want to have a good idea of what you can expect in the assessments. If your legal work experience is good-quality you might not cover all the practice areas of the law you are assessed on, but your experience will definitely help you. Read more in Chapter 4, Qualifying Work Experience, Good-Quality Work Experience (para **4.22**).

- *Fear of the Unknown for Client Interviewing*

6.22 It is natural to feel nervous going into the client interview and knowing you are being assessed adds more pressure, even if you are experienced.

The fear is primarily because you do not know what type of client you will encounter (ie demanding, upset or vulnerable) and what they may ask you. The fear is usually centred on not knowing the law or how to react confidently if the client asks you a question that you do not know the answer to or is unexpected.

If you are a qualified lawyer or have experience in client interviewing, just because it is an assessment does not mean you should necessarily be doing anything too different from what you do in practice. This is where your natural skill set and experience, should give you an advantage.

6.22 *Managing Nerves, Fear and Failure*

Having said that, many experienced lawyers I have coached treat the interview differently because it is an assessment. They sometimes forget to introduce themselves, do not engage in any small talk, act and behave very formally (because they want to come across as more professional). Their behaviour often comes across as cold and has the opposite effect of trying to build rapport and trust with the client.

When we discuss exactly what they do in practice when meeting clients and they demonstrate it, the whole introduction and exchange is different – it is more human and connected. Their body language is more relaxed (less stiff) and their facial expressions are softer. They come across as more natural and their nerves have disappeared by the time they start getting into the main part of the interview. That is a good strategy to remember if you do client interviews; do what you do by way of a greeting or introduction for the assessment. If you are a foreign jurisdiction lawyer, you want to make sure it is culturally appropriate. You can read more about this in Chapter 5, Communication Skills, Cultural Appropriateness (para **5.20**).

So, the strategy here is to behave as you would in practice (naturally you will feel more confident). If you do not have experience of client interviewing, you need to watch how it is done and practise it. Think about it in three stages:

(1) the introduction;

(2) the main body of the interview; and

(3) how to conclude it.

Having a structure will help you feel less nervous and more in control. There is more information in Chapter 8, Client Interviewing Skills which complements Chapter 5, Communication Skills.

During the interview, there will be an exchange of information. The client may ask you questions that are unexpected and may be unrelated to the matter. The first thing the client will notice after asking the question is your facial expression (body language). If you do not know what to say, you will have a panicked and startled expression (like a deer caught in the headlights), followed by a rambling attempt to answer, will not make you feel or come across confidently. What you might perceive as an awkward silence can actually be a useful pause where it gives you time to provide a more composed response and come across with credibility and confidence. It may also mean that the client adds some more information to what they have just said which could help you answer their question or ask a question in response.

If it is any comfort, regardless of the years of experience, you can never predict all your client's questions. Sometimes they are not related to what you are advising on and at other times they might be related, but you might not know the answer. More experienced lawyers may have the confidence to know how to handle this type of situation in practice. However, even they often do not do what they would do in practice because it is an assessment. It is natural that you may not know the answer to every question (even if it is an assessment) but you can learn how to deal with it so it puts less pressure on you. You should re-read Chapter 5, Communication Skills, Trust (para **5.21**) which explains what to do if you do not know the answer to a question, but still want the client to trust you and instruct you on their matter.

If you are a subject matter expert and very experienced at doing client interviews, you will already have a level of confidence. However, when you are assessed on a practice area of law that is outside your expertise, it can sometimes make you feel even more insecure because you are so used to confidently working in a subject matter that is within your comfort zone. The one advantage you have is being able to draw on your experience.

To make the client interview as authentic as possible, you might get a situation where the client asks you something outside the remit of the practice area you are assessed on (it would be part of their instructions). This is intentional to see how you will deal with it and whether you respond in a professional manner.

In real life, you have no idea what your client may be going through so if the client is a little demanding, upset or less talkative, you still have a duty to be professional. You have to try to understand what they want to do and offer them some preliminary advice (where appropriate). Remember, their behaviour is nothing personal against you.

First impressions count and a client ultimately wants a lawyer they feel they can trust to do what they want done, competently, efficiently and effectively. Managing your nerves will allow you to accomplish the key objective of winning the client over.

- ### *Fear of the Unknown for Advocacy*

6.23 Most people fear or do not like doing presentations and you can look at advocacy as a form of presentation but with courtroom formalities, so the language used is much more formal. If you are not a litigation lawyer or familiar with courtroom experience, then doing an advocacy submission can be out of your comfort zone and be a daunting experience which makes you nervous. Doing an oral presentation, in some respects, is easier because the language used is more reflective of how you might speak to a client. For example, you may state your own personal opinion in an oral presentation but you would not do that in an advocacy submission.

The assessments are done in a 'normal' room (not set up like a courtroom) so this can make it a little less intimidating.

> *'According to most studies, people's number one fear is public speaking. Number two is death.'*
> **Jerry Seinfeld**

The quote is a testament to how the majority of people generally feel about doing presentations. This seems to be the case regardless of the size of the audience or the style of the presentation (formal or informal). Having said that, the more you do them, the more confident you become and the easier it becomes to refine your presentation style. There is always room for improvement, but the whole experience of doing them does get a little easier if you practise, practise and practise. You will naturally develop a style that suits your personality, or see people who are role models whose presentation style you wish to imitate. They do presentations in a style that appeals to you and you can relate to, so you want to do it more like them.

The fear is usually focused on not knowing an answer to a question asked by the judge. They are entitled to ask you questions if they need clarification on a

6.23 *Managing Nerves, Fear and Failure*

point of law or something you have said. They can ask questions at any stage of the submission and will not get into a dialogue with you to challenge what you say. They may make a decision about your submission (if it forms a part of your instructions). It is impossible to try to guess every type of question you may be asked and by trying to do that you will increase your stress levels. It is a much better idea to practise a response or phrase that you can say confidently (and adapt it) when you do not know the answer to a question.

Remember, you still want to come across as confident and credible – which is possible even if you do not know the answer. Do not immediately start speculating or making assumptions, because you feel that you have to say something to try to answer the question to come across as confident; it can reduce your credibility. Sometimes, a short pause (known as the three-second silence), before you speak, is much more powerful. You can also avoid the pressure of 'silence' if you want time to think of a response by asking the judge for permission to look at your notes. Chapter 10, Advocacy, Handling Difficult Questions (para **10.12**) provides you with examples of what you can say. You will be marked down for not knowing the law, but marked up for using appropriate language and behaviour by demonstrating skilfully and professionally how to handle such a situation.

In a state of fear you could perceive the situation as a threat and end up in 'fight' mode and get defensive in your response. Never be rude, arrogant or sarcastic. You might think you would never do that, but sometimes when the pressure is on, you never know how you might respond or realise that is how you come across. It is absolutely fine to be assertive but your body language needs to be aligned with that response. So, it is important to practise your communication skills and understand how to handle your emotions and behavioural patterns.

No matter how nervous you feel, remember to smile softly at the assessor. It will immediately affect your physiology and is more likely to help rather than hinder you. The assessor is there to assess your performance and they are rigorously trained to do so. You want to make a good first impression and a smile will help you do that with confidence. Of course, the judge may not reciprocate but do not read into it.

Below are Top Ten Tips specifically for managing nerves and fear for client interviewing and advocacy.

Managing Nerves and Fear for Client Interviewing – Top Ten Tips

(1) If you do client interviews at work, introduce yourself in the assessment as you would at work.

(2) If you do not have experience of client interviews, you need to watch how they are done and practise doing them.

(3) Accept you will never know all the law or what the client could ask you and it will put less pressure on you.

(4) Have set phrases or sentences you can use if you do not know the answer to a question.

(5) A superior performance comes from being in a peak state. Learn how to manage your state.

(6) Have strategies to recognise what you are feeling when nervous and what parts of your body language and vocals are affected.

(7) The breathing and Six Second Pause exercises can recalibrate your state from feeling nervous to feeling calm.

(8) Always show empathy rather than defensiveness when you do not know an answer or you feel like the client is challenging you.

(9) Always be professional and calm, even if the client does not behave in the same way.

(10) Remember, first and last impressions count.

Managing Nerves and Fear for Advocacy – Top Ten Tips

(1) Practice is the key. There is no substitute for getting expert constructive feedback and then working on it and practising.

(2) Record yourself so you have tangible evidence to see how you progress.

(3) Recognise what your habits are when you get nervous and have a strategy for how you will deal with them.

(4) Superior performance comes from being in a peak state. Use the visualisation technique to imagine how you want the presentation to go.

(5) Learn from your failures and do not let them hold you back, but let them help you move forward.

(6) If you are not used to doing advocacy, practise reading out submissions aloud, get used to the language that might not come naturally to you.

(7) Breathing deeply is key to helping you remain calm and controlled.

(8) Your body language, voice and words are affected by your breathing.

(9) A smile confuses your brain about whether you are feeling fearful and nervous or happy.

(10) Remember, positive thoughts and feelings are as contagious as negative ones.

Failing the SQE Assessments

6.24 No-one wants to fail. However, it can happen and when it does it can be upsetting and you will experience a rollercoaster of emotions. It is best to let the emotions out rather than suppress them. This may take a while and it may not happen all at once. It can be quite cathartic to speak to someone or write down how you feel in the moment. If you speak to someone, ideally, that person should be a good listener who is not trying to offer you solutions, but just hears you out.

6.25 *Managing Nerves, Fear and Failure*

What you decide to do is the next step after you have had a chance to navigate your emotions. This is because you will probably be feeling low in confidence and self-esteem and may not make the best decisions for you in a heightened emotional state.

If you fail the SQE Part 1, there will be a breakdown of the results for each day. It is often less traumatic than failing the SQE Part 2 because that involves an interactive part to the way you are assessed which usually makes people feel more nervous.

For SQE Part 2, there is a breakdown of results against the Assessment Criteria. If you fail by a very small margin, it is more painful. If you have worked on your skills with an expert then often the scores for skills are high (which may be a reason why you failed marginally) and it was the law that let you down. When you know what areas you need to focus on (law or skills) it can help you decide what you want to do.

- **How to work out the SQE Part 2 results**

6.25 It can be very confusing when you see the breakdown of your results for all 16 assessments. Each assessment is graded against the relevant Assessment Criteria and you should read the Marking and Standard Setting Policy for more details.

For each assessment a percentage score for 'Skills' and a percentage score for 'Law' is calculated from the Assessment Criteria.

The average from your 'Skills' and 'Law' scores together provide a percentage score for an assessment. The final mark is the average score achieved across all the assessments.

- **Continue with the SQE**

6.26 For SQE Part 1, if you failed both days (FLK1 and FLK2) then it might be a good idea to re-evaluate your understanding of the law. If your scores were low do not rush to resit quickly.

For SQE Part 2, I suggest you sit down and do an autopsy on what happened and work out where you went wrong. You can see exactly how you did in each assessment and the practice areas of law. However, this is not a reflection of how you might do in future attempts but a good starting point.

You may realise that you did not dedicate enough time to study because of your personal and professional commitments. You may have realised your knowledge of the law or your level of experience was inadequate.

Do not beat yourself up, but recognise that what is done is done and you cannot change it. Hindsight offers lots of different things, which your real situation, at the time, did not allow. You would have done it exactly the same way, at the time. So, do not feel bad or guilty because it is not helpful. Concentrate on what is important, which is creating a new study plan (if that works for you). You should re-read Chapter 2, Preparing for the SQE, A Study Plan (para **2.25**) for guidance.

• Unsure about Continuing with the SQE

6.27 If you are questioning whether you want to continue with the SQE journey, it is a good idea to take some time out and have a break before you make your final decision. You may still feel raw and emotional about it, but in a better frame of mind you will make the right decision for you.

In Appendix 6B, I have included some powerful coaching questions I use when someone is undecided and needs some clarity as to what they want to do (not what they should do). These questions are ones you can attempt on your own or work through with someone else who might understand the coaching process. Some questions may lead to others not included so the flow of questions should be natural and connected to your answers. They do not have to be asked in any particular order.

If you decide to quit and feel like you do not want to continue on the SQE journey, there is no shame in it and it is your decision that is right for you. What counts is that you continue to carry on and do whatever you decide and move forward. Rather than see your failure as a waste of time, you should see it as an experience and you always learn something from your experiences. Also, the knowledge and skills you have learnt are not wasted and may be useful in ways you never imagined.

• Resits

6.28 If you fail SQE Part 1 or SQE Part 2 you will have two further opportunities to resit within a six-year period from the date you sat the assessments.

- **SQE Part 1**

    You will only be required to re-sit the FLK part of the assessment you failed (ie if you fail day one but pass day two, you only resit day one and vice versa). If you fail both days, you must re-sit them both in the same assessment window. See the table in Chapter 3, Functioning Legal Knowledge (FLK) Assessments (para **3.04**) for details of the subjects covered for each day.

- **SQE Part 2**

    The SQE Part 2 is classed as one single exam regardless of the fact that it is made up of 16 assessments. See the tables in Chapter 1, The SQE Journey (paras **1.18** and **1.22**) for details of the oral and written assessments.

If you use your maximum attempts within the six years, you will need to wait until the six-year period expires before you can re-apply. After six years, you can try again but any previous passes cannot be carried forward so, in effect, you have to start again.

> *'Success is not final, failure is not fatal: it is the courage to continue that counts.'*
>
> **Winston Churchill**

Managing Nerves, Fear and Failure – Top Ten Tips

(1) Understand the different zones and always aim to go from the comfort zone to the stretch zone and avoid staying in the panic zone.

(2) You want to be in a peak state when learning something new.

(3) It is natural not to be good at everything and practice is what makes you confident.

(4) Nerves are good, they are your ally – an alarm bell telling you it is time to focus.

(5) The breathing exercise and Six Second Pause exercise are great when you are becoming nervous or fearful.

(6) Practise, practise, practise is the key for mastering skills; start without the law.

(7) Do not let fear and anxiety dictate your past and future, they do not exist in the present moment.

(8) If you have failed SQE Part 2 do an autopsy on the areas you need to improve on and the areas you did well on.

(9) Do not dwell on failure, it may scar you, but it does not define you.

(10) Failure is just feedback telling you to do it again differently.

Chapter 6

Managing Nerves, Fear and Failure: Appendices

Appendix 6A: The Brain

Below is a brief and simple explanation provided by Dr Sue McNamara of Six Seconds which will be useful for you to read alongside the chapter.

> There is a lot written about the triune brain that is false. It is true however that the different regions of the brain, with different functions, are deeply connected.
>
> ***The Brain Stem***
>
> This part of your brain is responsible for your autonomic nervous system, our basic functions that are essential for protection and survival, such as respiration, digestion and heart rate.
>
> ***The Limbic System***
>
> This is a complex structure which deals with memory, attention and emotions. Within the 'limbic brain' there are three very important parts:
>
> - *The Hippocampus*
>
>   Its job is to pay attention to what is going on around you and what information is coming in from your senses.
>
> - *The Thalamus*
>
>   It is like an 'air traffic controller' within the brain. It has many functions including relaying sensory signals, directing attention and reactions.
>
> - *The Amygdala*
>
>   It is the brain's reaction centre and the source of our fight, flight or freeze reactions.
>
>   When the amygdala perceives a threat, it bypasses the 'thinking' part of our brain to trigger an emotional reaction, which then fires off messages that put our body into fight, flight or freeze mode. This causes an amygdala (emotional) hijack, which causes our heart rate to increase, blood rushes to the core and we are in survival mode! Our brain has perceived a threat and therefore needs immediate attention

Managing Nerves, Fear and Failure: Appendices

at this point. This happens even when there is no real danger, just perceived, for example in an exam situation.

The Cerebral Cortex

The cortex forms the outer layer of the brain and is responsible for synthesis, analysis, logic, language and symbols. This is the region that is the logical part of your brain which includes speech, decision making, problem solving as well as abstract thinking and self-reflection.

How Does the Brain Communicate With Each Part?

The brain does something called routing. Within the brain there are two routes: the long route and the short cut.

- *Long route*

    If you follow the long route the stimulus comes into your brain, via your senses. The thalamus sends the information to the cerebral cortex part of the brain to establish what you think or to access information. The signals then go to the limbic system to establish how we feel about the situation.

- *Short route*

    When our brain perceives a threat it reacts to protect us and hence sends the signals to the limbic system (the amygdala) to react quickly to survive. Depending on biology and experience that protection results in us fighting, fleeing or freezing. You are literally hardwired to react that way to defend against threat.

Appendix 6B: Failing the SQE Assessments

- ### *Uncertain about Continuing with the SQE*

This is a good coaching tool of powerful questions. Some are generic and some I have tailored to the SQE. They are in no particular order. They are designed to help you think about what you want to do, help you make a decision with clarity and also think about answers you did not think you had.

Do not rush through the questions; some will be easier than others and those you struggle to answer the most will usually be the ones that need the most attention – so persevere and do not give up so quickly on the question. Some answers may result in other questions, just go with it and see where the process takes you. These lists of questions are non-exhaustive and other questions that arise may be pertinent to you.

There is no standard right or wrong answer, just what is best for you. You may find it beneficial to work with a coach or someone else who understands the coaching process who can support you.

(1)   What are the pros and cons of continuing with the SQE?

(2)   What are the pros and cons of *not* continuing with the SQE?

Appendix 6B

(3) Which pros and cons list am I drawn to the most?
(4) What do I want?
(5) What could I do if nothing stopped me getting what I want?
(6) How can I laugh and take pleasure in what I do?
(7) What are my expectations here?
(8) Where am I being too hard on myself?
(9) What can I learn from this?
(10) What questions haven't I asked?
(11) What do I pay attention to?
(12) What are my interests and passions?
(13) What is blocking me from taking action?
(14) What other choices do I have?
(15) Who do I admire who can help me here?
(16) How will I know it is time to act?
(17) What actions do I need to take to help me?
(18) What am I doing right now?
(19) What is the positive intention behind my decision?
(20) Am I following my path or someone else's?

Chapter 7

Writing in Professional English

'If you can't explain it simply, you don't understand it well enough.'
Albert Einstein

In this chapter you will learn:
- ✓ How to identify your writing style: passive or active voice.
- ✓ How to recognise and understand the different effects of using punctuation.
- ✓ How to use plain English (as opposed to legal jargon).
- ✓ How to avoid misusing words.
- ✓ The positive impact of a good layout and structure.
- ✓ The power of the Four Cs to improve your writing style.
- ✓ The importance of proof-reading.

Introduction

7.01 This chapter will focus on the English language and will be a refresher for many of you regarding what you need to think about when writing in plain English. The chapter will not focus on technical legal drafting that may be required for a legal document (see Chapter 13), but more around how to write in 'clear, precise, concise and acceptable language', which is a requirement for all the written assessments in the SQE.

Other than the handwritten attendance note, which forms part of the client interviewing assessment, all the other written assessments will be computer-based. Bear in mind that computers may not have the full functionality of what you might expect in your normal day-to-day use. For example, there is no spell-check and highlighting function for the written assessments.

If you are working, then your writing style may be influenced by the business having its own 'house style'. A 'house style' ensures consistency among all employees when communicating in writing. However, for the purposes of the SQE assessments follow the UK English style suggestions below and make sure you are consistent.

7.02 *Writing in Professional English*

Written communication involves the ability to read and understand a person's meaning from what they have written. There are a range of different ways this can be done effectively, including:

- letters;
- emails;
- reports;
- facts and figures;
- diagrams;
- images;
- proposals.

In practice, you would use whatever method you think would be the best way for the recipient of the communication to understand its meaning and content.

For the written assessments, you might be required to produce an email, letter, memo or report. You should know the format of how to structure, set out and deliver the information in a clear, concise, comprehensive and correct manner. Some assessments will have a template and some may not.

The recipient of your written communication can range from a client, a third party, the other side or a partner within the firm (the list is non-exhaustive).

Unless you are provided with any hard copies of supporting documents, they will all be provided electronically because the assessments are computer-based. So, my advice when you are doing mock questions, is to practise them as if you were doing a real assessment. This means, rather than printing off mock papers and doing the assessment on hard copy, get used to flitting between open tabs on your computer. You may have several tabs open:

- the question/instructions;
- supporting documents (if any); and
- page to write your answer.

Examples of Application of Law

7.02 Below is a non-exhaustive list of examples where you will have to demonstrate your writing skills in a correct and comprehensive manner for any of the written assessments:

- Identifying relevant legal principles.
- Applying legal principles to factual issues. In effect, the best solution for a client's needs that reflects the client's commercial or personal circumstances (ie part of a negotiation).
- Interpreting, evaluating and applying the results of research.
- Ensuring that advice has appropriate legal analysis, identifies options and their consequences.
- Drafting documents which are legally effective.
- Applying understanding, critical thinking and analysis to solve problems.

- Assessing information to identify key issues and risks.
- Recognising inconsistencies and gaps in information.
- Evaluating the quality and reliability of information.
- Using multiple sources of information to make effective judgments.
- Reaching reasoned decisions supported by relevant evidence.

Identifying Your Writing Strengths and Weaknesses

7.03 Sometimes it is difficult to know what your strengths and weaknesses are without them being pointed out to you. A good self-reflective exercise to assess your writing skills is by answering the following two questions:

(1) **What areas of professional written communication skills do you find challenging?**

_____

_____

_____

There is no right or wrong answer. Below are some typical examples of challenges you might be able to relate to:

- 'I find it challenging to get across what I mean in a clear and articulate manner.'
- 'Not knowing how to address the client or someone senior.'
- 'Not knowing how to structure my emails and letters so they are to the point.'
- 'Wanting the tone of the written communication to come across as professional and not subjectively emotional to the reader.'
- 'I find it frustrating if there is incomplete information resulting in back-and-forth emails (or letters).'
- 'Not really knowing when to use certain punctuation to help make my point stand out or not come across as rude.'

(2) **What skills do you think are required to write in a professional style?**

_____

_____

_____

Below are some typical examples of what you might hear:

- 'Getting your meaning across clearly.'
- 'Not using legal jargon or technical language where appropriate – using plain English.'
- 'Writing using the active voice rather than passive voice.'
- 'Using correct, punctuation, spelling and grammar.'
- 'Articulate what you want to say clearly, concisely and correctly.'

7.04 *Writing in Professional English*

It is important to understand that the above examples are not exhaustive and you may have others. The point is to identify the areas you personally find challenging and how you can improve them to achieve what you have identified as good professional writing.

You might recognise that what you find annoying about someone else's writing style (eg they are too wordy, unstructured, write long sentences, typos etc) may be things that you are sometimes guilty of doing too, but you will not realise it until it is pointed out to you.

Your Level of English

7.04 You must be able to demonstrate confident use of English in your written communication. 'Confident' means the reader understands what you have written and it is done professionally, clearly and concisely: it should be a reflection of you. It also means that you should have a command of the language when writing. There is no room for any miscommunication by using incorrect words or punctuation which can change the whole meaning of the text. Such errors will undermine your credibility.

The SRA have said spelling mistakes and grammatical errors that do not impact legal accuracy, clarity or the certainty of your text will not be penalised. However, grammatical errors in the use of tenses could have an impact and affect how you are marked against the assessment criteria. They also say you should not be penalised for poor formatting but I believe layout is important and helps the reader.

You must aim to use correct grammar, punctuation and spelling which you can read more about from para **7.27** onwards. It may also be helpful to re-read Chapter 2, Preparing for the SQE, Your Level of English (para **2.44**) if you have any concerns around your level of English.

Exercise: Review Your Writing Style

Find an English language expert (who does not have to be a lawyer).

Ask them to review your English writing style, ideally from a practical (not academic) perspective. For example, give them a sample of a few documents you have written (emails, letters or memos) and get them to critique your work. It does not matter whether the examples are legal or non-legal work, but what is important is that you provide them with a decent selection of writing examples. This exercise and the others in this chapter will help you recognise your writing style.

Be specific as to what you want them to critique: conciseness, clarity of the message and correct use of grammar and punctuation.

Letters

7.05 Many law firms and businesses will have their own 'house style' so you may have your own preference as to how to write a letter.

In Chapter 12, Legal Writing, Letters and Emails (para **12.05**) you can see a suggestion as to how you can write a letter for the assessment, if no template is provided and you are not sure what to do.

Generally speaking, the following are usually included in a letter (and will be looked at in more detail below):

- client name and address;
- date;
- reference;
- salutation;
- subject heading;
- the content (importance of layout);
- the closing;
- signature;
- copy/enclosures (optional).

You should use the client's surname when writing their name and address and can also write above their name 'Private and Confidential'. For example:

Private and Confidential
Mr and Mrs Smith
79 Covenington Close
London
NW8 1DF

- *Reference*

7.06 When instructed by a client, most law firms will open a file for the client and give them a reference. Much of the referencing will depend on each business, but it may contain the initials of the client (eg JC) and numbers (eg 0123) or date (eg 140723) and may include the initials of the lawyer instructed (eg NH) such as:

JC/0123/NH or JC/140723/NH

For legal writing, you may be instructed to write a letter to the client and if you notice there is a reference in the instructions then you should include it in your letter. If you do not have a reference, then do not worry about including one. For example, in your client interviewing attendance note it would form part of the template but may not be completed until a file is open.

- *Salutation*

7.07 Normally, you would start a letter with 'Dear' and follow it through with your client's name. The name can be written in a number of ways depending on the relationship you have with the client (eg it is a new client or someone you know very well). For example:

7.08 *Writing in Professional English*

- Dear Sir/Madam – formal and do not know the name;
- Dear Mr and Mrs McNaughton (surname) – formal;
- Dear Ms McNaughton – you do not know her marital status;
- Dear Miss McNaughton – you know her marital status (single);
- Dear Mrs McNaughton – you know her marital status (married);
- Dear Annabel (first name only) – informal (you know the client very well).

When writing to a woman, it can sometimes get confusing because you could use any of the following: Ms/Miss/Mrs. There are no clear-cut rules, so if you are unsure use 'Ms' which is the most suitable and appropriate option. Normally in practice, you can ask the client how they would like to be addressed. This is especially important if you have a business client who is a married woman but uses her maiden name professionally.

If the person you are writing to has a title (such as, doctor or professor), you can write it like this:

- Dear Dr Hamilton,
- Dear Judge Roper,
- Dear Professor McNamara.

- **Subject Heading**

7.08 This usually comes immediately below the salutation and is important because it tells the recipient what the letter is about. Normally, the subject heading is in bold so it stands out.

- **Content (Layout)**

7.09 The most important part for the main body of the letter will be the layout. First impressions count. A good layout makes it easier for the recipient to read the document and it also looks professional. Use any of the following (appropriately) to help you with the structure and layout of your document:

- logical sequence;
- separate paragraphs;
- short sentences;
- the active voice;
- sub-headings;
- bullet points;
- tabulation.

Get confident with the idea of introducing what you think best shows your message in an easy and identifiable way. As soon as the reader sees your document, they make a judgement about you and your style.

- **The Closing**

7.10 This is how you 'sign off' the letter and will depend on whether you know who you are writing to and how you have addressed them in the salutation. For example:

- Yours faithfully

    If you do not know their name and have used 'Dear Sir/Madam'

- Yours sincerely

    If you do know their name and have used 'Dear Mr/Ms/Mrs/Miss McNaughton' or their first name.

- **Signature**

7.11 Normally, this will depend on the firm or business 'house rules'. Some 'house rules' state that people sign off using their name and others state that they sign off using the business name. For the purposes of the assessment, after using the appropriate closing, leave a gap and then sign off with your job title, in this case 'Solicitor' or read your instructions carefully to see what they say (ie are you writing a draft letter on behalf of a partner?). An example of how to set out the sign off:

- Yours sincerely/Yours faithfully

    Solicitor

- **Copy/Enclosures**

7.12 If you are writing to someone on behalf of the client and you copy them in, add their name at the end of the letter (after the signature). For example:

- Cc: Mr and Mrs Smith, 34 Trent Avenue, Newham, E14 6YU

If you are adding in any enclosures (Enc), at the end of the letter (after the signature and Cc), you should state 'copy' or 'original' to clarify the document and then state what it is, for example:

- Enc:
    1. Copy Witness Statement of Ruby Essie Jessa
    2. Copy Medical Records of Ruby Essie Jessa
    3. Original Marriage Certificate

As mentioned above, you can have a look at a letter template in Chapter 12, Legal Writing, Letters and Emails (para **12.05**) for guidance.

Remember, not everything will be relevant for your instructions, so only use what is required.

Emails

7.13 For the assessment, if you are asked to write an email you should follow the style suggested in the letter (as shown in the letter template in Chapter 12,

7.14 *Writing in Professional English*

Legal Writing). The content used in the letter template would be the same for the email. However, the name and address would not be required and a reference would be optional (if included as part of the subject heading).

Normally, in practice, if it is a lengthy matter, you might create a separate document and attach it to the email. You can then highlight what you would like the reader to focus on and include any deadlines (if appropriate) in the email.

Paragraphs

7.14 There are no strict rules about how long a paragraph should be. Where in the past, one-sentence paragraphs were frowned upon, they are acceptable now but should be used sparingly.

Think about each key issue or point you want to make and create separate paragraphs for them.

Paragraphs that are too long make the text look dense and impenetrable, and this is not easy to read. It can result in key information being lost in a sea of words. Make sure you use a range of different sized paragraphs, some short and some longer.

The content of the document is just as important as layout; they complement one another. The following Four Cs provide the foundation that you should have in mind for all your written communication. They are the formula to ensure your writing comes across in a professional manner.

The Four Cs

7.15 There is no strict definition of what the Four Cs mean generally and no particular order of importance as they all interlink. For the context of the assessments, you want to demonstrate all Four Cs, to come across as credible and confident. As mentioned, your writing is a reflection of you and you need to bear this in mind for all the assessments. Under the Four Cs, written communication should be Clear, Concise, Comprehensive and Correct, as discussed below:

- ***Clear Communication***

7.16 This means using language that is easily understood by the client and does not require re-reading or reading between the lines. It is also tailored to the person you are writing to and their level of understanding.

Clarity of writing follows from clarity of thought. When you understand something very well, that often means you can explain it simply, which does not mean it is simple or easy. It is evidence of your understanding of the matter or instructions (the skills) and application of your legal knowledge (the law) – using plain English.

Always have the reader in mind and consider how they will perceive the information you are giving them or requesting from them.

For example, when writing to a lay client, you would be expected to use plain English as opposed to writing to an expert or a barrister (counsel), where you may make reference to legal and technical language. However, generally, most law firms and businesses encourage the use of plain English.

- **Concise Communication**

7.17 This means being able to write in a lean style which is not so short that it comes across as rude or unclear.

A lean style of writing does not mean you exclude common courtesies (eg 'thank you' or 'please') or empathy (eg expressing feelings such as regret or compassion). Not including these would make the tone of your message seem abrupt and rude.

For example – compare the two sentences about cancelling a meeting. Both are saying the same thing, but one sentence is 22 words and the other sentence is 10 words:

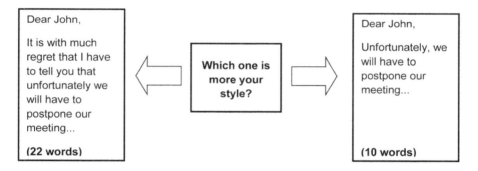

From my experience, if you are a (recent) graduate who has studied a non-law degree such as English Literature, History or Classics at university, you may have a wordier writing style than a Law graduate. There is nothing wrong with that in principle, but lawyers tend to be taught to write in a concise style at Law School and that means using the active voice.

Concise communication can be achieved by using the active voice style of writing rather than the passive voice. A passive voice style can make the written communication longer and can lose the impact of your message for the reader. Often, the reader will have to read what you have written twice, because the sentences might be long.

The use of an active or passive voice is to do with the structure of the sentence. Some people use the active voice naturally in their writing style whilst others use the passive voice. Sometimes, people are not even aware of what voice they use when writing.

The structure of the sentence when using an active voice is: subject (S), verb (V) and object (O).

For the passive voice the structure of the sentence is the reverse: object (O), verb (V) and subject (S).

For example, a very simplified way to illustrate this point is to explain it using a simple sentence:

Active voice: **The defendant hit the victim.** 5 words

Passive voice: **The victim was hit by the defendant.** 7 words

When the passive voice is overused in documents such as emails, reports, letters or memos, it lengthens them because each sentence is usually longer than it would be if written in an active voice. If the email or document is not very long it might not have such a huge impact, but if it is, then using the passive voice can make it less impactful.

> **Exercise: Identifying Your Active Voice and Passive Voice**
>
> Review a document you have written and identify your writing style.
>
> The goal of this exercise is to help you realise what style you use (unless you know already) and help you write in a concise style.

Also, try to avoid repetition and unnecessary words. For example, you may see in many contracts the words 'null and void'. For example: *'The contract will be null and void.'* can be written as *'The contract will be void'*. In this context null and void mean the same thing.

- ***Comprehensive Communication***

7.18 This means being able to understand all the relevant factual information the client provides on the matter, so you can offer complete legal advice. You may be expected to consider any commercial implications of taking any particular steps, depending on the practice area of the law. For example, in a business law scenario, if there is a dispute over a partnership agreement, you might want to point out the commercial risks and benefits of taking a particular course of action, in accordance with your legal advice.

This does not mean using legal jargon to provide 'comprehensive' evidence of your legal knowledge, but what it does mean is being able to explain the law simply and fully, in relation to the client's instructions or their matter. It means considering everything holistically and identifying issues or highlighting where more information may be required.

- **Correct Communication**

7.19 Being correct is a two-fold process: correct in law and correct in the use of the English language. You need to ensure the factual information from the client is accurately understood, so you can apply the law correctly. Make sure that your grammar, punctuation and spelling are correct, so your writing comes across as professional and the intention of the written communication is not misunderstood.

If you are worried about the level of your English, re-read Chapter 2, Preparing for the SQE (para **2.44**).

Exercise: Writing Concisely

To test your ability to write concisely, have a go at re-writing the paragraph below:

Original paragraph (Extract from an email)

I have changed my business address to that which is stated below in this email. I do not owe the amount of money which is claimed because I have completed all the work. I attach a summary of all the work that I have done. I would recommend that you contact me by email or phone in order for me to supply you with copies of all of the invoices relating to the work which has been carried out. I hope that I have been able to explain to you why I do not owe the money claimed. **[98 words]**

A suggested way of re-writing it more concisely can be found in Appendix 7A.

Commonly Misused Words

7.20 These are words whose pronunciation might be the same or very similar, but the spelling and meaning are different and depend on the context of the sentence. The incorrect use of words reflects badly on your credibility.

Exercise: Misused Words

Think of a sentence for each word using the correct context:

(1) Discrete/Discreet

(2) Complement/Compliment

(3) Stationery/Stationary

7.21 *Writing in Professional English*

(4) Effect/Affect

(5) To/Too

(6) Your/You're

(7) Practise/Practice

(8) Continually/Continuously

(9) Principal/Principle

(10) Then/Than

(11) Advice/Advise

(12) Its/It's

The goal here is to enable you to use these words correctly. There are some examples in Appendix 7B.

Contractions

7.21 These are words that have been shortened by dropping one or more letters. In the exercise above there are words 'You're' and 'It's' which are shortened versions of 'You are' and 'It is', respectively. There are many other contractions that are used in the English language (eg don't (do not), I've (I have), wouldn't (would not), should've (should have)).

Normally, contractions make the tone of the language less formal and are more likely to be used in conversation. So, if you are writing to a client it is not professional to include contractions. If you are writing an email, it might be more appropriate depending on who it is being sent to, the length of the email and the context.

For the written assessments, I would advise that you do not use contractions.

Archaic Legal Language v Modern Plain English

7.22 As mentioned most law firms and businesses prefer the use of plain English for written communication. Nonetheless, this may depend on the culture of the firm or business, so a lot of direction will come from your employers as to what the 'house style' of writing will be for the business.

For the assessments, I would advise you to write in plain English and to avoid legal or business jargon, where appropriate.

The following are typical examples of words associated with legal documents, known as 'legalese'. There is no real need to use them in general documents when plain English can convey the same message. It is not clever or knowledgeable to use legalese, if the person reading the document will struggle to understand it. Most modern-day law practices and businesses have moved away from it to make written communication more transparent and easier to understand.

Of course, studying law means you will inevitably come across it and tradition has meant that legalese was used as the norm in the past. However, in today's world, the preference generally is to use plain English – whether in legal or non-legal communication.

Exercise: Simplifying Legalese

Here are a few examples of legalese which can be replaced with plain English. Think about what these words actually mean and whether you use any of them. If you do, in what context do you use them and can you come up with an alternative using plain English?

(1) herein
(2) hereinafter
(3) hereafter
(4) hereby
(5) hereto
(6) hereunder
(7) forthwith
(8) notwithstanding.

You can find suggested alternatives in Appendix 7C.

US and UK English

7.23 There is no right or wrong use of either language style. Many legal departments use UK English (even if they are American companies or law firms). Sometimes the choice is influenced by culture and location, depending on where you work and the type of work you do. Different types of industries will dictate the language style used and lawyers should be mindful of this and, where required, adapt their style.

If you are an international student or lawyer qualified in a foreign jurisdiction where US English is your preference, for the purposes of the SQE I would advise you to use UK English. The main differences between them are the vocabulary and spelling. These can lead to different interpretations and meaning. So, train yourself to write in UK English for the assessments. Mixing the two styles, will make you appear inconsistent and may change the tone of what you are saying.

Below are some typical examples of differences in UK and US-style English for dates and spelling.

- ***Dates***

7.24 When writing the date, UK English starts with the date rather than the month. US English starts with the month followed by the date. For example:

7.25 *Writing in Professional English*

UK English: 25 (or 25th) December 2023;

US English: December 25 2023.

There are a range of other formats of writing the date, for example, using full stops (25.12.23) or forward slash (25/12/23). However, it is good practice to write the date in full to avoid confusion.

Modern UK-style writers prefer writing the date without the 'th' or 'st' – so '25th December 2023' would be written as '25 December 2023' and '21st December 2023' would be written as '21 December 2023'. Personally, in addition to that, I would add the day too for more completeness and clarity: 'Thursday, 25 December 2023'. This can help pick up any typos (ie did you mean Friday 25 December or Thursday 24 December?).

Usually in practice, businesses will have their own 'house style' which will be followed. However, for the purposes of the SQE assessments follow UK English style and make sure you are consistent.

- ***Spelling***

7.25 There are many differences in spelling and below are some common examples to bear in mind:

UK English	US English	Commentary
Honour	Honor	In US English the 'u' is omitted for many UK English words with 'ou' in them.
Pre-trial	Pretrial	In US English, no hyphen is used, where UK English tends to use a prefix to connect the word.
Practise (verb) Practice (noun)	Practice	In UK English, the spelling depends on its use. US English just uses the 'c' spelling of the word for both the verb and noun.
Specialised	Specialized	In US English the 'ize' endings used more commonly compared to the 'ise' for UK English.
Centre	Center	In UK English, many words ending in 're' are flipped to end using 'er' for US English.
Skilfully	Skillfully	The word 'Skill' is used by both with a double 'll', but when a suffix is added at the end, UK English drops one 'l' but US English continues to use both.
Defence	Defense	Many words in UK English with 'ce' will be 'se' in US English.

There is a lot more information and depth that can be explored about the differences between US and UK English. If you are interested in finding out more about the differences in the language then a search on the Internet will provide you with ample information.

Latin Phrases

7.26 There is often a tendency to use Latin phrases unintentionally in documents. This might be fine if it is common knowledge to other professionals, but if used in layman's documents it can cause confusion and make the reader feel alienated. Using Latin phrases does not make you look smart if the recipient does not understand what you mean. Modern writing styles avoid writing in old-fashioned English or using Latin phrases, instead preferring plain English. The following are examples of plain English alternatives that can work well:

Latin phrase	Plain English
Modus operandi	Method
Pari passu	Side by side/equal footing
Inter alia	Including but not limited to

Spelling

7.27 In the computer-based assessments you may not have the spell check functionality working. Under pressure to type quickly you may make more spelling mistakes, and will need to leave enough time to proof-read for errors which may not be highlighted automatically.

> **Exercise: How good is your spelling?**
>
> Sometimes when you see the spelling, you know it is correct just by looking at it: you may think *'it just looks right'*.
>
> Here is a quick exercise. Below are some typical words that can sometimes cause confusion or make you question the spelling, when you go to use them.
>
> From the 30 words, there are 10 words spelt correctly, can you identify them?

7.28 *Writing in Professional English*

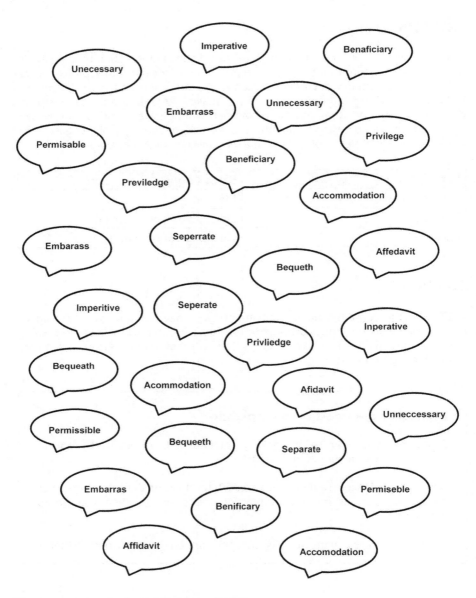

The answers can be found in Appendix 7D.

Punctuation

7.28 The incorrect use of punctuation can change the whole meaning and tone of your message. It can also be a costly mistake if the writing can be interpreted in a number of different ways. For example, a dispute over a contract may be caused by poor drafting and punctuation which affects the interpretation of the contract wording. Where the matter cannot be resolved amicably, the cost of going to court can outweigh the benefits of the contract.

Usually, in practice, businesses will have their own 'house style', so bear this in mind when you use it for the SQE.

Below is a grid containing commonly used punctuation marks and explaining their use with examples so you can see how to use them correctly.

Full Stop .	Comma ,	Colon :
Semi-colon ;	Square brackets [ ]	Hyphen -
Apostrophe '	Exclamation mark !	Capital letters **A**nd
Dashes A–B	Quotation marks 'Single' "Double"	Parentheses ( )

- **Full Stop**
    - A full stop should be used at the end of sentences not ending with an exclamation mark or question mark.
    - A full stop can also be used after abbreviations.

> **Example:**
>
> The Law Society represents solicitors in England and Wales and the Solicitors Regulation Authority regulates them.
>
> 'Sat. 30 Jan. 2023'.

- **Comma**
    - Shows a short pause within the sentence.
    - Be careful when using commas. A misplaced comma can change the meaning of the sentence.
    - Commas can clarify meaning and omitting them can lead to ambiguity.

> **Example:**
>
> Carlos hit Tony and Peter, then ran away. (So, Carlos ran away.)
>
> Carlos hit Tony, and Peter then ran away. (So, Peter ran away.)

- **Colon**
    - It points to information that follows it.
    - It may also be used to link two clauses in a sentence to show cause and effect.

7.28 *Writing in Professional English*

> **Example:**
> The following items are included in your mobile phone package:
> (1)   unlimited calls;
> (2)   1,000 texts; and
> (3)   256 | 8 GB storage data.
>
> A new legal director has been appointed: the direct result is the rise in share prices.

- **Semi-colon**
    - Used to separate parts of a sentence more distinctly than using a comma, where the sentence is too closely connected for separate sentences to be used.
    - In legal writing, it is used when using sub-clauses or paragraphs that are part of a longer sentence.

> **Example:**
> To err is human; to forgive, divine. (Alexander Pope.)
>
> You can choose any of the following locations for your work placement:
> (1)   Manchester;
> (2)   London;
> (3)   Bristol; or
> (4)   Leeds.

- **Square brackets**
    - These are used when referring to comments, explanations or notes not in the original text, but added later on.
    - In legal writing they are used to adjust the format of any quoted text.

> **Example:**
> The client will come in to sign the paperwork on Wednesday this week [make sure the figures are updated].
>
> This Agreement dated [date] will be enforced in [location].

- **Hyphen**
    - Used as a prefix to join two words together.

> **Example:**
> Pre-trial, non-statutory, re-distribute.

- **Dashes**
    - Used to enclose a sub-clause in the sentence and clarify a sentence more definitively than using a comma.
    - The longer dash can be used in place of the word 'to'.

> **Example:**
> Few – if any at all – enjoy working the long hours expected of city workers.
>
> London – Singapore – Hong Kong – London.

- **Apostrophe**
    - There are two uses for the apostrophe:
        (1) it shows shortened words/contractions/omissions; and
        (2) it shows possession.

> **Example:**
>
> | 1. | Contractions/omissions | |
> |---|---|---|
> | | **Uncontracted words** | **Contracted word** |
> | A | I will | I'll |
> | B | You are | You're |
> | C | Do not | Don't |
> | D | Cannot | Can't |
> | E | Should not | Shouldn't |
> | 2. | **Possession** | |
> | | **Description** | **Example** |
> | A | Single word for a person or thing | The client's money (one client). |
> | B | Plural words for people or things | The clients' money (all clients). |
> | C* | Single words ending with 's' | James' case or James's case |
> | D | Plural words not ending with 's' | The children's statement |
>
> *In row C you can see there are two ways the apostrophe can be used; both are correct, but usually it will come down to your preference or house style.

7.28 *Writing in Professional English*

- **Exclamation mark**
    - It should only be used once but people do use it in multiples (eg I already sent you the documents last week!!) Usually, multiple use is very informal and can change the tone of your message. Its use can be perceived as rude and come across as unprofessional. Therefore, if you want to use it, I would recommend once.
    - It is not often used in formal documents but can be used within square bracket comments to express the writer's feelings which do not form part of the document.

> **Example:**
>
> I already sent you the documents last week!
>
> The claimant will not settle for less than half a million pounds and the holiday home in Barbados. [No way – don't agree!]

- **Capital letters**
    - Used at the beginning of a sentence.
    - When referring to proper nouns, names, locations or abbreviations.
    - Defined terms in legal documents.

> **Example:**
>
> Thank you for your letter.
>
> It is noted that Maya is the CEO and will be travelling to London ASAP for the meeting.
>
> According to the Agreement, the Parties will have to provide a copy of the Policy.

- **Quotation marks**
    - Single quotation marks are used as the first quote.
    - Double quotation marks are used for a quote within a quote.

> **Example:**
>
> Single quote: He wrote 'this is great feedback'.
>
> Double quote: He wrote, 'Sarah said "this is great feedback".'

- **Parentheses**
    - These are used to enclose phrases, words or whole sentences.
    - Where a whole sentence is in parentheses, the closing punctuation stays inside.
    - Where only part of the sentence is in parentheses, the closing punctuation goes outside.

Example:

1. Penelope Xavier (call her Penny) wants you to ring her this afternoon.
2. (Halmegkar Panai Ltd is hereinafter referred to as 'the Company'.)
3. Halmegkar Panai Ltd (hereinafter referred to as 'the Company').

Grammar

7.29 There are so many statements made about grammar and this causes many people a great deal of confusion.

Are there grammar rules?

Are they fixed?

Can you start a sentence with 'And'?

Do you always have a comma after 'but'?

The English language is always changing. What was not acceptable grammar many years ago (eg starting a sentence with 'And' or 'Because') is now widely acceptable.

There are many free resources on the Internet if you want to polish up on and read more about grammar or the English language (UK). The 'BBC Learning English' website (www.bbc.co.uk/learningenglish) is a good resource and offers a range of courses at different levels of English with lots of other features that you may find helpful.

The aim of this chapter is to provide you with a quick refresher of the English language. It highlights the practical key areas to help you achieve the criterion that applies to all the written assessments which is to use: *'clear, precise, concise and acceptable language'*.

The Writing Formula: P.O.P

PURPOSE (reason why you are writing – what do you want to get across?)

ORGANISE (structure it, sub-headings, bullet points, layout)

PROOF-READ (check for spelling mistakes, typos, punctuation, active voice).

7.29 *Writing in Professional English*

> *'The most valuable of all talents is that of never using two words when one will do.'*
>
> **Thomas Jefferson**

Writing in Professional English – Top Ten Tips

(1) Practise your handwriting by doing attendance notes and ask someone to review them for accuracy and legibility.

(2) Be mindful of the Four Cs: Clear, Concise, Comprehensive and Correct.

(3) Test your typing skills and spelling with spell-check switched off.

(4) Write in the active voice, rather than the passive voice.

(5) Misused words – know the difference between similar words.

(6) Avoid using legal jargon, use plain English.

(7) A good layout helps the reader understand your message quicker.

(8) Refresh your memory with the punctuation grid and think about how you can make your writing more effective.

(9) Do not use contractions in formal documents. Although this is not a grammar 'rule' it is usually the preferred style professionally.

(10) Always bear in mind the writing formula – Purpose, Organise, Proof-read.

Chapter 7

Writing in Professional English: Appendices

Appendix 7A: The Four Cs

- ***Exercise: Writing Concisely***

Please note that there are many ways the paragraph can be written more concisely and ultimately it comes down to your writing style. The goal is to create an awareness of how to write concisely. This exercise forces you to think about what the relevant information is and whether there is any repetition. It encourages you to re-write the paragraph more concisely.

❖ **Original paragraph (Extract from an email)**

> I have changed my business address to that which is stated below in this email. I do not owe the amount of money which is claimed because I have completed all the work. I attach a summary of all the work that I have done. I would recommend that you contact me by email or phone in order for me to supply you with copies of all of the invoices relating to the work which has been carried out. I hope that I have been able to explain to you why I do not owe the money claimed. **[98 words]**

❖ **Suggested re-write**

> Please note the change of address below. I do not owe the sum claimed because I have carried out and completed all the work: see summary attached. Upon request, I will supply you with copies of the relevant invoices. **[39 words]**

❖ **Reflection/Notes**

You can see that you can re-write the paragraph more concisely in under half the words of the original paragraph.

Writing in Professional English: Appendices

Notice the tone of both paragraphs and how the use of punctuation means you can use fewer words. For example, by using the colon (:) you emphasise the statement made after it is very important.

Notice how the possible ways of contacting the writer are removed. If you offer the standard email and phone, then there is no real reason to keep it in there. If you have a preferred method of being contacted, then it makes sense to suggest it.

Appendix 7B: Commonly Misused Words

These are some sentences to help you understand how the words should be used in their correct context.

(1) discrete/discreet

We must be extremely **discreet** if we decide to go ahead with the plan.

There were a number of **discrete** issues that led to his resignation as CEO.

(2) complement/compliment

This book with help you because it will **complement** your studies.

She's not very good at receiving a **compliment**.

(3) stationery/stationary

The car stood **stationary** in the traffic jam for half an hour.

All the notepads and pens are in the **stationery** cupboard.

(4) effect/affect

Is there any adverse **effect** from taking that medicine?

How you look can **affect** what people think of you.

(5) to/too

I am going **to** finish working on this case before I go home.

That extra drink meant I was **too** drunk and had to go home early.

(6) your/you're

Thank you for inviting me to attend the Law Society ball as **your** guest.

You're always working so late and such long hours.

(7) practise/practice

Good public speakers **practise** their speech until it becomes natural.

One day, I would like to own my own law **practice**.

(8) continually/continuously

It has been noted that Ben is **continually** coming to work late.

The police worked **continuously** through the night to search for the missing child.

(9) principal/principle

The school **principal** is the person to contact about your complaint.

He believed in the **principle** that all men and women are equal.

(10) then/than

Children know more about technology **than** their parents.

We went to dinner and **then** went to see a movie.

(11) advice/advise

As a solicitor, my family and friends always ask me for free **advice**.

We strongly **advise** that you do not sign the agreement without further negotiations.

(12) its/it's

Exercise has **its** own physical and mental health benefits.

It's often the case that neither party will be happy with the decision.

Appendix 7C: Archaic Legal Language v Modern Plain English

Below is a suggestion of plain English that could be used to replace legal jargon.

(1) Herein – 'in this document'

(2) Hereinafter – 'later in the document'

(3) Hereafter – 'after this time'

(4) Hereby – 'by this action/means'

(5) Hereto – 'to this agreement'

(6) Hereunder – 'below' or 'after this'

(7) Forthwith – 'immediately'

(8) Notwithstanding – 'despite' or 'in spite of'.

Appendix 7D: Spelling

The correct spelling for the ten words you should have identified is as follows:

1	Affidavit
2	Unnecessary
3	Embarrass
4	Privilege
5	Separate
6	Beneficiary
7	Permissible
8	Bequeath
9	Accommodation
10	Imperative

Chapter 8

SQE Part 2

Client Interviewing Skills

'A customer is the most important visitor ... He is not dependent on us. We are dependent on him.'

Mahatma Gandhi

In this chapter you will learn:

✓ How to use your preparation time wisely.
✓ How to manage your time for the interview and take control of it.
✓ How to structure your interview notes so they complement the attendance note.
✓ How to build rapport and trust with the client.
✓ How to deal with common challenges and unexpected questions.
✓ How to deal with difficult, challenging or vulnerable clients.

Introduction

8.01 To get a better understanding of how to prepare for client interviewing, it would be beneficial for you to read Chapters 4, 5 and 6 before working through this chapter.

This chapter will help you think about how to prepare practically for the client interview and how to deal with unforeseen situations that you may encounter.

Although the quote above by Mahatma Gandhi refers to 'customer' the point is clear and applies to clients too; without which there would be no need for lawyers. Therefore, it is essential that you understand how to build trust and confidence in a client for them to instruct you by providing them with an exceptional service. In practice, this can lead to building your own reputation by getting client recommendations.

8.01 Client Interviewing Skills

My observations of common challenges are typically around the following areas (this is not an exhaustive list or in any particular order):

- **Challenges experienced for client interviewing:**
    - Failing to create authentic rapport – where the small talk with the client comes across as forced, unnatural and rushed.
    - Struggling to explain the law clearly and concisely – where too much legal jargon is used.
    - Speaking for too long and in depth very quickly – which comes across as an overload of information.
    - Running out of questions to ask the client – where lots of assumptions are made and closed questions asked, so not all the information is obtained.
    - Common courtesy etiquette – where no empathy is expressed authentically or re-assurance provided when concerns are raised.
    - Lack of emotional intelligence or empathy – where their language and behaviour is not congruent towards the client.
    - Not taking control from the outset – where they do not set out what will be done and how the interview is structured.
    - Thinking being professional means coming across as formal – where their behaviour reflects this formality when compassion and emotional intelligence is required.

These are just some examples and most of the lawyers I work with do not realise they do any of the above until it is pointed out to them. So, bear in mind and be open-minded to any constructive feedback, because you might do some of the above, without even realising it.

It makes sense for you initially to engage with a communication skills expert (eg a coach – ideally a lawyer, but this is not essential) who can properly assess your skills and help you improve where needed. After constructive feedback, when you are comfortable with practising your skills you can focus on applying them to the law because this helps build your confidence holistically. You can practise your client interviewing skills with a tutor, 'study buddy' or someone else who can play the role of the client. This is because once you recognise what you need to improve on from a skills perspective, you can practise reinforcing them correctly within the context of the law. Without any tailored constructive feedback on your existing skills you are blindly practising them without knowing if they are correct and effective. What you want the expert or coach to work on with you is how you:

- use the instructions and any supporting documents in the preparation stage;
- deal with the information presented to you by the client and what you do with it;
- ask relevant questions which are not assumption-based (many lawyers find this tricky);
- request ID from the client and explain the reason for it;
- ask a range of different types of questions to gather information;

- make small talk naturally with the client;
- explain any law or legal rules using plain English (many use legal jargon without realising it);
- alleviate the client's concerns;
- handle difficult or vulnerable clients with care and courtesy;
- deal confidently with unforeseeable questions or any documents unexpectedly handed to you in the interview;
- use empathetic language (where appropriate) which is congruent with your body language.

The above is a non-exhaustive list of areas on which I have helped many lawyers when coaching on how to do client interviews. Always think about what the assessment criteria will expect from you and adapt your behaviour accordingly to maximise your marks. You may think that is not being authentic. However, it is surprising how many lawyers are used to doing client interviews in practice and so used to their style that they do not adapt it for different types of clients. This is where your communication skills are tested and you have to show you can do this authentically and naturally.

Sometimes you may need to negotiate with the client about what they want to do and what you think might be better for them. How you approach this will depend on your experience and the type of client you get in the interview.

- ***Negotiation Skills***

8.02 The following assessments may include an aspect where you have to demonstrate your negotiation skills:

- Client Interviewing Skills (and the Attendance Note);
- Case and Matter Analysis;
- Legal Writing.

Although it will not be explicitly highlighted in any of the assessments mentioned above you should look out for any language that asks you to consider client-focused advice on potential options, strategies, risks and benefits.

Sometimes in a first meeting you might not have all the information you need. For example, on finding out about what the client wants to do, you might need more information or other documents to help you advise them properly. You may need to demonstrate your negotiation skills with the client if they are clear about what they want to do but you look at it from a different perspective. You will need to convince and persuade them of your reasoning and why. You should write it in your attendance note explaining what you said and what additional information you need (if any).

Chapter 11, Case and Matter Analysis, Negotiation Skills (para **11.09**) looks at negotiation skills in more detail to avoid duplication.

8.03 *Client Interviewing Skills*

The SRA has provided a sample of what you could get for this type of assessment for a wills and probate scenario. You can also find samples for all the other assessments on the SRA website (www.sra.org.uk).

Building Trust and Confidence

8.03 The client will be played by a professional actor and they will be briefed as to what their role is and how they are expected to behave. They will assess you on your skills only (not the law).

Many lawyers find the client interviewing assessment challenging. This is because, rather than focusing on the client and getting as much information as possible, they worry about advising the client on the law (in detail). Their focus is on the wrong aspect.

Without getting all the information you cannot offer any comprehensive advice. Based on the information you do get, you may be able to offer some preliminary advice (that is the level expected if you are asked to do so). Therefore, to worry about whether you will know enough about the law to advise the client in the interview is unnecessary. Your knowledge of the law is more relevant for the attendance note.

The interview is about being able to understand the client's matter comprehensively and what they want to do. When you have a good understanding of the client's matter, it provides you with the factual and legal issues you can include in your attendance note. The assessor (a solicitor) who marks your attendance note will be able to see the level of information you have elicited from the client which may result in any preliminary advice.

You need to recognise and focus on the criteria on which you will be assessed. The Assessment Specification can be read in Appendix 8A in detail but the key objective I want to point out is:

> 'In the interview candidates should aim to win the client's trust and confidence and to make sure that the client wishes to instruct or continue to instruct their firm.'

The key objective here is to *win the client's trust and confidence* and in the full description in Appendix 8A it is mentioned in the first and last sentence. How you do that is not necessarily by providing the client with in-depth legal advice on their matter. In fact, the chances are that you may not even have enough information to do that accurately. So, the point is: do not worry about knowing the law in detail (unless you can provide preliminary advice). The assessment overview states:

> 'Candidates do not need to provide detailed advice at this stage.'

By listening and asking good questions, you will have a better idea of any potential legal issues and can get clarification on any facts that may be confusing and/or inaccurate. These should be identified and referred to in the attendance note (you are assessed on the law and skills). Your focus should be whether you have the skills to connect with the client and gather all the relevant information to allow you to make a judgement call as to whether or not you can advise them. The goal is that you want the client to feel confident enough in your ability to instruct you. This means you have to make them feel that they were listened to and their concerns (if any) were addressed empathetically. You want them to leave the client interview with a clear understanding of what you propose to do if they instruct you on their matter.

The Assessment Criteria

You are required to conduct a client interview and obtain all the relevant information from the client whilst addressing any concerns and offering any preliminary legal advice where appropriate.

You can read about the more detailed version of the SRA criteria in Appendix 8A.

Below I have summarised and highlighted the criteria against which you are assessed.

- *Skills*

8.04

(1) Demonstrate listening and questioning skills (obtain good-quality information).

(2) Communicate and explain clearly so that the client understands (use plain English).

(3) Behave in a professional manner (be courteous, polite and respect diversity).

(4) Adopt a client-focused approach (understand the client's perspective, not just the legal perspective).

(5) Build trust and confidence with the client (rapport).

Although you are not assessed on the law you should always identify and resolve any professional conduct and ethical issues that may arise and you mention them in your attendance note.

You should assess yourself against these assessment criteria when practising client interviewing. These are assessed using the following grading scale:

Grade	Mark	Standard	Do you meet the competency requirements?
A	5	Superior performance	Yes, well above it
B	4	Clearly satisfactory	Yes, clearly meets it
C	3	Marginal pass	Yes, on balance, just meets it
D	2	Marginal fail	No, on balance, just fails it
E	1	Clearly unsatisfactory	No, clearly does not meet it
F	0	Poor performance	No, well below it

8.05 *Client Interviewing Skills*

As mentioned above, it makes sense initially to have a skills coach and share the assessment criteria with them. They should help you realise where you are in the grading scale for each of the key areas you are assessed on and how to get to superior performance (if you are not at that standard already).

In addition, a skills coach can also assist you in presentation skills (to help you with advocacy) which is also interactive. You can read Chapter 10, Advocacy in conjunction with Chapter 2, Preparing for the SQE, Practising Skills (para **2.43**).

The first thing you should aim for is grade A (5 marks) superior performance across all the skills criteria. Because on the day of the assessment, even with nerves, if you drop a grade, you would still be 'clearly satisfactory', grade B (4 marks). You want to avoid falling into the 'marginal pass' zone grade C (3 marks) for the skills. This is dangerous because it could tip your overall mark to fail if you are in the marginal standard for the law and skills in too many assessments.

There is no reason why you cannot try to achieve superior performance for the skills part, if you have worked at practising your skills, have relevant and sufficient work experience, together with expert constructive feedback. This is where you can have the edge on maximising on the marks, because this part is not based on assessing you on the law (unless you are required to give some preliminary advice). The skills are based on how you deliver your knowledge of the law (where required) and it really tests your communication skills. It is what you are expected to be able to do in practice. Your communication skills can be improved through legal and non-legal work experience. So, with expert feedback (for the context of the assessments), you should be confident in your ability to score high marks using your improved skills. The only thing that can really affect your performance, is feeling fearful or nervous on the day, because you have no idea what your client will be like and what you may be asked. You can read more about Managing Your Nerves, Fears and Failure in Chapter 6.

Remind yourself of the Competence Statement in Chapter 1, The SQE Journey, Appendix 1B which provides the context of what you are expected to know and be able to do in practice as a newly-qualified solicitor.

Unpredictable Clients

8.05 You have to be prepared to deal with a client who may be vulnerable, emotional, elderly, speak too much or not say much at all, together with anything else that is unexpected. The whole purpose of this assessment is to try to make it as authentic as possible to real-life work in practice. If you are a qualified lawyer, this is often more challenging for you because you are already comfortable with what you do and the types of clients you deal with in practice. However, you are required to show you have a versatile skill set and are able to deal with different types of clients in different practice areas of the law (even if you have no intention of changing the area of law you practise in).

Below are just some behaviours you might encounter from the client (it is all part of their instructions, so it is not personal to you). They may (not an exhaustive list):
- provide you with additional documentation or paperwork (related or unrelated) to the matter and push for you to look at it in the interview;

- make unreasonable demands about the matters that they think are reasonable;
- not like what you have to say about the matter and try to persuade you otherwise;
- not be very friendly or forthcoming with information, reluctant or dismissive about the matter;
- be pleasant and friendly, but talk too much and at a very fast pace – leading to information overload;
- be pleasant and friendly, but not say too much because they feel intimidated, nervous or shy.

Ideally, you want the client to be just pleasant and normal, which can happen too. However, if you are well prepared, you should be able to deal with any type of client. If you learn the strategies of how to handle the situation, you come away credibly and these skills will build your confidence in the long run too.

The daunting aspect of the interview is the unknown and how you will manage the time and get as much information as possible. This will then help you write your attendance note by identifying any factual and legal issues.

Regardless of how the client presents themselves you must always behave in a professional, empathetic (when required) and courteous manner.

The common challenges experienced vary hugely because each person is unique and so I cannot make generalisations. For example, some lawyers find it hard to build rapport authentically and others do this more easily. Others, find it hard to explain legal processes or procedures without using legal jargon and often do not even realise they are using it. Some lawyers may feel insecure about their level of English and pronunciation. Chapter 2, Preparing for the SQE, Your Level of English (para **2.44**) will provide some guidance and there is a pronunciation exercise you can do in the Appendix 2C.

You are assessed on two practice areas of the law:

- property practice; and
- wills and probate.

Many lawyers find it quite challenging to think about what they can ask the client in the preparation stage when there is little information. So, I will share a strategy I have created that will help you.

This strategy is contextual to each practice area of the law and simplified so that you can do it in the preparation time. Of course, the issues and questions will vary depending on your client's instructions, so you may need to adapt it and think of appropriate questions. The aim is to help you get as much information from the client as possible, so you do not get stuck and run out of questions to ask the client, or if you find yourself in a situation where a client is not offering you much information.

Preparation Stage

8.06 The preparation time is only ten minutes, so you do not have much time. A strategy will help you structure the interview, so you use your time efficiently

8.06 *Client Interviewing Skills*

and do not feel overwhelmed. This will also help you when it comes to writing the attendance note immediately after the interview has finished.

You will be presented with an email from a supervising solicitor, secretary or partner with some client instructions which may or may not include some supporting documents.

You should treat the instructions of what the client wants to do or discuss with you as your compass, to help you structure the content of what you want to ask and find out more about – this will help you with what you need to include in the attendance note. Be curious and do not make assumptions about anything you read. Instead, ask questions.

During the preparation stage, you will be able to write your own notes and use them in the interview and attendance note. It makes sense to have some idea of how you can leverage your time by writing your interview notes in a way that complements the attendance note, so you do not waste time duplicating information. You could use four separate sheets, number each one and add in the headings, like this:

1	2	3	4
Client's Personal Details	Professional Conduct	Factual and Legal Issues	Next Steps
			1.
			2.
Other People's Details			3.
			4.

You can read Making Notes During the Interview (para **8.23**) to see what information you might include on each page.

Then, after the interview when you go to write your attendance note, look at the layout of the template suggested which complements this approach. You can see the snapshot of how to write an attendance note in Chapter 9, Writing the Attendance Note, The Attendance Note Template (para **9.07**).

Ten minutes is not a long time. If there is very little information, do not panic – you need to be inquisitive with the client to understand what they want to do and address any concerns before considering next steps.

If there is a lot of information (eg some supporting documents), one approach is to skim read and add in question marks around the issue or points where you are confused, not clear or simply need more information. Make a note and ask the client directly for clarification about the point which saves you time trying to figure out what the law might be for issues which ultimately do not arise.

Whether there is very little information or too much, this is an intentional way to assess how you deal with the information you have in front of you in the given time. It will be helpful to write on the factual and legal page above some typical things you might want to discuss with the client around the practice area of law.

The danger of getting too fixated on writing a list of questions around a potential issue is that if the client gives you information that does not warrant the remainder of your questions to be asked, it can throw you off guard. This is because you were relying too heavily on an assumption you made which is now redundant. Also, do not feel the need to go down the list of questions in the order you have them. If a client raises something deal with it in the moment which helps the flow of the interview.

For example, in an interview for property practice, you may make a list of questions to ask the client around financing the property through a mortgage (your assumption) but realise in the interview that the client is a cash buyer. It is much better to have trigger words around which you can ask a range of questions. So, when asking about financing the property – trigger words could be: 'mortgage?', 'cash?', 'loans?', 'company?', 'insurance?' – then you have some flexibility to ask questions based on what the client tells you. The trigger words help you to avoid forgetting to ask about any key information in relation to a particular issue.

The strategy below may help you gather relevant information to provide any preliminary advice (if required). It will also be relevant for you to include any legal issues discovered in your attendance note.

Below is a non-exhaustive list of some typical questions or areas to consider for property practice and wills and probate, depending on the information you are given to help you to determine the factual and legal issues.

Property Practice

8.07 You must try to avoid making assumptions about the client's matter; instead explore by asking good questions.

8.08 *Client Interviewing Skills*

- **Some Practical Questions to Consider for a Property Practice Scenario**

  ❖ **Example**

  ➢ *Leasehold*

  8.08 If your instructions tell you the client already has a business set up and is looking to lease a new property to set up another business, you want to find out about both. The focus is on finding out more about the new business and if it involves the existing business. Do not make assumptions but ask questions which allow you to offer advice around the new business and any issues identified.

  ❖ **Questions to Consider**

  8.09
  - Do they own the existing business with anyone else? Is there a conflict of interest? Any non-compete issues?
  - Do they want to purchase or rent the property? Through the business or in their personal capacity?
  - What type of business will it be? Are there any licensing issues or requirements?
  - How long does the client want to lease the property? This will determine whether or not it needs to be registered.
  - Do they have the contact details for the agent, owner, other party's solicitors?
  - What is the yearly rental rate etc and how many years are left on the lease or has it expired?
  - Should the client renew the existing lease or create a new one? What are the pros and cons of either option for what the client wants to do?

  ❖ **Example**

  ➢ *Freehold*

  8.10 If your instructions tell you the client is a first-time home buyer and wants to know what the conveyancing process involves and the timescale, only talk about the stage they are at in the process. For example, if they are at the exchange stage, there is no point talking about the pre-exchange stage. The following are some general questions to think about in the preparation stage.

  ❖ **Questions to Consider**

  8.11
  - Who are they buying with – on their own or with somebody else?
  - What are the details of the new home? Price? Address?
  - Financial set-up: is there a mortgage approved or is the client a cash purchaser?

- Does a person who gives the client a cash gift need to get independent financial advice that they will have no beneficial interest or share in the home?
- If there is a mortgage approved, will you be representing the lender? How will any gift impact the lender's position?
- The three stages in the conveyancing process explained: pre-exchange – exchange/completion – post-completion.
- If more than one person, how do they want to hold the property? As joint tenants or tenants in common?
- What happens if the funds are not available on completion? What are the options and consequences?

Wills and Probate

8.12 You must try to avoid making assumptions about the client's matter; instead explore by asking good questions.

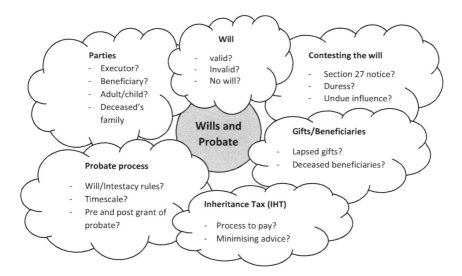

- ***Some Practical Questions to Consider for a Wills and Probate Law Scenario***

❖ **Example**

➢ *Instructions to make a will*

8.13 If your instructions are that the client is coming in to make a will you need to find out as much information as possible about their family and assets, without making any assumptions.

8.14 *Client Interviewing Skills*

❖ **Questions to Consider**

8.14
- What is their immediate and extended family set up?
- What do they want to do? List all their assets and any specific gifts etc.
- Are they elderly or vulnerable and do they understand what they want to do (have capacity)? Do you have any concerns? What will you do?
- Do you notice any language which suggests undue influence or duress?

❖ **Example**

➢ *Instructions for the Administration of an Estate*

8.15 If your instructions are that the client is coming in to ask you to help with the administration of an estate of a deceased member of their family or a friend, you need to find out as much information as possible, without making any assumptions.

❖ **Questions to Consider**

8.16
- Is there a will and is it valid? Procedure will depend on the validity of the will, the absence of one (intestacy rules), or where partial intestacy rules apply (ie there is a valid will but a change that affects the instructions, eg a beneficiary dies)?
- Is the client happy with their role as an executor? What are their options?
- Do you need to explain the probate process (pre-grant of probate – post-grant of probate)?
- Does the estate have enough to pay inheritance tax and any debts/liabilities?
- Are there any potential disputes over the beneficiary's gifts? Potential claims against the estate?
- How can you protect the interests of the executor?
- What happens when there is not enough money to pay the beneficiary or a specific gift has lapsed or does not exist anymore?

The Interview

8.17 For the actual interview with the client, in 25 minutes, you are expected to:
- meet the client;
- build rapport and trust;
- obtain their instructions;
- offer any preliminary advice (if required);

- try to convince them that you can competently and efficiently deal with their matter; and
- share what next steps you will take after the meeting.

It is a daunting prospect for many lawyers, but this is where your experience and the skills part comes into it. This section is split into three sub-sections:

- Beginning the Interview;
- the Middle (main body of the Interview);
- Ending the Interview.

You need to manage your time really well (without obviously rushing through it). You have to confidently and skilfully bring the interview back on track if the client goes off in a different direction or asks you to deal with something unrelated to the instructions. All of this can be done professionally and in an affable manner, so the client does not perceive you to be rude or unprofessional.

The Assessment Specification states you are not required to provide *'detailed advice at this stage'*, but do enough to win the client's trust so they want to instruct you. So, if you need to provide any preliminary advice, offer it. However, feel confident in telling the client that if you do not have all the information you cannot properly advise them and it could be negligent to do so. You should caveat any advice by saying the position might change, depending on a review of all the information. This may address the client's concerns, whilst still maintaining your credibility.

See the client interview as a fact-finding exercise to get you to a position where you can provide them with some preliminary advice (if required) and then explain what you propose to do in a follow-up meeting if the client is happy to proceed.

Below is a breakdown of the three parts to the interview with practical tips on how to deal with common client challenges you may encounter in the assessment.

I have provided you with ways to overcome some of the practical challenges and adapt them to suit your style and location (the context for small talk is travelling on the tube in central London). Therefore just reading them in a 'parrot fashion' way and learning the phrases will not be enough. You need to be able to say them with authenticity, which takes skill and you should re-read Chapter 5, Communication Skills.

- ### *Beginning the Interview*

> *'A smile is the shortest distance between two people'*
>
> **Victor Borge**

8.18 A smile goes a long way – especially when you only have 25 minutes and need to build rapport with the client. A smile is non-verbal and immediately makes you more approachable and affable. Obviously, your smile will be dictated by the scenario the client has come to see you about. It might be a more open and happier smile if your client is a first-time buyer of a new home or wants to purchase a property for a new business. Alternatively, it may be more subtle if

8.18 *Client Interviewing Skills*

they are coming in to see you about the administration of an estate or a potential dispute where a will might be contested. A smile with soft facial expressions should be appropriate for either type of situations.

Sadly, a smile alone is not enough to build rapport. Some small talk is essential too and helps you both relax. Even if you only have 25 minutes, small talk does not have to take long, but it does have to be authentic and not come across like it is a 'tick box' exercise. A client will see straight through it and it may offend them or you may appear disingenuous. It will have the opposite effect to building rapport and trust.

Although you do not have to introduce yourself by name, I think psychologically when you meet someone new it is natural to want to introduce yourself – it is what you would do in practice and it helps build a connection.

So, although it is an assessment and you do not have to do it, my advice is to include it. You may do it differently in work but have a good structure you can follow by practising it so even if you feel nervous on the day, it will boost your confidence because you know what you need to do at the start and how to do it.

A good strong introduction sets the scene. You could start by saying something along the lines of:

'Hello and thank you for coming in to see me today. My name is [your name] and I work in the [practice area] department.'

You do not have to use your name. However, if you do want to and you have a name that may be difficult to pronounce do not say it quickly. Sometimes lawyers say it quickly and quietly so it comes across as mumbled, as if they are embarrassed. That can make it difficult for the client to hear it and create an awkward situation where they do not want to ask you to repeat it. Although you might think this is a very minor point, it could affect how the client might feel from the outset.

You could also introduce yourself with your full name, but let the client know they can call you by a shortened version of it. Say your name with a smile, looking at the client, which can make both of you feel a bit more relaxed from the outset.

If the client has a name that you cannot pronounce or spell, ask them how you pronounce it and repeat it (this should be done with a soft facial expression and smile). On your paper, you can write their name down phonetically to help you pronounce it correctly.

Also, think about how you want to address the client. This will be a judgement call, but if you are unsure, use a more formal salutation and ask them how they would like to be addressed. For example:

'Would you like me to call you Ms Halai or Neeta?'

You may then follow that with some small-talk questions around their journey over to see you, the weather (the British are well known for talking about this subject!) or anything else you feel might be relevant. For example:

'Did you find the office OK?

It might be a good idea to look at Chapter 5, Communication Skills, Questioning (para **5.44**) to read more around different types of questions because I frequently hear the above type of closed question asked. This question is only relevant if it is a new client, not for one who has used the firm before, so read your instructions carefully. As it is a closed question, you can expect a limited response. If the client responds with a 'yes' or 'no' it can often make asking a follow up question difficult because there is no flow of information from a closed question. If you ask a range of closed questions, they need to be asked in a way that comes across as soft and aligns with your body language; otherwise the pace of asking them can come across a little quick, curt and unnatural (sometimes a little interrogatory).

'How was your journey in today?'

This question is an open, neutral question, and much better because it allows the client to speak a little more about their journey and that helps build rapport. If the client's answers to the small talk are quick, it is easier to move on to the main issues that need to be discussed. However, if the client goes into a lot of detail about their journey or whatever else you have asked them, do not stop them abruptly or tell them you only have 25 minutes or less. Even if that is true, the client may feel that you are rude or rushing them and that does not build rapport, trust or confidence. It is not a great start to the interview.

You do need to learn how to interject appropriately and skilfully, using empathy to take back control of the interview, so you can move it forward. For example: the client may explain that the journey into the office was a nightmare, and then proceeds to tell you details in a long-winded way. Your decision to interject has to link to something they say which allows you to hook it onto something else, to move the conversation forward, in a natural way. This allows you to take back control of the interview.

Once the client has said a little about their nightmare journey, getting lost or the weather etc, when it feels appropriate, you could interject, saying (the words), aligned with your facial expressions (body language) and using your voice congruently, something along these lines:

- **Example 1**

    'Oh dear, I'm sorry you got so lost – I remember when I first started here I got lost too! Hopefully, it won't happen again and the good news is at least you are here now. So, before we start, would you like a glass of water?

    (Client will respond)

    OK, so, you've come to see me about …'

- **Example 2**

    'Yes, I love the summer too! But travelling on the tube in the heat can be a nightmare in rush hour, but at least you're here now. Next time, we'll make an appointment for you outside of the rush-hour period. So, before we discuss why you're here, can I offer you a glass of water?

    (Client will respond)

    OK, so, I understand …'

8.19 *Client Interviewing Skills*

- **Example 3**

  'I know this must be a difficult time for you and I'm so sorry to hear about your loss ... So, I don't want to keep you here any longer than necessary. Before we start, can I get you a glass of water?

  (Client will respond)

  OK, so let's look at ...'

Responses similar to the examples above will very quickly make the client realise that you empathise and understand. The closed question about asking them if they would like a glass of water is the caring and connecting question which allows you to move away from what they were saying (their story) and focus on what you want to do (discuss the matter). It allows you to change the subject in a more subtle way that flows nicely and allows you to take back control of the interview.

Even though it is an assessment and you will not have access to offer the client any tea/coffee or water, you can still ask them which makes the conversation more authentic to what you would do in practice. The client will know that you will not be able to get them a drink but on the off chance the client does say they would like one, you can say something along these lines:

  'No problem at all, I will arrange for this to be brought in, until then, let's see how I can help you.'

Obviously, you will not be able to get them a drink, but this allows you to move on and start to deal with the matter in a natural way.

Although reading this may seem like the whole introductory part would take quite a large chunk of your 25 minutes, it can all be done effectively within a couple of minutes. That is why practising is key to making sure you are confident when you do the introductory part. There is no reason why you should not be when it has nothing to do with the law.

- **The Middle (Main Body of the Interview)**

  'Focus like a laser, not a flashlight.'

  Michael Jordan

8.19 You should be in control of the interview by this stage, even if the client does most of the talking by giving you the information you need. Being in control does not mean you come across as dictatorial, authoritative or too formal; it can be done in an approachable way and with empathy (where required).

You have to start confidently and let the client know what you intend to do (the structure) for the interview. This 'framing' technique lets the client know what to expect, helps you keep the client on track and interrupt, if they talk too quickly or stray off the topic. Obtaining the client's permission to interrupt them (when necessary), will keep the flow of the interview and help you manage your time better.

No-one likes to be interrupted and it can break the flow of the conversation. However, by framing it upfront, you can do it without coming across as rude or hesitant and you do not have to apologise every time. You can say something along the lines of:

'During the interview there may be times when I have to ask you to slow down or repeat something and it's not that I'm not listening or I'm being rude by interrupting you, it's purely to make sure I get everything down correctly. Is that OK with you?'

The closed question at the end, means that the client will most likely say 'yes' and give you their permission, if said affably and with authenticity. They want your help and your proactive stance is more likely to instil confidence in them than not.

If you are worried that a client might think you are rude for interrupting them quite a lot you are right, if you have not framed it upfront. If you forewarn them, I have never yet come across a client who might say something like *'No, don't interrupt me'*. Of course, it comes down to how skilfully the statement and question is asked. Their permission is the green light to allow you (if required) to interrupt their flow whenever you need to and do it confidently. They will not have a problem with it, because you have told them it might happen and you have their permission, so, it will not be perceived negatively.

You have to focus closely on what your client is telling you. That means be present and do not get distracted or start to worry about not knowing the law in relation to what they say. Such distractions will cost you in terms of time, missing important information and understanding the client's matter comprehensively.

You might be required to deal with client care in the interview. This can be dealt with at the beginning of the interview or at the end. My suggestion is to do it at the beginning so you can practise what you want to say before you get into the main reason for why the client has come to see you. Some key points to cover with the client might be:

- taking down the client's personal details;
- telling the client who will be working on their matter if instructed;
- telling the client about fees and other costs with any payment options;
- how the client can complain if unhappy with the service provided; and
- their communication preference (ie email or phone);
- asking the client for two forms of identification.

❖ **Client Identification (ID)**

8.20 If you need to cover client care then it will include the 'Know Your Client' requirement, where you need to ask them for two forms of ID if they are a new client. Ask to see their ID and, if they have brought it with them, state that you will take copies of it after the interview and return the originals to them.

8.20 *Client Interviewing Skills*

When a client says they do not have their ID on them or have one form of it but not the other, they may offer to email it to you after the interview. A mistake that many lawyers make is agreeing to accept email copies of the ID. You cannot accept them (unless they are certified copies) and you need to convey that to the client. You could say something like:

> 'Unfortunately, we can't accept email ID, we need to see the original. So just bring it in when convenient for you and we will take a copy and return it straightaway.'

Acceptable forms of original ID could be a:

- passport;
- driving licence;
- utility bill (less than three months old); or
- bank statement (less than three months old).

One form of ID should include photographic identification and another should show the client's address. A UK driving licence has both a photo and address on it. However, it can only be used as one form of ID. Either the client can:

- use it as proof of their photographic ID, so they need to provide another form of acceptable ID with their address on it, such as a bank statement or utility bill; or
- use it as proof of their address, so they will need to provide another form of acceptable photographic ID, such as a passport.

After doing the initial client care and taking down the client's personal details (if required), you should be ready to move into the reason why they have come to see you. Clients may not give you all the information you require: just as in real-life, a client rarely tells you everything you need to know, in the right order and perfectly articulated. This means you have to work for the information, by listening attentively and asking lots of pertinent questions. You can read more about listening and questioning skills in Chapter 5, Communication Skills (paras **5.43** and **5.44**).

If you are required to provide them with preliminary advice you should do it but caveat it with the fact that what you say is based on the information you have to hand. Below is a very simplified example just to illustrate the point of how to use language in a clear, concise and practical manner. Do not forget, you also need to be aware of when empathy is required. You could easily use the same style of dialogue for any of the practice areas of law.

In any interview where there are a number of options available for what the client wants to do you should suggest them. You will interview a client in property practice and wills and probate which are usually non-contentious areas of the law. However, you might find the preliminary advice you have to give could include elements of dispute resolution (eg if the client points out that there is a potential dispute over a property matter or the validity of a will). You should be able to explain the pros and cons of litigation by stating how expensive, timely and costly it is generally and that it is usually the last resort. You should be able to also discuss various other options available.

Below I will share brief examples of the two practice areas of law you cover for client interviewing to provide you with an idea of how to respond generally when you can or cannot provide preliminary advice. You should adapt the dialogue to a style that works for you and it is not provided for you to learn verbatim because it needs to be authentic to your speaking style. You want it to come across as natural and congruent with your body language and voice. You can read more about this area in Chapter 5, Communication Skills.

❖ **Example**

➢ *Wills and Probate Scenario*

8.21 The client has come to see you about disputing his father's will and wants to make an inheritance claim.

If you have a client who has come in with documents to support their claim, you may feel they do have a strong case and you can say something along these lines:

> *'On the face of it, you may have a claim against ... under the provisions ... because you can show ... Although you have strong evidence, it is very complex and challenging to argue ...*
>
> *Formally going down this route of contesting the will is not the best option to start with ... I suggest ...'*

If you cannot advise the client in any detail that is fine, do not panic and remember you are only expected to provide preliminary advice (where appropriate). Explain exactly why you cannot provide detailed advice, so it does not reduce your credibility with the client. You can say something along these lines:

> *'Unfortunately, without reviewing all the evidence in detail I cannot properly advise you on the strength of your potential claim.*
>
> *You have to understand that contesting the will can really further damage your relationship with ... and it is an expensive and lengthy process, which may not be financially worth it in the end.*
>
> *It is very complex and challenging to argue ...*
>
> *There are a number of options we can look at before this stage ... but I do need to review everything in detail and get back to you. I hope you understand?'*

Notice how by asking a closed question after your justification, you are asking the client to agree with you. In some scenarios, the client will agree, if you have made it clear why you cannot advise them in detail. In some instances, where the client may push you for an answer, you need to be assertive and ultimately do want the client to instruct you, so you have to explain your position again more empathetically. For example:

> *'I'm sorry, I know it is not what you want to hear today, but unfortunately, it would be wrong for me to offer you advice on the strength of your case without having all the information before me. Once I've had a chance to review it all, we can set up another appointment and I can talk you through all the options and my advice.'*

It is not helpful to try to please the client by making hypothetical suggestions. It means you often end up using non-committal language like 'I think ...' 'Maybe ...'

8.22 *Client Interviewing Skills*

'I'm not sure, but ...' or 'Possibly ...' This can cause confusion and misunderstanding. You need to remember that the goal is for you to gain the client's trust, so that they feel confident in instructing you on the matter. Therefore, it is best to refrain from giving any detailed advice, unless you are absolutely sure it is right, based on the information you are given, what documents you have seen and that you have the whole picture. What also happens when you start speculating is you become unsure of what to say, so you tend to use more gap fillers, such as: 'errm', 'umm' and this can raise doubts and affect your credibility.

❖ **Example**

➢ *Property Practice Scenario*

8.22 The client is a first-time buyer of a home and wants to know what the process entails and the timescale. The client's parents are paying for the deposit as a wedding gift. The client will finance the purchase with the help of a mortgage.

On the deposit issue, you can say something like:

'Unfortunately, we cannot accept the payment from your parents because they are not our client. What you need to do is ...

Also, as you are getting a mortgage your lender will require that your parents obtain independent legal advice and understand that they will not have any beneficial interest in your new home – that means it is an unconditional gift and they have no rights over the home. I appreciate it is a gift and this may not be the case, but the lender will insist on this formality.'

Then you can explain the conveyancing process in a structured way by saying something like:

'There are three key stages: pre-exchange, exchange-completion and post-completion. I will explain each part and you can ask questions at any time.

Firstly, the pre-exchange stage means there are a number of things we need to do to make sure that the seller actually owns the property and can sell it to you. We can do what is called a "title check" to ensure the property has a good and marketable title. It's a bit like doing all the checks on the property for you and [name of the lender]. The things we need to do include ...

Secondly, once we are happy to proceed to an exchange of contracts, we can also agree a completion date. Exchange of contracts is very important because the deposit is paid at this stage and you are legally bound to complete on the agreed date. If you decide to pull out at this stage the consequences are ...

After you have signed the mortgage deed [name of the lender] will release the money to us for completion to take place.

And finally, after completion we have to do a number of steps such as pay the stamp duty within [X] days to the HMRC and complete and file all the relevant paperwork which includes sending [state documents] ... to the Land Registry within [X] days. This is to register the property in your name and the mortgage with [name of the lender].'

Do not let the fact that it is an assessment make you feel like you have to be 'more formal' with the client. If you come across as too cold or unemotional rather than warm and approachable, this will not help you build rapport or trust. It may make the client defensive and the whole interview less enjoyable from both your perspectives. You may think it is an assessment so it will not be 'enjoyable' but if you treat the assessor as a client and do what you would do in practice, after the initial introduction stage, your nerves should have disappeared. You can read more around nerves in Chapter 6, Managing Nerves, Fear and Failure.

If you are used to doing interviews try to emulate those settings and make sure you take account of what is culturally appropriate in England and Wales too. You can read more in Chapter 5, Communication Skills, Cultural Appropriateness (para **5.20**).

Remember, the client will not assess you on the law, but on your skills. So do not overwhelm them with the details of the legal issues identified which you should mention in the attendance note. Anything relevant the client tells you should be included in the attendance note which will help shape your legal advice.

❖ **Making Notes During the Interview**

8.23 My top tip when making notes during the interview is to make them legible and structured and create a template that will help you when you have to do the attendance note (straight after the interview). You can read more about this in Chapter 9, Writing the Attendance Note.

You want to use your interview notes without duplicating them in your attendance note. If you scribble notes, use shorthand or if your writing is unreadable and all over the page, you will need to re-write the notes for the attendance note. This wastes your valuable time and may mean you do not complete it or cover everything you discussed with the client.

One strategy is that you have separate sheets of paper, and label and number them for your interview, as shown above in the 'Preparation Stage' at para **8.06**. Then when you write the attendance note, you can refer to a particular page from your interview notes, to save you re-writing the information. For example, page one could be split into two parts called 'personal details' and 'others' details'. On this page, you would note down all the client's relevant personal details (full name, address, date of birth, email address, phone number) and any other people mentioned that you think might be important to contact.

Then when you come to do the attendance note, read Chapter 9, Writing an Attendance Note, The Attendance Note Template (para **9.07**). It has four sub-headings within it and the first one is Personal Details and Other People's Details. If you wrote all the relevant information down during the interview on page 1, it means you do not have to re-write the information again. In your attendance note, you can say something like: 'Please see page one of the interview notes'. All page one should have on it is the contact details of the client and anyone else you think is relevant so the assessor can clearly identify who and what you mean.

It has to be absolutely clear where the information is (so number the pages) and it has to be easily legible and identifiable because the assessor will not make any assumptions in your favour if they cannot find the information or it is not clearly labelled where they can find it. It is probably unrealistic that you will be able to

8.24 *Client Interviewing Skills*

write a good set of comprehensive notes in a structured order during the interview for sub-heading three (Factual and Legal Issues). So, the rest of the attendance note will need to be handwritten in a clear, concise and legible style. See Chapter 9, Writing an Attendance Note, Attendance Note Template (para **9.07**).

- **Ending the Interview**

    'A good last impression is just as important as a good first impression.'

    Anon

8.24 There will be a clock in the room, so keep track of time. If you do not finish the interview in the allocated 25 minutes it will come to an unprofessional and abrupt end. For example, there may be a knock on the door, or the client may have instructions to end it when time is up.

Whether you have all the information or not, around the 20 minutes mark you should have a good idea of whether you will be on time or be timed out before you get a chance to end the interview. In the last five minutes you need to know what to do and how to do it professionally.

❖ **Running Out of Time**

8.25 You need to think about what to do if you know there is still a lot of information to cover, but you realise there is no way you will have enough time to cover it all. It is better to end the interview professionally, than to finish abruptly.

If you realise you will run out of time without covering everything you want with the client and you will not have time to summarise, what you can do is subtly warn the client that the interview is coming to an end. You can say something like:

> *'Thank you so much for all the information you have given me so far, it has been very helpful. I have enough for me to review and if you would like to instruct us, we can set up another appointment for you to come in. Is that ok?'*

Notice that this is actually making a statement to wrap up the interview rather than offering the client an option to carry on and give you more information. This is appropriate when you know you will be timed out and the interview will end abruptly, without you getting all the information anyway. It is much better to manage the situation and control the end of the interview than for it to end unprofessionally. The last sentence is a closed question and framed to justify a positive response from the client.

By this stage, you should have grasped enough information to address the client's key issues and concerns to write your attendance note. You should also be able to identify any factual and legal issues that impact them and what other information is required. You can add in the next steps part of the attendance note that you will make another appointment to see the client.

❖ **Ending on Time**

8.26 When you have all the information you need to draw the interview to a close, summarise briefly what you have discussed and state what you propose to do after the interview.

It is also an opportunity to ask the client if they have any questions about what has been discussed. You can let them know that the interview is coming to an end by saying something like:

> 'I have pretty much everything I need from you for now. So, before we finish, do you have any questions about what we have discussed today?'

Notice how the first sentence is telling the client that you have all the information you need and by saying 'So, before we finish' you are clearly telling them the interview is coming to an end. The following question is a closed question and only asking the client about anything that you have already discussed (ie not giving them the opportunity to ask anything new and outside the remit of the discussion). If the client wants you to go through a few things again decide what you can address and if you are really concerned about time, you can say something like:

> 'Please don't worry if you can't remember everything we have discussed. I will write to you explaining clearly what we covered, so you can go through it in your own time and come back to me with any questions. I appreciate it is a lot of information to take in.'

This type of statement offers the client reassurance and brings the interview to a nice and professional end. Be clear about what you will do or what the client is required to do.

Finally, thank the client for coming in again to see you and tell them you will be in touch. Shake hands with the client and do not forget to smile.

Below is the client interviewing structure that you should have in mind when practising your client interviewing skills:

Client Interviewing Structure

The Beginning

(1)　Introduce yourself.

(2)　Etiquette – small talk.

(3)　Explain the structure of the interview.

The Middle

(4)　Explore the factual and legal issues.

The End

(5)　Provide a summary and next steps.

Remember to read each scenario and any 'Notes to Candidates' carefully and only deal with any of the following issues if the instructions require it:

(1)　**Client care** (eg ID, the retainer, complaints)

(2)　**Funding** (eg legal aid, insurance, fees, disbursements and expenses)

8.26 *Client Interviewing Skills*

> *'People will forget what you said, people will forget what you did, but people will never forget how you made them feel.'*
>
> **Maya Angelou**

Client Interviewing – Top Ten Tips

(1) Read the Assessment Specification criteria and understand what you will be marked against for the interview.

(2) The key objective is to win the client's trust and confidence, to gain their instructions.

(3) Small talk is important and helps you connect with the client.

(4) Offer preliminary advice (if required); details of the law are not required.

(5) Smile (appropriately) and engage with the client to build rapport.

(6) Take control of the interview by structuring it and getting the client's permission when needed.

(7) Listen attentively to the client rather than worrying about whether or not you know the law.

(8) Do not make assumptions. Ask open questions initially and then 'drill down' questions to clarify your understanding.

(9) Read Chapter 5, Communication Skills to complement this chapter.

(10) Keep an eye on time and know when to start bringing the interview to an end.

Chapter 8

Client Interviewing Skills: Appendix

Appendix 8A: Assessment Specification

This has been reproduced with permission from the SRA:

Overview

Candidates will be given an email from a partner or a secretary stating who the client is and providing an indication of what the client has come to discuss. The email may, but will not necessarily, be accompanied by documents. The email may also indicate specific legal issues which candidates should have particular regard to in the interview and the subsequent attendance note/case analysis.

Candidates will have 10 minutes to consider the email and/or documents. They will then have 25 minutes to conduct the interview with the client. The client may be, but will not necessarily be, somebody in vulnerable circumstances.

An assessor who will play the role of the client will assess the candidate only on skills (not on application of law).

In the interview candidates should aim to win the client's trust and confidence. They should try to obtain all the relevant information and as full an understanding as possible of the client's concerns. Candidates do not need to provide detailed advice at this stage. They can conduct the interview on the basis that they will be advising the client in detail at a later date. However, candidates do need to give enough preliminary advice and to address enough of the client's concerns to establish the client's trust and confidence.

Assessment Objective

Candidates can demonstrate they are able to conduct an interview with a client.

Assessment Criteria

Candidates' performance in the interview will be assessed against the following criteria:

Client Interviewing Skills: Appendix

Skills

(1) Listen to the client and use questioning effectively to enable the client to tell the solicitor what is important to them.

(2) Communicate and explain in a way that is suitable for the client to understand.

(3) Conduct themselves in a professional manner and treat the client with courtesy, respect and politeness including respecting diversity where relevant.

(4) Demonstrate client-focus in their approach to the client and the issues (ie demonstrate an understanding of the problem from the client's point of view and what the client wants to achieve, not just from a legal perspective).

(5) Establish and maintain an effective relationship with the client so as to build trust and confidence.

You are not assessed on the law for the actual client interview. You should read this in conjunction with the Chapter 1, The SQE Journey, Appendix 1B which details what the Competence Statement includes and in particular the Statement of Solicitor Competence.

In Chapter 3, Functioning Legal Knowledge, Appendix 3A you can find an overview of the law covered for property practice and wills and probate.

More detailed information can be found on the SRA website (www.sra.org.uk).

Chapter 9

SQE Part 2

Writing the Attendance Note

'Good writing is clear thinking made visible.'
William Wheeler

In this chapter you will learn:

✓ How to use your client interview notes in an efficient way.
✓ What type of template might work for the attendance note.
✓ What to write in each suggested section to meet the criteria.
✓ How to use an appropriate layout.
✓ When it is appropriate to use bullet points.

Introduction

9.01 This chapter should be read in conjunction with Chapter 8, Client Interviewing Skills which deals with the practical aspects of the client interview. This is because after the interview you will have to handwrite an attendance note of what you covered with the client in the interview. It will also be beneficial for you to refresh your memory by looking again at Chapter 7, Writing in Professional English.

The first thing to do is understand what you are assessed against, so you can tailor your attendance note to cover the criteria. The Assessment Specification in Appendix 9A provides the full details but below is the key information that your attendance note should cover:

- all relevant information obtained from the client;
- an analysis of any legal issues that arise in the matter;
- a record of your initial advice (ie any preliminary advice offered);
- any specific factual or legal issues or questions raised;
- the next steps to be taken by you and/or the client.

9.02 Writing the Attendance Note

The actual client interview is assessed on the skills only, but the attendance note is assessed on the law and the skills equally. You will only be able to talk about any factual and legal issues in your attendance note if you gathered the information from the client. You can then provide a comprehensive and correct analysis based on it.

When lawyers who have failed the SQE Part 2 share their breakdown of results with me, I notice some score higher in the client interview (skills only) and lower on the attendance note (law and skills). A reason for this may be that the lawyer does not ask the right questions to gather information or makes assumptions about the client's matter. This is then conveyed in the attendance note and it means that the preliminary legal advice is not correct and comprehensive.

The SRA have provided a sample of what you could include in an attendance note for a wills and probate scenario (based on the client interview assessment sample). You can also find samples for all the other assessments on the SRA website (www.sra.org.uk).

The Assessment Criteria

9.02 You need to handwrite an attendance note based on all the relevant information you obtained from the client interview addressing any factual and legal issued identified. If you require any reasonable adjustments read Chapter 2, Preparing for the SQE, Fitness to Sit/Reasonable Adjustments (para **2.45**).

You can read about the more detailed version of the SRA criteria in Appendix 9A.

Below I have summarised and highlighted the criteria against which you are assessed.

- **Skills**

9.03

(1) Record all relevant information.

(2) Identify appropriate next steps.

(3) Provide client-focused advice on what the client wants to do and not just from a legal perspective.

- **Application of the Law**

9.04 You should note that, for all the assessments, your knowledge of the law needs to be applied:

- correctly; and
- comprehensively, identifying any professional conduct and ethical issues.

You should assess yourself against these criteria when you are practising writing the attendance note. These are assessed using the following grading scale:

Grade	Mark	Standard	Do you meet the competency requirements?
A	5	Superior performance	Yes, well above it
B	4	Clearly satisfactory	Yes, clearly meets it
C	3	Marginal pass	Yes, on balance, just meets it
D	2	Marginal fail	No, on balance, just fails it
E	1	Clearly unsatisfactory	No, clearly does not meet it
F	0	Poor performance	No, well below it

You can read more about the Competence Statement in Chapter 1, The SQE Journey, Appendix 1B which provides the context of what you are expected to know for practice as a newly qualified solicitor.

You have 25 minutes, so no time to waste. Have an attendance note template in mind. This will help you because you will need to do the attendance note from scratch and first impressions count. A well-presented attendance note that is legible with good layout is what you want the assessor to notice straightaway. It will make the assessor's job easier when marking it against the criteria. It also shows structure and clarity of thought, and that means you are less likely to miss out any important issues.

> *'Here is the golden rule ... Write legibly. The average temper of the human race would be perceptibly sweetened ...'*
>
> **Lewis Carroll**

I have suggested a template you can use for an attendance note. You do not have to use it or you can adapt it so that it works best for you. I would suggest that whatever template you use, have it in mind during the interview preparation stage (ten minutes) because it will help you save time if you want to refer to it for this part of the assessment. Remember, your interview notes and attendance note pages will need to be numbered if you intend to cross-reference between the two sets of notes for the attendance note.

Many lawyers may be used to typing or dictating notes for support staff to type up. However, this part of the assessment involves your handwriting, so it is a good idea to practise doing this exercise by hand.

The Purpose of an Attendance Note

9.05 After a client meeting or speaking to them over the phone, lawyers often place an attendance note on the client file. There are many reasons for this and some common ones are:

- It provides an accurate record of what was discussed with the client.
- It allows for another lawyer (in your absence) to pick up the file and know exactly what you have discussed with the client and what needs to be done.

9.06 *Writing the Attendance Note*

- It resolves potential disputes over what was or was not covered in the interview (at a later stage).

In practice, the attendance note is done straight after the client interview or any meetings. It summarises what was discussed and what needs to be done by which party and by when. It may also cover any advice, guidance or options offered as well as any risks and benefits. Attendance notes can vary in length so it will depend on what was discussed.

Normally, you would write to the client and cover what was discussed and what the next steps are on their matter. You may or may not provide the attendance note to the client – often it will depend on whether the client is charged for preparing it, in which case they would be entitled to it.

Post Interview – Failure to Address Key Issues

9.06 What do you do if you realise that you forgot (or ran out of time) to discuss an important point (factual or legal) with the client during the interview? Do not panic; be pragmatic. One way to deal with it is to write in your attendance note (in the appropriate sub-heading) something along the lines of:

'Need to discuss at the next meeting the issue of [state issue] and its [implications? options?].'

Notice this sentence is written using the future tense – it has not happened yet. This shows the assessor that you have identified a particular factual or legal issue that needs to be addressed with the client. You need to show that you can provide client-focused advice considering both their perspective and the legal perspective. If you did not get a chance to ask the client something that might affect any preliminary advice write down the advice and any potential options (to satisfy the legal criteria). You can then write in the next steps that a call or another appointment needs to be made for the client to come in and discuss the issues in more detail.

Just because this is an assessment, do not put anything in your attendance note that you did not actually say. If checked and your advice does not match up with it, you would be dishonest and not acting with integrity (two key SRA Principles). Read more about them in Chapter 3, Functioning Legal Knowledge Assessments, Appendix 3A.

Think about what you would do in practice, so be authentic and honest. Dishonest behaviour means you will have a very short career in law as a solicitor, if you actually make it past the SQE stage.

The Attendance Note Template

9.07 The attendance note template can vary. You can use one you are comfortable with or the one below which I have created to cover all the criteria that you are assessed against for completeness. An attendance note is not an essay. It usually has sections and sub-sections which can have bullet points, where appropriate.

The Attendance Note Template 9.07

The template below is just one example and the detail within it suggests some tips for what you might want to include in each section. It will also help you during the interview if you have in mind the sections during your preparation time (the ten minutes for the interview part), because it will guide you to ask relevant questions for each of the four sections. See Chapter 8, Client Interviewing, Preparation Stage (para **8.06**) for an example.

This is a snapshot of what your attendance note template can look like (remember you only have 25 minutes to complete it):

Attendance Note

Name: Client Name   **Date:** Today
Solicitor: Candidate   **Ref:** XX/01234/ABC
Time: 11am–11.25am   **Venue:** Office

Re: Subject Matter (what the client interview was about)

(1) Personal Details and Other People's Details

Sometimes it is easier to split this section into two parts, such as:

- *Personal Details*

Here you would write information such as: full name, address, date of birth, occupation, family set-up, financials etc (whatever information you think is relevant for the practice area of law).

- *Other People's Details*

Do you have to contact any other people, such as witnesses, the client's doctor, estate agent, other side's solicitors? Whoever is mentioned that you think you will need to contact, you can add their contact details in this sub-section or note down that the client needs to provide you with the details.

If you have made legible notes during the client interview, this is one section where you can easily refer back to your interview notes to avoid re-writing all the contact details again. For example, you could write something along these lines:

'See attached interview notes on page 1* for client's personal details.'

'See attached interview notes on page 1* for client's personal details and the witness's/doctor's details.'

*you must clearly cross-reference where the assessor needs to look on the interview notes (ie page 1) to find the information. They will not hunt for the information or second-guess where it might be in your notes or what you mean.

9.07 *Writing the Attendance Note*

You can see an example of how to use the cross-referencing style in Chapter 8, Client Interviewing Skills, Preparation Stage (para **8.06**). It shows you how to use four sheets of paper labelled with the four main sub-headings in this template.

(2) Professional Conduct

If there is more than one professional conduct issue, it is easier to use bullet points to deal with them. You can also add in any issue with identification (ID) here. For example:

'•   ID: client needs to bring in two forms of identification [state which ones] before the next meeting or any advice can be sent out. If they have only brought in one piece state what piece is outstanding and explain that email ID is not acceptable (if appropriate).

- Conflict of interest: is it a client, personal or a firm conflict of interest?'

Where there are no issues, you can simply write 'N/A' for non-applicable.

(3) Factual and Legal Issues

It might help you to split this into sub-sections:

- *Factual issues*

You can also write bullet points rather than full prose, essay style (where appropriate), as long as what you have written can be understood comprehensively. Here you would largely be referring to the information gathered from the client in your interview notes.

For example, in a property practice scenario for a leasehold property:

If the client brought in the lease then you can say it needs to be reviewed; or if they have not got it, you can write you have asked them to bring it in or email it. This request would be added to the next steps. You could write something like:

Client wants to purchase a shop to set up an events business which will provide high-end entertainment for special events. It will include offering themed parties. The client wants to do the following:

- *Buy the shop in her personal capacity – not through her existing business – with her friend Jamie. Jamie is aware of this new purchase and there are no issues such as a non-compete clause which affects the existing business.*

- *She will finance the purchase with her personal savings of [state amount].*

- *She would like to agree to a five-year lease and have the option to sub-assign. The existing lease has two years left on it.*

- *The client wants to do whatever option will be the quickest and most cost effective by either renewing the existing lease or creating a new one.*

- *Legal Issues*

This is where you provide any preliminary advice in a correct and comprehensive manner (law) by applying it to the client's instructions (skills).

State what the legal issues are specifically from the information the client provided you in the interview. Depending on what the client tells you (based on what you have asked them) you could write down any legal issues you identify. For example:

- Do you need to review the existing lease and what will you need to consider specifically (based on the client's instructions)?
- What are the pros and cons of renewing the existing lease or creating a new one?
- What negotiation points will you consider based on the client's instructions for a new lease as opposed to what is in the existing lease?

    Existing Lease

    (1)   [State details. Eg current lease rental, terms etc]

    (2)   [State any issues. Eg what can and cannot be done]

    New Lease

    (3)   [State suggestions and options]

- Are there any issues with what the client wants to do? Does the existing lease allow it?
- Will any licences be required?
- Do you need to do any legal research on a particular issue?
- What are the cost implications of a lease variation over creating a new lease?

If you decide that you prefer to deal with both the factual and legal issues holistically rather than split them, you should use sub-headings to clearly identify the key issues.

(4) Next Steps

Here you have to show the assessor that the following steps need to be taken after the interview.

There do not need to be seven of them, just whatever you feel is appropriate for the context. These are usually quite brief and confirm what you have told the client you will do and anything they will do. For example:

1. Client to provide ID – has said she will bring it in on [state date/next appointment].
2. Open file and send client care letter.
3. Call/write to the estate agent for the property and landlord's details and the lease.

9.07 *Writing the Attendance Note*

> 4. Client will bring in/email the lease for review.
> 5. Review the existing lease to see if it allows for what the client wants to do.
> 6. Research what type of licence may be required (if appropriate) and the process of obtaining it.
> 7. Arrange a follow-up call/meeting with the client to discuss both options.
>
> You may find that there may not be any next steps required. In this case you can say something like:
>
> > 'No further action is required now as the client came in initially for the complimentary meeting.'
> >
> > 'No further action is required at this stage because the client wants to think about how they want to proceed.'

Time is of the essence and organising what you want to say into the four sections suggested above are a good start. In 25 minutes, you do not have a lot of time to plan and think about layout and what you want to write and where it should go.

Also, if you feel you are running out of time (because the weightiest writing section is going to be section three (factual and legal issues), at least make sure you add in some bullet point next steps to correspond with what you have written (where relevant). It is better to show some level of completeness than stopping abruptly in the middle of another point which shows an incomplete attendance note. Therefore, when you realise time is nearly up, try to write something down for each section (where appropriate).

The SRA will not provide a template so if for the main part of the attendance note you prefer to use a different template make sure you practise your handwriting using that template so you familiarise yourself with it.

Remember, bullet points will help you get more information down as long as they are comprehensive enough to be understood and written in short sentences (not long paragraphs).

> **Writing the Attendance Note – Top Ten Tips**
>
> (1) Make sure you have an attendance note template in mind.
>
> (2) If you are going to use the suggested template format make sure you get used to reproducing it whilst practising in your handwriting.
>
> (3) If you want to cross-reference it with your interview notes (as mentioned in Chapter 8, Client Interviewing Skills) make sure you number all the pages.
>
> (4) Watch your spelling, grammar and punctuation. Minor typos will not be penalised.

(5) Make sure you have enough 'white space' in the layout so it makes it easier to read.

(6) If you make a mistake, just cross it out neatly.

(7) Write in a way that shows you applying the law to the client's instructions (facts) in a correct and comprehensive manner. Make it more advisory rather than academic.

(8) Do not state that you discussed something with the client if you did not. Use the future tense to suggest what you will discuss with the client in the next meeting.

(9) An attendance note should be an accurate reflection of what was discussed with the client as well as identifying any factual and legal issues and next steps.

(10) Try to review your attendance note before time is up.

Chapter 9

Writing the Attendance Note: Appendix

Appendix 9A: Assessment Specification

This has been reproduced with permission from the SRA:

Overview

Candidates will have 25 minutes to write, by hand, an attendance note/legal analysis of the interview they have just completed.

All relevant information obtained during the interview should be recorded in the attendance note/legal analysis. Candidates should provide an analysis of any legal issues that arise in the matter and record their initial advice for the client. The attendance note/legal analysis should also identify the next steps to be taken by the solicitor and, where applicable, the client, as well as any ethical issues that arise and how they should be dealt with. This may (but will not necessarily) include options and strategies for negotiation. If the email from the partner or secretary has asked the candidate to deal with any specific issues or questions, then advice on these issues should also be included.

Assessment Objective

Candidates can demonstrate that they are able to produce an attendance note recording a client interview and initial legal analysis.

Assessment Criteria

Candidates will be assessed against the following criteria:

Skills

(1) Record all relevant information.

(2) Identify appropriate next steps.

(3) Provide client-focused advice (ie advice which demonstrates an understanding of the problem from the client's point of view and what the client wants to achieve, not just from a legal perspective).

Appendix 9A

> *Application of Law*
> (4)   Apply the law correctly to the client's situation.
> (5)   Apply the law comprehensively to the client's situation, identifying any ethical and professional conduct issues and exercising judgment to resolve them honestly and with integrity.

You should read this in conjunction with the Chapter 1. The SQE Journey, Appendix 1B which details what the Competence Statement includes and in particular the Statement of Solicitor Competence.

In Chapter 3, Functioning Legal Knowledge, Appendix 3A you can find an overview of the law covered for property practice and wills and probate.

More detailed information can be found on the SRA website (www.sra.org.uk).

Chapter 10

SQE Part 2

Advocacy

> '... One must study three points: first, the means of producing persuasion; second, the language; third, the proper arrangement of the various parts ...'
>
> **Aristotle**

In this chapter you will learn:

- ✓ Tools and techniques for building on and improving your communication skills.
- ✓ How to structure the content to ensure you cover all the key legal issues.
- ✓ How a structure will help you manage your time.
- ✓ Your own communication skills, style and preferences.
- ✓ How to make persuasive legal arguments.
- ✓ How to deliver your advocacy submission confidently and persuasively.
- ✓ How to handle any difficult questions by the judge.
- ✓ What measures to take to gauge your levels of improvement.

Introduction

10.01 This chapter will help you think about how to prepare practically for the advocacy assessment and how to deal with any difficult questions you may be asked. It will be beneficial for you to read Chapters 5, on Communication Skills and Chapter 6 on Managing Nerves, Fear and Failure which complement this chapter.

Initially it really makes sense for you to engage with an expert (such as a lawyer who has advocacy experience and understands the assessments). They can properly assess your skills and help you with the areas in which you need to improve. Once

10.02 *Advocacy*

you recognise what you need to do, you can then practise reinforcing those skills, rather than blindly practising them generally, without any tailored constructive feedback.

Advocacy is an art of performance and unless it is something you already have experience of doing, it can be daunting, with all the courtroom formalities and language used. Although there is a heavy overlap with presentation skills, it is different and can sometimes seem unusual and awkward for someone who has no previous experience. It is a highly valuable skill which requires you to demonstrate your academic ability and critical thinking skills. With practice, it also improves your communication skills and confidence.

Advocacy is not easy. Sometimes you have to think quickly whilst making your submission if you are asked a question. However, it does become easier with experience, but you can never take for granted what might happen in a courtroom. Practice and having a structure in place will help you deliver a confident and persuasive performance. The role of the judge will be played by a solicitor who will be the assessor and remember that they are human too!

The room you do your advocacy submission in will not be an actual courtroom set up. The judge will already be in the room when you enter. For criminal advocacy, you will make your submission standing up and for dispute resolution you will make the submission sitting down.

You are assessed equally on the law and skills. Therefore, the skill of structuring and delivering your advocacy submission bears as much weight as your knowledge of the law. This means you need to know the law and present it articulately and persuasively to the judge.

The SRA has provided a sample of what you could get for this type of assessment for a criminal litigation scenario on the SRA website (www.sra.org.uk).

Challenges Experienced for Advocacy

10.02 My observations of common challenges are typically around the following areas (this is not an exhaustive list or in any particular order):

- Unstructured arguments or submissions presented without persuasion – when speaking there is very little expression or intonation.
- Body language not being aligned with what is said so it comes across as less credible.
- Incorrectly addressing the judge based on the court in which the hearing takes place.
- Not using the supporting documents interactively (if supplied and where appropriate) – not drawing the judge's attention to look at a document and instead just referring to it or reading from it.
- Not knowing how to respond to a question asked by the judge when they do not know the law or give a vague answer – so speculating, waffling or saying something irrelevant rather than dealing with it in a professional manner.

- Not finishing or ending appropriately – so the ending is abrupt and confuses the judge as to whether you have finished.

These are just some examples and many lawyers I work with do not realise they do any of the above until it is pointed out to them. So, bear in mind and be open-minded to any constructive feedback, because you might do some of the above, without even realising it.

The Assessment Criteria

10.03 You will be required to conduct an advocacy submission based on a file of documents and will be told what court you will be in. This will help you determine courtroom etiquette and what form of address to use for the judge. The role of the judge will be played by the assessor who is a qualified solicitor.

You can read about the more detailed version of the SRA criteria in Appendix 10A.

Below I have summarised and highlighted the criteria against which you are assessed.

- ***Skills***

(1) Use appropriate language and behaviour.

(2) Have a clear and logical structure.

(3) Present a persuasive argument.

(4) Engage with the judge.

(5) Include all the key facts.

- ***Application of the Law***

You should note that for all the assessments your knowledge of the law needs to be applied:

- correctly; and
- comprehensively, identifying any professional conduct and ethical issues.

You should assess yourself against these criteria when practising advocacy. These are assessed using the following grading scale:

Grade	Mark	Standard	Do you meet the competency requirements?
A	5	Superior performance	Yes, well above it
B	4	Clearly satisfactory	Yes, clearly meets it
C	3	Marginal pass	Yes, on balance, just meets it
D	2	Marginal fail	No, on balance, just fails it
E	1	Clearly unsatisfactory	No, clearly does not meet it
F	0	Poor performance	No, well below it

10.04 Advocacy

You can read more about the Competence Statement in Chapter 1, The SQE Journey, Appendix 1B which provides the context of what you are expected to know for practice as a newly qualified solicitor.

As mentioned above and in Chapter 8, Client Interviewing Skills, it makes sense initially to have an expert to help you assess your levels. The expert should (ideally) be a lawyer and be able to combine their expertise in communication skills and advocacy to help you realise where you are in the grading scale and help you get to superior performance (if you are not at that standard already). It will also help you realise how to approach the advocacy assessment which you can read in conjunction with Chapter 2, Preparing for the SQE, Practising Skills (para **2.43**).

You should aim for Grade A (5 marks), superior performance across the skills criteria. Because on the day of the assessment, even with nerves, if you drop a grade, you would still be 'clearly satisfactory' Grade B (4 marks). You want to avoid falling into the 'marginal pass' zone Grade C (3 marks) for the skills. This is dangerous because it could tip your overall mark to fail if you are in a marginal standard for the law and skills in too many assessments.

There is no reason why you cannot try to achieve superior performance for the skills part, if you have relevant and sufficient work experience and have practised your skills, together with expert constructive feedback. This is where you can have the edge. It may be harder to be correct and comprehensive on all the areas of the law to achieve high scores, as you may not necessarily know all the relevant law – or even if you do, you may not cover it adequately.

The skills are based on how you deliver the law and test your communication and interpersonal skills. The only thing that can really affect your performance is feeling fearful or nervous on the day. Typically this can happen if you do not know the law or sometimes nerves just get the better of you and affect the way you deliver your submission. You can read more about this in Chapter 6, Managing Nerves, Fear and Failure.

Preparation Stage: 45 minutes

10.04 During the preparation stage you may be told what application to make in your instructions or you may have to work it out. You will be able to write notes and use them in your submission. Overall, you need to understand the information to be able to use it effectively and correctly. Remember, any legal materials (eg legislative extracts) will only be provided to you where, as a newly qualified solicitor, you would be expected to look them up. You may also have supporting documents that might be:

- not relevant so you do not need to use them;
- relevant so you use them.

It is a good idea to have a template to help you structure your advocacy submission and it should have an introduction, middle and conclusion.

Advocacy Structure

For an advocacy submission the following provides an overview of a structure that you might want to use:

The Beginning

The four-step introduction:

(1) Form of address for the judge*.

(2) Introduce yourself (optional).

(3) Introduce the client.

(4) State the reason for the hearing.

* Note which court you are doing your submission in dictates how you address the judge:

- Senior Judges (Court of Appeal/High Court) – 'My Lord/My Lady';
- Circuit Judge (The Recorder in a Crown Court) – 'Your Honour';
- District Judge (Magistrates' Court/County Court) – 'Judge';
- Magistrates (non-legal members) – 'Sir/Madam/Your Worships'.

I have included 'Your Worships' because it is sometimes incorrectly used to address a judge when it is only used for non-legal members. Your assessment will be assessed by a solicitor (not a lay bench) unless your instructions tell you otherwise.

The Middle

There are many ways to present your submission. The aim is to make it structured and easy for the judge to follow. Make sure that whatever law or rule is relied upon you do not just state it but *apply it* to the facts. For example:

➢ State the law or rule relied upon and relate it to the facts or key issues. It may be one key issue and you apply the appropriate legal test/law which may be made up of several parts.

Alternatively:

➢ Split the key issues up (if possible) and deal with each of them:

- Key issue 1: present the issue and state the law relied upon:

    (1) State the first point and apply the legal test/law or supporting evidence

    (2) State the second point and apply the legal test/law or supporting evidence.

10.05 *Advocacy*

> **The End**
>
> It depends on how you have structured your submission as to whether you need to summarise or conclude.
>
> ➢ Summarise – highlight the key strengths that support your position.
>
> ➢ Conclude – reiterate the reason why the judge should find in your favour.
>
> ➢ Deal with costs (optional) and any questions.

The structure will be heavily dictated by the instructions and what issues you need to address. You need to use it by applying the law so it is easy to follow and understand.

Remember, you only have 15 minutes to deliver your message. So you want to do it well and without reading too much from your notes. You are unlikely to have time to write a script whilst reading the instructions and any supporting documents. Also, by writing a script you are more likely to be drawn to read from it. Read Chapter 5, Communication Skills (para **5.26**) for information on the ingredients that make up communication skills to help you with your delivery.

Think about where your submission would fit within the hearing. If it is a contested hearing and the other side would have gone first, think about how you might address the matter. For example, in a criminal law scenario for a bail application, if you are the prosecutor you would go first and make an application to remand in custody and would provide the facts and supporting legal authorities. If you are defending the application (when you start), you would not ask the judge if they would like to be *'reminded of the facts'* because you should know that the prosecutor would have gone first in the hearing. So, think about what questions are relevant to your submission based on the order of when you would speak.

The preparation time is 45 minutes so this should give you some idea of the amount of information you may have to read to plan what you want to say in your advocacy submission.

It is unlikely that you will have time to read all the documents in detail so your reading skills and attention to detail will be tested to determine relevancy. Try not to be overwhelmed or panic if there are a lot of documents or too much information. Look at them with the instructions in mind to see if the documents support your submission. If you know exactly what you are looking for in a document, go straight to it and then briefly make sure you are using it in the correct context. Always keep an eye on the time; there will be a clock in the room. Read Chapter 5, Communication Skills, Preparation Time for Oral Assessments (para **5.39**) to help you manage your time.

Should You Skim Read or Scan?

10.05 It is unlikely that you will have time to read every document in detail and some might not even be relevant. Therefore, you must get used to skim reading or scanning a document, depending on what you are looking for.

Should You Skim Read or Scan? **10.07**

You may have a range of documents that you have to read such as (non-exhaustive list):

Criminal Litigation

- Witness statements;
- CPS advance disclosure file;
- Pre-sentence report;
- Experts' reports;
- Extracts of legal materials (eg PACE 1984, Criminal Justice Act 2003, Sentencing Guidelines etc).

Dispute Resolution

- Particulars of Claim/Counter Claim/Defence;
- Witness statements;
- Contract/Agreement;
- Expert reports;
- Financial documents;
- Extracts of legal materials (eg CPR).

You want to know quickly what the documents say to see if they support your position or not.

Below I have explained how you might use both these reading skills in your advocacy preparation.

- ***Skim Reading***

10.06 Skim reading means that you look through some text quickly to get an idea or a gist of what it is saying.

- ***Scanning***

10.07 Scanning means looking through a text to find some particular information. For example, you may be looking for a particular section or rule from the legal materials provided to make a specific legal point.

From your instructions and any supporting documents you are given in the preparation stage, you should be able to weave in relevant facts for your advocacy submission.

A top tip is to make sure the documents you want to refer to are kept aside or open to the correct page. Keep them in chronological order, so you do not get flustered looking for them or finding the correct page during your submission.

Read through the scenario instructions properly to understand exactly what you need to do. For example, if you are asked to address three issues for the client – that is the structure for the main part of your submission. You just need to:

10.08 *Advocacy*

- identify the level of detail required for each issue;
- interweave any supporting documents or evidence for each issue;
- decide what you want to say in the introduction and conclusion.

Within each of the three key issues there may be some sub-points you need to make. Some key issues will be more straightforward and quicker to deal with than others. If there are too many sub-points for all the three key issues, you should choose the most important points first and then decide whether all the sub-points are necessary. You should only be referring to what is relevant, especially, because you only have 15 minutes and you do not want to get through most of your time allocation by going into great detail on only one or two key issues at the expense of others that require the same level of detail.

You must be strict with yourself over the content and allocate time equally if all the key issues are weighty ones. Knowing what you want to say for each issue will help you work out timings. Also, do not read out large sections of legal material (if provided) but apply it to the facts. This is more persuasive and engaging.

If you speak too quickly it can be frustrating for the judge because they have to work harder to follow what you are saying. So, you need to make sure you pause between each key issue and remember to slow your pace if you find yourself speaking too quickly because you are conscious of time. A good structure will help you keep on track by questioning the importance of the content required and will help you manage your time better.

You can always have some supplementary sub-points that can be dealt with in more depth if time allows. These may not be your most important points, but if you feel that you have enough time you can deal with them.

In reality, you are more likely to speak quickly in your submission due to nerves and timing. It is important to bear this in mind and have strategies in place when you realise you are doing it. Generally, Chapter 5 on Communication Skills and Chapter 6 on Managing Nerves, Fear and Failure will provide some guidance on this area.

Bullet points, short phrases or sentences and key words should be the triggers you rely on for your submission as opposed to long paragraphs.

Advocacy Submission: 15 minutes

10.08 When you enter the room the judge (the assessor, a qualified solicitor) will already be sitting in the room. Be prepared and know how to address the judge from your scenario instructions which will explain in what court you will make your submission (eg the magistrates' court, Crown Court, county court or High Court).

The temptation will be to read from your notes if they are in paragraphs, especially when you are nervous. It will not help you build rapport or deliver your submission with persuasion and confidence.

When reading your notes, you end up spending more time looking down at your paper than at the judge. This means the judge cannot see your facial expressions – which means you lose connection and rapport with them. It also means that you are unlikely to use your body language effectively (ie posture, hand gestures, etc) to emphasise a point to help you make a persuasive argument. If you do look up from your notes there is a chance you may lose track of where you were reading from which could cause you to panic and 'freeze' which can throw you off track. You can read more about this in Chapter 6, Managing Nerves Fear and Failure, The Brain (para **6.07**) and Stored Patterns (para **6.08**).

You may be asked to make one submission that deals with a number of issues and after it the judge may not make a decision (ie agree or disagree). Do not panic or read anything into their behaviour or body language if they come across as neutral. These are not signs of a good or bad performance. The judge is also entitled to ask you any questions in relation to your submission at any stage (not necessarily at the end), so be prepared.

You might also get a situation where you must make two separate submissions within your 15-minute assessment and the instructions tell you the judge will make a ruling on your first point (in your favour), so you then continue your second submission based on your instructions. Therefore, you must read the instructions carefully and figure out what you are being asked to do and weigh up how long you need to spend on each part.

Below is a breakdown of the language used for how you might present your submission. It is just an example and it should be adapted to your authentic style.

'All the great speakers were bad speakers at first'
Ralph Waldo Emerson

The Beginning

10.09 Start the submission with a confident introduction. This is where my four-step introduction in the Advocacy Structure (para **10.04**) helps you to avoid forgetting any steps before you get into the main body of your submission.

In my experience of coaching lawyers on advocacy, I find many launch straight into their submission without some or all of the four-step introduction. Some state they knew what they needed to do but forgot because of nerves. So, it is helpful to have a few trigger words that help you do the four-step introduction so you do not forget to do something you would otherwise have done. The introduction suggested is standard for courtroom etiquette and it can build your confidence, helping you to move smoothly into the main body of your submission. If you do not want to introduce yourself, you do not have to and will not be marked down. I include it to make the submission more authentic.

For example, in a courtroom advocacy submission the language used is more formal:

10.10   Advocacy

> Form of address based on which court

> Your name – use your surname only (optional).

"Good morning/afternoon Judge/Your Honour/My Lord/Lady, my name is Mr/Ms [surname] and I appear on behalf of my client [Mr/Miss/Mrs surname]."

> Your client's name.

> The reason for the submission

"Judge/Your Honour, ...

- ...we oppose the application for...

- ...Our application for... is made pursuant to...

- ...Today [client's name] is before the court to be sentenced for...

- ... [Client's name] should/should not be remanded in custody for...

In a submission you would not use phrases that are subjective such as *'I think'* or *'In my opinion'*; instead you might say *'It is submitted that ...'* or *'We submit ...'*

The Middle

10.10   Think about the order in which lawyers would speak in the hearing (ie would you go first or the other side?). If you know that you would go second in a hearing, even though the 'other side' or client will not be present in your assessment, you can still make your submission authentic by referring to them (see the examples below).

Once you are ready to provide your reasoning, then it is helpful to split your key issues and deal with them in a logical manner. A good structure is:

(1)   State the law/test relied upon.

(2)   Apply the facts to the law.

(3)   Conclude whether or not the facts satisfy or meet the law/test relied upon.

To make your submission persuasive you need to apply the facts to the law. Below is an example of the language you can use to introduce what you want the judge to do (in effect, be persuaded by your submission).

> '... The evidence presented supports my client's position and you will see that the test has been satisfied in favour of my client.'
>
> The [test/principle] relied upon is [state the law] ... and it is split into [number] parts, namely ...
>
> The first part, ... [state the first limb and then apply it to the facts]
>
> And the second part, ... [state the second limb and then apply it to the facts]'

If in your submission you want to refer to something said by the 'other side', you want to make it sound authentic. You would refer to the other side as *'My friend ...'*

for a solicitor, or *'My learned friend ...'* for a barrister. If you are not sure of the status because the instructions have not indicated it, you can use either.

For example, you might say something like:

> *'My friend makes the point ... this is disputed based on ...'*
>
> *'We submit that my friend will need to provide additional evidence, namely, ...'*
>
> *'My friend's assertion that ... is totally unfounded because ...'*

If you are referring to a supporting document you want to make sure the judge has it and you can draw their attention to it. This is the level of interactive engagement that strengthens your submission and makes it more persuasive. It also gets you marks for engaging with the judge. For example, you might say something like:

> *'Judge/Your Honour/My Lord/Lady, do you have a copy of ... [document]?'*
>
> *'May I draw your attention to page X at paragraph X where you will see it says ...'*

Remember to pause and look up whilst the judge finds the document. Do not carry on talking whilst they look for it.

> ***'The most precious things in speech are the pauses.'***
>
> **Ralph Waldo Emerson**

The judge should have a set of the same documents as you. If you are referring to a document they do not have, do not panic; you can always say something like:

> *'May I read out the relevant part of [X] and I can then hand you my copy?'*

The exchange between you and the judge should always be professional. You are always making suggestions or asking for permission rather than 'telling' the judge (eg you would not say *'Turn to page ...'* but say *'May I draw your attention to page ...'*): the former would be considered rude and not correct courtroom etiquette.

The End

10.11 When you have finished your submission, you want to let the judge know rather than just stopping abruptly.

A good way to make it clear that you have finished is to say something like:

> *'Judge/Your Honour/My Lord/Lady, these are my submissions unless I can assist you any further.'*

If the judge asks you questions, you need to be prepared for how to answer them – even if you do not know the answer. Do not let one response derail your performance for the remainder of the submission.

Remember, performance anxiety does not exist outside of you; it exists within you, so you need to know how to manage it. Chapter 6, Managing Nerves, Fear and Failure, Fear of the Client or Judge (para **6.16**) looks at this area.

10.12 *Advocacy*

Handling Difficult Questions

10.12 The judge may ask you a question at any stage during your submission. If you do not know the answer, that makes it a difficult question for you. Accept you will be marked down on the law for not knowing the answer. However, there is no reason why you should also be marked down for how you deal with it from a skills perspective. Remember, you are assessed equally on the law and skills and 'appropriate language and behaviour' is one of the criteria against which you are assessed. Therefore, you still have every opportunity to score highly in this area. The judge can ask you a range of different types of questions. For example, they may ask you to:

- clarify an issue;
- confirm the legal position of your submission;
- address them on the seriousness of the issue;
- specify exactly what section of the law/rules you are referring to;
- address them in relation to costs.

The above examples are a non-exhaustive list and you should be prepared to answer any questions. If you do not know the answer it is best to be upfront about it rather than bluff your way through it to disguise the fact that you do not know. The judge will see straight through that and it will reduce your credibility. You will also score lower on both the law and skills. However, if you deal with it professionally, your skills marks should not be adversely affected.

Many lawyers I coach get caught out by an unexpected question and instinctively respond by saying 'I don't know' (some shrug their shoulders) and this can come across as curt or defensive (in their tone) and unprofessional (in their body language) for a courtroom environment. You want to practise some phrases that you can confidently repeat and adapt if the situation arises. Having said that, you do not want to repeat them parrot fashion. You need to align your words with your body language and your voice for it to come across as authentic.

Below is an example of what you could say if you do not know the answer and adapt it to suit your style. Remember to use the correct form of address for the judge:

> *'Judge, I am sorry I do not have the relevant information in front of me at the moment.'*

> *'Judge, unfortunately, I am not in a position to provide you with an answer to your question without checking ... [with ... the client/the CPR rules/ PACE ... or the specific legislation] ...'*

If the question asked refers to a document you have mentioned in your submission and you need to refer to it in your response, ask for time to find the document. It may be harder to find it if your papers are not in order by this stage and the added silence puts more pressure on you to act quickly. You could say something like:

> *'May I have a moment to find the document in question?'*

Handling Difficult Questions 10.12

That immediately gives you more time, which means you feel less pressurised because the silence is permitted (by you asking for time), and so does not feel as long. The whole exchange can be done in seconds and helps you stay in control and shows confidence.

If you do not know the answer to a question, naturally you may not want to look at the judge and prefer to look down when responding. Make sure you make soft eye contact with the judge when answering their question, because you are still being assessed on your professional behaviour.

Passing SQE Part 2 is based on being tested on a range of different oral and written assessments which determine holistically whether you pass or fail, so do not let one assessment which you feel goes badly potentially affect the rest of them.

Advocacy is a challenging skill to learn and it does get easier with practice. You may decide you do not want to work in an area of law that requires it, but it is a valuable skill. In practice you may have to do presentations or public speaking and there is a lot of overlap between the two that can benefit you.

'Public speaking is a skill that can be studied, polished, perfected.'
Tom Peters

Advocacy – Top Ten Tips

(1) Read the assessment specification and understand what you are required to do.

(2) Read the instructions carefully. Use the correct form of address for the judge and work out whether you would speak first or second in the hearing.

(3) Mark any relevant documents you want to refer to and keep them in the order.

(4) Set out your structure, apply the key facts and information to the law/rules relied upon.

(5) Use the four-step introduction and trigger words and phrases to help you cover key issues.

(6) Engage with the judge by referring them to supporting documents (where appropriate).

(7) Pace yourself and pause between key sections.

(8) A persuasive submission requires application of the facts to the law – not just talking about the law.

(9) Practise responses in case you do not know an answer to a question.

(10) Practise your advocacy submission standing up and sitting down. You should record yourself to track your improvement.

Chapter 10

Advocacy: Appendix

Appendix 10A: Assessment Specification

This has been reproduced with permission from the SRA:

Overview

Candidates are given a case study on which they will conduct a piece of courtroom advocacy. An email asks the candidate to conduct the advocacy and tells them in which court they are appearing. Where relevant, candidates are also given a file of documents. Candidates may be asked questions during the advocacy. They have 45 minutes to prepare.

Candidates will then have 15 minutes to make their submission to a judge who is present in the room. The judge will be played by a solicitor of England and Wales who will assess the candidate both on skills and application of law.

Assessment Objective

Candidates can demonstrate they are able to conduct a piece of advocacy before a judge.

Assessment Criteria

Candidates will be assessed against the following criteria:

Skills

(1) Use appropriate language and behaviour.

(2) Adopt a clear and logical structure.

(3) Present a persuasive argument.

(4) Interacts with/engages the court appropriately.

(5) Include all key relevant facts.

Application of Law

(6) Apply the law correctly to the client's situation.

(7) Apply the law comprehensively to the client's situation, identifying any ethical and professional conduct issues and exercising judgment to resolve them honestly and with integrity.

Appendix 10A

You should read this in conjunction with the Chapter 1, The SQE Journey, Appendix 1B which details what the Competence Statement includes and in particular the Statement of Solicitor Competence.

In Chapter 3, Functioning Legal Knowledge, Appendix 3A you can find an overview of the law covered for dispute resolution and criminal litigation (ie criminal law and criminal practice and procedures).

More detailed information can be found on the SRA website (www.sra.org.uk).

Chapter 11

SQE Part 2

Case and Matter Analysis

'When you negotiate you must be prepared to compromise'
Nelson Mandela

In this chapter you will learn:

✓ How to read through documents quickly to glean key information.
✓ What information should be included in your report and how to structure it.
✓ How to demonstrate your negotiation skills in writing.
✓ How to write a report that is practical covering advice and analysis rather than an academic one.

Introduction

11.01 In this assessment you will be writing a report covering your advice and analysis for a client matter. You will receive the instruction from a partner in the firm, so it is an internal document as opposed to an external report for a client or someone else. This means that you may be reviewing the file based on:

- a client's initial instructions and what they want to do; or
- where key decisions need to be made weighing up all the options.

The report needs to be client-focused, so your advice must relate to the client's matter.

This assessment is computer-based, so you will be provided with an electronic case file of documents and you will need to address any issues raised in your instructions.

11.01 *Case and Matter Analysis*

You should have a clear understanding of the client's matter and then provide a legal analysis based on your advice. Therefore, you will need to spend a fair amount of time understanding the instructions and supporting documents. Read them carefully because the documents will help shape your advice. You may be asked to look at the issue from not just the client's perspective but also the other sides.

Pay attention to 'Notes to Candidate' carefully. It is very easy to be tempted to answer parts of a question when you know the answer, but it will not benefit you if you have been asked not to include it.

For the purposes of the assessment, a good report is comprehensive and concise and shows your legal, writing and analytical skills. Your report should allow the reader to make a confident decision based on it. You should read this chapter in conjunction with Chapter 7, Writing in Professional English.

There are many ways in which reports can be written and they usually contain an analysis of the facts which lead to your opinion. The facts are carefully analysed to provide logical opinions which help you reach a decision. The aim is to help the reader understand what you have to say about the matter and why.

This is not an academic writing exercise but a practical one. You need to demonstrate your knowledge of the law and apply it in a logical and methodical manner. Your report should:

- identify the relevant facts and legal issues; and
- provide client-focused advice.

Your advice should take into consideration what the client wants to do and the legal implications of doing it.

There are many things that you can include in your report, but you should only use sections that are relevant. Most reports will have the following sections, but they may be worded differently. For example:

- **Introduction**

    This is the aim/objective of what your report will cover.

- **Background**

    These are the facts that allow the reader to put your report into context.

- **Findings/Advice**

    This is your legal analysis of the facts.

- **Conclusion**

    This is your opinion or options based on your logical analysis of the issues.

- **Recommendations**

    These are the required next steps or action points based on your conclusion.

Your report may or may not use all the sections; this will depend on the instructions. However, you do want to set your report out in a structured way which makes it easy to follow.

You may be required to demonstrate your negotiation skills in writing. For example, advise the client to resolve a dispute by making, accepting or assessing an offer or justify your reasoning why they should or should not settle.

From your instructions and file of documents you should try to understand the client's underlying purpose and what they want to achieve and why. In practice, when you have to review a case not everything in the case file is always relevant so you have to be confident in deciding what to use in context when analysing the documents. You may also require information that is not in the file and should point that out in your report.

You will be required to demonstrate your strategic and analytical thinking skills by providing reasons for your advice.

The SRA has provided a sample of what you could get for this type of assessment for a business law scenario. You can also find the samples for all the assessments on the SRA website (www.sra.org.uk).

The Assessment Criteria

11.02 This is a computer-based assessment where you have 60 minutes to read through an electronic case file and produce a report. Some of the supporting documents may not be relevant for your report, so you have to read them quickly to decide on their relevance. You can read about skim reading or scanning documents in Chapter 5, Communication Skills (paras **5.37** and **5.38**) and Chapter 10, Advocacy, Should You Skim Read or Scan? (para **10.05**). These sections should help you where you have to review a case file or number of documents in the preparation stage because the principle is the same. You sift through the documents quickly and efficiently using the instructions as your compass to guide you on what to focus on. What you are asked to address in your instructions are usually the key issues that will help you structure your report.

You can read about the more detailed version of the SRA criteria in Appendix 11A.

Below I have summarised and highlighted the criteria against which you are assessed.

- ***Skills***

11.03

(1) Identify relevant facts.

(2) Provide client-focused advice.

(3) Use clear, precise, concise and acceptable language.

- ***Application of the Law***

11.04 You should note that for all the assessments your knowledge of the law needs to be applied:

11.04 Case and Matter Analysis

- correctly; and
- comprehensively, identifying any professional conduct and ethical issues.

You should assess yourself against these criteria when practising case and matter analysis (for any of the five practice areas of the law). These are assessed using the following grading scale:

Grade	Mark	Standard	Do you meet the competency requirements?
A	5	Superior performance	Yes, well above it
B	4	Clearly satisfactory	Yes, clearly meets it
C	3	Marginal pass	Yes, on balance, just meets it
D	2	Marginal fail	No, on balance, just fails it
E	1	Clearly unsatisfactory	No, clearly does not meet it
F	0	Poor performance	No, well below it

You can read more about the Competence Statement in Chapter 1, The SQE Journey, Appendix 1B which provides the context of what you are expected to know for practice as a newly qualified solicitor.

The SRA will not provide a report template in the assessment, so you should know how to set one out. Below I share with you a traditional and modern report style but you can choose whatever works best for you and adapt it.

A report will have facts and opinions and these are usually based on your legal analysis. You may be required to consider any of the following in your legal analysis of any issues (non-exhaustive list):

- pros and cons;
- strengths and weaknesses;
- risks and benefits;
- strategy;
- procedural issues;
- commercial risks;
- evidential issues;
- financial implications.

Reports build up to their conclusion by citing the facts, followed by the legal analysis and any evidence. That is what law schools traditionally teach you – in effect, your thinking followed by your conclusion.

However, in practice, whether you are dealing with a lawyer or a client, they want the answer. Therefore, it is natural to bypass the actual content (ie thinking) and go straight to the advice (ie conclusion or recommendation). So, there is some merit in looking at the different ways reports can be written, where the reverse order to the traditional approach could work equally well.

The modern approach stems from the Pyramid Principle established by Barbara Minto and used primarily in management consulting (eg McKinsey & Company).

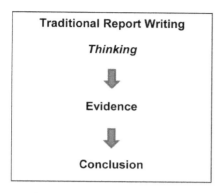
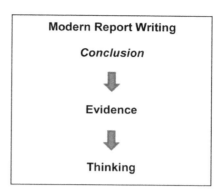

Many businesses will have their preferred 'house style' so adapt your style to make sure it covers what you are required to do. Below are examples of both ways of writing a report. Which approach you adopt will depend on your preference.

Report Templates

- *Report Sample 1 – Traditional Report Writing*

11.05

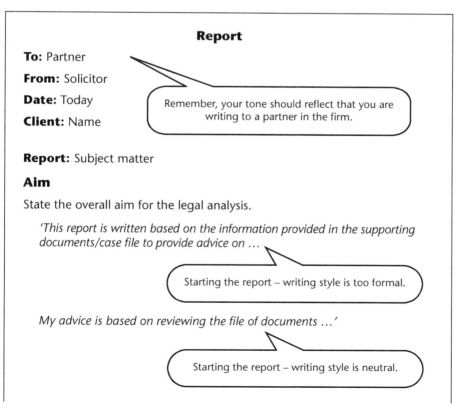

11.05 *Case and Matter Analysis*

Issues

List the issues making it clear how many there are and if you have any sub-issues use bullet points.

(1) Issue/Question

State the facts.

> 'The issue/problem is ...'

Risks

Identify any risks that could affect the client's position.

> 'As a result of what the client wants/does not want to do ...'
>
> 'The client could ...'

Thinking

Provide legal analysis considering any evidence/source (if appropriate) to support your opinion.

> 'The relevant section of the [state legislation/regulations] provides that ...
>
> The section makes specific reference to ...
>
> As the law stands at present ...
>
> The two-part test that needs to be satisfied is ...'

Evidence

Options/Strategies

If appropriate, from the risks identified, consider all the appropriate options for the client.

> 'The client's options are as follows ...
>
> The client could do ...
>
> The client cannot ...'

Conclusion

Recommendation/Conclusion

State what you think would be the best option/strategy for the client.

> 'I recommend the client accepts/rejects ...
>
> 'My advice is that the client does/does not ...'

(2) Issue/Question

Repeat the above format for any other issues you have to address.

> 'If you require any further clarification on any issues raised, please contact me.

Ending the report – writing style is too formal.

Please let me know if you have any questions.'

> Ending the report – writing style is neutral.

- ***Report Sample 2 – Modern Report Writing***

11.06

Report

To: Partner
From: Solicitor
Date: Today
Client: Name

> Remember, your tone should reflect that you are writing to a partner in the firm.

Report: Subject matter

Aim

State the overall aim for the legal analysis.

> *'This report is written based on the information provided in the supporting documents/case file to provide advice on …*

> Starting the report – writing style is too formal.

> *My advice is based on reviewing the file of documents…'*

> Starting the report – writing style is neutral.

Issues

List the issues making it clear how many there are and if you have any sub-issues use bullet points.

(1) Issue/Question

State the facts.

> *'The problem/issue is …*

Advice

Applying the facts, explain what you think would be the best decision for the client. For example:

> *'I recommend the client accepts/rejects …*

> Conclusion

> *'My advice is that the client does …'*

11.07 *Case and Matter Analysis*

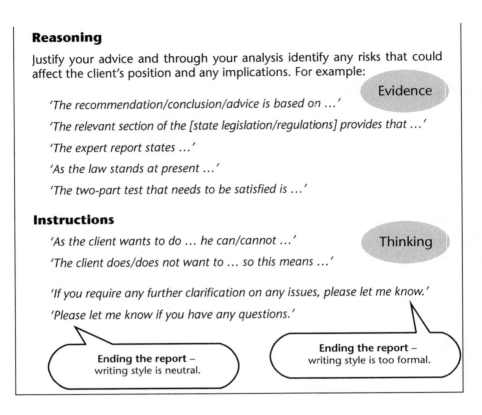

- ## *Example of a Modern Report – Dispute Resolution*

11.07 Below is an example of how to use the suggested modern report writing template because it is different to what you are usually taught at law school. You choose what works best for you as long as there is a structure that shows your advice and analysis.

The brief scenario provides you with a gist of the matter without too much detail. Where supporting documents would be included with the scenario, they have been omitted. Therefore, do not worry about additional information mentioned in the report that is not in the brief scenario.

The brief suggested answer and labels are just an example so you may add your own relevant points. The purpose is to allow you to see how to structure your answer identified by the labels 'conclusion', 'evidence' and 'thinking' to explicitly show you what is covered. You do not need to add labels for the assessment. Whether you need to use all three labels will depend on the type of advice required.

Brief Scenario

From: Partner

To: Solicitor

Date: Today

Re: Fix-it Contractors – Potential Claims

The client is James Powell who owns a business called Fix-it Contractors. His business does a lot of work with the chain of ABC restaurants owned by Mark Evans. Mark asked James to install six air conditioning units, one in each restaurant in London.

James agreed the contract terms with Terry, a commercial manager, employed by ABC restaurants. Terry insisted James use low energy units from Lite Suppliers whose managing director is Julie Townsend. James went to see the units in the Lite Suppliers warehouse and was impressed by them. He emailed Terry that they were not the correct specification but could work, however, he was not sure about their longevity. Terry still insisted on using them, so James paid £75,000 to Lite Suppliers for the six units.

Over a period of nine months, all the units started making a loud noise. Mark emailed James to fix them all at his own expense. James is upset that he is being held 100% responsible for the rectification work. James got an expert who works for him to look at the units.

Two days ago, James called Mark and his secretary answered saying that Terry had left the business and eloped to Spain with Julie. James had been calling and emailing Lite Suppliers with no response. He went to the warehouse last week and it looked derelict.

James wants to sue Lite Suppliers for the faulty units and sue Terry and (reluctantly) ABC restaurants (because Mark is his friend) for the rectification work. James does not believe he is fully responsible.

I have a meeting with James at the end of the week so please can you advise on:

(1) Any potential claims.
(2) Are Fix-it Contractors responsible for the rectification work?
(3) Any alternative options.

Attached*:

- Contract with Fix-it Contractors and ABC restaurants
- Purchase order with Lite Suppliers
- Email trail between James and Terry
- Expert report

*Not included here.

11.07 *Case and Matter Analysis*

Below you will see the suggested answer to the Brief Scenario which asks you to advise on three points. Each part is set out as a heading with its advice. The suggested answer is for illustration purposes only to show you how to write a modern report.

Suggested Answer

Report

From: Solicitor

To: Partner

Date: Today

Ref: FC/NH/01234

Re: Fix-it Contractors – Potential Claims

In preparation for your meeting with James, my advice is based on reviewing all the relevant documents.

(1) Any potential claims

Fix-it Contractors wants to sue Terry/ABC Restaurants for the rectification work and Lite Suppliers for the faulty units but the problem is as follows:

(a) Suing Terry

Fix-it Contractors does not have a claim against Terry for the rectification work. Terry was an employee of ABC restaurants and not a party to the contract that was signed... *(Conclusion)*

The contract shows that the parties are Fix-it Contractors and ABC Restaurants: [add in relevant extract] *(Evidence)*

Even if Fix-it Contractors wanted to bring a separate claim against Terry (in his own right)... it would need to weigh up whether it is a financially viable option and the fact that Terry now lives in Spain... *(Thinking)*

(b) Suing Lite Suppliers

Fix-it Contractors wants to make a claim against Lite Suppliers for the rectification work:

(i) If the units are faulty

Fix-it Contractors has a strong claim if it can be proved the units are faulty... *(Conclusion)*

[Add in relevant legislation / case law] states...

The expert report states *'although they looked externally impressive the quality of the motor and heat exchanger is poor'*. *(Evidence)*

As the expert is someone who works for Fix-it Contractors, it would strengthen the claim to get an independent expert's report for more credibility.

The evidence could also strengthen the position that Lite Suppliers could be responsible for the cost of the rectification work if proved the units are faulty. *(Thinking)*

(ii) **If the units are not faulty**

Fix-it Contractors would not have a strong claim against Lite Suppliers for the rectification work. This is because the units may be fine in principle but they chose to install them knowing they were different to the contract specification. *(Conclusion)*

James said to Terry in an email that *'they were not the correct specification but could work'*.

The contract states regarding specification… [add in extract] *(Evidence)*

James wants to sue Lite Suppliers but has found out Julie has eloped to Spain with Terry. He has had no responses to emails or calls and the warehouse is derelict. *(Thinking)*

A Companies House search and bankruptcy search is required to check whether any potential claim is a commercially and financially viable option.

(c) Suing ABC Restaurants

The contact was made between Fix-it Contractors and ABC Restaurants. So, ABC Restaurants could make a claim against Fix-it Contractors for the rectification work. Not the other way round like James seems to think. *(Conclusion)*

The contract states… [add in extract] *(Evidence)*

(2) Are Fix-it Contractors responsible for the rectification work?

Yes, technically Fit-it Contractors is responsible for the rectification work based on the contract they entered into with ABC Restaurants.

However, they could have a strong defence and counterclaim. *(Conclusion)*

The contract states… [add in extract].

11.08 *Case and Matter Analysis*

> The evidence that supports the defence and counterclaim is:
>
> - Terry insisted on using the units – [add in email extract].
> - The expert report on the quality of the units. *Evidence*
> - Terry was in a relationship with Julie so he did not act independently or in the best interests of ABC restaurants.
>
> James could check if Mark knew about Terry's relationship with Julie and suggest he obtain independent legal advice based on the evidence above as Terry is a former employee. *Thinking*
>
> **(3) Any alternative options**
>
> As James is friends with Mark, the best option would be for them to try and settle this between themselves. James can point out the defence and counterclaim evidence to explain why he is not 100% responsible for all the rectification work. Both could try to come to a compromise. *Conclusion*
>
> Based on the evidence mentioned above it could be suggested that 50/50 is a good starting point because... *Evidence*
>
> Alternatively, we could offer to set up a more formal meeting or write a letter to ABC Restaurants setting out Fix-it Contractors' position.
>
> It is important to highlight litigation should be the last resort because it is:
>
> - expensive;
> - emotionally draining;
> - a lengthy time-consuming process; *Thinking*
> - ruins relationships; and
> - damages reputations.
>
> Please let me know if you have any questions.

Contentious Matters

11.08 If your case is contentious or could potentially become contentious you may have to consider all the available options for the client. You could suggest alternatives to litigation, for example:

(1) Negotiation

This is where the parties try to agree on a settlement usually between themselves.

(2) Mediation

This is where a third party assists the parties' negotiation and an agreement is reached.

(3) Adjudication

An expert helps resolve a specific dispute, such as a valuation or a technical issue.

(4) Arbitration

This is an alternative to litigation and it is an adversarial process where a neutral third party issues a binding decision. Usually used for technical issues/ disputes.

Litigation is the last resort because it is a costly and lengthy process, not to mention emotionally draining. It is a legal process where the parties' resort to the court to settle a dispute. This could have huge commercial and financial implications for your client. Therefore, it should only be considered if all other options are exhausted and you have analysed holistically how the client's situation may be impacted.

Negotiation Skills

11.09 As mentioned in Chapter 1, The SQE Journey, Negotiation Skills (para **1.13**) the following assessments may include an aspect where you have to demonstrate your negotiation skills:

- Client Interviewing Skills (and the Attendance Note);
- Case and Matter Analysis;
- Legal Writing.

Although it will not be explicitly highlighted in any of the assessments mentioned above, you should look out for any language that asks you to consider client-focused advice on potential options, strategies, risks and benefits.

Negotiation skills are key for lawyers. Although commonly evidenced through oral communication, it is equally important that you are able to convey your message clearly and concisely in writing.

Generally, your negotiation style will be influenced by your personality and culture. The two common negotiation styles are competitive and cooperative (problem solving). I have trained many lawyers in negotiation skills in the UK and abroad. It is always interesting to see how many of them think their communication style is cooperative, but they actually come across as quite competitive (evident from observing their body language, tone and language). Rarely is a person wholly one style or the other, often being a blend of both. However, their default preferred style is what they show if or when the negotiation starts to become challenging.

'The ability to see the situation as the other side sees it, as difficult as it may be, is one of the most important skills a negotiator can possess.'

Roger Fisher

11.10 *Case and Matter Analysis*

There are many courses and books available on negotiation skills if you want to find out more. A good book to start with is *Getting to Yes* by Roger Fisher and William Ury. There is a great TED talk by William Ury called 'The walk from "no" to "yes"'. TED talks are short powerful talks online devoted to spreading ideas (www.ted.com).

In contentious situations it is very easy to lose perspective especially when emotions are heightened. It can be difficult to see beyond the immediate issue disputed and its wider implications (eg relationships and the commercial and financial impact etc). Therefore, sometimes it is harder in writing to make sure your message and tone accurately convey what you say and how you would like the reader to receive it.

Representing clients in any negotiations mean you are always acting on your client's instructions. That can be tricky if you do not agree with them and have tried to persuade them of your way of thinking.

In any negotiation, preparation is key and knowing everything about your client's matter is important. In the assessment, you will need to work out very quickly what information and documents are important and relevant to your instructions.

You have to consider the client's position and also try to see it from the other party's side too – you can never predict what will happen, so you have to assess the strengths and weaknesses of your client's case and weigh these up. If it is a contentious matter, you might also have to think about all the options including 'walking away' or 'carrying on'. Both of those options are viable if it means that it would be more detrimental for the client to settle. You will need to show you have considered the pros and cons and conducted a risk/benefit analysis.

If you identify you need more specific information or any other documents, you should explain what you need and why in your report.

Read Chapter 7, Writing in Professional English, The Four Cs (para **7.15**) to refresh your mind on the qualities of good written communication being:

- clear
- concise
- comprehensive
- correct.

You have to convey your advice and reasoning skilfully, clearly and concisely, ensuring that your legal analysis is correct and comprehensive. A high-level SWOT analysis can help you analyse the matter quickly, because it is unlikely that you will have time to do it in too much detail.

SWOT Analysis

11.10 This is a good tool to use when you have a question where you have to analyse the merits of what the client wants to do because it helps you try to find the right solution. It was created in the 1960s by Albert Humphrey at Stanford University. It is a versatile tool that can be used for any matters that require analysis. SWOT stands for:

SWOT Analysis 11.10

S = Strengths
W = Weaknesses
O = Opportunities
T = Threats

As you read your instructions, the SWOT could help you by noting down key information that fits into each quadrant. It may be that not every quadrant will have information in it. The aim is to help you provide an answer with credible reasoning. It may be useful for the business law assessment, but you could also use parts of it for the other practice areas too (where appropriate).

Below are some generic pointers for what to consider in each quadrant if you use the SWOT analysis:

Strengths	**Opportunities**
• Experience/Expertise?	• Growth/Expansion of business?
• Gain/Continue business?	• Reputation?
• Finance/Budget?	• Increase number of clients?
• Evidence?	• Referrals?
Weaknesses	**Threats**
• Lose control of business/Lose the case?	• No growth/Expansion of business?
• Evidence?	• Competition?
• Costs/Budget?	• Conditional financial support?
• Time frame?	• Service/Complaints?
• Lose business	• Lack of knowledge/Expertise?

The SWOT analysis could help you when shaping your answers for any legal analysis of a matter. It can help you emphasise strengths and identify weaknesses, as well as maximise opportunities and protect against threats.

This type of breakdown can help you work out your position for negotiating on various points or key issues. For example, in a business law scenario, are you fixed on a key issue (non-negotiable) or flexible about it? Does your position change if you concede on another issue etc?

On reading the report, the assessor should be able to see what stage the client's matter is at, what issues need to be discussed and how to proceed. They will be assessing it as if your report was done for a senior lawyer (partner) to read and then share that information with the client.

There should be enough information for you to provide a comprehensive report. Sometimes you might decide that you need additional information/evidence and you should state what you require and the reason why.

11.10 Case and Matter Analysis

'Writing is an art. But when it is writing to inform it comes close to being a science.'
Robert Gunning

Case and Matter Analysis – Top Ten Tips

(1) Know when to skim read or scan a document for the relevant information.

(2) Remember not all the supporting documents may be relevant or needed to be used in your advice.

(3) A SWOT analysis can help you assess the immediate and broader merits of the key issues for your report.

(4) Make the report client-focused and use the facts to logically form an opinion based on the evidence/analysis.

(5) Demonstrate your negotiation skills through options and a risk/benefit analysis (where appropriate).

(6) Where you need more information/evidence, explain what you need and why.

(7) Write in the active voice and keep your sentences short. Re-read Chapter 7, Writing in Professional English.

(8) Familiarise yourself with a report template that works for you. Layout is important so the information can be read easily.

(9) The language used should reflect the fact that you are writing to a partner in the firm who will rely on it.

(10) Remember to offer advice and next steps (where appropriate).

Chapter 11

Case and Matter Analysis: Appendix

Appendix 11A: Assessment Specification

This has been reproduced with permission from the SRA:

> **Overview**
>
> This is a computer-based assessment. Candidates will be given a case study with documents on which they will be asked to produce a written report to a partner giving a legal analysis of the case and providing client-focused advice. This may, but will not necessarily, include options and strategies for negotiation.
>
> Candidates will have 60 minutes to complete this task.
>
> **Assessment Objective**
>
> Candidates can demonstrate they are able to produce a written report to a partner giving a legal analysis of the case and client-focused advice.
>
> **Assessment Criteria**
>
> Candidates will be assessed against the following criteria:
>
> *Skills*
>
> (1) Identify relevant facts.
>
> (2) Provide client-focused advice (ie advice which demonstrates an understanding of the problem from the client's point of view and what the client wants to achieve, not just from a legal perspective).
>
> (3) Use clear, precise, concise and acceptable language.
>
> *Application of Law*
>
> (4) Apply the law correctly to the client's situation.
>
> (5) Apply the law comprehensively to the client's situation, identifying any ethical and professional conduct issues and exercising judgment to resolve them honestly and with integrity.

Case and Matter Analysis: Appendix

You should read this in conjunction with the Chapter 1, The SQE Journey, Appendix 1B which details what the Competence Statement includes and in particular the Statement of Solicitor Competence.

In Chapter 3, Functioning Legal Knowledge, Appendix 3A, you can find an overview of the areas of law that you will be assessed in the following way:

- dispute resolution or criminal litigation (either one of these);
- property practice or wills and probate (either one of these);
- business law (definitely this area).

More detailed information can be found on the SRA website (www.sra.org.uk).

Chapter 12

SQE Part 2

Legal Writing

> *'There are two things wrong with almost all legal writing. One is its style. The other is its content.'*
> **Fred Rodell**

In this chapter you will learn:

✓ How to set out a letter using appropriate structure and layout for the content.

✓ How to make the writing appropriate for the recipient.

✓ How to effectively adapt your communication style flexibly.

✓ How to improve your writing style from reading real examples with constructive feedback and suggested alternatives.

Introduction

12.01 This chapter will give you some practical advice on how to approach legal writing. You can use what you learn and apply it to your studies and mock practice papers. It would make sense to read Chapter 7, Writing in Professional English to support your understanding, as it complements this chapter.

If you are working, then your writing style may be influenced by the business having its own 'house style'. A 'house style' ensures consistency among all employees when communicating in writing. However, for the purposes of the SQE assessments follow the UK English style suggestions made in Chapter 7, Writing in Professional English and make sure you are consistent.

The examples used in this chapter are extracts taken from lawyers' written answers where I have provided constructive feedback. You may or may not be able to relate to the various writing styles, but they have been included to provide a wide range of styles. They will also help those who do recognise similarities to improve their writing style.

12.02 *Legal Writing*

You will need to have an idea of structure and layout in mind. Use the examples suggested or something similar that works for you to make it easy for the assessor to read and remember the Four Cs to cover all the issues. Written communication should be:

- clear;
- concise;
- comprehensive;
- correct.

You can read more about these in Chapter 7, Writing in Professional English.

The SRA has provided a sample of what you could get for this type of assessment for a property practice scenario. You can also find samples for all the other assessments on the SRA website (www.sra.org.uk).

The Assessment Criteria

12.02 The legal writing assessment will be computer-based and you will have 30 minutes to complete the exercise. You need to write a letter or an email as a solicitor to a client or someone else so you need to make your writing recipient focused. For example, the following could be recipients (non-exhaustive list):

- a client;
- a third party;
- the other side;
- a partner (in the firm);
- an expert.

You need to make sure that you use the facts in whatever you are asked to do. You may be asked to provide advice, guidance or instructions depending on the recipient.

You can read about the more detailed version of the SRA criteria in Appendix 12A.

Below I have summarised and highlighted the criteria against which you are assessed.

- ***Skills***

12.03

(1) Include relevant facts.
(2) Use a logical structure.
(3) Advice/content is client and recipient focused.
(4) Use clear, precise, concise and acceptable language which is appropriate to the recipient.

- **Application of the Law**

12.04 You should note that for all the assessments your knowledge of the law needs to be applied:

- correctly; and
- comprehensively, identifying any professional conduct and ethical issues.

You should assess yourself against these criteria when practising your legal writing (for any of the five practice areas of the law). These are assessed using the following grading scale:

Grade	Mark	Standard	Do you meet the competency requirements?
A	5	Superior performance	Yes, well above it
B	4	Clearly satisfactory	Yes, clearly meets it
C	3	Marginal pass	Yes, on balance, just meets it
D	2	Marginal fail	No, on balance, just fails it
E	1	Clearly unsatisfactory	No, clearly does not meet it
F	0	Poor performance	No, well below it

You can read more about the Competence Statement in Chapter 1, The SQE Journey, Appendix 1B which provides the context of what you are expected to know for practice as a newly qualified solicitor.

As the legal writing assessment is in the form of a letter or email, this chapter will look at how to approach both these formats, practically.

Letters and Emails

12.05 The details of what you should consider including in letters and emails are covered in Chapter 7, Writing in Professional English (paras **7.05** and **7.13**), respectively. Therefore, you should read them in conjunction with this section.

You have 30 minutes to complete this assessment and many lawyers have found the time allowed is challenging. The fact the assessment is only 30 minutes means you must have in mind how much you can practically do:

- read the instructions;
- read supporting documents (if applicable);
- write the letter/email.

Be mindful of any university or training provider's mock papers with suggested answers that are unrealistically too long or more academic stating legislation/case law. The answer may be provided to offer you revision points but it is not often a true reflection of what you can do in the time allowed or bearing in mind the criteria to make it recipient-focused. So, be confident that if you cover what you are asked, the length of your letter/email does not matter.

12.05 Legal Writing

You may be provided with a letter template in the assessment which will have the recipient's details already included. If you do not have a template then you should know how to set one out. Below is an example of a template with some comments of what you might want to include:

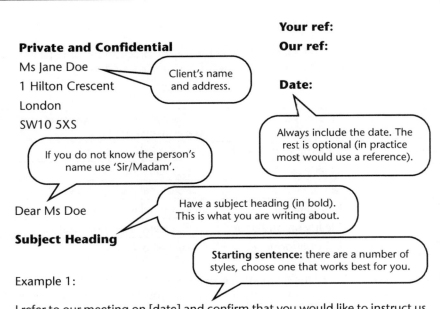

Example 1:

I refer to our meeting on [date] and confirm that you would like to instruct us on [the matter]. Below I will confirm the key issues raised and your concerns.

Example 2:

Thank you for coming to see me on [date]. I confirm we discussed the following key issues in relation to your matter:

Key Issue 1: [state the title]

These are the two options we discussed:

(1)   A and B; or

(2)   C and D

I would advise you to choose [(1) or (2)] because ... [state your reason/s].

Key Issue 2: [state the title]

As you work and earn more than [add in amount], unfortunately you fall outside the eligibility criteria and therefore will not qualify for ... We discussed a number of options available such as:

- Option A:
- Option B:
- Option C:

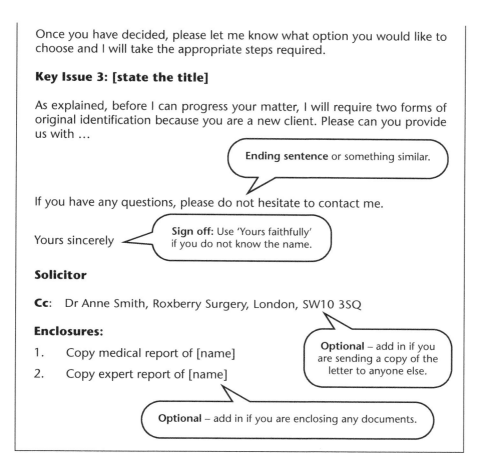

In the assessment, if you have been told in your instructions that you can assume some documents are attached or enclosed (but they are not actually provided), then you can take that as a hint that you might need to make reference to them or show you would enclose them in your letter or email (if appropriate). That does not mean you will always need to refer to them. Sometimes it may be to just let you know the correct protocol or procedure has been followed.

If you have to write an email, then the content used in the letter would be the same for the email. However, the template would not be the same so name, address and reference would not be required.

Legal Writing: Sample Extracts

12.06 I have reviewed and provided constructive feedback to many lawyers on their writing style. Below are some real extracts by anonymous lawyers of their writing style. These have been included to provide you with an insight into the different ways people write, where some styles may be influenced by their home jurisdiction, background and culture.

12.07 *Legal Writing*

To avoid duplication, samples of the content for one practice area have not been repeated for a different practice area. For example, the criminal litigation scenario extract shows a request for two forms of identification or deals with eligibility for legal aid and these may equally apply to other practice areas of the law. The constructive feedback offered aims to help you understand how the writing could be improved. You can have a go at writing the extracts yourself and then look at the alternative suggestions for the extracts in Appendices 12B to 12F.

The aim of the alternative suggestions in Appendices 12B to 12F is not for you to copy my writing style and replicate it, but compare it to your own style to notice any key differences. The alternative suggestions in the appendix are just guidance and by no means the only way or style – use what works for you. The letter-writing template and Chapter 7, Writing in Professional English should help you adapt your style (if required).

The 'Brief Scenario' just provides the gist of what the letter is about without going into too much detail. You will have more detailed instructions (and possibly supporting documents) in the real assessment. You are reading the extracts purely for illustrative purposes to see how some lawyers write and how the extracts can be improved. Do not worry about the additional information mentioned (in the extracts) that are not mentioned in the 'Brief Scenario'.

Some extracts are not written by the same person, therefore read each extract in isolation rather than as a whole letter and use what works best for you. There are extracts for all the practice areas of the law (Example 1 to 5) with alternative suggestions in Appendices 12B to 12F.

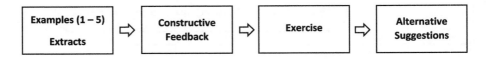

- **Example 1: Extracts of legal writing from a criminal litigation scenario**

12.07 Brief Scenario: Write to the client and confirm the advice given. The client has been charged with theft, the confession was obtained in breach of the Police and Criminal Evidence Act 1984 (PACE). The client will plead not guilty and does not qualify for legal aid.

These are original extracts so should be read with the constructive feedback.

❖ **Extract 1**

12.08 'I write you this letter in relation to our meeting that was held on 29 May 2020 ("the meeting"), to provide you with more clarity, and advice on the way forward, in the proceedings that have been instituted against you for theft.

Firstly, I would like to inform you once more, as our firm is regulated by the Solicitors Regulating Authority, we will need to be provided with proof of your identification. The document that can be provided as primary proof of your identification is your driving license or your ID or your passport, and as secondary proof of your identification, a utility bill or bank statement.

As it is necessary for our firm to make copies of the original documents, proving your identification, it will be highly appreciated if you can stop by our offices during the week to provide us with these documents.'

❖ **Extract 1 – Constructive Feedback**

12.09 The overall writing style is verbose which means that the lawyer has used more words than necessary. Also, use and apply the facts provided in your scenario.

In the first paragraph the words in quotation marks (ie 'the meeting') are unnecessary and the sentence is too long. Rather than just say 'theft', expand it to include what items were stolen and the value (which was provided in the original information).

In the second paragraph, check for accuracy and correctness: it is the Solicitors 'Regulation' not 'Regulating' Authority. The reference to primary and secondary identification could be interpreted differently when what you mean is that two forms of identification are required. Also, note the spelling of driving license is not with an 's' but with a 'c' (driving licence).

Paragraph 3 is correct but too wordy and informal (eg 'stop by our offices during the week').

❖ **Extract 2**

12.10 'I advise you to plead not guilty based on the confession. Every person has the right to be informed of his/her right to have a solicitor present during an interview at the police station. In the event that a person is not informed of such a right, or a solicitor is not provided to a person requesting the presence of a solicitor, the evidence obtained in such interview may be inadmissible.

It should also be noted that a confession that has been made due to oppression, or in circumstances which may render the confession unreliable, may also be inadmissible.

As you have indicated that you were not informed of your right to have a solicitor present, you were interviewed without legal representation, you were subjected to interviews from 6pm in the evening to 5am the morning, and influenced to make a confession, it is very likely that we will be able to have the confession omitted as inadmissible evidence.'

❖ **Extract 2 – Constructive Feedback**

12.11 The layout could be improved. There are a number of points made to support the argument that the confession is unreliable because of the way it was obtained. Illustrating them using bullet points would have worked nicely and been easier to read.

Also, when you use '6pm' and '5am' you do not need to spell out that it means evening and morning, respectively. This is unnecessary use of words.

12.12 *Legal Writing*

❖ **Extract 3**

12.12 'At the meeting you enquired whether your matter can be covered by legal aid. There are two requirements ("tests") that need to be met to enable you to qualify for legal aid i.e. the means test and the merits test.

To qualify in terms of the means test, you need to earn an income of less than 12475 pounds per annum. As you earn an income of 29500 pounds per annum, it seems unlikely that your matter will be covered by legal aid.

As you do not comply with the first requirement, there is no need to discuss the merits test, as you must comply with both "tests" to be eligible for legal aid.'

❖ **Extract 3 – Constructive Feedback**

12.13 The tone used to state that the client does not qualify for legal aid sounds a little harsh (eg 'there is no need to discuss the merits test') and could be worded more diplomatically. Also, when referring to a salary write it correctly: '12475 pounds' is '£12,475; and '29500 pounds' is '£29,500'.

❖ **Extract 4**

12.14 'Please feel free to contact me in the event of any uncertainty, or if there are any other queries you would like me to answer.

I am looking forward to hearing from you.'

❖ **Extract 4 – Constructive Feedback**

12.15 The closing paragraphs could be more concise. See the suggestion for the ending sentence in the letter template (para **12.05**).

Exercise – Example 1

Re-write the extracts for the criminal litigation scenario

Have a go at re-writing the above extracts more concisely by looking at the letter template suggested and incorporating the constructive feedback to help you.

See Appendix 12B for an alternative suggestion for the extracts.

- *Example 2: Extracts of legal writing from a property practice scenario*

12.16 Brief Scenario: A client called this morning and would like you to confirm the next steps after the exchange of contracts later today for the purchase of their

Legal Writing: Sample Extracts **12.20**

home. The client wants to complete in a week and is concerned how long the lender (British Bank) will take to release the mortgage funds.

These are original extracts so should be read with the constructive feedback.

❖ **Extract 1**

12.17 'It is my pleasure to inform you that we successfully exchanged contracts in relation to [add in address] ("the Property") and we are now moving onto the next stages of the conveyancing process, that is completion and post-completion stages. As requested by you, in this letter I will briefly set out a summary of these stages.'

❖ **Extract 1 – Constructive Feedback**

12.18 The instructions in the 'Brief Scenario' tell you that the client called, so using language like 'It is my pleasure to inform you' indicates that this is something the client did not know. It is a good idea to link the information in your instructions to your first sentence and then confirm what you will do.

Normally defined terms are used in contracts (eg 'the Property'), so I would not use it in the context of this letter. However, if you want to mention it, rather than put it in the first paragraph, you could add a subject heading stating the address and add 'the Property' after it, next to the property address.

❖ **Extract 2**

12.19 'I have already prepared the Transfer Deed, which is a document that reflects the terms of the contract of sale you signed. I will send the transfer deed to the seller's solicitors (SS) for the seller to sign. The transfer deed will then be submitted to the Land Registry after completion for purposes of registering the Property in your name and registering the mortgage in favour of British Bank.

After finalising the searches and enquiries, I will prepare a report on the property for your consideration, review and acceptance. Once this stage is completed we will move onto the completion stage which is where the purchase price for the Property is paid over to the SS and the title deeds and keys are handed over to you making you the legal owner of the Property.

The last stage will be the post-completion stage where I will attend to the payment of Stamp duty land tax at HM Revenue Services. SDLT is a tax payable on the purchase price of the Property. I will then proceed to register the Property in your name and the mortgage against British Bank and provide you with a copy of the transfer of title.'

❖ **Extract 2 – Constructive Feedback**

12.20 Although the information on the process is correct, it could be written in a more clear, concise and comprehensive manner. Check for accuracy as it is not HM Revenue Services but HM Revenue and Customs (HMRC). Also write SDLT in parentheses next to the full spelling if you want to refer to it later on.

12.21 *Legal Writing*

Splitting up the stages and using bullet points would also make it easier for the reader to understand the process.

Exercise – Example 2

Re-write the extracts for the property law scenario

Have a go at re-writing the above extracts more concisely by looking at the letter template suggested and incorporating the constructive feedback to help you.

See Appendix 12C for an alternative suggestion for the extracts.

- **Example 3: Extracts of legal writing from a business law scenario**

12.21 Brief Scenario: Two business partners are looking to protect their personal liability as their mobile accessories business expands. Advise them on whether a partnership or limited company would be their best option.

Below is an original extract so should be read with the constructive feedback.

❖ **Extract 1**

12.22 'A benefit of a private company is that the company is a separate legal personality and is able to enter into contracts and carry on a business for example. As a result, shareholders are not personally liable for the debts of the company, as the courts don't to go beyond this separate personality (behind the corporate veil).

If subsequently the company is wound up, and is insolvent, then the shareholders may be liable to contribute towards the shortfall in the assets of the company, but at most, only to the extent of any amount outstanding on their shares.

By contrast, s 9 Partnership Act 1890 (PA 1890) states *'every partner is liable jointly with the other partners for all the debts and obligations of the firm incurred while he is a partner'*. Thus, every partner is personally liable for partnership debts and obligations. Note that a partner is not liable for debts of the partnership before he became a partner.

The downside of a private limited company is the fact that much more information must be disclosed about it than about a partnership. For example, the company must be registered and it must make public the names of its directors. Limited companies are also required to file accounts and make other disclosures. Companies are more heavily regulated generally than partnerships, mainly by the Companies Act 2006, which states rules about how a company should be structured.

Companies are also required to have a written constitution (memorandum and articles of association) that govern how the company is managed for example.

There are however some exemptions from the heavy regulation for private limited and smaller companies, for example allowing flexibility in how shareholders make their decisions (eg by written resolution).

A written partnership agreement is not compulsory. However, lack of such an agreement for partners can lead to potential disputes or problems over how the running of a partnership should be.'

❖ **Extract 1 – Constructive Feedback**

12.23 This extract is written in quite an academic style for a letter, with little application of the law to the facts. Although the content is correct, the layout could be improved by including sub-headings, and for formal writing try not to use contractions such as 'don't'. The writing could also be better structured and more concise.

Exercise – Example 3

Re-write the extracts for the business law scenario

Have a go at re-writing the above extracts more concisely by looking at the letter template suggested and incorporating the constructive feedback to help you.

See Appendix 12D for an alternative suggestion for the extracts.

- *Example 4: Extracts of legal writing from a dispute resolution scenario*

12.24 Brief Scenario: Instruct the expert to assess the psychological injuries suffered by Carla Smith for quantum purposes. A list of various documents (not attached) will need to be included together with details of the issues on which the expert is required to provide an opinion. The expert will need to set up an appointment to see the client within two weeks and confirm that the report will be completed within four weeks of the appointment date. Fees agreed are £1,450 plus VAT.

These are original extracts so should be read with the constructive feedback.

❖ **Extract 1**

12.25 'I'm writing to you in connection with my client's civil litigation assault case. She has been attacked by a young man for whom a care home was responsible. In the case, negligence has been already admitted and the matter is currently proceeding on quantum only. In the case, our Client needs the clinical psychologist to prepare a report on the psychological impact of the assault on our client and we would like to instruct you to prepare such report. The report will be subsequently submitted in the court to support the Client's case.'

12.26 *Legal Writing*

❖ Extract 1 – Constructive Feedback

12.26 Using contractions (eg 'I'm') in formal letters may be considered unprofessional and informal, especially when instructing an expert or writing to a client. The use of 'In the case' at the start of two consecutive sentences is repetitive.

The first paragraph could start by stating the important point that the expert needs to see the client within two weeks.

The sentences could be more concise and accurate as the expert has already been instructed (ie '… we would like to instruct you …), and you could just follow through with the details.

You refer to 'the clinical psychologist' when you are writing to the expert. It would make the letter more impactful if you used the client's name 'Carla' instead of 'Client'.

❖ Extract 2

12.27 'We should be obliged if you would examine our client and let us have a full and detailed report dealing with any relevant pre-accident medical history, the injuries sustained, treatment received and present condition, dealing in particular with capacity for work and giving a prognosis.

It is central to our assessment of the extent of our client's injuries to establish the extent and duration of any continuing disability. Accordingly, in the prognosis section we would ask you to specifically comment on any areas of continuing complaint or disability or impact on daily living. If there is such continuing disability, you should comment upon the level of suffering or inconvenience caused and, if you are able, give your view as to when or if the complaint or disability is likely to resolve.'

❖ Extract 2 – Constructive Feedback

12.28 When providing instructions, the layout could be better. It is a good idea to list what you would like the expert to address because it makes it easier to read and ensures nothing is missed out when the expert meets the client and prepares their report.

❖ Extract 3

12.29 'We understand that you have agreed to see the client next week and prepare her report within four weeks after seeing her. We also understand that you have agreed a fee of £1,450 plus VAT for preparing the report. However, please let me know if any of these arrangements have been subsequently changed. Please also do let us know after you call with the client to make arrangements to see her and the date of appointment that has been agreed between you.'

❖ Extract 3 – Constructive Feedback

12.30 Separate the issues into different paragraphs – one deals with meeting the client and the other sets out the fees agreed and time frame for completing the report.

> **Exercise – Example 4**
>
> **Re-write the extracts for the dispute resolution scenario**
>
> Have a go at re-writing the above extracts more concisely by looking at the letter template suggested and incorporating the constructive feedback to help you.
>
> See Appendix 12E for an alternative suggestion for the extracts.

- ***Example 5: Extracts of legal writing from a wills and probate law scenario***

12.31 Brief Scenario: A charity is named as a beneficiary of Michael Shelby's will. It would like advice on its validity, specifically in relation to the deceased using only his initials to sign it and the number of witnesses. They were his sister Tina Shelby who has been left £3,000 and his best friend Paul Jones who has been left £1,000.

These are original extracts so should be read with the constructive feedback.

❖ **Extract 1**

12.32 'Dear Sirs

1. Introduction

We understand the following:

(a) The deceased died last week having made a short will prior to his death which bequeaths the following:

    (i) £3,000 to his sister,

    (ii) £1,000 to his best friend, and

    (iii) the residue to the charity

(b) The deceased only initialled his signature.

(c) The will was witnessed by two individuals (both of whom are beneficiaries and each of them signed the document in the presence of the deceased).'

❖ **Extract 1 – Constructive Feedback**

12.33 This layout looks more like a report and is not an appropriate way to start a letter.

You could use the person's name (Michael Shelby) instead of saying the 'deceased' to make it more personal (where appropriate).

Also, using the names of the witnesses throughout would make the letter easier for the client to read and understand.

12.34 *Legal Writing*

❖ **Extract 2**

12.34 'In order to execute a valid will, a testator must execute the will in the presence of two witnesses. A beneficiary should not, however, witness the execution of a will or the gift to that beneficiary will fail.'

❖ **Extract 2 – Constructive Feedback**

12.35 Apply the law more directly to the facts and use less legal jargon (ie 'testator'). It is inaccurate to say a will has to be witnessed by two people, it can be witnessed by two or more people.

Exercise – Example 5

Re-write the extracts for the probate law scenario

Have a go at re-writing the above extracts more concisely by looking at the letter template suggested and incorporating the constructive feedback to help you.

See Appendix 12F for an alternative suggestion for the extracts.

Remember, you can also practise testing your legal writing skills by using your own work-related scenarios (if they are practice areas you are assessed on).

Emails

12.36 The format of an email differs from letters (eg you would not write name and address, include the reference and the date in emails), but the main body of the content can follow the extracts suggested for the letters.

If you have to write a letter or email to a client on any given matter, it is a good idea to bear in mind that a structure is helpful. You can use the four points below and adapt the template in Chapter 7, Writing in Professional English to help you make sure you comprehensively cover all the key issues:

(1) Explain why you are advising ...

   (eg form a partnership over a company, plead guilty or not guilty to a charge)

(2) Describe how the advice applies or does not apply to the client's matter ...

   (eg application of the facts to the law)

(3) Outline what action you have taken (if appropriate) ...

   (eg what you have already done or who you have written to requesting ...)

(4) Outline the next steps

   (eg what you will do based on your actions, what you need from the client).

'Writing is the painting of the voice'
Voltaire

Legal Writing – Top Ten Tips

(1) Apply the scenario or instructions to your advice. Make the tone of your letter/email recipient-focused.

(2) Avoid using long sentences and write in the active voice to make your writing concise.

(3) Structure the content based on the instructions.

(4) Use bullet points or lists where you are requesting or listing a number of things.

(5) Write with the recipient in mind, so avoid legal jargon.

(6) Use headings and sub-headings when there are a number of issues.

(7) Write in a factual manner rather than a colloquial style.

(8) Using contractions in your letter can make it look more informal and less professional.

(9) Think about writing using the Four Cs: Clear, Concise, Comprehensive and Correct.

(10) Proof-read your work.

Chapter 12

Legal Writing: Appendices

Appendix 12A: Assessment Specification

This has been reproduced with permission from the SRA:

Overview

This is a computer-based assessment. Candidates will be asked to write a letter or an email as the solicitor acting in a matter, which clearly and correctly applies the law to the client's concerns and is appropriate for the recipient. This may, but will not necessarily, be in the context of a negotiation. Candidates will be given an email from a partner explaining what is required. The email may or may not be accompanied by electronic documents. The following is a non-exhaustive list of the possible recipients: a client, a third party, the other side to litigation or to a client transaction, or a partner within their organisation.

Candidates will have 30 minutes to complete this exercise.

Assessment Objective

Candidates can demonstrate that they are able to produce a letter or an email as the solicitor acting in a matter.

Assessment Criteria

Candidates will be assessed against the following criteria:

Skills

(1) Include relevant facts.
(2) Use a logical structure.
(3) Advice/content is client and recipient focused.
(4) Use clear, precise, concise and acceptable language which is appropriate to the recipient.

Application of Law

(5) Apply the law correctly to the client's situation.

> (6) Apply the law comprehensively to the client's situation, identifying any ethical and professional conduct issues and exercising judgment to resolve them honestly and with integrity.

You should read this in conjunction with the Chapter 1, The SQE Journey, Appendix 1B which details what the Competence Statement includes and in particular the Statement of Solicitor Competence.

In Chapter 3, Functioning Legal Knowledge, Appendix 3A you can find an overview of the areas of law that you will be assessed on in the following way:

- dispute resolution or criminal litigation (either one of these);
- property practice or wills and probate (either one of these);
- business law (definitely this area).

More detailed information can be found on the SRA website (www.sra.org.uk).

Appendix 12B: Example 1: Criminal litigation scenario

> **Brief scenario**
>
> Write to the client and confirm the advice given. The client has been charged with theft, the confession was obtained in breach of the Police and Criminal Evidence Act 1984 (PACE). The client will plead not guilty and does not qualify for legal aid.

> ***Alternative Suggestion for Extract 1 (para 12.08)***
>
> 'Further to our meeting on Tuesday 29 May 2020, I write to confirm that you have been charged with the theft of [state details] with a value of [state amount].
>
> **Identification**
>
> As we are regulated by the Solicitors Regulation Authority, I will require one proof of photographic identification and one proof of address – any of the following originals will be fine:
>
> - Photographic identification
>   - Passport; or
>   - Driving licence (UK)
> - Proof of address
>   - Utility bill (less than three months old); or
>   - Bank statement (less than three months old)
>   - Driving licence (UK)'

Legal Writing: Appendices

Alternative Suggestion for Extract 2 (para 12.10)

'Legal Advice:

- *Pleading not guilty*

I advise you to plead not guilty at court. This is based on the available evidence and your instructions.

- *Challenging the confession*

The confession can be challenged under the law* if it was obtained by oppression or is unreliable because of something that was said or done. In your case, the following facts support the argument that your confession may be inadmissible:

- You were not told about your right to access legal representation;
- The length of time and number of interviews conducted from 6pm to 5am; and
- The comments made by the arresting officer (which may be disputed).

The prosecution has to prove the confession was not obtained through oppression and is reliable. If they cannot prove this (beyond a reasonable doubt), then your confession would be excluded at your trial and would not form part of the evidence.'

*(Police and Criminal Evidence Act 1984, ss 76 and 78 (PACE).)

Alternative Suggestion for Extract 3 (para 12.12)

'Legal Aid

I explained that there are two tests (the means test and the merits test) and both need to be satisfied to qualify for legal aid. Unfortunately, you do not meet the means test because you earn £29,500 per year (you have to earn less than £12,475 per year), so you will not qualify for legal aid.'

Alternative Suggestion for Extract 4 (para 12.14)

'If you have any questions, please do not hesitate to contact me.'

Appendix 12C: Example 2: Property practice scenario

Brief scenario

A client called this morning and would like you to confirm the next steps after the exchange of contracts later today for the purchase of their home. The client wants to complete in a week and is concerned how long the lender (British Bank) will take to release the mortgage funds.

Alternative Suggestion for Extract 1 (para 12.17)

'Thank you for your call this morning to discuss the next steps after we exchanged contracts on [date]. The information below should provide you with the next steps between exchange and completion and post-completion.'

Alternative Suggestion for Extract 2 (para 12.19)

'Between Exchange and Completion

Now we have exchanged contracts you are legally bound to the purchase. As you would like to complete on [add in the date], I will do the following:

(1) Once you have signed the mortgage deed, I will ask British Bank to send me the mortgage funds which can take up to five working days.

(2) Prepare the transfer deed and send it to the seller's solicitor for completion.

(3) Send you a completion statement (which shows exactly how much money will be required to complete, pay the stamp duty and our fees).

(4) Pre-completion searches to ensure there have been no changes to the property.

Post-completion

Once we have completed the purchase, I will take the following steps:

(1) Complete the Stamp Duty Land Tax (SDLT) return and send it to the HMRC together with the amount payable.

(2) Register the following documents with the Land Registry:

   (i) The Transfer Deed (shows you are the legal owner of the property); and

   (ii) The Mortgage Deed (shows British Bank have a charge over the property).

Once the registration process with the Land Registry is completed, I will forward you a copy of the title register as evidence of your ownership.'

Appendix 12D: Example 3: Business law scenario

Brief scenario

Two business partners are looking to protect their personal liability as their mobile accessories business expands. Advise them on whether a partnership or limited company would be their best option.

Alternative Suggestion for Extract 1 (para 12.22)

'There are two options available to you and these are setting up a partnership or a limited company. Below I have explained both options and why a limited company would be the best option for your mobile accessories business.

Limited company

As both of you want to protect your personal liability then a limited company is your best option. That means you protect your personal assets outside of what you have invested in the business.

There is a formal set-up required which provides how the business is structured and is primarily governed by the Companies Act 2006 where the company must:

- be registered at Companies House and name all the directors publicly.
- file accounts and make other disclosures
- show how the business will be managed (memorandum and articles of association).

Small businesses (such as yours) can be exempt from heavier regulation where there is flexibility to adapt the articles of association.

Partnership

There is no formal set-up required, but it is advisable that a partnership agreement is made stating the roles and responsibilities of the partners and how any liabilities and disputes will be resolved.

There are two types of partnerships:

- General partnership

All partners are jointly responsible for all business debts and liabilities, so it does not offer you the same level of protection as a limited company.

- Limited liability partnership

All partners' personal liability is protected, so this option could work for you.

As your mobile accessories business is expanding, a limited company over a limited liability partnership would be the best option for you. Although both protect personal liability, the key difference is taxation. Also, in the future if your business required external financing or funding, lenders tend to prefer to do business with a limited company over a partnership.'

Appendix 12E: Example 4: Dispute resolution scenario

Brief scenario

Instruct the expert to assess the psychological injuries suffered by Carla Smith for quantum purposes. A list of various documents (not attached) will need to be included together with details of the issues on which the expert is required to provide an opinion. The expert will need to set up an appointment to see the client within two weeks and confirm that the report will be completed within four weeks of the appointment date. Fees agreed are £1,450 plus VAT.

Alternative Suggestion for Extract 1 (para 12.25)

'Thank you for agreeing to act in connection with this matter and seeing our client, Mrs Carla Smith, within two weeks. Mrs Smith is expecting you to contact her to arrange an appointment. Here are her contact details:

Address: [Client's address]
Tel: [Client's number]

Alternative Suggestion for Extract 2 (para 12.27)

'We represent Mrs Carla Smith in relation to her claim for personal injuries as a result of an assault on [date]. The main injuries appear to be psychological in nature and she has recovered from the physical impact of the assault.

Please find attached copies of the following documents:

- Statement of Carla Smith
- Carla Smith's medical records
- Counsellor [his/her name's] notes

We would like you to examine Mrs Smith and let us have your full report dealing with the following in general:

(1) Any relevant pre-accident medical history.

(2) The psychological injuries sustained.

(3) Treatment received and her present condition, dealing in particular with her capacity for:

  (a) daily living and caring for her family; and

  (b) her employment.

Alternative Suggestion for Extract 3 (para 12.29)

'You have agreed to provide us with a report within four weeks of seeing Mrs Smith. Please let us know what date you have arranged a meet her.

Legal Writing: Appendices

> We look forward to receiving the full report together with your invoice for the agreed fee of £1,450 plus VAT for this work.
>
> Please acknowledge receipt of this letter and its enclosures.'

Appendix 12F: Example 5: Wills and probate law scenario

Brief scenario

A charity is named as a beneficiary of Michael Shelby's will. It would like advice on its validity, specifically in relation to the deceased using only his initials to sign it and the number of witnesses. They were his sister Tina Shelby who has been left £3,000 and his best friend Paul Jones who has been left £1,000.

Alternative Suggestion for Extract 1 (para 12.32)

'Dear Sirs

Re: Advice on the Late Mr Shelby's Will

Thank you for your instructions. We confirm that you would like advice in relation to Mr Shelby's will and its validity. Namely:

1)   The fact Mr Shelby signed the will using his initials only; and

2)   The fact that there were two witnesses to the will

The charity is named as a residuary beneficiary which means that once any debts, liabilities and gifts are paid out, the remainder of Mr Shelby's estate goes to the charity. Below is our advice in relation to your concerns raised.

Signing a will using initials

The fact that Mr Shelby did not sign the will using his full signature and only used his initials does not invalidate the will.

Two witnesses

A will must be signed in the presence of two or more witnesses so the fact two witnesses signed this will in the presence of each other and Mr Shelby, means his will is valid.'

Alternative Suggestion for Extract 2 (para 12.34)

'In order to make the will valid, Mr Shelby must have signed it in the presence of two or more witnesses. They do not need to know the contents

Appendix 12F

of what they are witnessing, as long as, they signed it in the presence of each other and Mr Shelby.

However, a beneficiary should not witness the will or the gift to that beneficiary will fail. As Mr Shelby's best friend, Paul Jones and his sister Tina Shelby witnessed the will and both are named as beneficiaries, their respective gifts would fail (Paul's gift of £1,000 and Tina's gift of £3,000).'

Chapter 13

SQE Part 2

Legal Drafting

'Any fool can make things bigger, more complex ... It takes a touch of genius – and a lot of courage – to move in the opposite direction.'

Albert Einstein

In this chapter you will learn:
- ✓ What makes drafting easier for the recipient to read.
- ✓ The difference certain words make when drafting clauses.
- ✓ The importance of layout and how it should be consistent with what you are drafting.
- ✓ What to consider when drafting undertakings.
- ✓ When to use plain English (where appropriate).
- ✓ How to ensure consistency when defined terms are used in legal documents.

Introduction

13.01 This chapter complements Chapter 7, Writing in Professional English so it makes sense that you read these chapters in conjunction with one another.

Writing styles for legal writing and legal drafting do overlap a little, but they are different. For legal writing, you might have a more personalised writing style (eg writing to a client), but for legal drafting it is all about precision. A poorly drafted legal document can cause a range of complications and have major cost implications.

In this chapter no 'real' legal documents or precedents are used because they are frequently changed and updated. So, think of this chapter as providing you with general guidance on what to consider and think about practically when drafting legal documents. I have selected a few typical examples, but this is not a reflection

13.02 *Legal Drafting*

of their 'popularity' for the assessments. They are chosen because I have worked with many lawyers and these are some of the areas where we end up having a discussion about 'taking it back to basics'. This means understanding what the client wants to do or not do and what the law means in relation to it. As so many variables can affect the drafting, it would be unfeasible for me to cover every type of typical legal drafting scenario, form or document and how to complete it or draft it.

Your experience in practice and studying will provide you with a specific variety of examples where you can test your legal drafting ability and progress. The examples in this chapter are deliberately kept generic to make the principal point of what I want you to consider practically when you are drafting any legal documents, so use what works best for you.

The SRA has provided a sample of what you could get for this type of assessment for a dispute resolution scenario. You can also find samples for all the other assessments on the SRA website (www.sra.org.uk).

Legal Drafting – Business Law and Criminal Litigation

13.02 Legal drafting is a technical skill that is usually learnt at law school and your experience will grow whilst working in a legal department of a law firm or business. The practice areas of law that you work in will dictate what type of legal drafting you will frequently do. This chapter looks at legal drafting for two practice areas:

- **Business law**

    A commercial lawyer may be used to dealing with non-contentious work where they review and draft partnership agreements or commercial contracts, or set up and give legal effect to companies.

- **Criminal litigation**

    A criminal lawyer will be used to dealing with contentious matters where they may draft witness statements, a defence statement, review and negotiate on key issues affecting a client's case and weigh up the pros and cons of going to trial.

For the SQE Part 2, you will be assessed on what you should be expected to do as a newly qualified solicitor. Therefore, the degree of complexity and technical knowledge for a particular practice area of law will be assessed at the appropriate level (read Chapter 1, The SQE Journey, Competence Statement, Appendix 1B).

The Assessment Criteria

13.03 You will have 45 minutes to draft a legal document or a part of it (eg this could mean making amendments or re-drafting part of a document based on your client's instructions).

You can read about the more detailed version of the SRA criteria in Appendix 13A.

Below I have summarised and highlighted the criteria against which you are assessed.

- **Skills**

13.04

(1) Use clear, precise, concise and acceptable language.

(2) Structure the document appropriately and logically.

- **Application of Law**

13.05 You should note that for all the assessments your knowledge of the law needs to be applied:

- correctly; and

- comprehensively, identifying any professional conduct and ethical issues.

You should assess yourself against these criteria when practising your legal drafting (for any of the five practice areas of the law). These are assessed using the following grading scale:

Grade	Mark	Standard	Do you meet the competency requirements?
A	5	Superior performance	Yes, well above it
B	4	Clearly satisfactory	Yes, clearly meets it
C	3	Marginal pass	Yes, on balance, just meets it
D	2	Marginal fail	No, on balance, just fails it
E	1	Clearly unsatisfactory	No, clearly does not meet it
F	0	Poor performance	No, well below it

You can read more about the Competence Statement in Chapter 1, The SQE Journey, Appendix 1B which provides the context of what you are expected to know for practice as a newly qualified solicitor.

Types of Legal Documents

13.06 There are a whole range of typical types of documents you could be asked to draft, amend, re-draft or edit. The list below is not exhaustive, but offers you some ideas:

Business Law

13.07

- Adapting the Model Articles of Association to reflect specific instructions.

- Completing the forms required for the incorporation of a company.

- Drafting the minutes of a shareholders' meeting.

13.08 *Legal Drafting*

- Drafting or amending clauses in a partnership agreement or a shareholders' agreement.
- Drafting the allotment of shares.
- Completing a stock transfer form.
- Drafting or amending a director's service agreement.

Property Law

13.08

- Drafting the special conditions in the Standard Conditions of Sale.
- Drafting or amending a specific clause for a lease.
- Completing conveyancing forms (eg transfer deed, stamp duty, etc).
- Preparing and drafting a licence.
- Drafting an undertaking.
- Drafting a severance of a joint tenancy.
- Draft or complete a document in favour of a lender (eg protection of lender's security).

Criminal Litigation

13.09

- Drafting a defence statement.
- Drafting a witness statement (or a part of it).
- Drafting various applications (special measures for vulnerable witnesses, bail variations, exclude evidence, witness summons etc).
- Complete an application for a representation order.

Dispute Resolution

13.10

- Drafting particulars of claim (or a part of it).
- Drafting a witness statement (or a part of it).
- Drafting or amending a defence or counterclaim.
- Drafting a letter of claim.
- Drafting a request for further information.
- Drafting an offer to settle a claim.

Wills and Probate

13.11

- Completing different tax forms (eg IHT forms or supplementary forms).
- Drafting or amending a will (based on client instructions).
- Drafting various forms (eg deed of renunciation, reserve power or variation).
- Draft an oath/certificate for executor/administrator.

Remember, you must read the instructions carefully because this assessment is testing your skills on being able to interpret the client's instructions and reflect them in your drafting.

> *'If language is not correct ... then what ought to be done remains undone.'*
>
> **Confucius**

Language

13.12 If a dispute arises because the language used is unclear or open to interpretation, it can be very costly, time-consuming and bad for the business and your reputation.

Try to avoid using archaic legal language. Plain English is preferred for most businesses, especially for contracts. It makes them easier to understand and there is less chance of any misinterpretation.

In any legal drafting, when you properly understand your client's instructions and the reasons behind them, it makes it easier for you to ensure that they are reflected accurately and comprehensively. The language and terminology used should be consistent to avoid ambiguity. Never express the same point in two different ways in different clauses. Ambiguity or any difference in phrasing which could be open to interpretation can lead to costly disputes. For example, do not say in one clause:

'costs and expenses shall be borne by the Buyer'

and in another clause:

'costs shall be borne by the Buyer'.

Be consistent.

- ### *Similar words*

13.13 There are many synonyms (substitute/similar words) in law. For example, the following words mean the same:

- vendor and seller;
- purchaser and buyer;
- mortgagee and lender;

13.14 *Legal Drafting*

- mortgagor and borrower;
- lessor and landlord;
- lessee and tenant.

Be consistent with which pair of words you use. For example, vendor and purchaser/seller and buyer, mortgagee and mortgagor/lender and borrower. Do not mix the pairs of words (ie vendor and buyer or mortgagee and borrower). Generally, the latter words are more modern and easier to understand so it is a good idea to use them when drafting. However, make sure that the language is consistent throughout the whole document if you are adapting some clauses rather than drafting from scratch.

Make sure you think about how you refer to dates and currencies which can be open to interpretation if not made clear. For example:

- **Dates**

13.14 Clarify what you mean: 3/5/2023 could be 3 May 2023 (UK English) or 5 March 2023 (US English).

- **Currencies**

13.15 Clarify what you mean: the dollar ($) can refer to a number of different currencies. State clearly which one you mean: US$ (American), AU$ (Australian), S$ (Singaporean), HK$ (Hong Kong).

Your drafting should make it clear that the chosen currency is the only one accepted and how and when the currency is converted, who will bear the costs or fees.

- **Translation**

13.16 Language in contracts can have a different meaning to 'normal' everyday use. So, make sure any words used for international transactions are understood by all parties, especially if they have the contract translated to another language. Bear in mind, any vocabulary used will be context dependent but open to mistranslation. For example:

- Execution

    In a contract it can mean the parties' signatures to give the contract legal effect and in 'non-legal' language it can mean carrying out a sentence of death.

- Charge

    In a contract it can mean a security over a loan and in 'non-legal' language it can mean making a request for payment of goods or services or where someone has been charged with a criminal offence.

If you know the contract will be translated into other languages make sure you make it clear that the English language will prevail in any event (eg a dispute) and make it clear which jurisdiction is exclusively stated to hear any disputes. Without such clarity, the whole process can be extremely costly, time-consuming and inconvenient (if different cities or countries are involved).

- **Words**

  ❖ **'shall', 'must' and 'may'**

13.17 From your instructions, once the party's intentions are clear, think about whether you are making it obligatory for a party to do something or voluntary. Typically, the word 'shall' is commonly used in a range of different types of contracts, for example:

> 'The landlord shall let the tenant …'
>
> 'The claimant and the defendant shall …'

The word 'shall' is used in contracts to indicate what will or will not be done by the parties. A more modern alternative is 'must' which is more definite and imperative. For example:

> 'The landlord must let the tenant …'
>
> 'The claimant and the defendant must …'

An alternative word 'may' can be used where there is no definite obligation:

> 'The landlord may let the tenant …'
>
> 'The claimant and the defendant may …'

The word 'may' means that one party has the discretion to do or not do something – there is no obligation. Therefore, it should be very clear at the outset that the parties understand that they cannot rely on something to be done or not to be done. It goes back to the intention of the parties – so read your instructions carefully.

  ❖ **'by' and 'until'**

13.18 When you use the word 'by' to express a deadline the problem is it may not be clear what this means, for example:

> 'In line with the deadline, payment must be made by 25 June 2023.'

Does 'by' include the 25 June 2023 or not? It is much better to be more explicit:

> 'In line with the deadline, payment must be made on or before 25 June 2023.'

This makes it clear that payment can be made before the 25 June 2023, or on that date at the latest.

  ❖ **'before and after'**

13.19 This language is common when drafting delivery clauses where the contract might state, for example,

13.20 *Legal Drafting*

'The Company will deliver the Goods to the Supplier before 30 May 2023.'

'The Company will deliver the Goods to the Supplier after 30 May 2023.'

What happens if the Company deliver the goods *on* 30 May 2020? Are there any implications? Therefore, it is always a good idea to ensure that you cover that eventuality, making the clause more precise, such as:

'The Company will deliver the Goods to the Supplier on or before 30 May 2023.'

'The Company will deliver the Goods to the Supplier on or after 30 May 2023.'

The above are just a few examples of language to consider when drafting a contract or clause. If you are studying with a university or training provider, then they should provide you with relevant course materials.

'People know accuracy when they read it; they can feel it.'
Alan Furst

Layout

13.20 The layout of the legal document should also be considered and be consistent with the type of document you are drafting. Usually this may be dictated by the legal document, but if not, know what the layout should look like and adhere to it. For example, if you are drafting a contract or amending a contract then you should ensure that the whole document's tone is consistent and it is set out in a manner that makes it easy to understand and follow. This means checking that you have:

- a logical structure;
- paragraphs that deal with individual issues or points;
- appropriate headings and sub-headings;
- consistent numbering;
- accurate cross-referencing between other clauses and sub-clauses.

Note that although cross-referencing clauses can be inevitable for many contracts, it is a good idea to try to limit the number of cross-references. This is because flitting between clauses can make it more difficult to grasp the overall meaning. It also increases the chance that errors could be made in the cross-referencing where one clause might be changed, but the corresponding clause/s is/are not amended to reflect the change.

Business Law – Drafting Clauses

13.21 In accordance with your instructions, you may be asked to draft clauses around the interests, rights, obligations and powers of stakeholders/shareholders in a business. This could be from scratch or re-draft and adapt the Model Articles of Association or a partnership agreement (eg for resignation, appointment of director, transfer of shares, etc). Where I have referred to a contract it also includes any types of agreements.

Before you start to draft a clause, think about what your client wants and understand the context of the business and your instructions.

If you have to adapt a clause to your client's instructions and use a template, feel confident in adapting it to reflect what you need to do. That can mean you use plain English instead of legal jargon (where appropriate). If you are re-drafting, make sure that the tone and writing style are consistent with the rest of the document.

When you are very clear about what you need to do it makes it easier to express it, because you understand it better.

Depending on the course materials you use, you want lots of specific and practical examples of what to do and you need to be aware of the pitfalls of poor drafting, so as to avoid common mistakes.

- ### *Types of Clauses*

13.22 The key to drafting any clause is to make it comprehensive and precise. A contract is evidence of what the parties agree and it reduces the risk of any disputes. Most contracts will have the standard heading setting out the type of contract and parties' names and addresses, with a description of the goods/services as well as standard 'boilerplate' clauses. The end of the contract is where the parties sign and date it. Some contracts will also have appendices which details what the contract includes. The terms and conditions will vary depending on the circumstances, many will usually include the following (the list is non-exhaustive):

- Price, costs, fees, payment.
- Duties and rights of the parties.
- Warranties.
- Indemnities.
- Remedies (if a breach occurs).
- Confidentiality.
- Non-compete.
- Duration/termination of the contract.
- Force majeure.
- Governing law and jurisdiction.
- Arbitration/alternative dispute resolution (ADR).

- ### *Defined Terms*

13.23 After the named parties, many contracts have a defined terms section before the main clauses of the contract. If you are drafting from scratch make sure you think about whether you need to define any terms. There is a danger, if you

13.24 *Legal-Drafting*

define too many terms, that the document can become complicated and difficult to read. If you draft part of a legal document check to make sure that you are consistent with the defined terms used (if any).

Defined terms should be used only when you are clear and specific about what they represent throughout the whole document and their meaning and interpretation do not change.

When the defined term is used it starts with a capital letter throughout the whole document and serves as a reminder to anyone reading the document that the defined words have a special meaning. The defined terms in a commercial contract will be context dependent and vary depending on the type of contract. For example:

- 'Goods' means any products, articles or services and includes any components or materials incorporated in them …
- 'Seller' means a person, firm or company …
- 'Buyer' means a person, firm or company …

The examples below are of a costs/price clause and an alternative dispute resolution (ADR) clause simplified to illustrate how you might want to approach clear contract drafting. You can then apply the same thinking to drafting other clauses. Always bear in mind the Four Cs when drafting and you can read more about these in Chapter 7, Writing in Professional English (para **7.15**) which reminds you that written communication should be:

- clear
- concise
- comprehensive
- correct.

If it is a complicated scenario that involves a number of parties and you need to figure out what the duties and rights are and who has responsibility for what part of the contract, these questions will help you get some clarity:

- Who is your client?
- What is their role? (This can be broken down into key areas and who will do what part.)
- What do you need to do for them? (Understand their intention.)
- How can you draft clauses precisely? (Check against the Four Cs.)

- **Costs/Price Clause**

13.24 Depending on the type of contract, it may include a costs/price clause which will determine what one party's financial responsibilities will be to the other party and when and how payment will be paid.

13.25 Your instructions might ask you to draft a suitable costs clause in favour of the seller, for example:

'Vendor must cooperate with and assist the Buyer in this transaction herewith and all costs and expenses shall be borne by the Buyer and no costs or expenses will be borne by the Vendor.'

❖ **Example – Constructive Feedback**

13.26 The drafting is too wordy and the mixed use of vendor and buyer is incorrect. Be consistent in your language and use purchaser and vendor or buyer and seller. The latter terms are generally the preferred choice in modern drafting.

❖ **Example – An Alternative Suggestion**

13.27

'The Seller must co-operate and assist the Buyer throughout the whole process at the Buyer's expense.'

❖ **Example – Commentary**

13.28 You may think that this clause feels a bit too brief, but it actually states what the seller has to do and that the buyer will cover the cost. That does not mean that all clauses need to be as brief, they will all be context dependent. I have used a simple example to make the point that if your instruction is straightforward and simple, you can draft it simply. Therefore, feel confident about your ability to draft a clause more concisely and comprehensively, even if the template you choose is much more wordy or you are required to draft a clause from scratch.

If you have a clause where you are suggesting payment should be made in stages for any products or services, make it clear and comprehensive by including dates, amounts and time frames. For example:

'The Buyer must pay fifty per cent (50%) of the price of any order within [X] days of an order being accepted by the Seller and must pay fifty per cent (50%) to the Seller within [X] days of delivery of the ordered Goods.'

- ***Alternative Dispute Resolution Clause (ADR)***

13.29 This type of clause is found in contracts where parties want an agreement on what the protocol should be in the event that a dispute arises. Here are some questions to consider in the hypothetical situation of a dispute arising which can help shape the drafting:

- What are the different types of breach that could affect the business?
- What could be the difficulty in proving a fundamental breach?
- If there is a breach, what actions can be taken?
- What are the appropriate remedies?
- What types of damages would be appropriate?

13.30 *Legal Drafting*

ADR is encouraged to avoid costly litigation, which should always be the last resort. There are a number of different processes that can be used to attempt to reach settlement and the first should always be through negotiation. You can read more on the alternatives to litigation in Chapter 11, Case and Matter Analysis, Contentious Matters (para **11.08**).

- **Example**

13.30 Your instructions might be to draft an ADR clause on how any disputes will be resolved between parties, for example:

> 'In the event of a dispute, the parties shall use their best endeavours to resolve the dispute through negotiations in good faith. If the dispute is not resolved then the parties can …'

❖ **Example – Constructive Feedback**

13.31 On the face of it, the clause does make sense in the spirit of what the instruction has requested. However, the drafting is too vague and open to interpretation, which is likely to cause conflict between the parties if a dispute arises. Think about it: what does the clause actually require the parties to do? Without clarity, it is unlikely that there will be an agreement. Additionally, when a dispute does arise, the parties may not be able to agree on questions such as:

- What objective criteria can be used to judge whether a party has used their 'best endeavours' or 'all reasonable endeavours'?
- How long is a reasonable amount of time to try 'to resolve the dispute through negotiations'?
- Who decides and how will it be decided that one party has or has not used 'their best endeavours' and acted in 'good faith'?

Using 'best endeavours' places a mandatory (heavier) obligation on each party to try and resolve the matter through negotiations. However, many lawyers also use the alternative of 'all reasonable endeavours'. In deciding which phrase to use, it is worth ensuring that you use the phrase you can rely on that is supported by case law or precedents (for the context of your contract), in case of a dispute.

When a dispute arises, you might want to resolve it quickly. However, if the wording is ambiguous and open to interpretation, the other party may wish to raise these issues as a strategic delaying tactic (for whatever reason) and request an expert determination.

❖ **Example – An Alternative Suggestion**

13.32

> 'In the event of a dispute, the parties must use all reasonable endeavours to resolve the dispute by meeting to try and resolve the identified issue or issues at least [X times] within a period of [X months] before progressing to the next stage.'

❖ **Example – Commentary**

13.33 It is a good idea to try and contextualise what could be open to interpretation. So, using 'best endeavours' or 'all reasonable endeavours' implies different interpretations on their obligations to each other to try to resolve the issue or issues (ie by having a meeting). The stated time frame offers clarity over what period of time is agreed before next steps can be taken. If there are more specific issues relating to the main clause, then create sub-clauses. For example:

- The number of days or notice period required by which one party lets the other party know they want to request a meeting (eg in writing – by email?, letter? or both?)
- The request for a meeting must be made by [who – directors?] and a written response received within [X] working days.
- The meeting will be held in a neutral environment within [where – location?, city?]

The main clause may have sub-clauses to ensure completeness of what needs to be done (or not done) in conjunction with the main clause. The sub-clauses offer structure and clarity so there is little room for dispute based on ambiguity. In practice, before you start drafting a contract it is vital that you take your client's full instructions and ask good questions which probe deeper into what the parties' intentions are for the business and in the event that things go wrong. The spirit of both parties' intentions should be reflected in the contract.

Often terms or conditions towards the end of most commercial contracts are referred to as 'boilerplate' clauses and seen as standard, so may not be given the same level of importance as the rest of the agreement. It is important to make sure your client's instructions are reflected in the entire agreement.

Undertakings

13.34 Sometimes as lawyers you will be required to provide an undertaking to do or not do something. This is not something that should be given lightly. It is similar to a 'promise', but one that is taken very seriously and relied upon.

- ## *What is an Undertaking?*

13.35 The SRA Standards and Regulations Glossary states that an undertaking is:

> '... a statement, given orally or in writing, whether or not it includes the word "undertake" or "undertaking", to someone who reasonably places reliance on it, that you or a third party will do something or cause something to be done, or refrain from doing something.'

An undertaking is a commitment where you accept the legal consequences of entering into it. Note, it does not need to be given in writing. Sometimes, the circumstances when it is given verbally do not practically allow for it to be drafted there and then. However, it is good practice to promptly follow up and document it for clarity.

13.36 *Legal Drafting*

Some firms will have a strict policy on who can and cannot give undertakings (eg only partners). There will usually be some form of record, register or legal software system to keep track of what cases have 'live' undertakings and those that have been discharged.

They can be given in any practice area of law and whether or not one is required is context dependant. For example, these are two practice areas where undertakings are commonly used:

- Property law: for conveyancing transactions where one party's solicitor undertakes to release funds on a particular date to progress the transaction to completion.
- Business law: where one party undertakes to pay the costs of the other party.

There is a good business goal-setting model called SMART that can be used if you have to give or draft an undertaking. There are several interpretations as to what the acronym letters stand for and they can vary depending on the goal. For example, 'A' can be 'Agreed' or 'Achievable' and 'R' can be 'Relevant' or 'Realistic'. The model can be adapted to help you provide a smart undertaking, so it does not cause any costly or time-consuming disputes.

For the purposes of an undertaking, SMART can stand for:

- S = Specific (make it clear and unambiguous).
- M = Measurable (make sure you monitor how it will be achieved).
- A = Achievable (make sure you can fulfil it and it is agreed).
- R = Relevant (make sure it is relevant for what you want to do).
- T = Timed (make it time framed so you know when you have fulfilled it).

- ***Example***

13.36 Your instructions might be to draft an undertaking in a scenario where Company A will pay Company B's costs for the transaction and you draft something similar to this:

'Company A undertakes to pay Company B's costs for the transaction.'

- ❖ **Example – Constructive Feedback**

13.37 Although the undertaking is correct in principle, it is not comprehensive enough. Think about the intention behind the undertaking. It is to ensure that Company B's costs are paid for the transaction, so you should draft it to ensure that their costs would be covered in any event.

Assume, because of Company A's fault, the transaction does not complete and has fallen through. Could Company B claim for their costs up to the date of the transaction falling through? Company A could argue that they are not obliged to pay Company B's costs because the undertaking was only valid for the transaction (ie upon completion), and now it is not going ahead there is no obligation to pay as the transaction does not exist. Of course, this is open to interpretation. This is an example of how disputes can arise.

The key point is that when an undertaking is drafted ambiguously, it usually means it can be interpreted in more ways than one, which are likely to conflict. This can very quickly escalate into a costly situation and ruin business relationships.

In trying to be concise, you must ensure that you are comprehensive: any undertaking should always be worded specifically and contextualised.

❖ **Example – An Alternative Suggestion**

13.38

> 'Company A undertakes to pay Company B's costs in relation to the transaction in any event.'

❖ **Example – Commentary**

13.39 The additional key words 'in any event' ensure that whether or not the transaction completes, Company A would be liable for Company B's costs. This could mean all costs up to the point where the transaction fails to proceed or all the costs upon completion of the transaction. Either way Company B's costs related to the transaction will be paid by Company A.

When you have clarity of thought you have clarity of mind. This means that it is easier for you to draft something when you understand the intention behind it. So, make sure you understand what your client wants and, when you draft the undertaking, ensure that it is comprehensive and avoids any ambiguity leading to misinterpretation.

Criminal Law – Defence Statement

13.40 If your instructions are to draft a defence statement, make sure you complete all the sections that may precede the main part of the drafting because they count too.

You may be guided by what you are expected to include in each section, for example:

(1) provide details of the defence;
(2) the facts that you take issue with (as raised by the Crown Prosecution Service (CPS)) and why;
(3) the facts that you rely on for your defence and why;
(4) the points of law, admissibility of evidence or abuse of process relied upon, stating any authority that supports it;
(5) any alibis to support your defence, along with contact details.

13.41 *Legal Drafting*

- ### Statements (1) to (3)

13.41 Make sure your answers are clear and concise because they will form part of your client's case and there is no room for any misinterpretation. Write using plain English and keep sentences short and simple. Be clear what evidence your client takes issue with and why, then state their defence.

- ### Statement (4)

13.42 You will need to state the authority you rely upon to support your specific position. The more similar any case precedents are to your case, the stronger the evidence to help make your argument persuasive.

- ### Statement (5)

13.43 List the names of any witnesses and their contact details (eg address, mobile number and email).

Example

13.44 If you have a scenario where your client has been charged with assault and denies the charge, they may rely on self-defence. You will need to state:

(1) what defence is relied upon (ie self defence).
(2) details of the key evidence you dispute raised by the CPS explaining why.
(3) details of your facts relied upon explaining why it was self-defence.
(4) what case law and legislation supports your defence.
(5) names and contact details of witnesses relied upon.

It is your client's defence statement so it is written in the first person. For example, 'I did not intentionally stab [name] because I was acting in self-defence.'

Completing Forms

13.45 If part of your assessment involves completing any forms make sure you do not rush it by just completing the obvious parts like the client's or firm's contact details. There may be options where you need to delete or strikethrough what does not apply to your client – attention to detail does matter. For example, if you are asked to complete a Deed (or any legal document), where it may say something like: '[I][We] hereby ...' make sure that you strike out the option that does not apply. So, if you are representing one person, strikeout the 'We' (for example, [I] [We]) or vice versa if you are representing two or more clients. This may seem simple and straightforward, but I have frequently seen this level of attention to detail overlooked. These small, avoidable mistakes (made frequently) can lower your marks and could ultimately affect your overall SQE Part 2 mark.

Some forms have guidance notes, so make sure you complete the blank spaces with the correct information relevant to the application. For example, know which court you are sending the form to: county court or High Court, and populate the rest of the form with the relevant information required.

'Concision in style, precision in thought'

Victor Hugo

Legal Drafting – Top Ten Tips

(1) Read the instructions carefully to understand what you need to do.

(2) Be confident about adapting a template clause to make it more reader friendly (if appropriate).

(3) Pay attention to detail when filling out forms to avoid errors or omissions.

(4) In trying to be concise, do not overlook key information, draft precisely and comprehensively.

(5) Ensure that language is used consistently throughout any legal document.

(6) Use defined terms appropriately and sparingly.

(7) Understand what ADR processes are appropriate.

(8) Use precise and simple language (avoid legal jargon and archaic legal language).

(9) Clarity of thought is clarity of mind, which will help you draft accurately.

(10) Proofread your document.

Chapter 13

Legal Drafting: Appendix

Appendix 13A: Assessment Specification

This has been reproduced with permission from the SRA:

Overview

This is a computer-based assessment. Candidates will be asked to draft a legal document or parts of a legal document. This may take the form of drafting from a precedent or amending a document already drafted but it may also involve drafting without either of these.

Candidates will be given 45 minutes to complete the task.

Assessment Objective

Candidates can demonstrate they are able to draft a legal document or parts of a legal document for a client.

Assessment Criteria

Candidates will be assessed against the following criteria:

Skills

(1) Use clear, precise, concise and acceptable language.

(2) Structure the document appropriately and logically.

Application of Law

(3) Draft a document which is legally correct.

(4) Draft a document which is legally comprehensive, identifying any ethical and professional conduct issues and exercising judgment to resolve them honestly and with integrity.

You should read this in conjunction with the Chapter 1, The SQE Journey, Appendix 1B which details what the Competence Statement includes and in particular the Statement of Solicitor Competence.

Appendix 13A

In Chapter 3, Functioning Legal Knowledge Appendix 3A, you can find an overview of the areas of law that you will be assessed on in the following way:

- dispute resolution or criminal litigation (either one of these);
- property practice or wills and probate (either one of these);
- business law (definitely this area).

More detailed information can be found on the SRA website (www.sra.org.uk).

Chapter 14

SQE Part 2

Legal Research

> *'Research is creating new knowledge'*
> **Neil Armstrong**

In this chapter you will learn:

✓ How to write your legal research in a structured manner applying the law to the facts.

✓ How to confidently apply the legal research to the issues raised.

✓ Examples of how to present your legal research with the recipient in mind.

✓ What to do and how to review your own writing style and language.

✓ How to efficiently scan or skim read large amounts of legal documents/ extracts.

Introduction

14.01 Legal research is an essential skill for a lawyer. It is something that you are taught in law school. As a lawyer, you will never 'know' everything. There may be times when you encounter a situation which changes the dynamic of your advice and you need to see whether there are any precedents that could affect the advice. Some areas of law are likely to change more frequently than others, so legal research is an important skill to enable you to advise clients accurately.

Traditionally in law firms, senior lawyers tend not to do legal research themselves and have legal support staff (paralegals, trainee solicitors), junior lawyers or professional support lawyers (PSLs) who do that part of their work for them. That does not mean you underestimate the value of legal research because it is usually relied upon to advise the client, so it is very important that it is up to date and accurate. One reason senior lawyers have junior members of staff do it is that it is more cost effective for the client.

14.02 *Legal Research*

This chapter includes real sample extracts (para **14.08**) by anonymous lawyers, showing their writing style. There is constructive feedback on how to make the answers better, so they are presented in line with the Assessment Specification.

You will not have access to live legal databases and will be provided with primary and secondary sources (some that may not be relevant). Therefore you will need to confidently scan and skim read them and not get overwhelmed by the number of sources presented. Some of the sources may come from legal databases and you can read more about them and how to use the sources in para **14.05**.

For all the written assessments the Internet speed might not be the same as you are used to working with and this can affect your timing. The functionality of the computers may be different to what you are used to using (ie cut and paste) and you may not have spell check and highlighting. The SRA website does offer more guidance on this to make you aware of what to expect.

The awareness can help you better prepare for the written assessments and work out how to use your time efficiently and effectively.

The SRA has provided a sample of what you could get for this type of assessment for a criminal litigation scenario. You can also find samples for all the other assessments on the SRA website (www.sra.org.uk).

The Assessment Criteria

14.02 The legal research assessment is computer-based and you will have 60 minutes to complete it. Although there are no set rules as to how you split your time for the assessment, one suggestion could be:

- 20 minutes' reading, planning and writing;
- 40 minutes' researching.

This is just a guideline. It may well be that you do not need 40 minutes to do the research, in which case you have more time to write a comprehensive answer to a question. The more you practise the legal research questions with lots of primary and secondary sources the better you prepare yourself for the actual assessment. You may be provided with a contents page showing you all the sources listed in separate tabs. Not everything listed in the contents page will be relevant so go directly to the tabs you know that are relevant. You will not have time to read everything in a tab in detail. Any sources you are not sure about you can quickly scan or skim-read. You can read about the differences between them in Chapter 5, Communication Skills (paras **5.37** and **5.38**).

The danger is that you could lose track of time while reading the sources, so you need to be disciplined to allow yourself enough time to ensure that you cover all the questions rather than just focus on the one that takes the longest.

It also makes sense to split the time spent between the questions. Some may be easier than others, so you can adjust the time accordingly. Do not spend all your time on one question and run out of time for the others. That does not work in your favour.

Broadly speaking, you will be given an email from a partner which will ask you to do some research on an issue or issues for a client's matter. You will need to provide appropriate legal advice so the partner can use it to advise the client. You will write your answers on a template provided and your note should cover:

- the legal advice; and

- the legal reasoning including key sources or authorities.

The extract of the Assessment Specification description notes that you should be mindful of the following:

> '... the research will be within the broad heading of the practice area ... it may be outside the scope of the Functioning Legal Knowledge, thus requiring research.'

So, do not be too shocked by the fact that you might get a question that you do not have any knowledge about; that is the purpose of conducting the research. If you do know the answer, that is great and will make it easier for you to go to the correct source. However, the aim of doing the research is to discover something new that you are not expected to know so as to show the assessor that you have the necessary competence and know-how to conduct legal research.

You can read about the more detailed version of the SRA criteria in Appendix 14A.

Below I have summarised and highlighted the criteria against which you are assessed.

- ***Skills***

14.03

(1) Identify and use relevant sources and information.

(2) Provide advice which is client-focused and addresses the client's problem.

(3) Use clear, precise, concise and acceptable language.

- ***Application of the Law***

14.04 You should note that for all the assessments your knowledge of the law needs to be applied:

- correctly; and

- comprehensively, identifying any professional conduct and ethical issues.

You should assess yourself against these criteria when practising your legal research for any of the five practice areas of the law. These are assessed using the following grading scale:

14.05 *Legal Research*

Grade	Mark	Standard	Do you meet the competency requirements?
A	5	Superior performance	Yes, well above it
B	4	Clearly satisfactory	Yes, clearly meets it
C	3	Marginal pass	Yes, on balance, just meets it
D	2	Marginal fail	No, on balance, just fails it
E	1	Clearly unsatisfactory	No, clearly does not meet it
F	0	Poor performance	No, well below it

You can read more about the Competence Statement in Chapter 1, The SQE Journey, Appendix 1B which provides the context of what you are expected to know for practice as a newly qualified solicitor.

Legal Databases

14.05 For the purposes of the assessments you will not have access to any live databases. However, some of the sources may come from Westlaw Edge UK and Lexis Library. Both legal databases state on their websites:

- **Westlaw**

    'The only provider of fully consolidated, annotated legislation for UK, Scotland, Wales and Northern Ireland with legislative bills and bill trackers. Case Analysis documents help you digest the outcome and meaning of a case, fast.'

- **Lexis Library**

    'Lexis Library is a legal research platform which gives legal professionals up-to-date information, resources and expert opinion from established names such as Butterworths, Tolley and Halsbury's.'

Primary sources are the 'real' law – legislation and case law – and secondary sources are where you can find commentary and expert opinion on the law in textbooks, journals, *Halsbury's Laws of England* etc. It can help you with your legal advice for the research to start with secondary sources which can then point you to relevant primary sources.

Presenting Your Legal Research

14.06 The SRA sample suggests that a template will be provided and split into two parts:

(1) Advice to the client; and

(2) Legal reasoning mentioning any key sources or authorities.

Do not cut and paste large chunks of sources – it does not show any skill. Only use the relevant section or case law extract that makes the point.

- **Legal Research Note**

14.07 Below you will find a legal research note which offers guidance on what to include in each part.

1: **State the problem/question**
- **Advice to the client**

    State the facts and apply the law – this is what the lawyer reading the note wants to share with the client so it should be written in a client-focused style.

- **Legal reasoning (key sources and authorities)**

    State the case or legislation including specific sections – only cut and paste the relevant extract.

2: **State the problem/question**
- **Advice to the client**

    State the facts and apply the law – if one question has a number of issues to address – separate them.

    ○ Key issue 1

    State your legal advice applying the facts to the law. Split your advice into parts (if appropriate):

    – Point A
    – Point B

    (Use bullet points if you are making a number of points.)

    ○ Key issue 2

    State your legal advice applying the facts to the law.

- **Legal reasoning (key sources and authorities)**

    ○ Key issue 1

    State the case or legislation including specific sections for each part – only cut and paste the relevant extract.

    ○ Key issue 2

    State the case or legislation including specific sections – only cut and paste the relevant extract.

Legal Research: Sample Extracts

14.08 I have reviewed and provided constructive feedback to many lawyers on their legal research. These have been included to provide you with an insight into the different ways people write, where some styles may be influenced by their home jurisdiction, background and culture.

14.09 *Legal Research*

You will be provided with a template in the assessment but some extracts below were done without using one so this is reflected in some of the constructive feedback.

The samples of the extracts provided are for property practice and criminal litigation, not all practice areas of the law. The selected examples have been chosen to give you an idea of what you are required to do and how to do it. You can read the constructive feedback and, if relevant to you, apply it when you practise legal research exercises.

The alternative suggestions are just to give you an idea of how you might want to present your advice. This is just guidance and by no means the only way or style, so use what works for you.

You can remind yourself of the practical guidance offered when using the English language in Chapter 7, Writing in Professional English.

The 'Brief Scenario' provides the gist of what you have to research without going into too much detail. The reason for doing it this way is so you focus on what you need to do practically. Your real instructions would be more detailed and may also include supporting documents.

The sample extracts are provided purely for illustration purposes to show you how some lawyers write their legal research and how it can be improved with constructive feedback. Therefore, they may not be accurate and correct and may contain some additional information not mentioned in the 'Brief Scenario' below. The extracts are not written by the same person, so read each extract in isolation.

From my experience, there are three common mistakes lawyers make when writing their legal research answers. These are:

(1) They do not apply the law to the scenario/instructions (legal advice part).

(2) They repeat the facts unnecessarily (legal advice part).

(3) They 'cut and paste' large chunks of case law or legislation (legal reasoning, key sources and authority part).

The Assessment Specification tells you that you are assessed on two parts:

- **Legal Advice**

14.09 This is the part where you provide advice to the client on how the law affects the issues or problems raised. It is done for a senior lawyer to rely on your research to advise the client. Therefore, think of it as an advisory piece of work rather than academic. No research trail is required.

I have seen lawyers either state the law without referring to the facts, or vice versa where they repeat the given facts without actually applying the relevant law.

Stating the law without application to the facts does not fully demonstrate your skill set. If the law is correct, you show that you have the skills to research it, but you have not demonstrated how it addresses the client's problem, by applying it to the facts. Alternatively, repeating the facts without actually applying the law will waste a lot of your time. This approach does not show legal knowledge or skill, so will be marked low against the assessment criteria.

It is inevitable that you would probably run out of time if you typed out a lot of the facts (which have already been provided) before you actually start advising. Therefore, it is more efficient and effective to refer only to the relevant facts. If there are supporting documents, state in a clear and concise manner, which ones should be read in conjunction with your advice when making your point. For example, you could say:

> 'Please read the [state document] in relation to the
> advice around: [state the points/issues]'

This means that you do not need to provide the background or context in as much detail and can directly address the issues.

- **Legal Reasoning (Key Sources or Authorities)**

14.10 This is the part where you state the source which supports your advice. Identifying a correct source does not mean that you should 'cut and paste' the case law or legislation in large chunks. As mentioned above, this will not show evidence of your skills. You should use only parts of a relevant extract (where applicable).

You should provide the citation of what you are referencing (in context) and if, for example, it recommends a suggested official website, then add the website where the details of the information can be found.

This is a snapshot of what you will read:

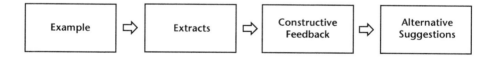

- **Example 1: Extract of legal research for property practice**

14.11 Brief scenario: You have received an email from a partner about the following matter.

Samira's father passed away and left his farm to her. She wants to sell the farm because she lives in the city. There is a lot of paperwork linked to it and she does not know what the process involves. In particular, it might be unregistered land, so please can you research the following points:
- How is ownership of the farm evidenced if it is not registered?
- What is the procedure to get the farm registered (if needed)?

These are original extracts so should be read with the constructive feedback.

14.12 *Legal Research*

❖ Extract 1

14.12 *1. How is ownership of the farm evidenced if it is not registered?*

'The Seller of an unregistered title must prove clean title going back to a good root of title at least 15 years old. A good root of title is an instrument which:

(a) describes the property; and

(b) deals with or shows the ownership of the whole legal and equitable interest; and

(c) contains nothing to cast doubt on the title. It should be noted that a grant of probate is not a good root of title as it does not describe the property.

Examples of good roots of title are:

(a) a conveyance on sale; or

(b) a specific devise in the will of a testator dying before 1926.

The purchaser will have to apply for registration on the completion of the purchase of the property to the registrar. Alternatively, the client, having authority to deal with her father's assets and estate could seek to transfer the title to the property in her name (by assent) and then sell the property with full registered title. However, even in such circumstances, the requirements from the registrar apply.

Land Registry Practice Guide 1.'

❖ Extract 1 – Constructive Feedback

14.13 *1. How is ownership of the farm evidenced if it is not registered?*

Barely any reference is made to the facts mentioned in the Brief Scenario. You are expected to be able to apply the law to the facts. So, if you write the law only (as above), it comes across as quite 'academic', rather than being specific to the scenario (ie to advise Samira). For example, where possible, use the facts in your advice: instead of saying 'seller' say 'Samira' or instead of saying 'the property' say 'the farm'.

The assessment criteria assess you on making the advice client focused (skills) and applying the law correctly and comprehensively (law).

It would also be useful to split the answer into two parts: 'Legal advice' and 'Legal reasoning'. Rather than just state the key source without explanation, provide a little context to it.

Also, if no abbreviations are mentioned in your instructions, do not abbreviate without first writing in full what you later go on to abbreviate. For example, you could spell out the Act and then abbreviate in parentheses, for example, 'Land Registration Act 2002 (LRA 2002)'.

❖ Extract 1 – Alternative Suggestion

14.14 *'1. How is ownership of the farm evidenced if it is not registered?*

Legal advice

As Samira is unsure whether or not the farm is registered, a search at the Land Registry will confirm the status. If the farm is not registered, it is called "unregistered land".

If the farm is unregistered, then her father's ownership of the property will need to be evidenced by the title deeds. A transfer deed from the previous owners of the farm to Samira's father will show its ownership. There may also be land charges that have been registered against the property. We can carry out a search of the Land Charges Register to establish this.

Legal reasoning (key sources or authorities)

For registering property see:

- Westlaw Edge UK 'Insight' document 'Unregistered land'.

The Land Charges Act 1972 (LCA 1972), s 2 sets out the different classes of land charges.'

❖ **Extract 2**

14.15 *2. What is the procedure to get the farm registered (if needed)?*

'Section 4 of the Land Registration Act 2002 (LRA 2002) sets out the requirements for the registration of unregistered land. The applicable provisions are:

- s 4(1)(a)(i) in respect of the sale of the property; or
- s 4(1)(a)(ii) in respect of any application for the registration of a property by means of an assent (ie the assent of the personal representatives to the property vesting in the beneficiary).

A qualifying estate for the purposes of the LRA 2002 is set out in s 4(2) and is:

(a) a freehold estate in land; or

(b) a leasehold estate in land for a term which, at the time of the transfer, grant or creation has more than seven years to run.

If the client is unable to provide full documentary title, evidence must be submitted to the registrar as proof that the applicant is entitled to apply under LRA 2002, s 3(2) or required to apply under LRA 2002, s 6(1); and where appropriate to account for the absence of documentary evidence.

Key sources

To register the property, Form FR1 must be submitted.

Good root of title: Law of Property Act 1925 as amended by the Law of Property Act 1969.'

❖ **Extract 2 – Constructive Feedback**

14.16 *2. What is the procedure to get the farm registered (if needed)?*

14.17 *Legal Research*

There is very little application of the law to the facts and that makes it less easy to read in relation to how to advise Samira. It is fine to say 'client', but to make it more relatable you could use the client's name (Samira). The note is for a partner to read and be able to use it to advise the client.

The way the answer has been written comes across as a little unstructured. Add in 'Legal advice' for the first part instead of for just the second part, 'Key sources'. The question is asking about the 'procedure', so although LPA 2002, s 4 sets out the provisions and requirements to register, you want to tailor your advice to make it relevant to what procedure is applicable if the farm is unregistered.

Rather than just state 'Good root of title' without referring to it in context, word it so that the assessor can see what you are saying about it.

❖ Extract 2 – Alternative Suggestion

14.17 *'2. What is the procedure to get the farm registered (if needed)?*

Legal advice

It is compulsory to register all land in England and Wales, so if the farm is unregistered it will have to go through the first registration process.

Samira will need to produce all the relevant paperwork which will need to be reviewed in relation to her father's ownership of the farm, which will need to show at least 15 years of evidence of title.

Samira could register as the owner of the farm. However, because she wants to sell it, the new buyer of the farm can make an application to the Land Registry by completing the FR1 form.

Samira would be responsible for the costs if there are any "gaps" in ownership and any buyer will probably want evidence of any rectification (if required) before completion.

Any application to register a property must be done within two months of completion.

Legal reasoning (key sources or authorities)

For information on making an application for first registration see:

- Westlaw Edge UK – Land Registry Practice Guide [state number, for example 1]

Good root of title (at least 15 years) is stated in:

- Law of Property Act 1925, s 44 as amended by the Law of Property Act 1969.

First registration timescale can be found in:

- Land Registration Act 2002, s 6(4).'

- **Example 2 – Extract of legal research for criminal litigation**

14.18 Brief scenario: You have received an email from a partner about the following matter.

Billy (aged 14) has been arrested for a robbery and he has never been in trouble before. He has been arrested with Damien (aged 21) who is separately represented. Billy's father is already at the police station. I will go down when the officers are ready to interview Billy. Please can you remind me of the following before I head down for the interview:

- Is the advice in relation to the interview different because Billy is 14 years old and what are the interview options?

These are original extracts so should be read with the constructive feedback.

❖ **Extract 1**

14.19 '1. Is the advice in relation to the interview different because Billy is 14 years old and what are the interview options?

(1) 'The client should be informed that, before the commencement of any interview at a police station, the interviewer should inform him of his entitlement to free legal advice and that the interview can be delayed for legal advice to be obtained, if he so wishes.

(2) If he chooses to be represented by a solicitor during the interview, the interviewer must provide him, and his solicitor, with sufficient information to enable them to understand the nature of the offence, and why he is suspected of committing the offence.

(3) As the questioning will most certainly relate to involvement or suspected involvement of the client in the robbery, the interviewer must also caution him before proceeding with the interview.

(4) In addition to the aforesaid, as the client is under the age of 18 years, he should not be interviewed regarding his involvement or suspected involvement in the offence in the absence of the appropriate adult.

(5) In the circumstances, the appropriate adult will be his father. If his father is present at the interview, he must be informed that he is not expected to act simply as an observer, and that the purpose of his presence is to advise his son while being interviewed, to observe whether the interview is being conducted properly and fairly, and facilitate communication with the person being interviewed.

(6) The Code specifically indicates the different procedure to be followed by the police in the event of an interview to be conducted with a juvenile.

(7) The different circumstances, and processes to be followed when a person is to be interviewed by the police is set out in Code C ("the Code") of the Police and Criminal Evidence Act 1984.'

14.20 *Legal Research*

❖ **Extract 1 – Constructive Feedback**

14.20   1. *Is the advice in relation to the interview different because Billy is 14 years old and what are the interview options?*

There are two parts to the question. The first part of the answer is comprehensive and correct, but it is quite long and too wordy. The answer could be shorter, more direct and concise. This level of detail for the first part of the question might mean that you run out of time to answer any other questions.

I have added in numbers for the paragraphs to make it easier for you to see what I have to say in relation to them; you do not need to do this in the assessment.

For example:

- Paragraphs (1)–(3):

    These are not that relevant because you know the partner is already going to attend the interview when the police are ready. The advice required was more specific to Billy being 14 years old. Make sure you read the instructions and information carefully.

- Paragraphs (4)–(5):

    These are more relevant because they actually relate to Billy who is 14 years old.

- Paragraphs (6)–(7):

    These refer to the 'key sources' but do not adequately provide the specific information required.

The second part of the question about the interview options has not been addressed. You would lose marks for this and this part of the question required more detail than the first part.

The layout could be better structured to deal with each part of the question more clearly. Just because it is one question does not mean that you cannot split it into two parts. The first heading should be 'Legal advice', then create sub-headings to show you have identified how many parts there are that need to be addressed and then deal with each of them. Some parts may require more detail and information than others. Then, create a separate section for the 'Legal reasoning' using the same layout, so it is easy to follow.

From the alternative suggestion below you will see that the interview options part required more detail than the level of detail provided to state Billy needed an appropriate adult because he is 14 years old.

It also makes it easier to read if you use the name of the client (Billy).

As it is a legal research exercise, you would be expected to be more specific and state exactly what part of Code C is being referred to as evidence that Billy will need an appropriate adult.

❖ Extract 1 – Alternative Suggestion

14.21 '1. Is the advice in relation to the interview different because Billy is 14 years old and what are the interview options?

The advice will be split into two parts:

Legal advice

(a) **Interviewing a child**

As Billy is 14 years old, he is classified as a vulnerable suspect and has special rights. An appropriate adult (parent or guardian) has to be notified of his arrest and asked to attend the police station. As his father is already there, we can ask him to act as the appropriate adult and explain what his role is during the interview with Billy.

(b) **Interview options**

The rules for children are the same as for adults. Billy's options are:

(a) answer questions in the interview; or

(b) provide a no comment interview (with a written statement (if appropriate)).

– *If Billy admits the robbery*

It is best to advise Billy to provide a no comment interview and, if charged, he can plead guilty at the earliest opportunity in court (and get maximum credit for his early guilty plea).

– *If Billy denies the robbery*

There are three options:

(1) He can provide his account and answer questions, which avoids any adverse inferences if he is charged and pleads not guilty in court.

(2) He can provide a no comment interview, but needs to be advised the court is entitled to draw adverse inferences (eg from the no comment interview, his presence near the scene of the robbery and/or items found).

(3) He can provide a no comment interview and submit a written statement. This is a good idea for two reasons:

   (a) it can get around the issue of the adverse inferences; and

   (b) justifiable, as Billy is a child who has never been in trouble before, so is not be used to interviews of this nature. Also, it could provide a consistent account of what he has to say about Damien's role.

If Billy is advised to give a no comment interview this advice and the inferences must be explained to him and he must be told that it is ultimately his decision.

It is good practice to make full and comprehensive notes which you can get Billy to sign and his father (as the appropriate adult) to witness, to show your advice was understood and agreed at the time it was given.

14.22 *Legal Research*

Legal reasoning (key sources or authorities)

(a) **Interviewing a child**

Under the Police and Criminal Evidence Act 1984, Code C para 11.15 – an appropriate adult is required for interview unless exceptions apply (eg an urgent interview is required). In this case, the exceptions do not apply.

(b) **Interview options**

The relevant sections of the Criminal Justice and Public Order Act (CJPOA) 1994 apply where an adverse inference may be drawn against Billy for his refusal or failure to:

- mention facts when questioned or charged (s 34);
- account for any objects, substances or marks (s 36);
- account for his presence at a particular place (s 37).'

Practical Legal Advice and Legal Reasoning

14.22 Hopefully the samples highlight that you must make sure you answer all parts of the advice required and some parts will require more detail than others.

The focus really is on providing client-focused advice and addressing the problems raised using relevant extracts of primary and/or secondary sources.

If your university or training provider has mock papers with suggested answers, they may be more academic to help you from a revision point perspective. You should use it but focus on making your advice more client-focused.

'Fast is fine, but accuracy is everything.'
Wyatt Earp

Legal Research – Top Ten Tips

(1) Set out your legal research clearly – have a structure in mind within the template provided.

(2) Apply the facts to the law for the Legal Advice section (para **14.09**).

(3) Provide specific details relied on in the Legal Reasoning (Key Sources or Authorities) section (para **14.10**).

(4) Only 'cut and paste' relevant extracts of the source on which you are relying.

(5) Application is key – apply your findings to the problem or facts. Your research note should be more advisory than academic.

(6) Use key words or phrases – legal words over factual words to help you scan or skim read for relevancy.

(7) Familiarise yourself with where to look within various legal documents, case law and legislation.

Practical Legal Advice and Legal Reasoning **14.22**

(8) You do not need to know about the law you are asked to research, just where to research it.

(9) Do not get overwhelmed by the number of primary and secondary sources provided – be confident in your decision that some might not be relevant.

(10) Using secondary sources first can help you and direct you to primary sources.

Chapter 14

Legal Research: Appendices

Appendix 14A: Assessment Specification

This has been reproduced with permission from the SRA:

Overview

This is a computer-based assessment. Candidates will be required to investigate a problem for a client. They will be given an email from a partner asking the candidate to research an issue or issues, so that the partner can report back to the client. Candidates will have to produce a written note explaining to the partner their legal reasoning and the key sources they rely on, as well as the advice the partner should give the client. They will not need to produce a research trail.

Please note that while the subject matter of the research will be within the broad heading of the practice area in which the assessment is set, it may be outside the scope of the Functioning Legal Knowledge, thus requiring research.

Candidates will be provided with sources for the legal research exercises. These may include both primary and secondary sources. Some of the sources provided may not be relevant.

Candidates will be given 60 minutes to complete the task.

Assessment Objective

Candidates can demonstrate that they are able to conduct legal research from a variety of resources provided and produce a written report.

Assessment Criteria

Candidates will be assessed against the following criteria:

Skills

(1) Identify and use relevant sources and information.

(2) Provide advice which is client-focused and addresses the client's problem.

(3) Use clear, precise, concise and acceptable language.

Application of Law

(4) Apply the law correctly to the client's situation.

(5) Apply the law comprehensively to the client's situation, identifying any ethical and professional conduct issues and exercising judgment to resolve them honestly and with integrity.

You should read this in conjunction with the Chapter 1, The SQE Journey, Appendix 1B which details what the Competence Statement includes and in particular the Statement of Solicitor Competence.

Chapter 3 Functioning Legal Knowledge in Appendix 3A has an overview of the five areas of law but this assessment will be outside the scope of what you are expected to know.

Do not panic if you see a problem for which you do not know the law, that is the purpose of legal research. The practice areas of law on which you will be assessed are as follows:

- dispute resolution or criminal litigation (either one of these);
- property practice or wills and probate (either one of these);
- business law (definitely this area).

More detailed information can be found on the SRA website (www.sra.org.uk).

Appendix 14B: Using Legal Databases

The whole purpose of legal research is that you do not know the answer, so you need to look for it. You are not expected to know about what you are researching. Therefore, you need to think about what printed or online sources are best and use key words or phrases that can help you find the answer. It is better to use terms lawyers would employ, rather than generic terms mentioned in the facts or problem.

For online sources, you can narrow down what you have to read by filtering all the relevant information you already have and then scanning for key words or phrases. For example, it would make sense to use key legal words and phrases like 'contract remedies' or 'breach of contract damages' rather than non-legal factual words or generic phrases. So, if the scenario is about a faulty [name of brand] computer, you would not benefit from searching through any extracts for words or phrases like '[name of brand] computer', 'faulty computer' or 'compensation' in the sources provided.

For the legal research assessment you will not have access to a live legal database so get used to reviewing documents in print format.

Many firms will subscribe to an online legal database and that is the modern and efficient way of doing legal research with huge amounts of information all stored

Legal Research: Appendices

in one place. Not only do they provide up-to-date information, but forms and precedents can be used and adapted too. However, some smaller firms may not be able to justify the cost and may rely on printed sources.

There are pros and cons for each format, but ultimately it will come down to your preference, based on where you work and what you do professionally, if you are working in legal practice.

The table below provides you with a few advantages and disadvantages for each format:

Advantages of Printed Sources	Advantages of Online Sources
Easy on the eye (rather than reading a screen)	Accessible from anywhere with internet access
No training required	Large capacity to store information in one place
No technical issues or failures	Easily and quickly check for updates and get alerts
Easier to compare two sources at the same time	Can 'cut and paste' relevant extracts into documents

Disadvantages of Printed Sources	Disadvantages of Online Sources
Does not allow for multiple users	Technical or internet issues
Not as efficient to keep track of updates	Training required
Need storage capacity	Initially may take longer to learn how to use the database effectively
Cannot 'cut and paste' from hard copy documents	Harder to browse or flick through a source
Not always up to date once printed and can miss updates	Expensive

Appendix 14C: Using the Internet

Although this option will not be available in the legal research assessment, I think it is important to mention it for good practice.

Instinctively, a common approach when researching anything is to use Internet search engines (the two most popular being Google and Bing) or artificial intelligence (eg ChatGPT). It is fast and can provide a whole array of answers, instantly.

Although there are websites that are reputable and reliable, it is dangerous to rely on sources from the Internet. The reliability and quality of the information can be questionable because anyone can publish information and it may be incorrect and out of date.

Appendix 14C

Be smart about what you search for on the Internet and do not take it at face value because it may not even relate to our jurisdiction (ie England and Wales). So, any legal research relied on for commercial purposes and advising clients should be done using reputable legal databases. They will provide you with comfort and confidence when giving any legal advice. Law firms and businesses invest a lot of money on subscriptions to legal databases for this reason.

If legal research could be relied upon by using the Internet (for free), every law firm and business would use it. The risks and stakes are too high because mistakes could give rise to negligence claims. Issues as to professional conduct might also arise (because your legal advice is dependent on obtaining good-quality information). Ultimately, mistakes could damage your reputation and credibility.

Testimonials and Reviews

The 1st Edition of this book has helped many people worldwide with reviews and testimonials on the Bloomsbury website, Amazon and my LinkedIn page (Neeta Halai).

Below I share a selection of first-hand experiences by some lawyers who chose to work with me. Not all lawyers provide testimonials, so I am very grateful to those who have shared their experience.

I have coached many lawyers for the SQE Part 2 (which is based on the OSCE, QLTS) and I have not needed to adapt my approach or standard. Therefore, you can feel confident that what you read is what you can expect for the SQE Part 2.

Europe

'Having Neeta as my coach was the best choice I made with respect to my OSCE preparation. She possesses a profound knowledge of the material and guided me step-by-step to the demanding OSCE test. Neeta was the one person who made me feel safe and confident for the exams.'

Stavros Michalopoulos, Associate, DLA Piper (Qualified in Greece)

'Neeta is a great coach. Her 1 to 1 training sessions helped me pass the OSCE exam. She gave me numerous practical tips. She was professional, encouraging and a real pleasure to work with. I recommend her without reservations.'

Alvaro Nistal, Counsel, Volterra Fietta (Qualified in Spain)

'OSCE 1 went particularly well for me and I think I owe a great deal to our coaching: It helped me put the right focus on skills (presentation/interviewing). To be very honest, even though I had done a number of mock exams before our coaching session, I didn't really know much about what to expect at the OSCE 1 and didn't realize how important demonstrating lawyers' skills would be. I also very much liked your positive and comforting approach, it helped me go into the exam much more confidently and confidence was what I needed most!'

Anonymous, Partner, Freshfields (Qualified in Germany)

'I wholeheartedly can recommend Neeta. She is an amazing coach! I had 1-1 session with Neeta just two days before the OSCE assessments. It was very intense but enjoyable at the same time. Neeta gave me a lot of useful tips which helped me to increase my level of confidence. She had a very individual approach that allowed us to focus on the points that were the most important to me. Neeta is a very skilled and highly professional coach and solicitor... Even if you have online support of your tutor, having a face to face session with a very skilled coach like Neeta is equally important. Thank you, Neeta!'

Magdalena Pilichowska, Legal Manager, St. James's Place Wealth Management (Qualified in Poland)

Testimonials and Reviews

'I would highly and warmly recommend Neeta as a QLTS coach and trainer in general. She is very professional, available and adaptive to your personality and needs. She combines excellent legal and interpersonal skills. The day we spent prepping together at my workplace was key to my success in the OSCE part of the QLTS. Thanks, Neeta!'

Elena Faloutsou, Associate, Skadden, Arps, Slate, Meagher & Flom (Qualified in Greece)

'Neeta is a very experienced and professional coach. I highly recommend using Neeta's services. I had an individual coaching session with Neeta ... I found her coaching extremely helpful. My day-to-day work does not require advocacy, and presentations are rare. It was easy for me to underestimate the challenges of those assessments, especially in a constrained setting of the actual exams. This is where the session with Neeta proved to be extremely valuable. She provided tailored advice, pointing out my flaws and areas for my improvement. She also gave me handy tips and hacks that helped to feel in control and confident at the exam.'

Taras Stadniichuk, Lawyer, Clifford Chance (Qualified in Ukraine)

'I found the 1-1 coaching session with Neeta for the OSCE exam very helpful. She helps you perfect your oral representation/advocacy/client interview skills by showing little tricks. Neeta adapts her session to your needs and pace ... and helpful to have a face to face session with her to double-check my understanding on certain points of the exam. I recommend taking her coaching session to all the candidates to increase their success rate in this exam.'

Asli Guner Paul, Assoc. General Counsel, Lightsource BP, (Qualified in Turkey)

'Neeta's approach was very practical and helped me to establish a structure for each of the modules. Also, we reflected together on my strengths and weaknesses, which helped to build more confidence. It was exactly what I needed at the time. And apart from her coaching qualities, Neeta has a very warm and generous personality, which she engages to help bring out the best in anyone she is working with. Therefore, I highly recommend Neeta!!'

Michiel René van'Landt, Lawyer, (Qualified in Netherlands)

'Thanks for all your help and advice in the workshop and follow up coaching session, Neeta. The preparation with you had helped me to follow through with the assessments with more confidence ... and putting theory to practise. You had put to me a few times that I should throw in a smile here and there and show I am still in the room as a person. I remembered this during the exams, and am sure to have benefitted from it.'

Anonymous, Lawyer, Siemens, (Qualified in Germany)

'I cannot recommend Neeta highly enough! I have never met a coach so committed to getting the right results ... and being there as a sounding board for a very isolated (and often underestimated) process. Neeta provided me with the right tools to pass the OSCE the first time and I would not hesitate to recommend her to anyone taking on this challenge! Thank you doesn't truly convey how grateful I am for Neeta's coaching.'

Sarah Melaney, Partner, Brown Rudnick, (Qualified in Scotland)

Testimonials and Reviews

'Neeta's powerful coaching skills, practical tips and individualized teaching approach helped me greatly with sitting the oral assessments in OSCE with a high level of confidence. She manages to turn a highly intense day into an enjoyable and interactive learning experience. I highly recommend training with her!'

Duygu Tanisik, Head of Legal, Limejump (Qualified in Turkey)

'One of the reasons I did so well this time round is because of your training session. I think this really helped me feel more confident and prepared.'

Anonymous, Lawyer, Hill Dickinson, (Qualified in France)

'Neeta coached me for the Qualified Lawyers Transfer Scheme OSCE Interviewing and Advocacy. She is very hands-on and professional. Neeta has boosted my scores by providing constructive feedback, practical tips and sharing her wealth of knowledge and experience. I cannot recommend her highly enough.'

Anna Sukhanova, Director, Y&YSV Limited (Qualified in New York (US) and Russia)

Asia

'Neeta is truly amazing! When preparing for the OSCE examination ... I had anxiety around the presentation and client interview aspects, which I felt I had not focused on, nor practiced enough for. Neeta guided me through these challenges and gave me practical tips which ended up helping me immensely during the exam itself. And I ended up passing the OSCE on the first try!! I would very much recommend Neeta's services, especially if, like me, you are concerned about the oral aspects of the OSCE assessment.'

Avishai Ostrin, Head of Privacy, Asserson, (Qualified in Israel)

'Neeta coached me for the England & Wales foreign lawyer qualification exams (QLTS). The only thing better than Neeta's videos that are a must watch for anyone attempting the QLTS is Neeta herself! I ended up working with Neeta very, very close to the time of my assessments and I am grateful that she made the time for me and was such an excellent coach. I highly recommend her.'

Suraj Sajnani, Associate, King & Wood Mallesons (Qualified in Hong Kong)

'I attended a group class taught by Neeta. ... I had only studied the law being tested on the exam, and was extremely nervous and unsure as to how to approach the skills based areas being tested. Neeta's group class was extremely helpful – she has a no nonsense, marking rubric-based approach to ensure that you tick all the right boxes ... Most importantly, it gave me the peace of mind as well as the confidence boost I needed to walk into the exam room and know what exactly to expect.'

Amanda Yim, Associate, Linklaters (Qualified in Singapore)

Testimonials and Reviews

> *Neeta is a wonderful coach and a very highly motivated lawyer. She has great work ethics as well.*
>
> *Thank you for your help Neeta!*

Nila Gibb, Compliance Advisor, BP (Qualified in Indonesia)

> *'Neeta is a great coach...and Neeta is excellent in encouraging candidates to improve their skills for the assessments and also undertakes participative feedback which is highly useful. I would recommend anyone interested in improving their skills to take training sessions with Neeta.'*

Riya Kaul, Lawyer, (Qualified in India)

> *'Professional, encouraging and effective.'*

Samantha Groffman, Senior Legal Counsel, Travelodge Hotels (Qualified in China & US)

Africa

> *'Neeta is a dedicated professional with an intuitive ability to get her clients to perform at their best. It was a pleasure to work with her and would highly recommend her!'*

Daniel Mwihia Mburu, Advocate, (Qualified in Kenya)

> *'Neeta was completely invested in my training which was fantastic. I could see that she really cares and wanted to ensure that I was thoroughly prepared and comfortable with the assessment. I would highly recommend Neeta to anyone who wants to get a clear understanding of what to expect and how to prepare for the OSCE assessments '*

Reghard Smith, Associate, Walkers (Qualified in South Africa)

North America

> *'Passing the OSCE exams is no small task, but I am grateful to Neeta and her expertise in helping me find success. Neeta is an experienced solicitor and helped me prepare for the OSCE. She not only gave me useful tips, but also helped me in feeling confident that I can perform the tasks that the OSCE requires. I think Neeta is a primary reason I passed. Thanks Neeta!'*

Carolyn K. Van den Daelen, Managing Partner, Quorsus (Qualified in Illinois, US)

> *'I took OSCE for the first time in May 2019 and passed it. I made the wise decision and had the pleasure to work with Neeta in a few individual interview and advocacy sessions. Neeta is very patient, encouraging and positive and at the same time very efficient in pointing out areas where I could make improvements. I felt that after each session I grasped new ways in which I could gain additional points. Studying for the exam was a stressful process and I really appreciate the help and support Neeta gave me. I would highly recommend her to anyone who plans to take the exam.'*

Lin Jacobsen, Lawyer, Ogier, (Qualified in New York, US)

South America

'My 1:1 coaching session with Neeta in preparation for the OSCE 1 was invaluable. Neeta gave me the confidence I needed before the exams. She provided excellent resources and advice on how to better engage and communicate with clients and prepare for advocacy. The coaching she provided has helped me with my exams, but beyond that it will, without a doubt, help me in my career.'

Gabriela Roque, Senior Associate, Watson, Farley & Williams (Qualified in Brazil)

'Neeta is a superb coach. She tailored the workshop to my needs and provided me with tangible added value. The various techniques shared with me were key to feel better prepared for the oral assessments. Her coaching clearly made a difference. Not only that, she was a pleasure to work with! I would highly recommend Neeta.'

Mariano Soto Gajardo, Founder, Trancura Legal (Qualified in Chile and New York (US))

Australasia

'I attended a New Heights Training workshop on "Client Interviewing Skills & Advocacy/Oral Presentation Skills" in November 2019 while I was preparing for the QLTS OSCE. Neeta is a highly knowledgeable and professional coach and her training greatly assisted me with applying my existing knowledge to the practical OSCE assessments. The workshop was kept to a small number of people so we were all able to participate in practice interviews and advocacy while pinpointing areas of improvement. If you are preparing for the OSCE (or incoming SQE) I highly recommend coaching from Neeta.'

Emma Kemp, in-house lawyer, Allen & Overy (Qualified in New Zealand)

Neeta's training helped to focus my studies for the OSCE 1 part of the QLTS conversion program. She provided me with confidence and structure for the exams. … her help was invaluable and I would highly recommend her.

Michelle, Big Four Accounting Firm (Qualified in Australia)

Index

All references are to paragraph numbers and appendices.

A

Advocacy
  assessment criteria 10.03, App 10A
  assessment specification App 10A
  challenges 10.02
  emotional intelligence 5.34
  generally 10.01
  handling difficult questions 10.12
  managing nerves and fear
    fear of judge 6.18
    fear of unknown 6.23
  oral assessments and client
    interviewing 1.21
  preparation time (45 minutes) 5.40; 10.04
  scanning 10.05, 10.07
  skim reading 10.05, 10.06
  submission (15 minutes)
    beginning 10.09
    end 10.11
    generally 10.08
    middle 10.10
Alternative dispute resolution (ADR)
  clause
    drafting 13.29–13.33
Appearance
  first impressions 5.24
Aspiring lawyers (working)
  preparing for SQE
    generally 2.20
    Practical Legal Skills (PLS)
      Assessments 2.42
    qualifying work experience (QWE) 1.30; 4.07
Attendance notes
  oral assessments 1.20
  writing *see* **Writing attendance notes**

B

Business law
  legal drafting
    alternative dispute resolution (ADR)
      clause 13.29–13.33
    costs/price clause 13.24–13.28
    defined terms 13.23
    generally 13.02, 13.21
    types of clauses 13.22

Business law – *contd*
  legal drafting – *contd*
    types of legal documents 13.07
    undertakings 13.34–13.39
  legal writing: sample extracts 12.21–12.23, App 12D

C

Case and matter analysis
  assessment criteria
    generally 11.02
    law 11.04, App 11A
    skills 11.03, App 11A
  assessment specification App 11A
  contentious matters 11.08
  generally 11.01
  negotiation skills 11.09
  report templates
    dispute resolution 11.07
    modern report writing 11.06, 11.07
    traditional report writing 11.05
  SWOT analysis 11.10
  written assessments 1.23
Character and suitability
  requirements for admission to Roll of Solicitors 1.34
Client interviewing skills
  actual interview
    beginning 8.18
    end
      ending on time 8.26
      generally 8.24
      running out of time 8.25
    generally 8.17
    middle (main body of interview)
      client identification (ID) 8.20
      examples
        property practice scenario 8.22
        wills and probate scenario 8.21
      generally 8.19
      making notes during interview 8.23
  assessment criteria 8.04, App 8A
  assessment specification App 8A
  attendance note
    oral assessments 1.20
    writing *see* **Writing attendance notes**
  building trust and confidence 8.03

Index

Client interviewing skills – *contd*
  challenges 8.01
  communication skills
    emotional intelligence (EQ) 5.33
    preparation time 5.39
  generally 8.01
  managing nerves and fear
    fear of client 6.17
    fear of unknown 6.22
  negotiation skills 8.02, 11.09
  oral assessments
    advocacy 1.20
    attendance note 1.21
    client interviewing 1.19
    generally 1.18
  preparation stage 8.06
  property practice
    generally 8.07
    practical questions to consider: examples
    freehold 8.10, 8.11
    leasehold 8.08, 8.09
  unpredictable clients 8.05
  wills and probate
    generally 8.12
    practical questions to consider: examples
    instructions for Administration of an Estate 8.15, 8.16
    instructions to make a will 8.13, 8.14

Coaching
  generally 2.14
  performance coaching 2.15

Common law system of England and Wales
  understanding App 1A

Communication skills
  challenges
    amount of experience 5.05
    generally 5.04
  communicator
    communication
      generally 5.26, App 5A
      verbal 5.29
      visual 5.27
      vocal 5.28
    emotional intelligence (EQ)
      advocacy 5.34
      client interviewing 5.33
      generally 5.30, 5.32, App 5B
      generally 5.08, 5.25
      intellectual intelligence (IQ) 5.30, 5.31
    time management
      generally 5.35
      preparation stage 5.36

Communication skills – *contd*
  communicator – *contd*
    preparation time for oral assessments
      advocacy 5.40
      client interviewing 5.39
    preparation time for written assessments 5.41
    scanning a document 5.37
    skim reading a document 5.38, App 5C
  connector
    appearance 5.24
    generally 5.07, 5.10
    rapport
    building
      authentically 5.14
      generally 5.13
    commonality 5.19
    cultural appropriateness 5.20
    definition 5.12
    generally 5.11
    overcoming superficiality 5.15
    perception 5.16
    small talk
      environment 5.18
      topics 5.17
    trust
      building 5.23
      definition 5.22
      generally 5.21
  convincer
    generally 5.09, 5.42
    impact: persuasion and influence 5.45, App 5D
    listening 5.43
    questioning 5.44
  description 5.02
  generally 5.01
  importance of successful communication 5.03
  practising 5.06
  written *see* **Writing in professional English**

Competence Statement
  generally 1.36, 2.32
  practising certificate 1.35, App 1B
  Statement of Legal Knowledge App 1B; 2.35
  Statement of Solicitor Competence App 1B; 2.33
  Threshold Standard App 1B; 2.34
  understanding 2.31

Conduct *see* Character and suitability; Professional conduct

Criminal litigation
  legal drafting
    defence statement 13.40–13.44

Criminal litigation – *contd*
  legal drafting – *contd*
   generally 13.02
   types of legal documents 13.09
  legal research: sample extracts 14.18–14.21
  legal writing: sample extracts 12.07–12.15, App 12B
Currencies
  legal drafting and language 13.15
Curriculum vitae (CV)
  qualifying work experience (QWE) 4.01, App 4A

D

Dates
  legal drafting 13.14
  writing in professional English 7.24
Disclosure and Barring Service (DBS)
  admission to Roll of Solicitors 1.33
Dispute resolution
  drafting documents *see* **Legal drafting**
  legal writing: sample extracts 12.24–12.30, App 12E

E

Education or training provider, choice of *see* Preparing for SQE
Emails
  legal writing 12.05, 12.36
  writing in professional English 7.13
English language skills *see also* Legal drafting; Writing in professional English
  generally 2.44
  International English Language Testing System (IELTS) 2.44
  pronunciation exercise App 2C
Ethics
  Functioning Legal Knowledge (FLK) Assessments
   generally 3.04
   SQE Pt 1 App 3A
  generally 1.12
Exemptions for SQE
  agreed exemptions 1.07
  generally 1.06
  individual exemptions 1.08

F

Failure *see also* Managing nerves, fear and failure
  continuing with SQE
   generally 6.26
   resits 6.28
   uncertainty 6.27, App 6B

Failure – *contd*
  Functioning Legal Knowledge (FLK) Assessments 3.08
  generally 1.14; 6.24
  working out SQE results 6.25
Fear *see* Managing nerves, fear and failure
Fitness to sit/reasonable adjustments
  expert evidence 2.46
  generally 2.45
  typical examples of reasonable adjustments 2.47
Functioning Legal Knowledge (FLK) Assessments
  assessment specification
   generally 2.37; 3.04
   SQE Pt 1 App 3A
   SQE Pt 2 App 3B
  failing 3.09
  generally 1.15; 2.36; 3.01
  multiple choice questions (MCQs)
   generally 3.01
   practical tips 3.08
   studying 3.06
  multiple choice tests (MCTs)
   distractors 3.03
   generally 1.15; 2.38; 3.01, 3.02
   intellectual thinking/intuitive thinking 3.07, App 3C
   managing nerves 6.20
  negotiation skills 1.13
  professional conduct and ethics 1.12; 3.05, App 3A
  results 1.16
  studying for 3.06

I

Internet
  use and legal research App 14C

L

Language *see* English language; Legal drafting; Writing in professional English
Language patterns
  managing nerves 6.05
Law Society
  role of App 1C
Legal databases
  accessing/using for research purposes 14.05, App 14B
Legal drafting *see also* Writing in professional English
  assessment criteria
   generally 13.03
   law 13.05, App 13A
   skills 13.04, App 13A
  assessment specification App 13A

Index

Legal drafting – *contd*
  books available on subject
    App 13B
  business law
    alternative dispute resolution (ADR)
      clause 13.29–13.33
    costs/price clause 13.24–13.28
    defined terms 13.23
    generally 13.02, 13.21
    types of clauses 13.22
    types of legal documents 13.07
    undertakings 13.34–13.39
  completing forms 13.45
  criminal litigation
    defence statement 13.40–13.44
    generally 13.02
    types of legal documents 13.09
  generally 13.01
  language
    currencies 13.15
    dates 13.14
    generally 13.12
    similar words 13.13
    translation 13.16
    words 13.17–13.19
  layout 13.20
  types of legal documents
    business law 13.07
    criminal litigation 13.09
    dispute resolution 13.10
    generally 13.06
    property law 13.08
    wills and probate 13.11
  words
    'before' and 'after' 13.19
    'by' and 'until' 13.18
    'shall', 'must' and 'may' 13.17
  written assessments 1.25
Legal research
  assessment criteria
    generally 14.02
    law 14.04, App 14A
    skills 14.03, App 14A
  assessment specification App 14A
  generally 14.01
  Internet, using App 14C
  legal databases, accessing/using
    14.05, App 14B
  presenting
    generally 14.06
    legal research note 14.07
  sample extracts
    generally 14.08
    legal advice 14.09
    legal reasoning (key sources and
      authorities) 14.10
    legal research for criminal litigation
      14.18–14.21

Legal research – *contd*
  sample extracts – *contd*
    legal research for property practice
      14.11–14.17
    practical legal advice and legal
      reasoning 14.22
  written assessments 1.26
Legal writing *see also* Writing in
  professional English
  assessment criteria
    generally 12.02
    law 12.04, App 12A
    skills 12.03, App 12A
  assessment specification App 12A
  emails 12.05, 12.36
  four Cs of written communication
    see **Writing in professional**
    English
  generally 12.01
  letters 12.05
  sample extracts
    business law scenario 12.21–12.23,
      App 12D
    criminal litigation scenario 12.07–
      12.15, App 12B
    dispute resolution scenario 12.24–
      12.30, App 12E
    generally 12.06
    property practice scenario 12.16–
      12.20, App 12C
    wills and probate law scenario
      12.31–12.35, App 12F
  written assessments 1.24
Letters
  legal writing 12.05
  writing in professional English
    closing 7.10
    content 7.09
    copy/enclosures 7.12
    generally 7.05
    layout 7.09
    reference 7.06
    salutation 7.07
    signature 7.11
    subject heading 7.08

M

Managing nerves, fear and failure
  advocacy
    fear of judge 6.18
    fear of unknown 6.23
  brain 6.07, App 6A
  breathing 6.12
  confidence 6.03
  controlling nerves: peak state 6.04
  failing SQE assessments
    continuing with SQE
      generally 6.26

Index

Managing nerves, fear and failure – *contd*
  failing SQE assessments – *contd*
    resits 6.28
    uncertainty 6.27, App 6B
    generally 1.14; 6.24
    working out SQE results 6.25
  fear of client or judge
    advocacy 6.18
    client interviewing 6.17
    generally 6.16
  fear of failure
    direct experience 6.14
    indirect experience 6.15
    generally 6.13
  fear of unknown
    advocacy 6.23
    client interviewing 6.22
    generally 6.19
  generally 6.01
  language patterns 6.05
  pain/comfort/stretch zones of experience 6.02
  SQE Pt 1: Functioning Legal Knowledge (FLK) and multiple choice test (MCT) 6.20
  SQE Pt 2: Practical Legal Skills (PLS) 6.21
  stored patterns
    fight 6.09
    flight 6.10
    freeze 6.11
    generally 6.08
  symptoms of nerves or fear 6.06
Marketing and advertising
  misleading, education and training providers 2.07
Masterclasses
  studying formats 2.13
Motivation
  generally 1.10
Myers-Brigg Type Indicator
  communication skills 5.45, App 5D

N

Negotiation skills
  case and matter analysis 11.09
  client interviewing 8.02
  SQE assessments 1.13
Nerves *see* Managing nerves, fear and failure

O

Oral assessments *see* Practical Legal Skills (PLS) Assessments

P

Practical Legal Skills (PLS) Assessments
  assessment specifications
    aspiring solicitors (working) 2.42

Practical Legal Skills (PLS) Assessments – *contd*
  assessment specifications – *contd*
    generally 2.40
    qualified lawyers 2.42
    students 2.41
  generally 1.11, 1.17; 2.39
  managing nerves and fear 6.21
  marking criteria 1.27
  negotiation skills 1.13
  oral assessments
    client interviewing
      advocacy 1.21
      attendance note 1.20
      generally 1.19
    generally 1.18
  practising skills 2.43
  professional conduct and ethics 1.12
  results 1.27
  written assessments
    case and matter analysis 1.23
    generally 1.22
    legal drafting 1.25
    legal research 1.26
    legal writing 1.24
Practising certificate
  continuing competence
    Competence Statement *see* **Competence Statement**
    generally 1.36
  generally 1.35
Preparing for SQE *see also* Studying for SQE
  aspiring solicitors (working) 2.20
  Competence Statement *see* **Competence Statement**
  decision process when choosing a course provider
    generally 2.03
    SQE data 2.04
    understanding course provider 2.06
    understanding yourself 2.05
  fitness to sit/reasonable adjustments
    expert evidence 2.46
    generally 2.45
    typical examples of reasonable adjustments 2.47
  level of English
    generally 2.44
    International English Language Testing System (IELTS) 2.44
    pronunciation exercise App 2C
  Miller's pyramid 2.28, App 2B
  misleading marketing/advertising 2.07
  Pearson VUE centres 2.48
  Pt 1: Functioning Legal Knowledge Assessments *see* **Functioning Legal Knowledge (FLK) Assessments**

Index

Preparing for SQE – *contd*
 Pt 2: Practical Legal Skills Assessments *see* **Practical Legal Skills (PLS) Assessments**
 qualified lawyers 2.21
 registration 2.02
 students
  alternative routes 2.19
  generally 2.16
  law degrees 2.17
  non-law degrees 2.18
Professional conduct
 Functioning Legal Knowledge (FLK) Assessments
 generally 3.04
 SQE Pt 1 App 3A
 generally 1.12
Property practice
 client interviewing skills
  actual interview: example 8.22
  generally 8.07
  practical questions to consider: examples
   freehold 8.10, 8.11
   leasehold 8.08, 8.09
 drafting documents *see* **Legal drafting**
 legal research: sample extracts 14.11–14.17
 legal writing: sample extracts 12.16–12.20, App 12C

Q

Qualified lawyers
 preparing for SQE
  generally 2.21
  Practical Legal Skills (PLS) Assessments 2.42
 qualifying work experience (QWE) 1.29; 4.06
Qualifying work experience (QWE)
 aspiring lawyers (working) 1.30; 4.07
 authentication 4.16
 best time for taking SQE Pt 2
  after QWE 4.21
  before QWE 4.18, 4.19
  during QWE 4.20
  generally 4.17
 completion 4.24
 curriculum vitae (CV) 4.01, App 4A
 duration and location 4.13
 finding
  additional qualifications increasing your chances 4.10
  generally 4.09
 generally 1.28; 4.01, 4.05
 good-quality work experience
  assessing 4.23

Qualifying work experience (QWE) – *contd*
 good-quality work experience – *contd*
  generally 4.22
  legal work experience 4.12
  opportunities 4.11
  organisations 4.14
  qualified lawyers 1.29; 4.06
  SRA regulation 4.15
  students 1.30; 4.08
  template App 4B
 types of lawyers
  generally 4.02
  O-shaped lawyer 4.04
  type of lawyer you want to be 4.03

R

Rapport
 building
  authentically 5.14
  generally 5.13
  commonality 5.19
  cultural appropriateness 5.20
  definition 5.12
  generally 5.11
  overcoming superficiality 5.15
  perception 5.16
  small talk
   environment 5.18
   topics 5.17
Registration for SQE
 generally 2.02
Report writing templates
 modern report writing
  example: dispute resolution 11.07
  generally 11.06
 traditional report writing 11.05
Roll of Solicitors, admission to
 character and suitability requirements 1.34
 Disclosure and Barring Service (DBS) 1.33
 generally 1.32
Routes to qualification *see* SQE journey

S

Scanning a document
 advocacy 10.05, 10.07
 time management 5.37
Skim reading a document
 advocacy 10.05, 10.06
 time management 5.38, App 5C
Solicitors Regulation Authority (SRA)
 regulation of QWE 4.15
 role of App 1C
SQE assessments
 failing
  continuing with SQE

SQE assessments – *contd*
  failing – *contd*
    generally 6.26
    resits 6.28
    uncertainty 6.27, App 6B
    generally 1.14; 6.24
    working out SQE results 6.25
  generally 1.11
  negotiation skills 1.13
  professional conduct and ethics 1.12
  Pt 1: Functioning Legal Knowledge Assessments *see* **Functioning Legal Knowledge (FLK) Assessments**
  Pt 2: Practical Legal Skills Assessments *see* **Practical Legal Skills (PLS) Assessments**
SQE journey
  admission to Roll of Solicitors
    character and suitability requirements 1.34
    Disclosure and Barring Service (DBS) 1.33
    generally 1.32
  choosing to qualify as solicitor in England and Wales 1.03
  different routes to qualification 1.09
  exemptions
    agreed exemptions 1.07
    generally 1.06
    individual exemptions 1.08
  introduction 1.01
  Law Society, role of App 1C
  motivation 1.10
  post-SQE journey 1.31
  practising certificate
    continuing competence Competence Statement App 1B
    generally 1.36
    generally 1.35
  pre-SQE journey 1.02
  qualifying work experience (QWE)
    aspiring lawyers (working) and students 1.30
    generally 1.28
    qualified lawyers 1.29
  reasons for becoming a solicitor 1.10
  reasons for qualifying as a solicitor in England and Wales 1.03
  reasons for SQE 1.04
  replacement for existing routes to qualification 1.04
  results 1.14
  'snapshot' 1.01–1.36
  Solicitors Regulation Authority, role of App 1C
  SQE assessments *see* **SQE assessments**
  transitional period 1.05

SQE journey – *contd*
  understanding common law system of England and Wales App 1A
  Welsh language 1.03
Statement of Legal Knowledge
  generally App 1B; 2.35
Statement of Solicitor Competence
  generally App 1B; 2.33
Students
  preparing for SQE
    alternative routes 2.19
    generally 2.16
    law degrees 2.17
    non-law degrees 2.18
    Practical Legal Skills (PLS) Assessments 2.41
    qualifying work experience (QWE) 1.30; 4.08
'Study buddies'
  generally 2.27
Studying for SQE
  formats
    classroom/lectures 2.11
    coaching
      generally 2.14
      performance coaching 2.15
    digital technology/apps 2.10
    generally 2.08
    law books 2.09
    masterclasses 2.13
    online 2.12
  full-time students 2.29
  Functioning Legal Knowledge (FLK) Assessments 3.05
  generally 2.28
  pillars of learning 2.28
  study plan
    fixed or flexible 2.26
    generally 2.52
  support groups/'study buddies' 2.27
  time management
    distractions and disrupters 2.23, App 2A
    generally 2.22
    Pareto's rule 2.24
    study plan 2.25, 2.26
  working full- or part-time 2.30
Support groups
  studying for SQE 2.27
SWOT analysis
  case and matter analysis 11.10

T

Threshold Standard
  generally App 1B; 2.34
Time management
  communicator skills
    generally 5.35

Index

Time management – *contd*
  communicator skills – *contd*
    preparation stage 5.36
    preparation time for oral assessments
    advocacy 5.40
    client interviewing 5.39
    preparation time for written assessments 5.41
    scanning a document 5.37
    skim reading a document 5.38, App 5C
  studying for SQE
    distractions and disrupters 2.23
    generally 2.22
    Pareto's rule 2.24
    study plan 2.25, 2.26
Translation
  legal drafting 13.16
Trust
  building 5.23
  definition 5.22
  generally 5.21

U

Unpredictable clients
  interviewing skills 8.05

W

Welsh language
  generally 1.03
Wills and probate
  client interviewing skills
    actual interview: example 8.21
    generally 8.12
    practical questions to consider: examples
    instructions for Administration of an Estate 8.15, 8.16
    instructions to make a will 8.13, 8.14
  drafting documents *see* **Legal drafting**
  legal writing: sample extracts 12.31–12.35, App 12F
Writing attendance notes
  assessment criteria
    generally 9.02
    law 9.04
    skills 9.03
  assessment specification App 9A
  generally 9.01
  post interview and failure to address key issues 9.06
  purpose of attendance note 9.05

Writing attendance notes – *contd*
  template 9.07
Writing in professional English *see also* Legal drafting
  archaic legal language v modern plain English 7.22, App 7C
  commonly misused words 7.20, App 7B
  contractions 7.21
  emails 7.13
  examples of application of law 7.02
  four Cs of written communication
    clear communication 7.16
    comprehensive communication 7.18
    concise communication 7.17
    correct communication 7.19
    exercise: writing concisely App 7A
    generally 7.15
  generally 7.01
  grammar 7.29
  identifying writing strengths and weaknesses 7.03
  Latin phrases 7.26
  letters
    closing 7.10
    content 7.09
    copy/enclosures 7.12
    generally 7.05
    layout 7.09
    reference 7.06
    salutation 7.07
    signature 7.11
    subject heading 7.08
  level of English 7.04
  paragraphs 7.14
  punctuation 7.28
  spelling
    generally 7.27, App 7D
    US and UK English 7.25
  US and UK English
    dates 7.24
    generally 7.23
    spelling 7.25
Writing reports
  modern report writing
    example: dispute resolution 11.07
    generally 11.06
  traditional report writing 11.05
Written assessments
  case and matter analysis 1.23
  generally 1.22
  legal drafting 1.25
  legal research 1.26
  legal writing 1.24